Doing What WORKS

An Integrative System for the Treatment of Eating Disorders from Diagnosis to Recovery

ABIGAIL HORVITZ NATENSHON

NASW PRESS

National Association of Social Workers
Washington, DC

James J. Kelly, PhD, ACSW, LCSW *President*
Elizabeth J. Clark, PhD, ACSW, MPH, *Executive Director*

Cheryl Y. Bradley, *Publisher*
Lisa M. O'Hearn, *Managing Editor*
Hyde Loomis, *Copyeditor*
Susanna Harris, *Proofreader*
Lori Holtzinger, *Indexer*

Cover by Dever Designs
Interior Design by Xcel Graphics
Printed and bound by Cadmus/Port City Press

Library of Congress Cataloging-in-Publication Data

Natenshon, Abigail, 1947–
    Doing what works : an integrative system for treating eating disorders from diagnosis to recovery / by Abigail Horvitz Natenshon.
        p. ; cm.
    Includes bibliographical references and index.
  1. Eating disorders.   I. National Association of Social Workers. II. Title.
    [DNLM: 1. Eating Disorders—diagnosis. 2. Eating Disorders—therapy.
3. Psychotherapy—methods.   WM 175 N273d 2009]
    RC552.E18N385 2009
616.85'2606—dc22

                                                                        2009021705

*This book is dedicated to my mother, Zelda Ehrenkrantz Horvitz,
who was the embodiment of mindful wisdom, action, and connectedness
in her life as she lived it and as she inspired others to live theirs.*

Contents

Foreword

I can remember the moment.

I had been told all too many times that I needed to make the decision between listening to the eating disorder and listening to my own voice, yet for seven long years it was difficult to distinguish between the two. Through multiple hospitalizations, months at intensive day hospital programs, and years of therapy, weigh-ins, doctors' appointments, and nutritionist visits, I never lost the hope that one day the decision to recover would seem easier and that living a full and healthy life would be within my reach. I was on a path to complete self-destruction; without the enduring support of my family, friends, and treatment teams along the way, I would have succeeded. My journey was filled with many losses—the loss of a true college experience, the loss of many friends, the loss of a fully functioning heart (working now, thanks to a pacemaker), and the loss of the innocence that I was invincible, as in fact I learned that I was not.

Thankfully, I managed to make it to that magical point in time when my own voice prevailed. It was the summer between my first and second year of graduate school. I hit my own personal rock bottom and finally accepted the help that had been right before my eyes all along my journey—including embracing the recommendations made so frequently to accept the support of medication. Eight weeks after my first true medication trial, I woke up and made the decision no longer to listen to the voice of the eating disorder. I remember the moment vividly.

After that point in time, my mind and my body finally began healing together. It took years of adopting new patterns, taking on new challenges (including a move across the country), making new friendships, establishing myself in a new career, and using adjunctive healing supports before I could feel confident in my recovery. But it did happen. I did recover. The journey was long and the pathway at times painful, but the results have been both rewarding and long lasting. Over 10 years have passed since that special moment, and with a wonderful, loving husband, two healthy children (born without fertility assistance), and a fulfilling career, I can say that I am stronger and more present as a result of my struggles through my eating disordered years.

My success story is not isolated. Long-lasting recovery from an eating disorder is possible, although not simple or easy. Fighting through an eating disorder is as complicated as the treatment it requires. One must have tenacity, patience, endurance, and continual hope to sustain the momentum for change. Recovery involves taking risks, being humble, asking for help when needed, and remaining connected with others who are committed to helping one grow each day. Support and connections to others are critical. Being open to using adjunctive approaches, thinking outside the box, and problem solving are all at the core of success throughout treatment and recovery.

What is required of clients for recovery from an eating disorder is essential for those providing the treatment as well. It is therefore no surprise that the field of eating disorder treatment is filled with clinicians who have completed their own recovery journeys and have been blessed to feel the beauty and joy of life without battling eating disordered thoughts or behaviors. We become involved in this difficult work because we have been able to experience firsthand the power of the therapeutic connection, the challenges and possibilities of recovery, and most of all the real belief that recovery is possible. This has been my motivation to enter the field of clinical social work and to mentor novice clinicians in becoming more present, caring clinicians.

I met Abbie Natenshon 18 years ago, when I was first diagnosed with anorexia nervosa and had to return home from my first semester in college. At 18 years of age, I had just been released from my first hospitalization and had just begun the grueling task of recovery. For almost six years, through four years of college and my first years of work as a teacher, Abbie listened, supported, and cared for me unconditionally. I never once doubted her commitment to my full and enduring recovery. Through her kindness, wisdom, and encouragement, and mostly through her continual presence in the moments of our sessions, I learned that there was too much to lose from the eating disorder and too much possibility for losing hope in myself.

A quick Internet search 10 years after I finished treatment led me back to the therapist who not only built my endurance for the long recovery tasks ahead, but also first exposed me to the field of clinical social work, a field that is at the core of who I am today. I e-mailed her to thank her for her unconditional support during a difficult time in my life and to let her know about her impact on me through the years.

What happened after I pressed the send button was in itself magical. Abbie responded. Not only did she remember who I was after all of those years apart, but she also remembered the details of my experiences as if they had happened yesterday. She continued to show the same interest and enthusiasm in my recovery as she did in my years of treatment. And since the time of our reconnection, she has continued to be a source of support and guidance, but this time in the role of professional and personal mentor as I continue to grow as a therapist, a wife, and a mother.

On behalf of your clients over the past 40 years, Abbie, I thank you. And on behalf of the clinicians who can now also hear your compassionate, honest, patient, and present voice through the pages of *Doing What Works*, I thank you as well. I know clinicians around the world will be better prepared for working with clients with eating disorders as a result of reading this book, and I know hundreds and thousands of individuals like me will recover and lead healthy and fulfilling lives as a result.

This book gets to the heart of the healing process—what it means and what it takes. It describes a uniquely human process, spoken through the voice of a uniquely experienced and committed practitioner. Within this book, you will discover and learn how it all works in becoming best prepared to do what works for your clients, their families, your team, and yourself, in life as well as in your professional encounters.

Kimberly Israel, LCSW, MPH, PPSC

Acknowledgments

I wish to thank my husband, Lou, the love of my life, my best friend and companion, confidant and mentor, my 'mother, father, and son' all rolled up into one extraordinary human being. Thank you, Lou, for your infinite kindness and patience, for offering this writing project the infinite respect and latitude it required, while offering me the security of your constant and loving presence during the occasional stumble. Your enthusiasm, encouragement, and heartfelt pride in me and my work have nourished me throughout my life, as they have through this writing project.

I wish to acknowledge and thank Kimberly Lambert Israel, my dear past client, and now colleague, friend, and mentor. As my professional advisor/editor during this project, you have been teacher and student, sounding board and cheerleader; your wisdom, experience, and keen insights have sustained me, while your excitement about the developing manuscript spurred me forward and buoyed me, refueling my internal coffers as they would become depleted. You are an inspiration to me and to every person who has ever experienced an eating disorder.

I want to thank my sister Barbara, a brilliant human being and therapist, who so lovingly read and learned, edited and taught, listened and shared, offering deep and wonderful insights, as always; and my sister Nina for being so precious to me. And thank you, my daughter, sweet Elizabeth for the constant inspiration you have provided me throughout your extraordinary life, and thanks to my technological guru, your loving husband, Harris Stein. Both of you have rescued me time and time again through your high-tech help. Many thanks to my son Adam and his endearing wife Debra, for the personal and professional support, guidance, wisdom, and love you have afforded me through life as well as through this process. How marvelous it is when the tables get turned and a mother has the privilege of reaping what she sows, enjoying the wisdom and mentoring of her own children! Much love and gratitude to my sweet beloved grandsons, Gabriel Benjamin and Zachary Raphael, who have provided my fondest (and at times, only) distraction from my work this past year. They are a continual source of sheer joy.

I would like to thank Lynn Freedman, my talented nutritionist partner in this work of ours through the decades, for her enduring friendship, her masterful skills and wise consult and bolstering through our tough cases together. Thank you, Lynn, for listening so well to me; inevitably, our discussions leave me knowing more about myself as a professional and who I wish to become.

Many thanks to my clients, who, through these four decades, have offered me the gift of "work" that feels like pleasure; for your precious relationships, for sharing your lives, and for teaching and stimulating me to become a better person and therapist, always.

Many thanks to Lisa O'Hearn, my editor at NASW Press, who steadfastly midwifed the birthing of this project through the thick and the thin of it all—no pun intended. This book was a highly ambitious process for both of us, and I am grateful to her and to NASW for having been part of still another gratifying team effort in my life.

Thanks to my Academy of Eating Disorders colleagues from whom I have learned and continue to learn so much about eating disorders and their treatment. They have provided a life-line to me within the context of a private practice that might otherwise have become a lonely and far less productive experience. These colleagues continue to provide the fruits of their brilliance and experience through their infinite generosity.

Last, I would be remiss if I did not thank Ethan Oberman and his wonderful remote computer back-up company, Spider Oak©. Ethan saved me from the jaws of a virtual publishing nightmare, as at the very moment of book completion and preparation to transmit the text to my publisher, I learned that my frozen computer had contracted a virus that corrupts and deletes files. It was a never-to-be-forgotten moment when Ethan calmly pulled up my entire book on his Blackberry, while standing in line at O'Hare Airport, and blithely sent it to my publisher just before boarding a plane for California.

SECTION 1

PREPARING YOURSELF TO TREAT EATING DISORDERS

1

A Treatment Field in Transition: Where We've Been and Where We're Going

If we do not change our direction, we are likely to end up where we are headed.

—Chinese proverb

Within a 2-day period, I received two calls from mothers of teenagers with anorexia. The first had taken her daughter, who had lost a great deal of weight precipitously, to her pediatrician, who declared the girl to be "fine" because her weight was still on the growth charts. She instructed this mother "not to worry," that there was "no problem to speak of . . . aside from amenorrhea," and referred the client to a gynecologist. This physician declared that it is normal for girls not to have regular periods until age 21 and not to be concerned. She prescribed birth control pills to replace the estrogen necessary to restore and maintain her bone density, despite research that shows hormone replacement therapy to be ineffective in treating anorexic women (Seidenfeld & Rickert, 2001). The girl's father did not "believe in therapy" and felt that if there were to be any medical implications at all, she clearly needed to be in the hands of a medical doctor, not a psychotherapist. "I am calling you now," this mother told me in our first phone contact, "Because I can't bear the thought of going to still another doctor who will ignore or misunderstand P's situation. I can't risk it," she said, "in terms of her health, and for my own sanity."

The second call was from a mother who had asked her pediatrician what she should do to support her daughter, for whom the alarm bells were sounded by her boarding school headmistress when she requested that the girl return home to recover and to avoid setting a poor example in the dining hall for peers. "What do I do now?" this mother asked. "How can I help her in the face of her disbelief that anything is wrong?" "Just support her. . . . *You're* the mother . . . *you'll* know what to do" was as much advice as this doctor could offer. But simply loving a child is not enough for a parent seeking to support recovery from an eating disorder. Parents and families need guidance; it is for health care professionals to provide it.

From the perspective of close to 40 years in my therapist's chair, I have been unintentionally rendered a virtual fly on other professionals' office walls listening to clients' war stories of their past therapy encounters. Physicians are not alone in failing to comprehend fully the implications of eating disorders, which are shrouded in myths and misconceptions. They are joined by some of the best and brightest mental health professionals who participate in eating disorder treatment teams, along with the parents of child clients, who have the most powerful investment of all.

Suffering from her own misguided beliefs, the first caller spoke of "plea bargaining" with God: "So if she could just gain two or three more pounds—it would be OK if she has some compulsions, if her coping might be a bit off. We could *live* with that." This mother was wrong: I made it clear to her that this youngster, and this family, really could *not* afford to live with anything less than a life without an eating disorder. This young woman needed and deserved to achieve a full recovery, to nourish and care for herself physically and emotionally through free choice and without fear, not only with regard to food and eating, but in all life functions. She needed to develop a healthy relationship with food to fuel her body, to live a balanced and quality existence, and to menstruate naturally if she wished to become a parent herself one day.

In this chapter, I define the problems professionals face in treating eating disorders in preparation to propose solutions in the chapters that follow. I describe some of the most salient issues in the field of eating disorder treatment, including the misunderstood role of food and weight, the pervasiveness of risk factors, inadequate professional education, insufficient treatment resources, and insurance coverage for eating disorder treatment. Finally, I review the research–practice divide and summarize the field's best practices as they are currently understood.

STATE OF THE FIELD

Eating disorders do not come with instructions, either for victims or therapists. Because of symptom variability and inconsistency as seen through the majority of cases that fall into the eating disorders not otherwise specified category of the *Diagnostic and Statistical Manual of Mental Disorders* (4th ed., Text Rev.; American Psychiatric Association, 2000) and because "eating disorders often coexist with other mental health disorders, these disorders often go undiagnosed and untreated" (Hudson, Hiripi, Pope, & Kessler, 2007, p. xxx). A low number of sufferers obtain treatment for their eating disorder. Although early detection is important for successful outcomes, practitioners typically fail to make an early diagnosis and establish a relevant course of treatment (Hudson et al., 2007).

Compounding the problem, many health professionals treating eating disorders fail to recognize both *that* they do not know and *what* they do not know, thereby losing sight of what they need to learn—about themselves, their clients, the disorders, and the obstacles that could impede sound and effective treatment. Because of this failure, they often practice what they know by default, doing what is familiar and comfortable and relying on generic practice principles. Many professionals acknowledge that treating eating disorders is a separate field in itself about which they know little or nothing, yet they offer treatment just the same in the assumption that lethal behaviors can be ameliorated sufficiently through treating the emotions underlying and driving them. The following sections describe factors contributing to the current state of the field.

Misunderstood Role of Food and Weight

The greatest impediment to diagnosis and treatment is that eating disorders are not what they appear to be, surrounded as they are by the smokescreens of food and weight. We have heard it before and we know it well: Eating disorders are not about food. Yet food and weight issues confuse and confound clinicians throughout the treatment labyrinth. Food- and weight-related behaviors are useful diagnostic mechanisms, offering access to pivotal underlying emotions and providing invaluable opportunities to access and integrate healing behavioral changes. At the same time, eating and weight issues can distract and deter practitioners from the need for constant vigilance of the deeper issues and comorbidities that underlie and drive these disorders. How easy it is to lose track of the reality that though the issue of weight in diagnosis and treatment is of consequence, by itself it is by no means indicative of recovery from an eating disorder.

Though weighing in is an important accountability tool, it is counterproductive for clinicians to seek an "ideal weight" or to offer anorexic patients the "carrot" of reaching a specific "target weight" as their goal. No one . . . not a nutritionist, not the patient, nor a physician . . . can set a goal weight arbitrarily and expect it to lead to recovery. When a nutritionist or doctor says, "It is important for you to gain another five pounds" (to reach the low end of normal on the charts), the patient hears, "Five pounds is all I need to gain in order to get everybody off my back; five pounds will let me stay skinny without being considered 'sick.'"

The body itself is the only accurate determiner of appropriate weight; an attachment to any weight less than the body's set point weight is a distraction to complete recovery. Each person has a set point weight to which the person naturally gravitates; bodily fluctuation may span from 5 to 10 pounds, but the fit body at its set point weight will rarely gain beyond its natural range. Attaining one's set point weight marks full weight restoration, a normalized internal function of brain and body, and the reversal of amenorrhea. The set point concept counteracts the commonly held misconception that the more one eats, the more weight one gains; that food is fattening; and that when it comes to food, less is more. I think of the set point weight as being like an ocean's tide. When the moon is new, gravitational forces may not pull the body of water as high as it comes in when the moon is full. The rising tide, be it slightly higher or lower, always approaches, (but does not exceed), a certain point on the shore, with the exception of hurricanes or other natural forces. So is the set point equally consistent, expected to fluctuate ever so slightly, but always hovering close to the water line.

By failing to remember that food and weight are but two of many significant elements of these diseases, practitioners may inadvertently enable disease. For example, an internist highly experienced in the treatment of eating disorders saw a client of mine and remarked that her motivation to renew her recovery effort now "could surely not be the result of any physical problems," as her weight was "fine" and her lab tests "excellent." He directed these remarks to a woman who purged every morsel of food, multiple times a day, with the exception of breakfast. She chose never to return to the internist's care (as he failed to demonstrate an understanding of eating disorders and the severity of her condition. By applauding her weight, he reinforced her distortion that eating disorders are defined by weight and that she would need to lose more weight to maintain her anorexic status). It took extensive therapeutic work to repair the emotional damage done.

Routine physical exams or lab tests provide "evidence" of an eating disorder only in the direst stages of the disorder. The therapist's reliance on body mass index (BMI) to determine the existence of an eating disorder can act as a diagnostic decoy. BMI is a measure of body fat based on height and weight. Normal weight is at 18.5 to 24.9; overweight is at 25 to 29.9; obesity is at 30 or greater. Waiting until a BMI becomes low enough to warrant a diagnosis of anorexia may seriously threaten opportunities for early intervention. BMI offers only an approximation of a diagnostic standard and does not take into account natural variations in physique among ethnic groups, bone structure, fat–muscle ratios, or genetic components.

Pervasiveness of Risk Factors

Myths and misconceptions about eating disorders are rampant in a society where dieting and exercise have become a norm and even obsession. Many people consider food restriction to be normal or even a healthy sign of enviable self-discipline. Considering themselves experts on food and eating simply because of their own personal life experiences, some practitioners subscribe to subjectively based truths about healthy eating and weight management. Everyone eats; everyone knows what he or she considers to be healthy and normal behaviors with regard to eating and weight control.

But in the face of ever-changing dietary trends that arouse attention and fear, "normal" eating in today's world is no longer necessarily "healthy" eating. It becomes increasingly difficult for clients and professionals to recognize pathology in the face of a myriad of contradictory theories about how to become and remain fit and thin. Adding to the confusion, those with clinical disorders appear to be doing precisely what everybody else is doing [by]—skipping meals, having coffee and a doughnut and calling it breakfast, or grabbing a soda or protein bar for lunch on the run.

A recovering anorexic high school student spoke of her frustration at having to fulfill the requirements of her food plan: "*None* of my friends eat breakfast; *nobody* eats seven grains a day, three dairy exchanges! Why do *I* have to? It's not normal. I *see* what's normal, all around me, observing my friends in the cafeteria!" Unfortunately, she is not far off the mark. Eating healthfully becomes a hard pill to swallow, particularly in the face of irrational fears evoked by a fat-phobic society.

An adult client with anorexia described her childhood eating habits as being "unhealthy." When I asked what she meant by unhealthy, she replied, "You know. . . . My mother had me eating things like red meat, dairy products. . . ."

Professionals, like all human beings, tend to become increasingly bodily aware and health conscious as they experience the effects of aging, pregnancy, injuries, and the insults of daily life. People need not be eating disordered to restrict or abuse food at times or to eat in response to emotional cues such as stress, sadness, or boredom. Over the years, in conducting many informal surveys about what constitutes healthy eating, I have observed that the majority of those questioned, young and old, lay and professional, believe that healthy eating is fat-free and sugar-free eating and that dieting is the best and only way to lose weight and keep it off. In seeking data about what triggered clinical disease in my clients, invariably the trigger to disease onset is "I started an innocent diet; then, I just kept on eating 'healthier and healthier.'"

It becomes increasingly difficult to consider eating disordered behaviors pathological in light of their prevalence. Misconceptions leading to dysfunctional eating run deep and know no age barrier. Fully 40 percent to 50 percent of girls on American college campuses skip meals, diet, and binge eat in an attempt to become healthier and more fit. Many of them are at risk of developing anorexia or bulimia (Ann, 2007). One of my college-age clients insisted that this statistic is vastly underestimated: "Seeing what girls eat and don't eat in my sorority house, I'd say 70 percent is more like it." Box 1.1 lists statistics that indicate how widespread disordered eating is in the United States.

It is up to the practitioner to remind clients that they have a life-threatening disease that, at least temporarily, sets them apart from the freedom that others have to abuse food [or engage in disordered eating]. Just as a glass of red wine can be healthful and relaxing for most, that same glass of wine for the person recovering from an addiction to alcohol can mark the beginning of a downward spiral into recurring alcohol abuse.

Inadequate Professional Education

Eating disorder professionals come by their lack of treatment preparedness honestly. For those of us schooled before eating disorders became a field in itself in the 1970s, there was virtually no information available to be taught. Now, some 40 years later, despite the increasing accessibility of scientific research about eating disorders, treatment of these diseases continues to fall between the cracks of formal education. Opportunities for training are few, and there is a lack of clarity within the health professions about what constitutes adequate preparation to treat eating disorders. A survey showed that "researchers and clinicians both felt that they had received inadequate training [in eating disorders] to engage in integrated clinical-research activities" (Banker & Klump, 2007, p. 3). Graduate social

---

BOX 1.1

Eating Disorder Statistics

- 42 percent of first- through third-grade girls want to be thinner.
- 81 percent of 10-year-olds are afraid of being fat.
- 46 percent of 9- to 11-year-olds are "sometimes" or "very often" on diets, and 82 percent of their families are "sometimes" or "very often" on diets.
- Over half of teenage girls and nearly one third of teenage boys use unhealthy weight control behaviors such as skipping meals, fasting, smoking cigarettes, vomiting, and taking laxatives.
- 91 percent of women recently surveyed on a college campus had attempted to control their weight through dieting; 22 percent dieted "often" or "always."
- 25 percent of American men and 45 percent of American women are on a diet on any given day.
- 35 percent of "normal dieters" progress to pathological dieting. Of those, 20 percent to 25 percent progress to partial- or full-syndrome eating disorders.
- Girls who diet frequently are 12 times as likely to binge as girls who don't diet.

Source. Reprinted with permission from the National Eating Disorders Association (n.d.).

---

work programs in the United States tend to be oriented towards social welfare rather than clinical practice, and clinical curricula all too typically overlook the unique treatment requirements of eating disorder care in not offering specialty courses. A survey showed that 42.3 percent of practitioners received formal education in the context of graduate training; the most common training in eating disorders treatment consisted of workshops or seminars (71.2 percent), followed by self-education/reading (53.8 percent), and informal supervision (57.7 percent) (von Ranson & Robinson, 2006).

A student recently trained at one of the most highly reputed graduate schools of social work inquired why there were no courses dedicated to the treatment of eating disorders. She was informed that specialty training for eating disorders is "unnecessary and redundant" based on the proliferation of more generic courses that address the issues underlying these disorders, such as human development, self-esteem, mood disorders, and issues of control and identity. This response reflects the misconception that an eating disorder is not a disease in itself but merely a symptom of deeper issues. In fact, successful eating disorder treatment requires highly specific and clearly intentional protocols.

In this attitude, graduate schools of mental health are not alone. My colleague, a highly skilled nutritionist, described the advice she received from her graduate school advisor, who discouraged her from working with eating disorders. Her mentor made the case that "the work is tough, the clients resistant, the changes minimal, and the liability risks enormous. . . . People die from these disorders!" The advisor went on to caution her about the high rate of professional burnout in the field of eating disorder treatment, which in fact is more likely to be directly correlated with the failure of clinicians to understand the requirements of eating disorder treatment and the failure of clients with eating disorders to thrive with inadequate treatment.

Partly in response to pressure from organizations that fund research that demands legitimized, quantifiable, and predictable outcomes, as well as from insurance companies and legislators, the field is faced with a demand for an increasing commitment to evidence-based therapy approaches over the harder-to-measure relationship capacities of the therapist. The training that does exist for clinical practice traditionally prepares therapists to function as autonomous, self-directed professionals, leaving them unprepared (and often unwilling) to commit to the logistics, time, and effort it takes to accomplish the ongoing demands of team collaboration. Improvements are needed in the education of professionals who will treat eating disorders to ensure that this vulnerable population receives adequate treatment.

On a positive note, the very best resource of all for education about eating disorder treatment exists right under our noses. The Academy for Eating Disorders is a worldwide community of 1,400 inspired, dedicated, and energetic experts whose work and contributions comprise the heart and soul of research and treatment advances in this field. Members participate in animated and impassioned dialogue, sharing rich personal and professional experiences as a form of peer consultation through a membership listserv and through annual conferences that integrate the best and brightest minds in the field. The Academy for Eating Disorders is at the cutting edge of treatment change and progress in both clinical practice and scientific research. I urge all practitioners who treat clients with eating disorders or who wish to learn to treat these disorders or contribute to the growth of eating disorder research and clinical practice to become active participants in the resources provided by this and other national eating disorder organizations as a best practice for learning.

Insufficient Treatment Resources

With tongue in cheek, a colleague observed, "Of 500 psychotherapists in any given area, about 490 would claim competence in treating eating disorders." The treatment requirements of eating disorders, however, are far more rigorous than most clinicians recognize. In light of the voids in formal and informal education, it is hardly surprising that the majority of people with these disorders do not receive any form of treatment (Hudson et al., 2007), and research shows a substantial client and doctor delay in seeking and finding treatment (de la Rie, Noordenbos, Donker, & van Furth, 2006). In addition, clients do not obtain the quality of treatment they deserve in locations where there are simply not enough adequately trained specialists available to meet client numbers and demands.

A survey found that the majority of people with eating disorders are not receiving the recommended level of care and that 55 percent of those with the conditions were not treated by a specialist. For some, the nearest appropriate specialist service could be up to 150 miles away. Only 14 percent of clients, caregivers, and professionals in one survey had found eating disorder treatment close to home, and only 17 percent of young people had been treated in settings that were age appropriate (BBC News, 2005b). In the United States, it is reported that only one third of people with anorexia nervosa receive mental health care, only 6 percent of people with bulimia receive mental health care, and the majority of people with severe eating disorders do not receive adequate care (National Eating Disorders Association, n.d.).

The source of the misconception that eating disorders are not curable may be that, to date, too few professionals have been adequately trained to treat and heal them. Eating disorders *are* curable, however. Studies conservatively indicate that "50 percent of clients with anorexia remit within one to three years and never require inpatient care. Of the remaining 50 percent who require inpatient care, an additional 50 percent to 70 percent will recover, depending on the duration of follow-up. Thus, an estimated 75 percent to 85 percent of clients with anorexia completely recover. If clients who experience significant improvement are included, the rate of positive outcome rises to over 90 percent" (Johnson, Lund, & Yates, 2003).

I believe that when clients suffer for decades from an eating disorder, it is not about the tenacity of the disease, or even about the resistance of the clients. It's about us—the treating professionals—and it is an indicator of how imperative it is that we upgrade the quality of our understanding and caregiving. Our first job is to educate ourselves.

Insurance Coverage for Eating Disorder Treatment

In December 2006, a landmark statement by the Academy for Eating Disorders affirmed that "eating disorders (anorexia and bulimia nervosa) are biologically based mental illnesses" involving a "neurobiological disorder of the brain . . . that significantly impairs cognitive function, judgment, and emotional stability and limits the life activities of the person with the illness." Researchers who are working to redefine how diseases are classified are now looking less at symptoms or physiological measurements and more at their genetic underpinnings (Bulik et al., 2003; Kaye et al., 2000). According to Bryan Lask, an expert researcher in the field of anorexia,

> "The biological cause has been underemphasized and the sociocultural pressures have been overemphasized. There has to be a biological contribution; otherwise, everyone would be anorexic given the sociocultural pressures in our society." (cited in Laurance, 2005, p. 22)

Finding disease origins in biology and genetics lends credence to eating disorders as legitimate diseases that are coverable by insurance companies. In a 2006 press release, the Academy for Eating Disorders' president, Eric van Furth, issued the position statement that "Eating disorders clearly fit the criteria for biologically based mental illness. Parity for coverage should occur throughout the U.S. health system" (Academy for Eating Disorders, 2006). The struggle for parity in insurance coverage for mental health disorders, and especially for eating disorders, has been a sore spot in the profession for years. A lobbyist for insurance coverage for individuals with eating disorders and their families spoke of the biased attitudes she regularly encounters among federal and state legislators, who typically do not consider eating disorders to be "real diseases" at all, but rather "healthy eating gone wild" or unique forms of dieting at the discretion of the individual. Considered to be conditions of volition and intention, eating disorders have been denied disease status.

Until recently, insurance coverage was restricted to situations where medical or physiological complications required hospitalization, irrespective of whether there might also be a diagnosis in the *Diagnostic and Statistical Manual of Mental Disorders* (4th ed., Text Rev.; American Psychiatric Association, 2000), even if services were delivered in a psychiatric setting. The average recovery time required for a hospitalized individual with anorexia is seven years; the average length of stay anorexics need to fully restore weight and provide relapse-prevention treatment is 90 to 120 days; the average number of inpatient treatment days covered by insurance plans is 31 days for anorexic clients and 14 days for bulimic clients. In countless instances, families have depleted their retirement accounts and life savings or have been forced to take out second mortgages on their homes because insurance companies refuse to cover a child's eating disorder treatment.

In October 2008, Congress succeeded in eliminating discrimination in health care coverage against people who have mental disorders, with House and Senate coming together to pass mental health parity (see Emergency Economic Stabilization Act of 2008). According to the Eating Disorders Coalition for Research, Policy & Action (2008),

> This bill requires group health plans that currently offer coverage for mental health and substance-use disorders to provide those benefits in the same manner as benefits provided to all other medical and surgical procedures covered under the plan. It also prohibits group health plans from imposing discriminatory annual/lifetime dollar limits, co-pays and deductibles, or day and visit limits unless similar limitations or requirements are imposed for other medical and surgical benefits.

"Every day we get calls from parents whose kids are on the verge of death due to an eating disorder, yet they cannot get their health insurance companies to pay for this life-saving treatment," said Jeanine Cogan, policy director of the Coalition. "This law will change that" (Eating Disorders Coalition for Research, Policy & Action, 2008).

The parity legislation passed in 2008 will not take effect till January 1, 2010. The Federal parity law was written in such a way that it honors already existing state laws that are stronger. For states where eating disorders are not defined as mental illness, the federal parity law will not remedy that, but there is still a possibility that eating disorders will be treated, as the law leaves it up to the plans to decide what mental illnesses are covered.

A number of organizations are continuing the fight to expand insurance for eating disorder treatment (see Box 1.2 for a list of these organizations). As a result

---

BOX 1.2

Eating Disorder Organizations

- Families Empowering and Supporting Treatment of Eating Disorders (F.E.A.S.T.) is an organization of and for parents and caregivers to help loved ones recover from eating disorders by providing information and mutual support, promoting evidence-based treatment, and advocating for research and education to reduce the suffering associated with eating disorders.
- The National Association of Anorexia Nervosa and Associated Disorders (ANAD) is the oldest association aimed at fighting eating disorders in the United States. ANAD assists people with eating disorders such as anorexia nervosa and bulimia and also assists their families. Headquartered in Highland Park, Illinois, ANAD is a nonprofit organization working in the areas of advocacy, family support, therapist referrals, research, education, prevention, and hotline help for those with anorexia and bulimia.
- Family Resources for Education on Eating Disorders (FREED) is a parent-founded nonprofit organization committed to educating the community about the serious nature and growing prevalence of anorexia, bulimia, and binge eating disorder (http://home.comcast.net/).
- The National Eating Disorders Association (NEDA) STAR (States for Treatment Access and Research). This program promotes awareness among local legislators about the challenges in accessing adequate medical care to battle an eating disorder because of unfair practices by insurance companies and seeks to change state law to address those inequities (http://www.nationaleatingdisorders.org).
- The Academy for Eating Disorders (AED) is an international, transdisciplinary professional organization. The AED promotes excellence in research, treatment and the prevention of ED and provides education, training, and a forum for collaboration and professional dialogue (http://www.aedweb.org).
- The Eating Disorder Referral and Information Center provides information and advocacy for the uninsured and underinsured seeking health insurance coverage (http://www.EDReferral.com).
- The CoverMe Foundation [makes] available a resource database and corporate partners to inform and assist the uninsured with low-cost and no-cost options available in and around users' communities (http://www.covermefoundation.org).

---

of their efforts, for example, on October 9, 2008, President George W. Bush signed Michelle's Law (H.R. 2851), designed to ensure that dependent college students who take a medically necessary leave of absence do not lose health insurance coverage. Box 1.3 lists some strategies for procuring health insurance coverage for eating disorder treatment.

For clients without health insurance, some residential care facilities offer scholarships, and occasionally government-sponsored programs offer financial support for participation in research projects that pair clients with resources. In communities where there are research hospitals and universities, clinical studies may be available that provide opportunities to participate in low-cost, high-quality treatment. Nonprofit organizations, such as the National Association of Anorexia

---

BOX 1.3

Strategies for Procuring Insurance Coverage for Eating Disorder Treatment

- Speak directly with an appeals specialist at the insurance company.
- List medical complications. In procuring insurance coverage for eating disorder care, the International Classification of Diseases codes for bradycardia, hypotension, malnutrition, and severe malnourishment may be used additionally where there is evidence of anorexic brain imbalances.
- With employer-provided health insurance, human resources departments can sometimes become successful insurance advocates.
- Focus on cost–benefit analysis. Relate the successes the client has known.
- Be aware that "benefit substitutes" may be a possibility in certain situations when benefits are running out. As an example, you might check to see if outpatient days may be swapped for available inpatient days, or vice versa, to allow for a more extended tenure in either of the milieus.

Nervosa and Related Disorders or the National Eating Disorders Association, as well as individual psychotherapists, can be instrumental in connecting people with viable treatment sources.

BEYOND THE RESEARCH–PRACTICE DIVIDE: CURRENT BEST PRACTICE

Central to the failure of current efforts to properly educate clinicians treating eating disorders is the unworkable disconnect between eating disorder research and its application to clinical practice. Academics and scientists, who make the most significant contributions to the clinical literature, typically have had limited access to the treatment venue. The focus on scientific evidence typically leaves the research inaccessible, and in many cases irrelevant, to the more intuitive style of practitioners on the front lines of treatment. In addition, the eating disorder professional literature tends to focus on disparate and nonintegrative elements of care in the face of highly complex, systematic, multifaceted disorders that demand a fully integrative basis of care.

According to a 2007 survey, eating disorder clinicians revealed that they considered research findings to be largely irrelevant to the realities of clinical practice and cited the need for empirical guidelines for adapting empirically supported treatments to 'real-life' treatment and for changing course when they are ineffective (Banker & Klump, 2007). The author of the survey report highlighted "the need for researchers to study what clinicians do in their treatments rather than simply expecting clinicians to do what researchers study" (Banker & Klump, 2007, p. 4).

There is much that is compelling about the certainty of statistics and hard evidence that arise out of pure science. Although evidence-based research in the field clearly points to better efficacy with cognitive–behavioral therapy (CBT) than with less-specified approaches, exclusive CBT practice and a rigorous adherence to a single method are considered inadequate to produce optimal outcomes. As humanistic psychologist Abraham Maslow noted, "If you only have a hammer, you tend to see every problem as a nail" (cited in Germer, Siegel, & Fulton, 2005, p. 69). "The danger of excess loyalty to one method of treatment is summarized in the concept of 'theory countertransference,' in which the therapist imposes his or her theoretical predispositions on the client. The result is therapy that confirms the therapist's assumptions, and where 'stalled treatment tends to be chalked up as client resistance'" (Germer et al. 2005, p. 69).

Evidence-based guidelines alone do not necessarily motivate change in the client or the practitioner's creative process in seeking ways to liberate the client's tyrannized soul. Consistent with evidence-based psychological therapy for other clinical disorders, it has been shown that evidence-based treatment is relatively rarely implemented in routine clinical practice (for eating disorders) (Wilson, 2005).

If CBT and evidence-based practice alone are not sufficient to cure an eating disorder, however, neither are random or purely intuitive approaches, including psychodynamic psychotherapy. It is increasingly evident that eating disorders, with their diverse and systemic etiology, symptom presentation, treatment systems, protocols, modes, and milieus, defy scientific reductionism and compartmentalization. Psychiatrist David Brendel spoke of the "myth of psychiatric scientism" in arguing that "psychiatry needs to adopt a wider view of evidence, one more akin to the ideas of quantum physics. Physicists have moved beyond a mechanistic Newtonian view of the world," he observed. "They talk about chaos and uncertainty and about the effect that the observer has on what is being observed" (cited in Pettus, 2006, p. 38).

Eclecticism and inclusion are key to achieving positive outcomes in treating eating disorders. When and how to combine methodologies become decisions of nuance and accrued skill sets. The authors of one research study concluded that therapists need "to show flexibility and breadth of understanding in adapting symptom-management techniques to the unique constellation of transference themes that exist with each patient" (Johnson, Connors, & Tobin, 1987, p. 675).

Since the 1990s, which has been called the decade of the brain, the greatest single factor influencing the treatment of eating disorders is evidence-based research proving that biologically and genetically based eating disorders affect, and are affected by, brain and genetic structure and function. Ironically, the science of the brain is increasingly lending legitimacy and credence to the importance of the "art" of human connection in therapeutic healing. The field of psychoneurobiology has proved that healthy therapeutic connections result in structural and functional brain changes that can influence and even change gene structure. The implications of these findings for eating disorder treatment are vast and yet to be plumbed, but the discoveries support the importance of the human relationship, along with practicable, eclectic, and proven treatment skills, in healing eating disorders. So the art of human connection turns out to be scientific after all, and a bridge to help clinicians breach the chasm between research and practice appears to be enticingly within reach. This research is discussed in greater detail in Chapter 11.

Combining the positive effects of empirical and anecdotal data promises to optimize treatment efficacy. New clinical trends include the growing popularity of mindful practice and of somatic–sensory, synergistic, mind–body approaches; these trends are derived from research on brain plasticity demonstrating that the human brain is capable of changing throughout life (Doidge, 2007, p. 43). Combining elements of science and humanity makes treatment more palatable for professional consumption and outcomes more potent for clients with eating disorders.

Therapists do not cure eating disorders or their clients; clients cure themselves through recovery assets that congeal and accrue from within. It is through the healing relationship, nourished by the unique and versatile use of the self, that practitioners provide the means and incentive for the client to heal herself. It is for the therapist to inspire the client to learn and to motivate the individual to take in and take charge of new information, to become transformed by it, and to use it to further discover and enrich herself. The eating disorder therapist, through the healing connection, becomes the medium to the client's return to the exiled core self.

It has been my observation throughout the four decades of my own practice, that the therapist's versatile use of self is the most critical took in his or her arsenal. There is no such thing as a good idea that has not been thought of before. The uniqueness of the therapist's use of self in relationship with clients with eating disorders has been corroborated in research about the efficacy of mindful psychotherapy that took place during the mid-1990s, which we consider in Chapter 13. I believe that the 2,500-year-old practice of mindful awareness is rapidly on its way to becoming the heart of combining CBT and psychodynamic treatments. An in-depth discussion of the integration of mindfulness in psychotherapy, CBT techniques, and healing aspects of the therapeutic relationship is found in Chapter 8.

CONCLUSION

The field of eating disorder treatment is still in its adolescence, as are so many of its clients. As treatment techniques continue to evolve, practitioners struggle to stay abreast of best practices and how to apply them. In the face of the treatment field's crisis of identity, clinicians find themselves very much on their own, seeking to find their own way as definitive training mechanisms continue to elude them. The field is at once enriched and compromised by the divergent viewpoints of clinicians and researchers and by a sense of benign chaos that arises out of a diffuse diversity of approaches, limited resources, and in some cases, personal biases and misunderstanding regarding eating disorders and their unique requirements for treatment.

Eating disorder treatment depends on rules and protocols, but with a clear overlay of intention and action, humanity and instinct, integrative skills and a creative and knowledgeable use of the practitioner's self in seeking life-saving changes. In psychotherapeutic treatment, and perhaps especially in the treatment of eating disorders, therapists need to learn how best to access their most valuable personal resource of all—themselves—in developing the optimal treatment relationship.

2

Eating Disorders 101:
Knowledge Is Power

Leadership and learning are indispensable to each other.
—John F. Kennedy

A peddler cannot sell from an empty cart: We have to know before we can teach. Knowledge is power. By fully understanding eating disorders, professionals are in a better position to empower their clients. They become better able to anticipate, interpret, and respond not only to what they encounter but also to what eludes them. As educators, clinicians need a clear understanding of eating disorders before they can effectively teach clients and families to heal from them. In this chapter, I provide a brief description of eating disorders and their implications for clients and families, followed by a review of the fundamental characteristics of the ways in which eating disorders work, an understanding that is essential to effective treatment.

EXTENT OF THE PROBLEM

According to the National Eating Disorders Association (n.d.), as many as 10 million women and girls and 1 million men and boys have an eating disorder in this country. Included in this figure are individuals diagnosed with anorexia nervosa, bulimia nervosa, and eating disorders not otherwise specified (Part 2 discusses these diagnoses in more detail.

According to a 10-year study by the National Association of Anorexia Nervosa and Associated Eating Disorders (n.d.), in 86 percent of individuals with eating disorders, the eating disorder began before age 20. An estimated 11 percent of high school students have been diagnosed with an eating disorder (Cedric Centre for Couselling, n.d.), but there is evidence that the problem is more widespread. An additional "15 percent of young women not diagnosed with an eating disorder have substantially disordered eating behaviors or attitudes" (*Weighing the Facts— Eating Disorders: Information and Resources,* 2008). Rates of diagnosed eating disorders have doubled since the 1960s. An increase in rates of eating disorders among young women ages 15 to 19 has occurred in each decade since the 1930s, and the incidence of bulimia in girls and women ages 10 to 39 has tripled between 1988 and 1993 (Engel, Reiss, & Dombeck, 2007).

Although eating disorders occur most often in children and young adults, adults of various ages are sometimes stricken; most, however, have carried their disease with them, unhealed, from earlier life. Chronicity (long-term disease) and adult status have been associated with a worse prognosis (Guarda, 2008). Despite their suffering, however, many adults with eating disorders manage to function effectively as professionals, as parents, and as life partners, and many are talented and highly achieving individuals. They hide their symptoms from friends, families, husbands, and children, fighting their fight in isolation and loneliness. A client with bulimia in her 50s saw a highly regarded psychiatrist for 20 years to deal with her "life issues." When I asked whether he had addressed her eating disorder, she responded, "Well, he said, "In the 20 years I've known you, your weight has never fluctuated more than five pounds up or down. This is clearly *not* an eating disorder." In fact, her diagnosis clearly *was* an eating disorder; she engaged in compulsive overeating, periodic fasts, and abuse of laxatives and diuretics, and she struggled with a pervasive sense of misery and resignation, because as long as her eating disorder remained undiagnosed, there would be no cure.

Although most individuals with eating disorders are women and girls, about 10 percent to 15 percent are men and boys (Zerbe, 1993). Studies show a ratio of about two female to every one male anorexia client and a three-to-one ratio of female to male bulimia clients (Andersen, 2004a), though men are less likely to recognize their own symptoms as an eating disorder; whereas women are concerned predominantly with weight, men tend to be concerned with shape and muscle definition, seeking to become bigger and more muscular (virile), rather than thinner. By high school boys are almost equally dissatisfied with their bodies as are girls; half want to gain muscle weight and to lose fat. An equal or smaller number want to lose weight, also with a goal of becoming leaner and more muscular (Andersen, 2004a).

Eating disorders and the passion to be thin in men are at least as tenacious and life threatening as in women. Men with eating disorders more frequently display impulsive behaviors such as bingeing and purging, and men display higher rates of drug and alcohol abuse and sociopathy and gender identity disturbance (Andersen, 2004a). Men with eating disorders manifest a high frequency of gender identity disturbance, homosexual orientation, and asexuality (Zerbe, 1993). Andersen (2004a) explained that when very ill, males and females suffering from medical complications require similar treatment, but when patients become healthier, the individuals' life stories unfold to reveal differences between the sexes in predisposition, course, and onset. Andersen suggested that we need to examine the roots of the issue and look at gender diversity. Keep in mind that because of the differences in the nature of eating disorders symptoms in males and females, because eating disorders are considered to be "female" disorders, because of the requirement of specific bodily standards in athletics, and because of symptom variability in the eating disorders not otherwise specified diagnosis, eating disorders in males are often missed. It is critical that practitioners develop a heightened awareness to clinical and subclinical eating disorders in males.

DISORDERED VERSUS HEALTHY EATING

For both diagnostic and prevention purposes, it is critical that practitioners recognize the distinction between disordered eating and eating disorders. *Disordered eating* is immoderate or unbalanced eating. Examples include overeating, skipping meals, grazing, or dieting. Though in most people, disordered eating is a benign enough behavior, any form of disordered eating has the potential to metamorphose into a clinical eating disorder in the presence of a genetic susceptibility and a precipitating environment trigger.

On first assessment, it may be difficult to distinguish disordered eating from an incipient or clinical eating disorder, so it is necessary to monitor disordered eating closely, with an emphasis on nutritious and balanced eating, set point weight restoration, and the reduction of compulsive behaviors. Making the assumption that disordered eating is a benign phenomenon, particularly in young children, constitutes playing with fire.

Healthy eating is the ability to eat anything, at any time, as long as it is with moderation. Healthy eating consists of three nutritionally dense and balanced meals a day, including varied foods representing all the food groups, as well as snacks. Healthy eating is pleasurable eating; it is the ability to eat without fear, compulsion, excess, or connection to one's emotional well-being. It is eating for the purposes of fueling the body, satiating hunger, and sociability.

A client with whom I had had a close relationship for a decade, asked what I had eaten for lunch that day. I told her. The meal started with leftover cold pizza and a piece of barbecue chicken from the night before, both of which "spoke to me" when I opened the refrigerator door. That, along with a plum, a bowl full of overly ripe raspberries that needed to be eaten, and two handfuls of nuts that I nibbled while feeding the cats, became my meal. Any "balance" that may have been missing would be made up through other meals that day. For the most part, anything goes, anytime, when it comes to nutritiously dense foods. Food is God's gift to mankind. It is a sensuous delight, our reward for hard work, our excuse to sit and talk with loved ones, our refueling refresher to make us feel good and energized, and our brain's best enabler to function at its best. In the best of all worlds, food should be an inalienable right for all people living on this earth.

A commonly held belief is that "instinctive eating"—eating when hungry and skipping meals when not—is the key to healthy eating. Advocates of instinctive eating assume that all individuals are equally competent and capable of making smart decisions about food choices and self-care if left to their own devices as a result of an inborn internal compass. It is my belief that accepted notions about the efficacy of purely intuitive eating simply do not apply to the myriad of children and adults lacking the capacity to sense internal cues and regulate themselves. Some cues may not be accurate; some perceptions of accurate cues may be distorted. In addition, once an individual develops a clinical eating disorder, perceptual distortions and dysfunctional hunger gauges render that person incapable of calibrating hunger and satiety signals.

It is far less problematic to occasionally eat too many cookies than it is to be afraid to ever let a cookie pass one's lips. What is unhealthy is compulsion and extremism of any kind and lack of self-control. In fact, there are no "unhealthy foods," just unhealthy ways to relate to food and approach the eating process.

A young woman engaged in compulsive nightly bingeing on sweets in bed before going to sleep. There was nothing intrinsically problematic about eating ice cream and cookies as part of her daily diet. What became problematic was what her ritualistic behaviors represented; the choiceless, compulsive quality of her eating; and why she felt compelled to eat these foods in this same manner every night, and in this place, without fail. For her, as her treatment progressed, the excesses of obsessive–compulsive disorder ultimately became a more likely diagnosis than an eating disorder.

For the individual with an eating disorder, attempting to follow prescriptions for healthy eating at appropriate times, in appropriate proportions, and on a consistent basis becomes a more complex task than it first appears, particularly because an optimally healthy relationship with food and eating demands approximation, ultimately taking the place of precision and prescription. The healthiest diets are ones in which the individual is able to improvise, allowing for some indulgences. It is normal to overindulge during holidays such as Halloween and Thanksgiving, accommodating for excesses on one particular day by compensatory eating the next. Compensatory eating is not restrictive eating, but a return to normalized eating. Box 2.1 lists the characteristics of healthy eating appropriate for clients recovering from an eating disorder.

A healthy eating lifestyle goes hand in hand with good sleep and study or work hygiene, requiring a balanced existence in life in general. Getting adequate sleep, exercise, and relaxation makes a person more likely to feel and look better, to lose weight and gain health, and to awaken at breakfast time to eat the first and most important meal of the day.

Normalized eating is healthy eating that has become an integrated part of the fully recovered eating lifestyle. For lunch, a young woman with anorexia consistently chose turkey with a sweet potato on the side as her starch rather than choosing a turkey sandwich. Nothing is wrong with turkey or with sweet potatoes or with the combination of the two. What is significant is how she made her food choices and why she was unable to vary her routine. Fear still dictated her choices, and it is apparent that she had not yet become a normalized eater.

BOX 2.1

Characteristics of Normalized Eating

- Healthy eating is not fat-free eating, nor is it instinctive eating, particularly for individuals with eating disorders, whose sensory gauges are dysfunctional.
- Normalized eaters should have no need to weigh themselves with any degree of regularity. People with disordered eating or eating disorders typically weigh themselves daily, responding to weight gain with the determination to decrease it and to weight loss as a reinforcement to dieting.
- People who are not normalized eaters cannot rely on hunger and satiety cues to determine when to eat or stop eating.
- Getting in shape for a sport is not synonymous with self-starvation and getting thinner; rather, it requires caretaking of the body through healthy, regular, and consistent fueling; appropriate exercise; and sleep hygiene. The body and brain require fueling, nurturance, and responsible care for optimal function.
- There is no cure for an eating disorder better than food itself. Eating three meals and at least one major snack per day is the prescription of choice.
- Humans need to eat approximately every four hours.
- The best way to maintain a healthy eating regimen is to "front-load" caloric intake, taking in a goodly portion of nutrients early in the day rather than waiting until dinner and evening snacking to supply the lion's share of daily nourishment (see "The Most Important Meal of the Day," 2008).
- Some healthy eaters prefer to eat six small meals (as opposed to three meals and snacks in between) throughout the day. Eating six small meals a day is often recommended for slow gastric emptying and/or hypoglycemia. This eating regimen must be distinguished from "grazing," which is less conducive to re-establishing the circadian body rhythm required to restore the healthy functioning of a sluggish metabolism.
- Regular eating facilitates reversal of a delay in gastric emptying typically seen in underweight clients, thereby reducing their propensity to feel full.
- Veganism in clients with eating disorders (particularly in young children) is invariably a therapeutic issue, making recovery more difficult in that it presents fewer opportunities to consume adequate proteins and fats and allows little room for flexibility.

Normalized eating for people recovering from an eating disorder involves the following:

- eating normal portion sizes—sometimes bigger, sometimes smaller, depending on availability and circumstance;
- eating varied food choices, in no particular order of consumption;
- letting go of food rituals such as not permitting foods to touch each other on the plate; cutting food into very small pieces, spitting out chewed food, eating the same thing at the same time every day, emotional eating, or restricting food items and food groups;

- eating regular meals and snacks and eating them consistently, everyday, day after day;
- letting go of ritualized excesses such as flavoring iced tea with 12 packets of artificial sweetener, drinking six or more Diet Cokes a day, regularly substituting granola or power bars for meals or snacks, carrying one's own food to parties and events to be assured that one can be in control of exactly what one ingests, and refraining from excessive exercise;
- experiencing joy and pleasure from eating.

HOW EATING DISORDERS WORK

The central notion of eating disorder treatment is that the compulsion to manipulate food intake correlates with a person's rigidity, compulsions, and fears of imperfection in other life spheres. In response to a pervasive sense of low self-esteem, powerlessness, and lack of control, the individual with an eating disorder manipulates her external environment (controlling food consumption) to create the sustaining illusion of internal self-control and well-being. Through an ironic transfer of power, self-determined habits transform into tyrannical compulsions that take up residence at the client's core, displacing her authentic self. Recovery from an eating disorder restores the integration and resiliency of the authentic self, freeing the individual to exercise genuine self-control and self-determination and to accommodate the spontaneous and changing needs of the moment through her own resourcefulness rather than through reliance on a rogue disease.

P, a talented speaker with a real interest in politics, felt too fat to join the debate team: "I can't risk ever having my picture appear in the school newspaper. I would be disgraced." As a result, she was socially isolated, with her eating disorder providing her only dependable relationship. At the same time, she took great comfort in the knowledge that she remained a vital part of a wider community of the calorie and thinness obsessed, a community within which she had earned a rightful place. Her eating disorder provided her with a secure sense of safety but essentially put her life on hold.

For some emotionally healthy individuals, an eating disorder may represent a fleeting coping glitch at a critical time in life. A 14-year-old youngster became anorexic, depressed, and emaciated after moving to a new town with her family, changing schools, and leaving all of her friends. Once she had recovered, she described herself as "acting and feeling psychotic" when she was in the throes of the disorder. Within two months of the start of her treatment, she had gained back her original weight and reported feeling as if she was "waking up from a bad dream."

For others, an eating disorder represents a lifelong struggle with their relationship with food; in these instances, the eating disorder typically occurs in tandem with co-occurring disorders and mood instability. Many adult clients describe always having had an issue with food, from their early childhood years on. One woman could not remember a time in her life when she was not dieting.

Eating Disorders Involve Both Nature and Nurture

The origins of eating disorders exist in the biology of gene clusters (nature) and the environment of the individual (nurture). A study showed that siblings of individuals with an eating disorder were about 10 times as likely to develop anorexia or bulimia, reflecting the importance of genetic factors in these disorders (Lilenfeld et al., 1998). Genetics explains why one child in a family may have an eating disorder whereas another does not; it also explains why, in at least 50 percent of cases, it is that when one twin has an eating disorder, the other will, as well (Lilenfeld et al., 1998). Conversely, in the absence of a genetic propensity for an eating disorder, no amount of influence, from family, peers, or society in general, will be sufficient to bring about a clinical disorder, and why in the face of pernicious media influences, only 5 percent of adolescents become clinically eating disordered (Adolescent Medicine Committee, Canadian Paediatric Society, 1998). Women may be more at risk of developing eating disorders than men because of the way their brain processes information. Scientists have found that a woman's brain responds differently than does a man's when exposed to certain words concerned with body image (Ramsey, Ward, Treasure, & Russell, 1999). The findings may explain why 10 times as many women develop anorexia and bulimia as do men (BBC News, 2005a).

In individuals with a genetic susceptibility, disease onset may be triggered by a single event or by an ongoing stressor over time. Environmental triggers may take the form of unavoidable life transitions such as geographic moves, divorce, death, or the onset of puberty. Family systems that are chaotic, abusive, or lacking in normal boundaries, and parents who role model their own unresolved issues about eating and weight management can become elements in a wide array of triggers leading to the onset of disease. Some parents, even from healthy family systems, may intentionally or unintentionally give their child the clear messages that they approve of the child's excessive thinness or restrictive behaviors.

Eating Disorders Are Diseases

A recent survey showed that a third of the United Kingdom population believes that people choose to be anorexic (Bennett, 2008). In fact, eating disorders clients do not bring their disorders on themselves; these disorders result from a disease process that deprives the individual of the internal resources required to withstand and combat it. Eating disorders are biopsychosocial diseases, a concept that holds significant implications for both prevention and cure. Believing she had brought her disorder on herself, a client with anorexia expressed amazement that others had come up with the same "creative" idea as she for losing weight. It seems odd to consider a behavioral–nutritional dysfunction a disease, particularly when its symptoms are acceptable to and shared by so many people who are in no way ill. What makes an eating disorder a disease?

I conceptualize eating disorders to be diseases by virtue of their being systemic, taking life and altering life quality, affecting diverse populations, and interrupting social and emotional development. As systemic diseases, eating disorders affect every aspect of a client's mood and function; for these clients, a "good" day is one on which the scale shows weight loss; a "bad" day shows weight gain. A 15-year-old did not feel free to shop for underwear with her mother because she had eaten a piece of candy earlier that day and felt that her entire body was hugely distorted and distended as a result. Eating disorders are diseases too, in their potential to take life and alter life quality, as well as to become cured. One young client described her illness as being like a cancer, with tentacles that metastasize and spread out to infect every aspect of the body and function, causing destruction in its wake. She described healing as the process of separating out and disentangling, "thread by thread," every aspect of disease from every aspect of her life function.

Eating disorders take on the quality of disease, too, by afflicting victims of every gender, age, racial, ethnic, and socioeconomic background. Scientist Anne Becker discovered a sharp rise in the incidence of eating disorders in the Fiji islands with the advent of television in that part of the world ("Fat-Phobia in the Fijis," 1999). A study reported that Black girls were 50 percent more likely than White girls to exhibit bulimic behavior, including both bingeing and purging, but also less likely to seek treatment because of their assumption that these are "White girls' diseases" (Bennett, 2008).

Eating disorders are diseases, too, in their capacity to interrupt normal development and to stunt a person's growth, both physically and emotionally at whatever age and life stage they occur. These disorders arrest the development of the self and the achievement of personhood and self-determination. Like other diseases, eating disorders are often accompanied by and may trigger co-occurring disturbances, such as depression, anxiety, heart disease, and osteoporosis.

W, a college student, did not realize that she had anorexia nervosa or depression, even though she had lost 20 pounds in 3 months and had become a social recluse. Though she had been engaged in psychotherapy for two semesters, she could not understand why she felt so depressed and was increasingly unable to concentrate on her studies or make decisions. Because no health care professional could come up with a diagnosis of any sort, she felt frightened and discouraged that there would be no way out of her misery. Once I was able to diagnose an eating disorder, she felt relieved in the knowledge that identifying the problem would enable recovery interventions.

Eating Disorders Can Be Lethal

Anorexia has the highest mortality rate of any psychiatric disorder; 8 percent to 18 percent of persons with this disorder die as a result (Zerbe, 1993, p. 170). The mortality rate of individuals with bulimia appears to be lower, although electrolyte imbalance, cardiac arrhythmias, esophageal tears, gastric rupture, and acute recurrent pancreatitis can be life threatening (Zerbe, 1993, p. 171). Its lethality is ironic in the face of the patient's reliance on the disorder as a survival tool, as a primary device for coping with adversity.

Eating disorders take the lives of victims in the prime of life who may appear to be in perfect health. Many die suddenly in their sleep from cardiac arrhythmias and stoppages brought on by electrolyte imbalances. Compared with the general population, people with anorexia are at a heightened risk of death not only after hospitalization but many years later; their long-term risk of death stems not just from anorexia but from a number of other causes as well.

Women with anorexia are reportedly 12 times more likely to die than women of a similar age in the general population and up to twice as likely as women with any other psychiatric disorders (Work Group on Eating Disorders, 2006). The suicide rate among women with anorexia is as much as 57 times higher than that for women of a similar age in the general population, and the methods they use tend to be highly lethal with a low potential for resulting in rescue (Holm-Denoma et al., 2008).

When a human body is reduced to approximately 65 percent of ideal body weight, the risk for mortality becomes heightened. No one knows how long it takes for a person's body and vital organs to succumb; no one can predict when and how complications of eating disorders will lead to a body's demise. Compounding these problems, warning symptoms are often hidden from the clinician. Prisoners have lived for years on meager rations in prisoner of war and concentration camps, illustrating the endurance of the human body in adjusting to adversity, starvation, deprivation, and physical torment. A colleague of mine, speaking of two deaths in her practice, stated, "It took one of my clients 8 years of severe malnutrition and the other 15 years to get there."

Eating disorders are capable of killing off life quality even without extinguishing lives. A young woman who was a brilliant student at a prominent university fell into a bulimic coma for three months, from which she emerged with permanent and global brain damage. Never able to return to school, this young woman will spend the rest of her life in a facility for people with brain dysfunction.

Eating Disorders Are Systemic Diseases

An eating disorder is a system that encompasses every aspect of a person's function and existence—cognitive, behavioral, physiological, nutritional, emotional, sensory, attitudinal, social, and cultural. Each overlapping sphere demands skilled (and simultaneous) attention from knowledgeable experts offering treatment attention to all facets of disease, all at once. Treating dysfunctional behaviors alone, restoring weight alone, appealing to the cognitive mind alone, managing underlying mood dysfunction or low self-esteem alone, and engaging in a friendly and comfortable therapeutic connection alone are insufficient to bring about healing. No aspect of an eating disorder exists in isolation; similarly, none will heal in isolation. The client herself becomes a system of disparate (exiled) parts of the self that, through recovery, become reorganized and reintegrated into a unified personality and core self. Box 2.2 lists the many facets of the client system that are affected by eating disorders.

One client described her disease as follows:

> It was like I was running a science experiment where I was my own experiment. I never knew who was doing what . . . was I running the disease, or was the disease running me? My eating disorder and I had become one and the same, taking turns egging each other on. The person that I really am got lost in the shuffle.

BOX 2.2

Eating Disorders: A Multifaceted Disease System

Facet of the Eating Disorder System	Aspect Affected
Body	Nutrition, physical health
Mind	Cognition (thinking), behaviors, sensing, body image perception, attitudes
Psyche	Developmental milestones, feelings, emotions, self-esteem, mood
Social self	Family relationships, other personal interactions
Soul	Quality of life, capacity to enjoy inner peace; eating disorder symptoms can be considered the voice of the soul
Self	Detachment or disconnect from one's inner core
Brain	Neurochemistry through heredity, environmental factors, and the onset and process of disease

Source: Natenshon, 1999.

With clients who have eating disorders, therapists enter a relationship triangle consisting of you, me, and the eating disorder. Initially, the clinician can expect the disorder to speak for the client, through her mouth and in her voice. Recognizing and calling attention to this dynamic will help the clinician sustain the client's hope and motivation throughout treatment.

The systemic nature of these disorders demands an integrative perspective in offering care. Any form of reductionist treatment that excludes the larger disease picture can be expected to trivialize the pervasive enormity of the effects of the illness on clients and families. For example, the father of an anorexic woman described her care at a treatment center where she had undergone classical Freudian psychoanalysis. Ignoring the multidisciplinary demands of treating anorexia and the disturbed perceptions of her malnourished brain, her analyst had her lying on the treatment couch for months, waiting for her to initiate and direct her own care. The therapist never attended to the physical, behavioral, and emotional aspects of the eating disorder.

Eating Disorders Are Disorders of Sensing and of Loss of Self-Reference

The client who has an eating disorder has little access to real feelings and accurate sensations. The distorted sensation of being fat masks genuine feelings of anxiety, sadness, or fear whose recognition is essential to resolving the underlying problems. A client with an eating disorder told me, "Neither day nor hour goes by without my awareness of the tyranny of my disorder. I can't even drink a cup of tea without being concerned about whether it might make me feel unpleasantly full, creating a 'fat feeling' and, therefore, an intolerable day." This young woman was completely out of touch with her true self and incapable of sensing her needs.

Clients who have eating disorders describe a profound, total loss of the self. They are unable to sense or accurately experience the self and the surrounding world, exacerbating shame and self-loathing. In her book, *Sensing the Self: Women's Recovery From Bulimia*, Reindl (2001) described this inability as follows:

> People with bulimia nervosa avoid turning their attention inward to consult their needs, desires, feelings, and aggressive strivings because to do so is to encounter an annihilating sense of shame. Disconnected from internal, sensed experience, bulimic women need to develop a sense of self . . . to become attuned to their physical, psychic and social self-experience. . . . What emerges as the core experience of recovery is the process of developing a sense of self, where the word 'sense' is as important as the word 'self.' (see book jacket)

My clients have described the loss of sensing and of self-reference time and again. One confided,

> I would be lost without my eating disorder. What would I do with my life if I wasn't trying to look perfect? What else would I think about? How could I know who I am? What I need? I need something to aspire to, to give my life a direction, a purpose.

Without access to her senses, this woman could not allow herself the aesthetic pleasure of a plate of food, smelling the aromas as she cooked, tasting the tastes, feeling the textures on her tongue and in her cheeks. The thought of "womanliness" was repulsive and shameful to her; she could not consider the disgrace of developing breasts, hips, buttocks, or thighs, yet she remembered with regret a boyfriend she had once loved.

Recovery involves a newly renewed capacity to learn through sensing (differentiating) distinctions; clients create alternative options for thinking and action by reorganizing and reintegrating disparate aspects of their personalities. In discerning what does not work for them, their brains learn to distinguish options that might work better. It is significant to note that imaging studies have found evidence of brain changes associated with the regulation of appetite, indicating that the sense of taste differs in women with anorexia nervosa. With clients, I purposefully speak of my own "sensing" of what might be occurring within the treatment dynamic as it occurs in the moment, based on what the client says and how she says it. In this way, I illustrate how the senses are called up and brought into use through listening, nuanced thinking, and instinct, and how sensing derives from approximations, from personal and visceral impressions.

Eating Disorders Are Disorders of Control

According to Nelson Mandela, "Our deepest fear is not that we are inadequate. Our deepest fear is that we are powerful beyond measure." During the process of recovery from an eating disorder, through a growing capacity to self-determine and regulate food and behaviors, illusory external control (thought to be accessed through the symptoms of the eating disorder) is replaced by the client's acquisition of genuine internal controls.

The control issues accompanying eating disorders sometimes take the form of the client's manipulating and wielding too much power over others despite her feelings of powerlessness. Most such attempts at controlling others, however, are inspired by the desire to assume control over the self.

Eating Disorders Are Disorders of Excess, Compulsion, and Dysregulation

Eating disordered behaviors are imbalanced, immoderate, and excessive, both around food and appetite and in other life spheres. Clients tend to eat too little or eat too much, sleep too little, recreate too much, socialize too little, or exercise too much. Driven by compulsion, thoughts and behaviors take on an all-or-nothing, black-and-white, choiceless quality.

Promiscuity and shoplifting are typical compulsions of bulimic hypomania. Jail does little to deter compulsive stealing; it is not uncommon for even affluent clients to find themselves in trouble with the law after shoplifting a worthless and unneeded item from a retail store.

Compulsive workouts for individuals with activity disorders, a form of bulimia, can compromise daily life function and may result in self-injury. An adult client who had anorexia and an activity disorder developed shin splints from running 10 miles a day. When instructed by his doctor to curtail his morning workout routine, he began to wake up at 4:00 A.M. every day to swim several miles instead before getting on the train to go to work (Natenshon, 1999).

Excess, compulsion, and the undifferentiated lack of self-awareness that defines them are benchmarks of an eating disorder. A person who is incapable of discerning hunger or satiety, for example, is likely to be incapable of differentiating or moderating other sensations, thoughts, feelings, or urges. The following are examples:

- J, a young woman with anorexia, not only felt compelled to stay at a job she hated; she disciplined herself to work 16 hours a day, seven days a week, without adequate financial remuneration or acknowledgment from her superiors. She felt as victimized by her bosses and peers as she did by her eating disorder. In her mind, quitting her disease, like quitting her job, was simply not an option.
- While in the throes of anorexia, D had become socially isolated; her greatest fear in contemplating recovery was that if she were to let go of her ultra-strict food restrictions, she would engage in out-of-control gorging and become obese. As she began to restore her weight and associate once again with friends, she went to opposite extremes, staying out all night and becoming "passing-out drunk," then sleeping the entire next day and missing classes, meals, and study time. Her fears of losing control were realized in multiple contexts.
- U, an anorexic eighth grader who got perfect grades, was a concrete, black-and-white thinker. Her goal was to eat the least she could in order to stay alive and excel in school. She feared that if she studied less than six hours

a night, she would not be able to get herself to study at all, which would lead to failure at school, jeopardize her chances to get into college, and preclude a happy and fulfilled adult life.

- K, a college student with anorexia who was compulsive about restricting calories, wrote her term papers the day they were assigned, and then edited them every day until they were due. She edited one paper 60 times before she handed it in.

- A client with anorexia, P, described needing three trunk-size suitcases for a weekend visit to a friend at college. Fearing that she might be missing something or somehow not look presentable enough, she brought her entire wardrobe "just to be safe." One trunk just carried just shoes and boots, another held all the clothes in her closet that were appropriate for the weekend, and another was just for toiletries, lotions, and hair and skin beautifiers.

Eating Disorders Are Disorders of Fear

Most of us do not relish dealing with life's ambiguities, transitions, and changes; the unknown naturally gives rise to some degree of fear in its uncertainty. Extreme fear and dread of the unknown and the unpredictable lie at the heart of eating disorders, explaining why individuals who have eating disorders would rather remain sick than risk a recovery that might require them to cope with life without the security of this crutch.

One young woman observed that to imagine her life without her eating disorder aroused feelings of desperation akin to what it must feel like on the first day of nursery school for the defenseless and desperate child torn from the protection and guidance of an ever-constant mother. Genetically based anxiety plays a critical role in creating the fears that give rise to EDs; the malnourished brain and the dynamic of treatment and recovery exacerbate these fears and create resistance to recovery. Although anxiety may precede the onset of an eating disorder, it will diminish significantly with weight restoration.

For the individual with an eating disorder, the fear of food and eating is no ordinary fear. One of my clients compared her fear of becoming fat to her fear of handling a poisonous snake with bare hands, being pursued by a killer with a gun, or jumping out of an airplane without a parachute. She feared remaining anorexic, but she also feared a recovery that would leave her "stranded." She was afraid that if her progress was moved along too quickly, it would leave her bereft and overweight; if too slowly, she might be forced to enter a treatment program.

A youngster with anorexia was so anxious about having eaten two sugar cookies that two days later she continued to perseverate about how scary it was to have them "contaminating" her body. She could think of little else but about having "poisoned" herself and how she would need to refuse all food now as a result. Many individuals with anorexia refuse to eat food that they do not prepare personally, because, as one client observed, "Who knows what might be in it and how it could hurt you?"

It is important for therapists to interpret to clients that what might seem like obstinacy and stubborn sabotaging of treatment are simply signs of anxiety and fear. This will reassure clients that what may sound irrational and "crazy" (even to themselves) is largely a manifestation of anxiety. Keeping this fact in mind may also help therapists minimize their own frustration.

Behind every "fat" thought, feeling, or fear, there are other thoughts, feelings, and fears awaiting discovery. R refused meals for fear of "becoming fat." When pressed to describe her fears more precisely, she admitted that she would not eat breakfast for fear that she would "eat too much, appear bloated, need to purge at home, be late for school, need to purge again at school, miss classes, feel badly about herself all day, be unable to concentrate and learn, and have to eat with her peers who might then discover her secret in the school cafeteria."

Panic attacks are not uncommon as individuals with eating disorders face food and the act of eating. Symptoms of panic attacks might include nausea, tingling hands, shortness of breath, rising blood pressure, lightheadedness, and blacking out. A young woman with anorexia described sitting down to dinner at an Italian restaurant with her family. She described the experience as follows:

> When they brought the whole pizza to the table at once and put it down in front of us, I was nauseated with panic in not knowing what to do, how to react, what to say. I broke into a cold sweat. It was a horrific and overwhelming moment. It was not until my sister cut off a small slice and put it on a plate in front of me that I could feel less terror and figure out what I had to do next.

Eating Disorders Are Triggered by the Thin-Is-In Culture

It is ironic that despite the health consciousness that pervades society, triggers to eating dysfunction and eating disorders are to be found everywhere. It becomes increasingly difficult to consider dysfunctional behaviors and attitudes as pathological in light of their prevalence. A chic pasta bar in New York City sported an advertisement in its window that read, "Our food comes up as easily as it goes down." A billboard for a popular franchise restaurant boasts of serving "Clean Food" and advised customers to "ingest no evil," inspiring fear and paranoia in an increasingly eating-disordered population where food is seen as fattening and where less is considered more.

A survey of college students from six campuses across the United States found that 30 percent would be willing to take a nutritional pill if they could forgo eating (Nichols, 1999). More than 10 percent of the female respondents reported feeling embarrassed to be seen buying a chocolate bar (Nichols, 1999). Disordered eating is not restricted to women on college campuses. A study conducted by Cornell University found that 40 percent of male football players engaged in some sort of disordered eating behavior (Cedric Centre for Counselling, n.d.). Myths and misconceptions surrounding eating disorders, food, and weight management are rampant; Box 2.3 lists some of the most common. It is up to psychotherapists to anticipate, recognize, bring to awareness, and dispel prevalent myths and misconceptions that threaten to sabotage treatment outcomes.

The pernicious messages of the media are inescapable; turning on the television, seeing a movie, or standing in line at the supermarket, we are reminded that

---

BOX 2.3

Myths and Misconceptions About Eating Disorders

The following are some of the most common myths and misconceptions surrounding eating and weight-related issues (all are false):

- Nobody eats breakfast.
- It's OK to skip meals if you aren't hungry.
- Dieting is the best way to lose weight.
- If a person's weight is within the range of normal on a weight chart, an eating disorder can be ruled out.
- People with anorexia are thin and easy to diagnose.
- When weight has been restored to "normal," recovery has been achieved.
- Food is fattening.
- Fat-free eating is "healthy" eating.
- Eating fat makes you fat.
- There is no such thing as "too much exercise."
- It is normal for teenage girls to dislike their bodies and to go on diets.
- It is normal for teenagers not to have regular menstrual periods
- Victims who die from an eating disorder are always emaciated.
- A person needs to exercise to burn calories.
- A person with an eating disorder can quit the disorder once she is as thin as she wants to be.
- Diets geared to weight management or health issues in adults (e.g., fat-free or low-fat diets for those who are obese or have heart disease) are also appropriate for children, teenagers, and young adults.

---

thinness is deemed central to a happy and successful life. Another study (performed in 1995) found that three minutes spent looking at a fashion magazine caused 70 percent of women to feel depressed, guilty, and shameful (see "Health matters," n.d.). One of my anorexic clients spent about $45 a month on fashion magazines, and many consider fashion to be their expertise and plan to seek careers in the fashion world.

Although parents cannot protect their child from exposure to harmful media messages, they can teach their children how to recognize such influences and not be taken in by them. Children need to be taught to become critics of the media rather than victims of it. They need to understand that the models they see are thinner than 98 percent of women viewing them (National Eating Disorders Association, n.d.). Practitioners need to educate themselves, so that they can educate parents, and so that parents, in turn, can educate their children.

In combating the influence of society and the media, it is critical that practitioners, parents, teachers, and coaches become cognizant of what healthy eating really is and what constitutes disordered eating. There is nothing abnormal about exhibiting food preferences. It is the extremes in behaviors motivated by fear or driven by compulsions that mark pathology. Professionals need not be exemplary eaters themselves in order to function as eating disorder practitioners. As client advocates and educators, however, they must be ready and willing to talk the talk of healthy eating and living, even if they do not feel personally capable of walking that path themselves; having said that, I believe that no amount of discussion will be convincing if the therapist's own conflicting emotional issues about eating and weight management remain unresolved.

Eating Disorders Affect the Entire Family

Whenever a client who is identified as having an eating disorder walks through my office door, I envision a virtual crowd awaiting treatment and needing care. Parents and families will potentially require intervention, collaboration, education, and therapeutic support along with their child. The following e-mail from a parent speaks with eloquence and poignancy to the reality that parents of child patients become your clients, too:

> All your life you love something. Because you love it, you take care of it. You know what you need to do to make it whatever it is. You know how to provide for it, change it, feed it, and care for it. You know how to fix what has gone wrong. Then, something like this comes, and you can't fix it, no matter how hard you try. She doesn't feel she needs fixing or changing. And I can't fix it. So I feel frustrated, helpless, angry, and guilty. I can't do anything about it when she feels so unhappy with herself that she hurts herself, or she takes laxatives. I can't stop it, because I can't be there 24 hours a day, 7 days a week, wherever she is. I don't know how to help her.

Eating disorders are family diseases for the following reasons:

- The great majority of eating disorder cases involve children whose lives, diseases, and recoveries play out at home—at kitchen tables, in family bathrooms and bedrooms—alongside and in full view of parents and siblings.
- By virtue of the family's physical proximity to their recovering child, parents and siblings find themselves on the front lines of diagnosis and care, observing and participating in the child's battle with disease.
- Families and siblings typically become targets of the client's volatility and irascibility, particularly around mealtimes. They must deal with the onslaught of mood instability, which may run the gamut from depressive withdrawal to impulsive acting out against the self and others.
- Because issues giving rise to eating disorders are largely developmental, it is the natural role of parents to address, foster, and repair developmental tasks and milestones in their children. In some cases, the attitudes of overly controlling parents vis-à-vis their own disordered eating and weight management concerns can be damaging to the susceptible child attempting to recover.

Parents of children with eating disorders can be expected to be, in some respects as needy as their child. As parents begin treatment, it doesn't take long before the inevitable questions arise: "So, what have we done wrong as parents?" and "How have we created this problem for our child?" In response, I am quick to help parents recognize that the more relevant and constructive questions to ask are "What have we as parents done right in countering this illness?" and "What can we do to continue to enhance our child's recovery?" I help them see that they are performing nobly and creating an opportunity for their child's complete recovery by facing these unpleasant realities; bringing their child to care; demonstrating the courage, integrity, and loving tenacity it takes to initiate and stay with the tough conversations with resistant children and resistant disorders; and offering themselves in whatever capacity they can to enhance their child's healing. I help them to learn that the nature of their support for their child will need to change substantively through the various stages of their child's healing. Box 2.4 lists common misconceptions among parents that reflect teaching opportunities for therapists.

The family system provides context and container for the child's emotional and physical development from childhood into young adulthood. The best way to facilitate change in any one particular aspect of any system is to foster parallel

---

BOX 2.4

Meeting Parents Where They Are

Anticipating, recognizing, and countering parental disempowerment and ignorance about eating disorders are key to the child's healing. Therapists can expect parents to be misguided; it is for treaters to enlighten and educate them. Anticipate that parents will make the following mistakes: Parents will typically:

- Believe they are the cause of their child's problem and that by becoming involved, they will make matters worse.
- Believe that health professionals alone cure these diseases.
- Hesitate to "accuse" a child of having an eating disorder when there is no "definitive evidence."
- Believe that eating disorders are minor problems as compared to alcohol or drug abuse.
- Be afraid to confront their child because they assume that angering the child might exacerbate the problem or provoke the loss of the child's trust or love.
- Not see an eating disorder as a disease (if their child had diabetes or cancer, they would feel no such ambivalence about making demands for healing)
- Believe that what their child eats is none of their business and that intervention is synonymous with interference and fosters dependency.
- Believe that their child's recovery changes should be clearly and readily observable.
- Believe that because treatment can be such an extended process, they cannot know if a therapy relationship is effective until at least several months into it.
- Believe that children don't want their eating disorder "secret" discovered.
- Believe that therapists breach their child's privacy rights and confidentiality through any form of communication with them.
- Believe that once children become adolescents, they no longer need or want their parents' help or influence.

changes within other aspects of the system. In cases where a resistant child refuses to participate in some aspects of treatment, interventions with the child's family system (even in the absence of the child) can be powerful enough to stimulate changes within the child. The naturalist John Muir said, "When we try to pick anything out by itself, we find it hitched to everything else in the universe." Inclusive family involvement supports the needs and emotional well-being of all members of a family system in flux. Family therapy sessions generally result in family members making connections to each other and to the treatment process. In developing the family's courage to practice new skills and find solutions to long-standing problems, conjoint treatment typically results in feelings of catharsis and well-being.

In family treatment, it is not unusual for the identified patient to prefer (or demand) not to focus on herself and her eating disorder but instead to address general family issues. In such a case, it behooves the therapist to begin with the agenda that feels most comfortable for family and child, then to meander with the evolving dynamics of the session to discussion about the implications of the eating disorder as it impacts the family dynamics. In the interest of reducing fears, and reinforcing strengths, I make a point to be forthright and generous in pointing out whatever positive signs I observe immediately within a family system (bonded, problem-solving, communicative and/or mutually supportive) that portend a successful outcome. Parents need support and nurturing not only to boost their own knowledge and self-confidence but also to empower and motivate them in facilitating their child's healing.

In some instances, family belief systems can exacerbate an eating disorder. Over the years, C's anorexia was resistant to healing. As C ultimately began to nourish herself, it started to become clear that underlying the tenacity of her disorder was the family belief that a person always needs someone (or something) to care for her; although her parents had been separated for over a decade, they chose never to divorce, as neither could face life without a caretaker. Always feeling like an outsider in her family, she turned to her eating disorder to assume this protective role for her. Her disorder also provided secure boundaries to shield her from intrusive family members.

In my psychotherapy practice, I make it my business to come face to face with parents as soon, and as often, as possible. Parental involvement is an asset to diagnosis, information gathering, knowledge sharing, and family bonding, as well as to the functioning of the professional team. Sessions that include grandparents or older siblings provide invaluable education for family members while bringing to light new or previously undiscovered therapy issues for the child. The quality of the therapist's relationship with parents can be a pivotal factor in fostering the quality of the relationship between the therapist and the child.

Unfortunately, eating disorders by their very nature strip parents of their executive function as protectors and supporters of their child, denying them authority, authenticity, and confidence in the face of the afflicted child/stranger now possessed by this tyrannical "monster within." The same can sometimes be said of previous treatment experiences in which professionals excluded parents from participating in the recovery process; one parent described being instructed by her child's therapist to "take both hands off the wheel." When parents are excluded, they are denied the opportunity of learning how the process of psy-chotherapy works, what change looks like, and what it really takes to heal an eat-ing disorder. By investigating what families have taken from past treatment expe-riences, the goal of the current clinician is to highlight and underline the client's and family's prior learning and growth in determining a purposeful direction for continuing change.

Effects on the Marital System When a Partner Is Ill

Adult eating disorders can become a "third wheel" in the process of choos-ing a mate or life partner. Whether consciously or subconsciously, partners invari-ably seek mates who share issues, attitudes, values, and preferences. It is not unusual to find a fiancé of an anorexic client colluding with his partner to ensure that weight management or eating issues remain underground in the company of other secrets.

Partners of anorexic women often tend to prefer thin women, are comfort-able looking the other way rather than confronting problems, and typically strug-gle with their own addictions, eating dysfunctions, perfectionism, and compul-sions. After 25 years of marriage and three children, the husband of an anorexic woman would pinch her waist to measure her fat; appearance and perfection were important to him. It is not unusual to find that husbands who divorce anorexic women seek out other women with similar appearance and issues.

Unique behavioral patterns may develop between such couples. For exam-ple, anorexic women may be averse to being touched or embraced by their partner after having eaten. One anorexic wife retired for the night at 4:00 P.M. to avoid fur-ther eating. An anorexic client claimed that her husband knew about her struggles to recover though contended that he still didn't have "a clue as to what recovery *really* is about." After years of therapy, she said, "Just as he awakens and wants to have sex, I awake feeling fat and obsessing about what I can eat that day. It doesn't lend itself to sexual compatibility." I invited her to ask him to join her in treatment, but she claimed she didn't want her disorder to become a "burden" to him.

Treaters need to be aware that unless partners are recruited to treatment and involved to some degree in alleviating the eating disorder, the partnership itself is likely to become a factor in inadvertently perpetrating or prolonging disease. Likewise, when positive changes happen within the partner with the eating dis-order, to ensure the homeostasis of the marital system, both partners need to be brought into treatment to accommodate and reconfigure the changing marital sys-tem. As a young woman with bulimia achieved wellness, her increased empow-erment made her less willing to be victimized by her husband's alcoholism. As she became more self-possessed and assertive, she became less tolerant of his abu-sive behavior, and he became increasingly threatened by and intolerant of her emerging core self. Worried that in individual treatment she might outgrow him, he preferred that she not seek treatment at all. Together, this couple and I decided that the husband would join her in sessions periodically to keep an eye on the potential need for conjoint marital sessions to stabilize a marital system in the throes of imbalance. Through these sessions, her husband learned to appreciate and respect that his wife was regaining herself, the importance of his marriage to him, and his own investment in growing healthier alongside her to preserve the marriage that he so valued.

Effects on the Marital System When a Child Is Ill

An eating disorder that emerges within a family system represents a crisis for all members of the family, including parents and siblings. The crisis takes the form of fear for their afflicted child, guilt for believing they may have caused the problem, and frustration in not knowing how to fix it. In addition, families deal with disruption of mealtimes, with parents needing to monitor and police every food encounter. Pressures are brought to bear through financial insecurity and the need to participate in a recovery process that they do not understand (and may be excluded from.) Most painful of all, parents of children with eating disorders have temporarily lost emotional access to the withdrawn, depressed, defensive, and preoccupied child. Because of the nature of family systems, the diversion of the eating disordered child can, in some instances, distract and shield parents from the need to confront their own personal and/or marital issues. In the face of a child's recovery, underlying and previously unexpressed marital issues may emerge in direct proportion to the child's stabilizing health. If partners are not open to their own and the family's growth and change alongside their recovering child's growth and changes, the emotional status of the child, the wider family system, and the marital partnership are at risk for disruption.

As a client with anorexia began to make recovery progress, her parents began to look more clearly at their own marital problems, which had taken a back seat to the emerging eating disorder. In an effort to protect the marriage, they began to subtly sabotage the girl's progress in her recovery. In another instance, a 10-year-old child with anorexia found that she was a powerful influence in her parents' marriage. Because her father was so actively intent upon helping her to get well and her mother was so passively intent upon keeping her sick (perhaps to deflect attention from the marriage), the child's choice was to stay sick. This choice may have been at least partly a dynamic of wanting to bring about balance in the marital relationship by supporting her mother, whom she saw as the more vulnerable partner.

Effects on Siblings

Do not underestimate the stress on children living side by side with a client who has an eating disorder. Siblings have no choice but to live closely with the fear, frustration, and powerlessness of an eating disorder within their family system. It is typical for siblings to feel anger at the attention being lavished on the child with the eating disorder or to feel compelled to hide their own neediness in deference to the needier siblings and to parents who are already emotionally overwhelmed. In an attempt to caretake their parents, some children may act prematurely "adultified," becoming overly compliant or solicitous and asking too little of their parents for themselves. Therapists need to be attuned to such tensions within family systems.

For example, the younger brother of a teenage with anorexia bore the brunt of his sister's moodiness and secrecy about "the secret that everyone knew." In response, he became hostile and sometimes insulting to his sister with regard to her weight, mimicking their father's behavior. In so doing, he enjoyed an alliance with his otherwise rejecting father but suffered his sister's abusiveness. Most unfortunately, as a result of his having been intentionally excluded from knowing his sister's "secret that everyone knew," each sibling missed out on a chance to support and be supportive, one to the other.

The 20-year-old sister of a young woman who had been anorexic for four years broke down in tears in a conjoint session with her sister. She described how frightened and "creeped out" she felt by her sister's emaciation, to the point of feeling unable to touch her or show any sign of affection. Though her sister was currently doing well, she anticipated that history would repeat itself and that her sister would relapse time and again. She admitted to feeling intensely angry at her sister for not taking care of herself, for endangering her life, for being untruthful, for worrying their parents, and for making their family life so disruptive and unpleasant for so many years; Most difficult of all, she felt guilty for being unable to help her effect change.

Sisters and brothers who come to understand eating disorders and are included in the process have the potential to become the struggling child's greatest ally and support resource; in so doing, they benefit by learning the courageous art of facing and resolving problems with wisdom and sensitivity. Within a relationship rooted in trust and based in loving concern, their encouragement of their sibling to eat heartily and healthfully can be sustaining and reinforcing. In being told by her sister, "Take another piece of pizza; it's good for you and delicious and clearly won't make you fat," the client described her sibling as being "a saving grace." As part of her admission about her difficulties trying new foods, her sibling offered reassurance about the many other positive changes she *had* made. The client reported feeling supported and loved.

For another client, one of the most significant forces in her persistent body image concerns and fears of eating was the competition she felt with her younger sister, whom she envied for her smaller stature. Through treatment, the two girls experienced a significant change in the quality of their relationship. As the bonds between them deepened, the client began to see and accept her sister as a whole human being, with needs, feelings, and vulnerabilities of her own. Their increasing intimacy, along with more secure boundaries, diminished their sibling rivalry as well as the internal conflict between them that had contributed to triggering the eating disorder.

Effects on Blended Families

Divorce and remarriage cause problems even for the healthiest of children, who must navigate the stressors of changing parents, family, house, school, and peers, aside from living out of a suitcase on weekends. Children with or without an eating disorder bring to new living arrangements a sense of loss and, potentially, a lack of belonging and identity, of attachment and trust. The loss of privacy in being required to share bedrooms and bathrooms is particularly acute for the child with the eating disorder. Reclusive, abusive, attention-getting, and self-destructive behaviors are not atypical for children with an eating disorder facing difficulties in adapting to change. Problems can be exacerbated if the new stepparent has limited knowledge about eating disorders and their implications for the child and the family as a whole, particularly when boundaries are shaky.

A healthy relationship between the biological parent and the child is critical in achieving favorable outcomes. Although family dynamics may be complex, they remain clearly resolvable where there is love and concern and a willingness to participate in family therapy. Box 2.5 lists questions clients frequently ask of therapists and appropriate responses.

BOX 2.5

Questions Commonly Asked by Clients

Q. If I lose weight by eating *less*, how is it possible that by eating *more* in recovery, I can remain thin?

A. When you restrict food, you're more likely to become extremely hungry, which leads to gorging and, therefore, to gaining weight, Eating nutritious foods at regular meals will improve your metabolic function and help you develop a healthier eating lifestyle, both of which lead to *sustainable* thinness. Once you've reached your set point weight, you'll stop gaining weight, and this healthy weight will stay with you throughout your lifetime.

Q. How is it possible that eating fats won't make me fat?

A. Your body requires fats to maintain a healthy reproductive system and to grow neural pathways in your brain, among many other functions. If you eat with balance and moderation, no food will make you fat.

Q. How can I be sick if my medical tests show that I am normal on all counts?

A. Medical tests typically won't show evidence of eating disorder until you are very, very sick. Even when close to starvation, the human body is highly resilient and inventive in surviving on too little food.

Q. How can I be sick if I feel better than ever?

A. It is normal to feel better when sick with an eating disorder than during the process of becoming well. The eating disorder gives you a false sense of power and control. As you recover, you may initially feel uncomfortably anxious as you lose this sense of power and control. With time, this anxiety will lessen, and you will feel better than ever.

Q. Are 100-calorie packs of cookies healthy snacks for limiting caloric intake?

A. There are no bad foods. Even "junk" foods are fine to eat in moderation, as long as you also eat nutritious meals. Healthy eating is not determined by the number of calories you ingest but by your ability to eat all food groups in a balanced way. The most sustainable good eating habits are those that you and your body determine together, based on your healthy eating lifestyle, your appetite at the moment, and your food preferences.

Q. Why do my parents have to be involved in my treatment? They're really annoying.

A. You may feel that your treatment is none of your parents' business. It's as if your eating disorder is putting up a fight so that it can remain in control over your life. Your parents, however, have an obligation to look out for your well-being until you are able again to resume control of your own life. Once you're able to care for yourself, we can help your parents learn to step back and give you more responsibility for yourself.

Q. Why do I need to get my period back naturally if hormone replacement therapy will do the trick? (This question pertains to clients with anorexia)

A. Although your gynecologist may be willing to prescribe birth control pills to bring on your period, a healthy reproductive system and your ability to give birth to a baby one day, along with your body's capacity to grow healthy, strong bones will stay compromised unless you can restore enough weight through eating to bring on your period naturally. (Seidenfeld & Rickert, 2001). A normal period is a signal that your body is happy and fully functional and doing what it is designed to do.

Eating Disorders Are, by Nature, Counterintuitive

Eating disorders leave the rational mind reeling. A mother repeated her daughter's proclamation, "I'm not sick, there's nothing wrong with me!" which was followed in quick succession by, "Mom, am I ever going to recover from this?" There is contradiction in the notion of anorexia as an attempt to eat "healthfully to an extreme." No extreme is healthy. Practitioners need to resolve a lot of confusion by alerting clients and families to the idiosyncratic and contradictory nature of eating disorders.

With eating disorders, the pain of disease feels comforting, even as the realities of weight management and recovery inspire fear and dread. J sat in my office weeping in frustration that her school's headmistress and her mother believed she was struggling with an eating disorder. The evidence was clear: She had a pathological fear of gaining weight, she had lost 20 pounds in six weeks as a newly declared vegetarian, and her mother had discovered diet pills in her dresser drawer. But the client pointed to the fact that her body mass index was in the normal range, at 18.6 (the normal range is 18.5 to 25). When told that she needed to recover, she claimed,

> But I'm not even sick—My behavior is no different from any of my friends at school! When I restrict food, I feel happy and in control; when I eat normally, I feel unhappy and out of control. It's just not fair!

Clinicians need to anticipate and interpret illogical aspects of these diseases and their treatment to their client in order to minimize cognitive dissonance and distortions that become blinders to recovery. Such discussions sustain the integrity of the treatment process. By keeping expectations realistic, therapists legitimize clients' feelings, clarify beliefs, reassure, motivate, and instill trust in the integrity of the treatment process. The lists that follow describe the multitude of eating disorder–related elements and processes that are counterintuitive, by their very nature.

Counterintuitive Behaviors

- Because eating disordered behaviors occur along the continuum of normal human behavior, they often disguise themselves as indicators of a healthy lifestyle and an enviable display of self-discipline.
- Studying nutritional labels can be considered a sign of enlightenment though it may indicate food compulsions and fears.
- By causing fluid retention, laxative abuse results in apparent and temporary weight gain, not loss (as is the common misconception).
- Food restriction leads to weight gain; dieting children are more likely to become overweight adults, because dieting damages metabolic function and creates an unhealthy relationship with food.
- The more nutritiously dense foods one eats and the more regularly one eats (within the structure of meals and snacks), the less weight one gains, with the ultimate achievement of set point weight.

Counterintuitive Beliefs

- The eating disorder and its symptoms render the client powerless, even while offering the illusion of control.
- Although perceived as a survival tool, eating disorders kill and maim. To the client, the eating disorder represents both savior and tormentor, best friend and abuser.
- Clients believe that restoring lost weight will trigger unstoppable weight gain to the point of obesity and that, once they have lost control of their weight, they will lose control in every other life sphere.
- In our society, it is considered healthy to be weight conscious and nutrition focused.
- It is commonly believed that not everyone with an eating disorder needs help to recover. The issues that underlie eating disorders are indicators of problems that have essentially gone underground. Unless the client gets help, these problems are apt to fester and smolder, finding other outlets.
- Exercise, in the absence of sufficient caloric intake, will not increase a person's metabolism, nor will it contribute to weight loss. "Muscles, in response to malnourishment, "donate" protein to sustain brain function and become smaller; as a result, the body's ratio of fat to muscle increases.
- "Radical weight-loss efforts such as dieting, use of appetite suppressants and laxatives, and vomiting are more likely to lead to greater weight gain over time and a higher risk of obesity" (Stice, Cameron, Killen, Hayward, & Taylor, 2000).

Counterintuitive Aspects of Diagnosis

- Eating disorders are generally not disclosed or diagnosed in the doctor's office or by lab testing until their most advanced stages. A clean bill of health from the medical doctor enables the client's denial about being sick.

- Practitioners need to diagnose not only the client's pathology, but also his or her strengths to tailor treatment to the ever-changing status of recovery progress and goals.
- Clients with anorexia who rarely consume fats are more likely to suffer from high cholesterol levels. High cholesterol is a well-known side effect of malnutrition, with an abnormal lipid profile placing patients at risk for cardiovascular disease (Matzkin, Geissler, Coniglio, Selles, & Bello, 2006).

Counterintuitive Aspects of Treatment

- Practitioners need to retrain themselves to identify sometimes elusive optimistic outcomes and signs of progress as well as pathology.
- Most clients enter treatment not accepting that they are sick and emotionally unprepared to give up a disease process that feels empowering and life enhancing.
- Resistance to care characterizes all stages of treatment.
- Long-term emotional goals are served by attending to the details of small, short-term behavioral tasks.
- Imposing external controls becomes the practice ground for the eventual development of internal controls. Changes are sustainable only when they originate from within the client and when the client owns them.
- The best learning is typically derived from mistakes. Learning inspires change.
- Therapists treat family systems in an effort to best affect individuals.
- Although the issues underlying and driving the disorder are not about weight, the manipulation of food and weight becomes a diagnostic tool and the primary intervention for bringing about changes in physiology, emotions, and behaviors.
- The clinician must at once be an expansive, conceptual, and integrative thinker, envisioning the big picture of disease and recovery, while remaining attentive to the small details that accrue to become far-reaching outcomes.
- Treatment involves short-term, concrete, and immediate behavioral tasks to facilitate the achievement of long-term, ambiguous, and far-reaching recovery goals.
- Therapists must be authoritative and limit setting at the same time as loving and nurturing.
- The professional must be fully present in his or her humanity, lending ego and sharing self while remaining consistently and professionally boundaried.
- Treatment involves the dual challenges of seeking physiological stabilization while actively seeking changes in emotional, behavioral, and attitudinal paradigms.
- Therapy treats emotions to enhance behaviors and behaviors to bring about emotional growth.

- The clinician plays to the client's strengths and internal resources even while attending to the client's vulnerabilities.

Counterintuitive Aspects of Recovery

- Weight restoration by itself does not indicate healing, although recovery cannot happen without it.
- Recovery progress typically involves both forward and backward movement; regression or weight loss does not necessarily imply failure.
- The disease process invariably feels better to the client than does the process of becoming recovered; clients in recovery can count on feeling worse (i.e., more anxious, fearful, and out of control) before they begin to feel better.
- In recovering, clients may need to restore more than the desired amount of weight before their body is able to recalibrate to its set point weight. It takes a counterintuitive leap of faith for clients to understand that at set point, the body can handle food intake without restriction of any kind and without weight gain.
- The client has to learn to give up control of the eating disorder to regain genuine control of the self.
- The internal resources required to recover will not be available to the individual with the eating disorder at treatment outset; these clients approach treatment with limited and skewed sensory awareness, capacity to perceive bodily cues, ability to discern differences (learn), and to self-regulate.

Counterintuitive Aspects of the Treatment Relationship

- Many clients come to the professional seeking to be "fixed" rather than to learn how to fix themselves. Clients need to become acquainted with their own accruing strengths so that they can heal themselves and stay healed.
- Professionals must learn to avoid making statements such as, "Hey, you're looking really great these days!" I find myself having to bite my tongue not to make comments like this when I observe sunken cheeks beginning to fill out, hair looking shiny, nails becoming stronger, and faces smiling more easily and more often. Statements like these are typically taken to mean, "You look fat. It's time to go back on a diet," leading to a resurgence of anxiety that can cause a setback in eating. For this reason, it is important to be sensitive to the need for many clients in recovery to choose blind weighing.

CONCLUSION

Eating disorders are not about food. They are complex and systemic diseases affecting all aspects of a person's existence and functioning. Eating disorders are a reflection of the client's quality of life and are reliable predictors of a compromised existence if left untreated and unhealed. Understanding food use and abuse provides insight into diagnosis and treatment, personality assessment, and under-lying emotional issues. How we eat is a metaphor for how we live, how we solve problems and make decisions, how we monitor and care for ourselves, how we regulate our internal world and our internal feelings, and how safe we feel both in our body and in the world around us. Improved eating behaviors lead to emo-tional healing, enabling clients not only to enjoy improved eating patterns but also to reconnect with the self. The following statement was made by a recovered client of mine:

> I might still be suffering in silence with all of my insecurities had it not been for the opportunity and incentive my eating disorder provided to seek help. The recovery was tough to go through, but it certainly beats having killed myself! Best of all, the new me is so much better than the old pre–eating dis-ordered me. This has been the best and most productive, even if the most painful, life experience I have ever lived through.

3

Soul Searching: Assessing the Personal Side of Professional Challenges

Success is the ability to go from one failure to another with no loss of enthusiasm.

—Winston Churchill

Professionals rarely feel neutral about treating clients with eating disorders. Those who work with these clients tend to love what they do, preferring it to all other specialties and in many instances approach it as a calling. Other practitioners flatly refuse to treat this population. This chapter discusses the personal demands on therapists of treating clients with eating disorders. Here I describe how I became involved in this practice area, and I set out the personal factors therapists need to succeed in treating this population. Discussion of transference and countertransference issues follows, and guidelines are offered for therapist self-disclosure. Finally, I discuss the unique challenges to the professional's personhood of treating eating disorders.

The reputation of these lethal disorders precedes them; eating disorders are notorious for creating professional burnout in the face of client resistance, ambivalence, and prevarication. It stands to reason that countertransference issues pervade this work. At any given moment, an incoming phone call may oblige a practitioner to spring into action to manage a many-faceted crisis affecting client and parents, all the while juggling privacy and confidentiality issues, treatment plan revisions, and possible milieu transitions. Some professionals wonder, Why even try? For me, there are so many reasons.

Infinitely gratifying and never boring, this work presents ongoing challenges that demand to be met and obstacles that demand to be overcome. An almost palpable interpersonal energy empowers the human connection between client and professional that this work requires and evokes. The population of clients with eating disorders is, for the most part, made up of consummately delightful individuals—bright, talented, well-intentioned people. Many of these highly achieving individuals excel at anything they attempt, including their commitment to their disorder. They come to treatment as clay, unformed and vulnerable, awaiting a kind of rebirth into life through a re-entry into themselves. I can honestly say that I love many of my clients, and I consummately respect and enjoy working with the rest, as well as with their parents and families.

Some of my clients are among the finest people I know. I appreciate and empathize with their struggles and revel in their successes. I feel privileged to have had the opportunity to treat and, in many respects, to "parent" these extraordinary human beings—to weed, cultivate, nurture, and water them into full bloom as whole human beings and then to say good-bye as they mature and move on, just as it should be.

It has been said that the Judaic scholar is not fully equipped to study Kabala until the age of 40, when accrued life learning and experience permit sufficient maturity and wisdom to handle the complexity of a profound and heady body of knowledge. Similarly, for novices in the eating disorder treatment field, this specialty may present challenges that are too intense for comfort. A social worker just out of graduate school for whom I was providing consultation reported becoming severely depressed at the start of her first job doing intakes at an eating disorder clinic. She found herself dreading going to work because of the helplessness she felt in the face of the hostility and resistance of these clients and the intractable and self-destructive nature of their conditions. This young woman lacked the "mileage" and treatment experience she needed to develop a clear sense of the process of treatment sessions and the arsenal of skills required to treat this client population. The clients may also have triggered in her some unresolved issues of her own.

MY STORY

I wish I had a penny for every time someone has inquired of me what first propelled me toward this field. Have I ever had an eating disorder? Have my children? It is almost with a sense of treason that I admit that I never have personally experienced an eating disorder, nor have my children, though personal struggle is no stranger to me. I know well what it is to face challenges in life that cause great angst and the need for problem solving and emotional resiliency. In asking such questions, prospective clients seek to know whether or not I am qualified to treat them, the assumption being that one must have personal experience with an eating disorder in order to treat one. Although their intentions are legitimate in seeking quality care, their standard of judgment is misguided. Successful treatment more legitimately depends on understanding these disorders, their ramifications, and their unique treatment demands; on the acquisition of integrative skill sets; on impassioned and genuine caring; and on an open receptivity to diverse and inclusive resources, including the creative and courageous use of one's own self as a practitioner

A certain depth of understanding and know-how does legitimately emanate from origins that are experiential in nature. My own passion for this work arises out of a combination of personal qualities and preferences, but ultimately out of a deeply meaningful life experience from my own role as a parent faced with problems demanding solutions with the birth of my daughter 30 years ago, who at the time had special needs that put my husband and I on the front lines of life crisis and survival. As parents, we understood quickly enough that we would need to learn to find appropriate help and manage our daughter's highly unique case virtually on our own. In seeking to salvage her life quality, for us, necessity would become the mother of invention and we were ultimately able to accomplish our mission through the exquisitely honed expertise of Moshe Feldenkrais and Anat Baniel, whose methods I will discuss in Chapter 11.

In the early 1980s, my passion and expertise in the area of parent advocacy led me to approach my community hospital in search of a few weekly family psychotherapy cases to round out my private practice. The hospital placed me on their eating disorder day program unit. There I became immediately hooked, smitten with these clients and their families who were hungry to discover possibility in a mire of belief systems that spoke of impossibility, who sought a way out where there appeared to be none in sight. My daughter's recovery has been the impetus behind my passion to empower and embolden parents in their own life quests; it has created a sensibility and responsiveness to the poignancy of parents' needs, to their raw fear in the face of the danger to their child, to the complexities of family relationships in times of crisis, to the perils of depending on professionals who may not fully understand the condition they treat, and to the pressing needs of the afflicted child.

The drive to discover workable solutions in the face of overwhelming odds is as primal to human survival as the need for air and water. Creative innovation, along with the resolve never to say never, is a critical ingredient in the determination to do what works. Personal experience has taught me to envision possibility in all of life's most pessimistic places, an awareness that I strive to share with my eating disordered clients, whose condition renders them blind to optimistic perspectives about body and future. As practitioners, we use the lessons of our own life struggles to touch the lives of others.

Where does your own passion come from? Before reading on, I suggest that you pause to consider what might be your own motivation to treat clients with eating disorders. Whatever the calling that challenges, invites, drives, or welcomes you to this expertise, it is worth recognizing, as it can offer significant insight into how and why you do what you do, say what you say, and think and feel the way you do in the context of this work. Conversely, it is essential for you to know what might underlie your motivation to refuse to treat these cases. In the words of Moshe Feldenkrais, engineer, physicist, inventor, martial artist, and student of human development, "We need to know what we do in order to do what we want." Box 3.1 provides questions to help you in your self-examination.

BOX 3.1

Introspection in Preparation to Treat Eating Disorders

The process of becoming aware stimulates learning and growth and creates options for choice making. Ask yourself the following questions:

- What sparked your interest in treating eating disorders?
- Are you aware of any life experiences that may have been instrumental in pointing you in this direction?
- Are you aware of any personal issues that might be worth your special attention as you prepare to treat eating disorders?

   If you have ever struggled with an eating disorder or dysfunction or compulsive exercise, now is a good time to pause to consider the following:

- In what ways do you feel that working with eating disorders is even more of a challenge by virtue of your having lived with the disease and its recovery?
- How does your history with the eating disorder or dysfunction make you more attentive, attuned, appreciative, and, perhaps, responsive to the needs of these clients?
- How aware are you of the internal self-talk that might determine how you might make decisions about the best direction to take a client—which issues to pursue, when, and how best to do so?

ART AND SCIENCE OF EATING DISORDER TREATMENT

Human connections heal. Children who feel connected at home and at school are the ones most likely to succeed and to stay out of trouble. In a similar vein, the most predictive factor of better health in old age is social involvement with friends, family members, or clubs, particularly those that involve intimate relationships. The field of neuroscience has provided convincing support for the healing power of the relationship in clinical practice by exploring ways in which human beings are hardwired to connect with other human beings, as explained through Judith and Allan Schore's (2008) discussion of modern attachment theory, in which they emphasize right-brain systems that underlie attachment and developmental change.

   Evidence-based research supports the healing capacities of the treatment relationship as one of the most critical predictors of successful treatment outcomes. A healthy, collaborative treatment relationship can ameliorate a client's dissociation from aspects of self that contribute to poor self-esteem and negate self-acceptance, basic self-trust, and self-determination. Studies have shown that "differences between therapists (in their practice style and versatility in the use of self within the therapeutic relationship) are more important to treatment outcomes than the particular treatment method or theory embraced by the therapist" (Germer, Siegel, & Fulton, 2005, p. 57).

Germer et al. (2005) quotes Samuel Butler in describing the use of self with the client as follows: "Life is like music; it must be composed by ear, feeling and instinct, not by rule. Nevertheless, one had better know the rules, for they sometimes guide in doubtful cases, though not often" (p. 68). In 1925, a nurse named Adelaide Nutting summarized this critical duality in caregiving:

> We need to realize and affirm a view that medicine is one of the most difficult of arts. Compassion may provide the motive, but knowledge is our only working power. We need to remember that growth in our work must be preceded by ideas, and that conditions that suppress thought must therefore retard growth. Surely we will not be satisfied with merely perpetuating methods and traditions: surely we should be more and more involved in creating them. (Leichner, 2005, p. 22)

Over dinner one night, a colleague of mine voiced her concerns about what she considered to be a disconnect between the science of treatment and the art of psychotherapeutic practice. Because she considered treatment to be an art that demands talent as innate as are aptitudes for music, sculpting, or painting, she believed that one cannot "teach" another person to be a masterful therapist. We discussed what makes a therapist great and what accounts for that chemistry between people that makes therapy compelling and that inspires learning and change in another person. We discussed the qualities that separate the true genius of a Paganini or a Heifetz from the fine musicianship of the thousands of fiddle players who play in symphony orchestras, and whether genius factors are quantifiable or teachable.

It is my sense that what sets the true artist apart is his or her capacity to combine professional and personal assets and to initially master, and then transcend, left-brain technical skills through the creative genius of the instinctive right brain. The therapist who treats eating disorders *does* need to stand apart in his or her level of skill mastery, becoming somehow differentiated from the cadre of "symphony player" practitioners. Mastery is liberated, not learned. Whether concertizing, skiing with agility down a mountain slope, or treating a client with an eating disorder, the capacity to connect cognitive left-brain skills with the instinctual creativity of the right brain is the stuff of true mastery. These qualities allow the musician to reveal the true voice of the composer. For the eating disorder practitioner, a similar grounding in technical skills along with the freedom to know and fully use a liberal, differentiated and integrated personal self, facilitates the emergence of a newly acquired, developing, and integrated voice in the client.

As practitioners, we do not need rarified skills or genius to achieve a measure of artistry. We just need further education and greater understanding of these diseases and what sets them and their treatment apart. I believe the tools of this treatment trade are actually supremely accessible; in many respects, they are disarmingly simple, and they are hardly strangers to us. We know them all; we know how to implement them. We are good at making connections. We have the skills in our repertoire. What we have to learn is simply which to use, when, where, and how, in the unique context of these disorders—in what sequence, in which combinations, and in what manner.

SUSTAINING THE MINDFUL AND LOVING CONNECTION

It is through a developing trust in the therapist and the therapy process that the client ultimately develops the capacity to trust her own self. The therapy relationship provides the opportunity and context for the client to resume and repair interrupted developmental processes through her relationship with the therapist to achieve wholeness and life quality.

The practitioner's capacity to realize a full connection with his or her own self is prerequisite to establishing a potent connection with clients who have eating disorders. Although techniques and strategies for treatment are for the most part eminently teachable for those choosing to learn, it clearly takes a special kind of person to find gratification in a journey that is typically as arduous as it is extended. Eating disorder diagnosis and treatment do demand special personal characteristics that cannot be gleaned by reading textbooks alone; these qualities exist within one's own character, within one's humanity and experience of growing, learning, and responding to the world around us. Practitioners need to be capable of accessing instinctual radar in recognizing what is apparent and what is hidden, discerning what is not said as clearly as what is said. They need to be capable of rolling with a treatment process whose rhythm and pace will be determined collaboratively with the client, a virulent disease, and the dynamic of the therapeutic moment. The therapist requires courage, confidence, and competence in using himself or herself with intention, flexibility, and most of all genuine caring in fearlessly standing up to the challenges of resistance, ambiguity, and unpredictability.

The following is an example of a mindfully caring treatment encounter. When the economy soured during the winter of 2008, a client e-mailed to tell me that she could no longer afford to come to treatment weekly. I e-mailed back, suggesting that she become twice as proactive in propelling her *own* recovery now through self-help techniques and through journaling her feelings, challenges, and accomplishments. I suggested that she try to become more self-aware than ever, developing her own internal voice that would take the place of mine, that would systematically poke holes in her irrational and compulsively deprecating thinking. "You have heard the phrase, fake it till you make it?" I asked. "This is what I am inviting you to try to do for yourself now."

She responded as follows:

> I, too, am genuinely disappointed that I can't do sessions more frequently. But I do have to thank you for your e-mail. Your words make me feel like you believe in me, and that's the feeling I get when I'm with you. It actually gives me hope. I've been trying to be proactive in reframing negative thoughts (and mostly the punitive words my eating disorder has for me about every decision I make) into gentler statements. I'm not always successful, but I hope I'm getting better at building a stronger voice! But I'm just going to find ways to keep myself in recovery if I begin to get stressed. Thanks again for all the warmth you exude to me.

We negotiated a reduced fee for services, allowing her to ultimately continue her treatment with me, now more motivated than ever before.

The loving connection, the source and origin of productive psychotherapeutic treatment, is an action-based connection that entails hard-nosed reality-testing, probing, and confrontation. In effective eating disorder treatment, sleeping dogs rarely have an opportunity to lie. True caring may be demonstrated in the therapist's fierce advocacy for a client's strengths.

In response to a client's pronouncement "I can never commit to anything," I pointed to her own past description of having staunchly committed herself to an exercise program that had proved to be unpleasant and self-defeating. In not being able to choose a kinder course for herself, she had indeed demonstrated her capacity to stick it out in the face of hardship; the task remaining for her was to choose to commit herself to more benevolent activities. In listening closely and taking her experiences to heart, I was able to feed back her own observations about herself that prompted a newly restored and more realistic cognition that would motivate her to growth and change.

In a sense, psychotherapy becomes an intimate encounter. In Paul Russell's word s "Therapy is a love relationship. . . . It does not work to try to somehow 'be' loving. The only thing that can work is to feel the love that is already there" (Germer et al., 2005, p. 135).

As Germer et al. (2005) noted,

> Russell's words aptly convey that love is not something that we generate; it is found in the activity of intimately attending. Constancy and care in attention have a quality of love. There is a refinement and subtlety to such attention, as well as genuine warmth and interest. The quality of attention can be cultivated as we learn to bring wholehearted attention to more of what occurs, more of the time. (p. 135)

The quality of the therapeutic alliance has consistently been shown to be the most important factor in therapy outcome and is

> more important to treatment outcomes than the particular treatment method or theory embraced by the therapist. . . . Overall, empathy accounts for as much and probably more outcome variance than does specific intervention. Empathy may be even more influential in intervention-based treatment than in relational-based therapy. It might almost be said that the relationship *is* the treatment. (Germer et al., 2005, p. 57)

In Chapter 11, we will learn that neuroscientific evidence points to the power of the human relationship to bring about changes within the brain's structure and function.

To date, the "human" side of clinical preparedness has, until recently, been considered unteachable. But with the advent of more mindful treatments during the past decade, more effort is being made to address this gap in the education of clinicians. For example, Harvard Medical School has instituted a course that attempts to teach "bedside manner" and sensibility to improve the doctor's responsiveness to the emotional needs of the dying patient. The course instructs medical residents how to connect personally with their patients, how to achieve a better quality of listening, and how to encourage hope (Ruder, 2006).

EATING DISORDERS AMONG TREATING PROFESSIONALS

When a practitioner has personally experienced eating disorders and the emotional issues that underlie and drive them, it can become a powerful motivator for this specialization. In fact, a substantial proportion of professionals in this field are themselves recovering or recovered victims of eating disorders, a phenomenon peculiar to this specialty (Barbarich, 2002).

This reality carries implications not only for clients but also for the well-being of these professionals. Relating to eating disorders from firsthand experience can enhance a practitioner's sensitivity to these issues and a positive identification with the client. On the downside, the insinuation of countertransference into the treatment process could cloud the clinician's capacity to observe and respond effectively unless self-awareness is high and pivotal, and unresolved issues have been worked through to sufficient resolution.

Some institutions make a point of employing practitioners who have personally experienced and recovered from eating disorders. A treatment facility in California describes itself as being "designed and created by recovering professionals." A New England–based eating disorder organization restricts its intern program to students and practitioners who have personally recovered from an eating disorder. In a preliminary survey of recovered professionals in the eating disorder treatment field, Barbarich (2002) found that

> the lifetime prevalence of an eating disorder among professionals was 33.2 percent for females and 2.3 percent for males; 38.8 percent of treatment facilities reported hiring clinicians with a history of an eating disorder. Three factors . . . the duration of illness, a history of anorexia nervosa purging type, and a history of more than one eating disorder . . . predicted an increased rate of relapse for practitioners. The longer the recovery time prior to entering the field as a professional predicted a decreased rate of relapse. (p. 1)

This survey also reported that clients felt that the hope and motivation recovered staff provided were one of the most important aspects of the program for them and that "a history of an eating disorder is only one among many personal and technical factors that determine the suitability and competence of the individual as a clinician" (Barbarich, 2002, p. 305).

As human beings, we all struggle with emotional issues of different kinds, and we are all, hopefully, healing and growing throughout our lives. The introspective therapist with clear insight into his or her own functioning has the greatest potential to fully discover and grasp the client's experience, to sustain clear boundaries, and to exercise intentional self-containment. To treat eating disorders effectively, clinicians who have experienced an eating disorder need a level of personal knowledge that hovers at least largely in the realm of "for the most part already healed" to optimize perception and the quality of response. Johnson et al. (1987) found that staff members who had not personally experienced an eating disorder sometimes could become preoccupied with the process and dynamics and neglect the need for symptom improvement (e.g., weight gain, abstinence from bingeing and purging or exercise). Guidelines are clearly needed so that professionals who have made personal recovery can have benchmarks to evaluate their readiness to enter the field.

Recovered professionals and those who struggle with the remnants of an old eating disorder need to be exquisitely attuned to themselves as they become involved in therapeutic relationships. A former client who had been in treatment with me for severe and enduring anorexia ultimately made a complete recovery, went on to graduate school in the field of social work, married, and bore two beautiful and healthy children. She eventually became a highly effective practitioner, administrator, and supervisor of social work interns. As she began her professional practice, she was reluctant to treat clients with eating disorders. In discussing her reluctance, she spoke of "that eating disordered piece that remains with me . . . that appears through occasional fleeting thoughts of food restriction . . . that I typically will recognize and then choose to dismiss." In describing a lack of confidence that emanated from this remnant of her disease, she questioned whether people could learn from her if she still entertained such thinking, even on a superficial level.

Initially, she believed she might still be at risk personally of taking on and integrating the anorexic thoughts or feelings of prospective clients. She doubted that her extensive personal experience of having been in treatment for over a decade would prepare her for what she knew to be the unique requirements of providing professional care. Having lived with her disorder, she described feeling more highly vulnerable to the mysteries and challenges of defenses and resistance and less assured in dealing with them. She feared she would miss some signs of disease, overlooking them in mistaking them for normal; that she would miss vitally important physical components (that even under the best of circumstances remain elusive to therapists); and that she would not be able to be as directive and limit setting as she would like in response to compliance difficulties.

Interestingly, after reviewing a draft of this book (for which she provided valuable feedback), she reported "a newfound confidence" that "my knowledge of self and recognition of client countertransference issues, along with my ability to be more assertive and honest in my current role as supervisor to interns and clinicians in training, prepare me well for working with this client population." She stated, "I am amazed to find how much I actually do know!"

TRANSFERENCE AND COUNTERTRANSFERENCE

Transference is particularly relevant to the treatment of eating disorders. A client of mine described her work with a therapist who had recovered from anorexia: "Her eyes would well up with tears each time I would begin to speak about my disease," she explained, "so I made sure to steer clear of the topic." A social worker who had suffered from anorexia treated a client of mine in a hospital day program; she confided in me that she "can't bear to look at her for how emaciated she is." The messages of disgust and rejection (and perhaps envy) would not have been lost on my client, compromising treatment effectiveness. Therapists who are parents of children with eating disorders may find themselves at risk of losing their objectivity and professionalism in treating children with eating disorders and in becoming involved in parent–child issues within the context of family treatment.

When the client transfers feelings about a person from his or her past onto the therapist in the present, transference is occurring; such phenomena add complexity to treatment relationships but need not be destructive to the process when the therapist recognizes, understands, and deconstructs the transference for learning purposes. Positive transference can bring quick improvements in the client; negative transference may be experienced as client resistance. [An example of negative transference might be seen in one of my client's past relationship with a therapist. The latter gave this obese client the "feeling of being judged and disapproved of because I could not lose weight. I got the feeling she didn't like me," she said, which led to an unsuccessful treatment experience. Positive transference happens when the therapist finds strengths in the patient that leads to a sense of collaboration, excitement, and motivation in the treatment process for both parties. The interpretation of transference phenomena can be critical to the client's self-awareness and learning.

I worked for a decade with an anorexic male (purging type) who, in the course of treatment, examined his childhood issues of secrecy and detachment from his parents. Over time and with growing familiarity, he found himself increasingly reluctant to disclose the truth to me about the frequency and depth of his dysfunctional behaviors. In a transferential response, he unconsciously feared that my response to his difficulties would mimic his parents', so he withheld information to avoid the disapproval and rejection he anticipated. In pointing out this dynamic, I called upon his cognitive strengths to differentiate the reality of now with the reality of then, stressing the importance of keeping the eating disorder always at the front and center of our work.

In an act of tough love, I brought pressure to bear on him to finally enter a day program. In accordance with his early childhood attachment issues, he assumed that this was a sign of my rejection, that I must be "sick of him" and his intractable disease, and that our relationship was therefore no longer viable. By helping him interpret this transference in light of his attachment issues, he regained enough security within our relationship to step outside of it temporarily to enter a program, which brought him to new level of healing.

Countertransference patterns reflect the complexity of the clinician's unconscious emotional response to the client's transference. It is incumbent on the professional to be aware of countertransference reactions and to monitor, contain, and control them as a means to integrate his or her own emotional reactions effectively into sessions. By observing one's own reactions objectively, practitioners can use countertransference as a vehicle to stimulate their own and their clients' learning and growth.

For example, in treating families, I am aware that my own intolerance of injustice and victimization of a scapegoated family member makes me particularly reactive in support of the more vulnerable, bullied, and manipulated members within any family system. My own countertransference issues typically inspire me to support or become the voice of the family member who has until that point been deprived of a voice; sometimes this person may be someone other than the identified client. By bringing the dynamic to the awareness of the family system, my intention is to stimulate an increasingly mindful recognition of a structural dynamic, offering the family the option to choose another, more humane and effective pattern. By doing so, I act the part of role model, educator, and advocate for the home environment to become a haven for greater safety and mutual kindness and for parents to assume greater responsibly to become enlightened and "parental." I am a firm believer that children should not be granted permission to be vicious to and bully their siblings just because they are "moody adolescents." I encourage parents to understand what I feel, see what I see, and express themselves as I model self-expression in sessions.

Box 3.2 will help you assess the attitudes about food and weight you've formed over a lifetime; this self-examination will help you process transference and countertransference in ways that will benefit your client. In developing an awareness of potential projections of your own, consider whether they might have interfered with treatment: Did it ever occur to you that you may have had a question in mind for your client that you failed to ask? It is important to discern what stopped you from inquiring and from following your instinct. Might you have been afraid to deal with your client's anticipated anger, believing that it would interfere with your working relationship together? Might you have avoided discussing something that might have been tough for you so you could spare yourself the discomfort?

Recognizing countertransference offers the practitioner an unparalleled source of understanding about the self and the client, providing direction for the session and perhaps even supplying clues as to the potential for co-occurring diagnoses in your client. Missing the opportunity to use countertransference productively can deter the healing process.

For example, a group therapist at a day program working with a client of mine found this client "too intimidating" to approach in the group because of her "hostility" and her "clear message to stay away." The client, however, confessed to me that she was in fact the intimidated person in feeling that she had "no right to take up group time or space" that should belong to others. The group therapist's reaction denied my client the conditions she required to feel the motivation and permission she needed to participate in the group. This therapist made an erroneous assumption based on her own interpretation (and fear) of what she interpreted as hostility in the client. So as to avoid potential confrontation, she denied the client and the group the advantage of her engaging in a healing dialogue that might have taken her to a new level of growth. This situation was rectified through my intervention.

Another client had been in treatment for 6 months with a therapist who reacted with anger toward intervening parents. The therapist instructed these parents to "back off" and "butt out" in the interest of letting their daughter "feel more in control of her life." By not allowing the parents a role in their child's treatment, this therapist denied this family the opportunity to support their daughter and to mentor her recovery. The inflexible defensiveness of this therapist is likely to be the result of unresolved countertransference issues regarding her own parents or

---

BOX 3.2

Assessing Your Attitudes About Food and Weight, Then and Now

Know thyself is inscribed above one of the entrances into the shrine of the Delphic oracle. As professionals, our most valuable asset is a resource we need not go far to access: It is ourselves. Mindful self-awareness and intention, accurate self-appraisal, and self-determination ensure clear and workable boundaries and lead to an integrated and deft use of the self. Not coincidentally, these are the same qualities we seek in our recovering clients.

The attitudes of your family of origin will influence your attitudes today and the way in which you might interact with a child who has an eating disorder in your professional practice. The following exercise, taken in its entirety from *When Your Child Has an Eating Disorder: A Step-by-Step Workbook for Parents and Other Caregivers* (Natenshon, 1999), facilitates the therapist's effort to "know thyself." To review your early childhood attitudes and experiences with food and eating, read and contemplate the following questions:

- How did you feel about your body while growing up?
- Were you ever teased or criticized by others because of the way you looked? If so, why?
- Did your family of origin have rituals concerning food? If so, what were they?
- Was food ever used as a device to threaten or motivate you? If so, how?
- What kinds of eating behaviors and meal patterns did you see in your role models (e.g., parents, siblings, counselors, coaches)?
- How did these childhood events affect your attitudes and values then? How do they affect them today?
- What messages did you get from your parents about how people are supposed to look?
- How did your parents perceive you physically? How do you know?
- Who made dinners for you as a child? Who ate with you?
- What were dinner times like? What kinds of things were discussed?
- Draw a picture of your family dinner table. Who sat where? Was anyone often absent?
- What were your family's food traditions, rituals, and quirks?
- How were troublesome issues handled? Were problems resolved? Give examples.
- Could people express themselves honestly and openly? Explain.

---

of her projection that parental involvement would represent intrusive interference. At a time when she most needed help from her parents, this child was encouraged to diminish her parents' role in her life. The youngster ultimately cited "privacy rights" in choosing to ignore their "inappropriate and intrusive" interest in her personal safety around self-injury. After 8 months of unsuccessful treatment for depression and bulimia, this father expressed frustration at having been put in the "parenting penalty box," where their hands had been tied.

It is not unusual for the client with an eating disorder to stir up turbulent feelings of despair and hostility in the therapist when struggling with life and death concerns, a process that can be hard to witness. It behooves clinicians who work with clients who have eating disorders to be particularly aware of their own countertransferential feelings, using specific techniques to help contain and constructively process powerful affective states mobilized in treatment.

Loving Too Much

Transference issues can create experiences where practitioners love or connect too much with a client or nurture the client in ways that fall short of eliciting change and learning.

> Becoming mindful as a practitioner can help root out ingenuous attempts to bolster one's own sense of self through the need to be loved by one's clients, a process that can threaten healing. The therapist's feeling of helplessness in the face of an intractable problem can also undermine treatment; therapists are armed with many techniques that can be used to mask this helplessness, distracting himself and the patient from the dread that the limits of therapy have been reached. (Germer et al., 2005, p. 65)

Therapists need to beware of the temptation to become their client's friend, to avoid uncomfortable topics of discussion for fear of losing the patient or arousing her anger, or to be diverted or distracted by more pleasurable conversations about boyfriends, movies, and what she did with her friends last weekend. Soft pedaling, or omitting pointed remarks and difficult topics, can reinforce the client's sense that certain problems should not be discussed because they are too painful. Repudiated feelings need to be brought out to center stage to define, address, resolve, and integrate them. If a client resists taking the discussion to real and pivotal places, that dynamic deserves attention as a therapeutic issue loaded with learning potential.

A meaningful connection enables therapists to enter all dimensions of their client's experience. A quality therapy relationship allows clients to move into new and often raw, painful, or lonely inner experiences. Asking the client to report her ongoing vision of the therapy relationship can offer critical information about the felt quality of treatment, the client's resistance to recovery and underlying personality structure, and the efficacy of the therapist's use of self.

Practitioners must remain sufficiently alert and responsive in order to avoid collusion, not only with the powerful client who refuses to focus on healing her disorder but also with the helpless and passive client who demands that the therapist do the work for her:

> A sincere desire to help may lead a therapist to try to "fix" the situation for the patient, to be overly ready to prescribe answers and solutions. There is a time for expert opinion, but not in the place of first building the patient's own motivation as an active, not a passive participant. (Miller & Rollnick, 1991, p. 68)

Knowing when, why, and how to remain purposefully and meaningfully intentional in the face of a client's manipulations can be a difficult, but pivotal task.

Over the course of 15 years, I guided a young woman through intractable anorexia, programs and hospitalizations, neurological complications, the death of both parents, the trials and tribulations of employment experiences and of relationships, mood instability, and periodic regressions. My nutritionist partner and I had become like surrogate parents for this young woman in some ways. During a stressful life event our client suddenly lost a substantial amount of weight and became resistant to altering her eating lifestyle.

Aware of the danger she was in and of her resistance to feeding herself, in a true demonstration of tough love, my partner and I insisted that she commit herself to a contract for weight gain; lending each other the strength, we stayed firm to our demands in the face of her resistance, refusing to provide further treatment unless she complied with the terms of the contract. Through a conjoint intervention, we created a united front against disease and a supportive and loving (though limit-setting) safety net for our beleaguered client.

Countertransference may affect the professional's willingness to set limits, confront the client's resistance, probe and seek disclosure, and integrate parents and loved ones into treatment as resources and advocates. Some practitioners fear that the client might misconstrue meaningful and appropriate confrontation as judgment or hostility, becoming alienated and losing affection or trust. (In such a case, I am always sure to inquire about the client's response, to process and to learn from it.) When might a therapist's reluctance to confront uncomfortable truths risk the life of a noncompliant client? How does the therapist know if and when the relationship is strong enough to weather confrontation that the client may consider harsh? How best to choose one's words, timing, and messages to convey and which tangents to pursue? The nuances of the myriad of varied and integrative elements affecting each individual case guide the answers to these questions with each client. Though the choice always lies with the therapist, the response ultimately rests with the client.

Gender Issues

A young woman diagnosed with eating disorder not otherwise specified who worked with a male therapist for several years described comments he would make about her appearance as a woman, such as suggesting that she straighten her hair and have rhinoplasty if she was seriously concerned about looking better. This contributed to her preexisting paranoia that her looks were unacceptable but also aroused transference issues of her own about her relationship with males. She felt she couldn't talk freely about her weight obsession because "he'd never relate to it as a man." She also felt that she needed to please him "because he was a man and she was a woman."

"On the days that I went to therapy," she confided, "I dressed for him, knowing that he would be derisive about my not caring about my appearance if I dressed in oversized clothing to hide my fat."

In asking her why she stayed with him for so long despite the negative messages she picked up from him, she confided that his poor view of her paralleled her own feelings about herself so perfectly that she felt it was a good match. She believed there were no alternatives for someone as "badly off" as she. She described him as being like "an uncle" who "needed to have some slack cut." The fact that this therapist was a male reinforced her out of control feelings, first as a woman, then as an eating disordered woman. So much could have been gained (for both therapist and client) from processing these issues together as they arose.

Gender issues take many forms and should be considered inevitable facts of life, as well as learning tools. Though highly critical with eating disorder treatment under any circumstance, boundary issues become even more salient when therapist and client are of different genders.

Therapist Weight

Therapists and nutritionists who are overweight or who have a disability may engender a lack of trust in clients with eating disorders, who typically demand perfection in themselves and everyone with whom they identify. An overly thin therapist may arouse feelings of competition or anxiety in the anorexic client. If a therapist is gaining or losing appreciable weight (because of pregnancy or illness), he or she should consider bringing the issue of weight variance up in session as this reality might have the potential to adversely affect the quality of the treatment environment; if the client assumes that the practitioner hasn't figured out his or her own weight problems, that could interfere with her trust in this person's ability to figure out hers, as well. Though the client may or may not be consciously aware of any sense of competition, envy, disrespect, or anger toward a treating professional who looks excessively thin and who can "get away with it," should such feelings exist and go undetected and unresolved, the client may resist engagement in treatment.

Clinicians need to consider the possible interference of such perceptions and projections and to bring the potential for such dynamics out in the open through nonjudgmental observations and questioning. Offering invitations to speak about such concerns and their implications promotes the healing process. Therapists need to live what they teach, modeling openness and honesty in communication. No topic is off limits for discussion within the treatment context if it furthers the goals of teaching and learning and has a potential bearing on the healing process. The therapist may offer hunches, guesses, or ponderings, describing possible scenarios about concerns that may or may not turn out to be relevant. Always, the goal is to assist clients' knowledge of themselves.

Delinquent Payments and Countertransference

For practitioners in private practice, dealing with fee collection can be uncomfortable, even if clearly delineated protocols are in place. Transference and countertransference issues arise partly because of what may appear to be an intrinsic contradiction in the eyes of some clients and professionals about the provision of social services and caregiving within the context of a business venture.

A client in a nearby college whose treatment was being funded by out-of-town parents graduated and left the country. The parents had allowed the bill to grow, allegedly because of complications with the insurance company, though they promised to pay as soon as they could straighten out the problem. In the end, they told me that their insurance would not cover any of the charges and that, having run into financial problems, they would leave a sizable bill unpaid.

A practitioner's sensitivities and attitudes concerning money often stem from early childhood learning, weighing in as transference and countertransference sometimes as potent as those concerning eating or weight management. Complicating matters, payment arrangements for eating disorder treatment are unique in that clients are often children who cannot be financially responsible for their own care. For parents who are absent from the process, those who are divorced or separated from the family and out of the picture, and college students whose parents live out of town, separateness from the treatment process may create a greater tendency for them to lack a sense of personal responsibility for paying therapy fees.

When therapists fail to clearly delineate financial expectations, they may be forfeiting an opportunity to prevent sudden termination and failure to pay fees. The arrangement to treat and be compensated for treatment should become part of a contractual arrangement, with financial guarantors and/or patients held fully accountable. In cases such as the ones discussed above, the private practitioner's capacity to process credit cards could potentially minimize the opportunity for nonpayment of accrued amounts.

Transference: A Case Study

I had a close treatment relationship with a young man who had anorexia for many years as he struggled to keep his weight above the point of emaciation. Five weeks before his wedding, he had lost 12 pounds, despite having signed a contract with me and his nutritionist in which he agreed to gain a half pound a week. A month before his wedding, it became apparent to me that we needed to have an honest conversation about this to refocus his goals for treatment. He became defensive about discussing eating and weight and refused to include his future wife in the discussion. Using diversionary tactics in an effort to reassure both me and himself, he reported, "I didn't lose any more weight this week, and I ate crab cakes for the first time." I reminded him that eating better is something that has to happen predictably, meal after meal, day after day, week after week to be lasting and effective.

He stormed out of the session in a huff, implying that I would not be seeing him again. He did not contact me for close to two weeks despite my attempts to contact him (on several occasions) to see what was keeping him from returning to process what had been such a fertile session. When he finally did return, he learned a great deal about his responses to problem solving under stress, confrontation, and anger management. He recognized that by shutting down and becoming emotionally unavailable, he mimicked similar responses in his deceased father.

His issues touched many chords within me, raising significant countertransference issues. I had envisioned the time before his wedding as a motivational window of opportunity to rethink his life priorities and goals for the future. It was my own projection that this fertile life experience (his wedding) should provide an incentive for self-care. Positive life experiences that would otherwise be joyous, however, typically also bring increased pressure and anxiety. In addition, I was aware of experiencing an adrenal response to his insistence on dictating the agenda of treatment. I helped him see that if my words to him sounded harsh, they came from genuinely caring feelings and true concern that my attachment to him was deep throughout our protracted treatment relationship. I spoke of my respect for his inventiveness and energy in accomplishing as much as he had and of my frustration in watching him risk such marvelous potential.

His connection to me was reminiscent of his early childhood attachments and had a strong approach–avoidance element—it would be his way or the highway. Was my response overly motherly? Was his response overly childlike? Were our mutual bonds over a decade of attachment helping or hindering this situation? Ultimately, I persuaded this young man to bring his fiancée in for a session, alerting her to the depth of the problem. Following that session, he chose to leave treatment for a time. Refusing inpatient care, he vowed to heal on his own and to return to my care once he had begun to restore his weight and turn his recovery around. He did just that, with the assistance of a new physician who saw him weekly, with a great deal of resolve and with the support of his bride. In addition, the next time I confronted him with a truth that was hard for him to hear, he made a point of discussing and resolving potentially contentious situations with me sooner rather than later, having let go of his childhood obstinacy and withdrawal in the face of frustration. Because we were able to process his transference issues and my countertransference issues thoroughly, our relationship became even more viable.

Lessons in This Case

The following are the "bottom lines" in the treatment of this client:

- I would have been enabling his disease if I had avoided a focus on the eating disorder at that moment, though he complained that my choice to confront him at a time so close to his marriage upset him.
- He needed medication, an intensified treatment program, and weight gain; he needed change of some kind—soon—to save his life and restore life quality.
- He needed an alarm to go off within his family system so that his loved ones might assume some responsibility for him while he was incapable of doing so.
- He needed to become more self-aware and self-determining in his approach to frustration tolerance and anger management.
- He needed the opportunity to appreciate that relationships can, should, and do survive and prosper from interpersonal stressors and disillusions when they are substantive and genuine; such learning would be a boon to his upcoming marriage.

Afterthoughts

I am always an observer of myself as I treat others. I observe myself from a cognitive place, though I essentially treat clients from a connection with self and other that is firmly rooted in sensing and intuition. The more spiritual among us may consider this meaningful responsiveness a form of psychic energy emanating from the depth of my core. Whatever its origin or its name, I know I can trust my brain's right hemisphere to fly me quite respectfully by the seat of my therapy pants, having first mastered the substantive diversity of left-brain skills so essential to the treatment process. I also take great comfort in the confidence that there is generous room for error within healthy and loving human relationships. Contrary to the perspective of the individual with an eating disorder, who believes that a person is no more than what he or she appears outwardly to be to others, I believe that personhood lies within, and that it is one's personhood, with all of its strengths and vulnerabilities, that gets communicated within the connection of the therapy relationship. Treatment quality, originating cognitively and extending into the sensory realm, demands our full and constant presence not only in the moment but also in our characters.

With regard to the case of this young man, I fully own what I consider to be legitimate feelings of anger and frustration in response to his resistance to change after those many years of relationship and treatment. His commitment to an intractable illness was as tenacious as my own commitment to his recovery. The humanness of genuine feelings, his and my own, was real and valid, providing invaluable information for the recovering client about himself and his relationships, and about how both work. There is a legitimate place for all feelings within a deeply intimate and loving therapy relationship. I am certain that taking on emotional conflict as we did, when we did, was largely responsible for inspiring his subsequent move forward into recovery, releasing him from his stuck point. Could this discussion have taken place and had the same impact just after the wedding, in hindsight? Perhaps. But in the end, my demand and insistence on change at this moment brought movement to what had become a static if not deteriorating process. It took a lot of love to make these demands and a lot of courage to carry them through (though I admit it would have taken even more courage to continue to treat him if so doing enabled a potentially lethal outcome). It took disruption and discomfort to uncover and decipher palpable and powerful transference and countertransference issues, to induce this young man to face himself, and to shake out a recovery process to a point where movement, change, and resolution would become not only possible, but likely.

THERAPIST SELF-DISCLOSURE

Clients with eating disorders are hypersensitive and in most instances, exquisitely attuned to the nuanaces of the therapy relationship. The therapist's self-disclosure potentially adds fuel to the fire. In the interest of preserving the relationship, it is always better to "give words" to something that a hypersensitive client knows and feels, recognizing "the elephant under the chair," particularly when the eating disordered client may be prone to assume responsibility for any relationship problem that may ensue. The therapist should model every opportunity to test reality, as these clients are quick to distort and tend to use denial as a preferred coping tool.

After my beloved dog—which had been my constant companion and a presence in all of my sessions for 14 years—died suddenly, a client asked where he was. It was therapeutic for both of us to discuss and grieve; as hard as it was for me to talk about it at that raw moment, it would have been harder on the client if I had not. The discussion modeled the depth and breadth of human feelings and the benefits of sharing them with loving others. It modeled humanity, intimacy, mutual trust, and vulnerability, illustrating how we all are subject to the same degree of lack of control in many aspects of our lives. Most of all, it modeled coping—the determination to move forward at a time of emotional depletion and the knowledge that pain can be made easier to endure with a supportive person beside you. I openly processed the dynamic of that session with her while it was happening and during the following session. My presence in the moment made that session a highly rich and meaningful experience.

Therapists' self-disclosure can help clients become more self-reflective and self-accepting, but self-disclosure must always be in the interest of the client and never self-serving. Some practitioners question the ethics of self-disclosure. Revealing the past existence of an eating disorder has been shown to be of benefit to some clients; doing so requires great sensitivity to the feel and timing of the relationship and the needs and capacities of the client to assimilate this information and benefit from it. After disclosing an eating disorder history, it would be wise for the therapist to check in with the client at critical points in the treatment to investigate potential transference responses that could derail the treatment process.

A nuanced sharing, with clear boundaries, of the therapist's self inspires human connection, even as it is inspired by familiarity and connectedness. The therapist's disclosure of vulnerability can be particularly significant if the client tends to idealize the professional or treatment relationship. Therapist self-disclosure needs to be purposeful and motivated by intentionality to enhance the client's self-awareness, learning, and change. When effective, it can deepen the client's own access to affect and the promotion of self-regulation.

Effective self-disclosure never brings attention to the practitioner for the benefit of the practitioner, nor does it create alignments that could result in rifts within the client's other pivotal relationships. Following self-disclosure, the therapist should immediately shift the focus back to the client and her response.

UNIQUE CHALLENGES TO THE PROFESSIONAL'S PERSONHOOD

Eating disorders are disorders of perception, judgment, thought, attitude, values, and attachments. Essentially, they are disorders of the qualities that are most profoundly human. Establishing a good treatment relationship provides the therapist with access to the finest aspects of the client's humanity, and vice versa, encompassing many levels and degrees of human intimacy, emotion, and feeling. It is for this reason that practitioners need to know and model for clients what it means to be truly human, which involves the capacity to grow, to change, to learn, to solve problems, to err, to recover, to heal oneself, and to use one's self with kindness and compassion to positively influence the lives of others. The rigors of the personal experience of conducting eating disorder treatment set this treatment specialty apart from generic practice, raising the standard of excellence for care.

Tolerating Ambiguity With Patience

Ironically, the variety and intensity of personal and professional issues that eating disorders evoke in clinicians clearly parallel the emotional tasks and challenges of their clients. Eating disorder treatment demands that clinicians inhabit the same uncomfortable gray areas and fuzzy approximations of life that they persuade and embolden their clients to confront. Eating disorder practitioners need to learn to tolerate the same sensation of the "free fall" in the face of the unpredictability of the healing process, as does the client. Ambivalence and resistance create unevenness in the client's capacity to heal and stay healed, making this process clearly not for the chicken-hearted. There are precious few opportunities in eating disorder treatment to let one's hair down

Like their clients, practitioners are called upon to function amid the murky realities of ambiguity and feelings of powerlessness as they traverse borders in family systems while maintaining clear and definitive boundaries. Eating disorder professionals regularly field manipulation, resistance, impatience, pessimism, power struggle, and denial. Professional tasks require the same degree of patience that clients and families are forced to muster in what seems like an endless recovery ordeal. Professionals need to learn to use themselves as whole and complete individuals, with flexibility that comes out of seasoned maturity and with confidence in solving problems—all goals that the health professional shares with his or her clients with eating disorders.

The field is not a good fit for the practitioner who thinks linearly, avoids multitasking, prefers to abide by pre-established protocols or agendas, or feels uncomfortable with the ever-changing reality of eating disorder recovery. The greatest challenges of all are for the professional who fears conflict and prefers to avoid risk as much as the therapist's clients do. Effective eating disorder therapists believe in the human capacities for change and self-repair and exercise resourcefulness and self-reliance in devising creative and sometimes unconventional solutions to tough problems. They need to use themselves and available resources deftly and to know where to turn for help when the well appears to be running dry and how to teach their clients to do the same. Box 3.3 lists the personal resources required to treat eating disorders.

Forgiving Yourself

Even when practitioners are acutely sensitive to the workings of the malnourished brain and the distortions that are the benchmark of eating disordered thinking, conversations intended to be therapeutic can become minefields. Some of the mistakes practitioners make in treating clients with eating disorders are virtually unavoidable in light of their exquisite sensitivity and projections. Try not to be too hard on yourself in such instances.

BOX 3.3

Personal Resources Required of Eating Disorder Therapists

- Professionals require the stamina and courage to stay afloat in the midst of the dynamics and turmoil of functional and dysfunctional family systems in flux, traversing clear and definitive boundaries even while maintaining them.
- Professionals require adeptness at navigating within the parameters of clearly determined goals while remaining alert to the need to alter them.
- Professionals need to learn to use themselves as whole and complete individuals, with flexibility that comes of emotional differentiation, seasoned maturity, and confidence in solving problems, a goal they share with their clients.
- Professionals need fortitude to withstand the denial and potential hostility of clients and families who may resist the demands of recovery.
- Practitioners, like their clients, typically find themselves thrown off balance by counterintuitive treatment realities intrinsic to this work (see Chapter 2) that can prevent recovery. By anticipating and recognizing contradictory elements of these diseases and enhancing their clients' capacity to understand, accept, and confront them, the therapist sustains the integrity of the treatment process and provides the reassurance and motivation clients need to remain invested in a confusing and sometimes discouraging process of healing.

How a professional says things is as important as *what* he or she intends to convey because the malnourished brain is so prone to distorting incoming information. In working with an individual with an eating disorder, a professional's presentation of information needs to specifically accommodate the client's reactivity to appearance and weight issues and other inevitably distorted interpretations and projections.

For example, a pediatrician who specializes in work with eating disorders was attempting to educate a 12-year-old client and her mother about the benefits of eating fish with omega fatty acids. The girl reacted with acute fear about ever eating fish again, assuming that fatty acids make a person "fat." In the same examination, this doctor told the youngster that her metabolic function was "normal," provoking her fear about its not being "fast." The doctor described the fats in a single avocado as being not only healthy but sufficient to meet one's daily requirements. All of these facts frightened the girl sufficiently to cause a reversal in her eating progress. She and her mother left her office infuriated, never to return.

Preserving Your Integrity

At times, a therapeutic response can stimulate change and growth in the client or family system even if it sabotages a treatment process. A client may choose to leave treatment because the therapist has taken a carefully considered professional "risk" in offering sensitive feedback to preserve the integrity of the treatment process. In such instances, therapeutic lessons taught may need to become grist for a therapy mill elsewhere, on someone else's treatment couch.

I recently spoke with an 18-year-old woman with anorexia and her parents about the urgency of her receiving intensified care as she prepared to leave home the following year for college. In that session, her resistance to change had become increasingly apparent, and it was clear to me that "push needed to come to shove" in establishing a new direction if she were to recover. I spoke of her need to accept nothing less than a quality existence, which she richly deserved. I recommended that she be evaluated by a physician for medication to treat her severe anxiety and that she consider entering a treatment program to stimulate change.

Following that potent session, the client never returned to treatment. Neither she nor her parents would commit to the rigors of the recovery process, no matter what the benefits it held for the girl's future. This mother, who had micromanaged her daughter's life, dictating what she would eat, who she could and could not play with, what she should think, what she should wear, and how she should learn (she did her child's homework with her every night), had confessed during a prior session that she would have "nothing to live for" after her daughter's departure for college. There is the likelihood that this mother was deeply invested in keeping her daughter sick and at home by her side. My agenda, in not running parallel to hers, was rejected, keeping this young woman victimized and infantilized, if not by her mother, than by her eating disorder.

Finding Professional Support

Professionals working with clients who have eating disorders need to become students not only of themselves, their clients, and the treatment process but also of other more experienced professionals through consultation, always maintaining humility in the face of the complex and far-reaching effects of these disorders and their recovery. Continuous and accurate self-monitoring and treatment appraisal are greatly enhanced by peer consultation and professional supervision, be it formal or informal. Fellow team members are an excellent source of necessary and sustaining support through ongoing treatment complexities and pitfalls. In some instances, the practitioner may require the wholly objective ear of a non–team-related consultant who has some emotional distance.

Obtaining the support of colleagues is a way of caring for oneself, of replenishing empty coffers, of sustaining a clear and optimistic voice, of shoring up efforts and confidence even as one attempts to shore up that of one's clients. Eating disorder professionals need to become perpetual learners, and they can depend on clients and the therapeutic process to provide the most potent teaching of all. Clients, who feel invisible everywhere else in life, need to feel embraced, seen, heard, and fully understood by the professional, who in turn, needs to do whatever it takes to keep himself or herself equal to this task.

CONCLUSION

Eating disorder practitioners find unique personal challenges piggybacking on already daunting professional treatment tasks. It is through a loving therapeutic connection that the treatment environment becomes a safe and trusting place to learn, allowing the seeds of successful treatment outcomes to germinate and come alive. The eating disorder practitioner needs to encounter himself or herself first to connect with others who seek to do the same. By attending to the humanistic aspects of treatment—by nurturing the self-awareness, compassion, and empathy that bind people together and inspire personal greatness—the odds that clients will achieve full recovery are improved. The best listeners to others are those who are best at listening to themselves.

SECTION 2

DIAGNOSTIC NUTS AND BOLTS

4

Eating Disorders and the *Diagnostic and Statistical Manual of Mental Disorders*

I have a saying about all psychiatric diagnoses made in people who have ongoing eating disorders; 'You can't be sure what's wrong with their head until they're fed.'
— Edward P. Tyson, MD, Medical Director of Cedar Springs
Austin Treatment Center for Eating Disorders in Austin, Texas

The diagnostic bible for mental disorders is the American Psychiatric Association's *Diagnostic and Statistical Manual of Mental Disorders.* In this chapter, I refer throughout to the most recent version, Fourth Edition, Text Revision (*DSM–IV–TR*; American Psychiatric Association, 2000). In introducing this most widely used diagnostic reference, I also explore the most common co-occurring disorders in individuals with eating disorders. Determining accurate diagnosis is critical to a quick and potentially life-saving response of the therapist with eating disordered clients. The manual is a pivotal diagnostic tool, and practitioners need to intimately acquaint themselves with it and with the information it provides, not only about eating disorders but also about frequently co-occurring conditions. Having said this, it is important to be aware that currently, among eating disorder professionals, there is an ongoing dialogue about upgrading the definitions of eating disorders as they stand, to match the ever-growing knowledge of these disorders through research and practice. The information provided in the *DSM* should be regarded as a guideline in arriving at a complete and comprehensive diagnosis for an eating disorder. This chapter is meant to acquaint you with the terms and conditions that you are likely to confront in treating these disorders.

The *DSM* offers definitions that differentiate personality quirks from symptoms of mental illness and that establish eligibility for insurance reimbursement or the status of disability. Its multi-axial assessment system offers five separate domains of information that help the clinician plan treatment and predict outcomes. The system is comprehensive in its consideration of mental disorders, general medical conditions, and psychosocial and environmental problems. Because eating disorders affect so many levels of functioning, it is particularly important for therapists to accurately assess them all in establishing an accurate diagnosis of a typically broad-ranging presenting problem.

Because of the complex nature of eating disorders and their diagnosis, and in light of the ongoing research and ever-increasing understanding of their origins and implications, practitioners can anticipate the newly revised *DSM–V* (with a scheduled 2012 publication date) to reflect an evolving set of increasingly accurate diagnostic criteria for eating disorders. As an example, a candidate for a new category of eating disorder is "purging disorder." This category describes people of normal weight who purge after eating normal or even small amounts of food. Currently, a common and understandable error of diagnostic judgment occurs when a normal-weight client denies a history of binge eating, thus leading the interviewer to disregard investigation into the use of vomiting, laxatives, or diuretics to control weight (Henig, 2004).

Typical co-occurring disorders would include addiction; physical, sexual, and emotional abuse; mood disorders; anxiety; and depression. The simultaneous presence of eating-specific pathology and personality psychopathology is typical of an eating disorder (McLaren, Gauvin, & Steiger, 2001). The client with an eating disorder is a complex, multifaceted human being who cannot be defined or understood fully through any combination of diagnoses—a perfect example of the whole being greater than the sum of its parts.

By way of introduction to the *DSM*, my suggestion is to read it, know it, understand it, and then consider the possibility of integrating an even more nuanced, comprehensive picture of the person sitting before you, recognizing that no two people with an eating disorder are alike. Strict interpretation of *DSM* criteria may work against clients who are of normal weight or who are overweight; inexperienced clinicians might tend to overlook these client groups, perpetuating the problem. Fairburn (2008) points out that

> the implication of the *DSM-IV* scheme is that each of the eating disorders requires its own form of treatment, which is not the case. Because eating disorders evolve in form suggests that "transdiagnostic" mechanisms play a major role in maintaining eating disorders psychopthology and treatments that are capable of addressing these mechanisms should be effective with all eating disorders, rather than just one. (p. 18)

DSM DEFINITIONS OF EATING DISORDERS

The *DSM–IV–TR* defines three types of eating disorder—anorexia nervosa, bulimia nervosa, and eating disorder not otherwise specified. In describing prevalence of these types, Fairburn reveals that "the most commonly neglected diagnosis of EDNOS [eating disorder not otherwise specified] comprises between 50 and 60 percent of adult outpatients. BN [bulimia nervosa] comprises about 30 percent of cases and least common is AN [anorexia nervosa], which comprises the remaining 10 to 15 percent" (Fairburn, 2008, p. 8). Symptoms vary throughout the life of any single disease and recovery process, rarely if ever precisely matching clinical definitions. Clients with bulimia may purge 30 times a day or once every three months. They may take 150 laxatives a day or never use laxatives at all. Some clients with anorexia are painfully thin; others are of normal weight.

Because it is not unusual for symptoms of all three disorders to exist within the same individual, and because they typically transmute into one another during an individual disease and recovery experience, symptoms of anorexia and bulimia defy strict categorization. Clients with anorexia and bulimia share psychopathology, which includes the urge to be thin and a fear of becoming fat, emotional and behavioral compulsions, distortions in body image and self-perception, and the inability to moderate their functioning vis-à-vis food and other life spheres. They also experience the loss of power, control, self-worth, and the ability to sense them.

As aspects of the same disease syndrome that share a great diversity in symptoms and issues, anorexia and bulimia differ in the basic structure and function of clients' personality. Treatment needs to reflect this difference. Clients with bulimia are driven by impulsivity, purging in an attempt to undo out-of-control behaviors so as to restore a sense of self-control. These clients typically abuse diuretics, diet pills, ipecac, or laxatives and exercise as methods of undoing. Clients with anorexia, in contrast, are driven by compulsivity and restriction. They keep a tight rein on themselves, adhering to precise rituals around eating and exercise in order to contain rather than act out urges. In this way they avoid the risk of facing the need to undo an out-of-control behavior, which they believe would surely lead to a fully out-of-control existence.

Another major difference between anorexia and bulimia is the relative balance of undereating and overeating and its effects on body weight. In bulimia, body weight is usually unremarkable because overeating and undereating cancel each other out. With anorexia, attempts to restrict are more successful, and the client typically (but not necessarily) remains significantly underweight (Fairburn, 2008).

It is not atypical for clients with anorexia, when the drive for hunger overcomes their drive for thinness, to simultaneously overeat and purge. Likewise, individuals with bulimia, who typically overeat and purge, may also restrict food or starve themselves for days on end. Some purge; others do not. Clients with bulimia may become anorexic to maintain their weight as they cease purging behaviors. Most people with bulimia, binge eaters included, are of normal weight. Bulimic behaviors may take different forms, including overexercise, compulsive overeating, and abuse of laxatives, diet pills, diuretics, and ipecac, though most fail to recognize these behaviors as being purge related.

Anorexia Nervosa

The lifetime prevalence of anorexia nervosa is 0.9 percent in women, and 0.3 percent in men (Hudson et al., 2007). Although only 10 to 15 percent of people with an eating disorder have anorexia (Fairburn, 2008), it is the most highly recognized of these disorders because of the severe emaciation of some of its victims. The *DSM–IV–TR* edition complete definition of anorexia nervosa (307.1) is too lengthy to include here. Significant criteria for this diagnosis would include "the refusal to maintain a minimally normal body weight, intense fear of gaining weight, and a significant disturbance in the perception of the shape or size of one's body. Postmenarchal females with this disorder are amenorrheic. The individual maintains a body weight that is below a minimally normal level for age and height. Usually weight loss is accomplished through reduction in total food intake, and individuals with this disorder intensely fear gaining weight or becoming fat. The experience and the significance of body weight and shape are distorted in these individuals (*DSM–IV–TR*; American Psychiatric Association, 2000, pp. 583–584). The *DSM–IV–TR* also defines two subtypes of anorexia: restricting type, in which weight loss is accomplished primarily through dieting, fasting, or excessive exercise, and binge-eating/purging type for those who regularly engage in binge eating or purging behaviors (or both). Most anorexics who binge eat also purge through self-induced vomiting and the misuse of laxatives, diuretics, or enemas. Some purge after the consumption of small amounts of food (*DSM–IV–TR*; American Psychiatric Association, 2000, p. 585).

Anorexia nervosa has been defined as "a behavioral disorder characterized by ego-syntonic self-starvation, denial of illness and ambivalence towards treatment" (Guarda, 2008, pp. 113–120). A British Broadcasting Company reporter who spent six weeks engaging in anorexic behaviors in an effort to better understand the dynamic of this disorder called the pursuit of thinness "a way of losing yourself in one problem—weight loss—and ignoring all the other issues in your life" and "a seductive and all-consuming addiction when the figures on the scales are a simple, if nutty, method of measuring your success as a human being" (Spicer, 2007).

Anorexia has been described as follows:

> an adaptive attempt by the individual to meet the demands of self, family, and development. Most anorexics would acknowledge that the decision not to eat is the first time in their lives that they have asserted their own will. Developing anorexia nervosa in this culture offers a woman a peculiar opportunity to consolidate an identity around a socially sanctioned psychiatric disorder. (Johnson, Sansone, & Chewning, 1992, p. 737)

Bulimia Nervosa

The lifetime prevalence of bulimia nervosa is 1.5 percent in women and 0.5 percent in men (Hudson, 2007). According to the *DSM–IV–TR*, essential features of bulimia nervosa (307.51) are "binge eating and inappropriate compensatory methods to prevent weight gain. Self evaluation of the individual with Bulimia Nervosa is excessively influenced by body shape and weight. To qualify for the diagnosis, the binge eating and the inappropriate compensatory behaviors must occur, on average, at least twice a week for 3 months" (American Psychiatric Association, 2000, p. 589). The *DSM–IV–TR* defines a binge as "eating in a discrete period of time an amount of food that is definitely larger than most moist individuals would eat under similar circumstances. The context for the binge is significant. Binges typically include sweet, high-calorie foods. Individuals with bulimia nervosa are usually ashamed of their problem and conceal the symptoms. An episode is accompanied by a feeling of lack of control. Another essential feature of BN is the recurrent use of inappropriate compensatory behaviors to prevent weight gain, including vomiting and the misuse of laxatives, diuretics, ipecac, or enemas. Exercise becomes excessive when it interferes with important activities or when the individual continues to exercise despite injury" (American Psychiatric Association, 2000, pp. 590–591). In my experience, individuals with bulimia commonly display impulsivity, co-occurring mood disorders, intractable compulsions, and bulimic hypomania, and may typically engage in promiscuity, self-mutilation, substance abuse, or other forms of self-numbing.

In committing self-destructive behaviors, many individuals with bulimia enter trancelike states reminiscent of dissociations they may have experienced during emotional, physical, or sexual abuse in their past. Individuals with bulimia nervosa are reported to have experienced higher rates of other types of trauma besides childhood sexual abuse, including adult rape and molestation, aggravated assault, and physical neglect. The onset of bulimic symptomatology is often caused by periods of prolonged calorie deprivation (Johnson & Maddi, 1986).

Many clients with bulimia have a history of laxative abuse (estimates range from 40 percent to 75 percent), and 28 percent have used ipecac at least once to induce vomiting. Those who abuse laxatives have poorer behavioral, cognitive, and psychological outcomes than those who do not (Franzen et al., 2008).

Bulimic behaviors vary widely. One bulimia client described consuming 10,000 calories in a single sitting; she confided that she would regularly fill one quarter of a bathtub with her vomit from a single binge. Bulimic binges, however, are distinguished not necessarily by the amount of food consumed, but by the compulsive nature of these episodes. To someone with restricting bulimia, five grapes may constitute a binge. When she experienced mounting anxiety, one client with bulimia would find herself behind the nearest convenience store in a trancelike state, frantically forcing a single cupcake down her throat (Natenshon, 1999).

Purging can take many forms, including vomiting, spitting out chewed food, excessive exercise (including sexual behavior), or squirming in one's chair, as well as the abuse of laxatives, colonics, diuretics, diet pills, or ipecac. One of my clients awakened several times a night to satiate a tremendous thirst for carrot juice or orange juice, which she claimed would become too acidic for her stomach to handle, causing a purge. Noncompensatory exercise (that is not related to previous food consumption) typically functions as a routine form of weight control or mood regulator for bulimic individuals.

Bulimic behaviors are an apt metaphor for how clients approach life in general; the binge–purge cycle parallels compulsive behaviors in other life spheres. V struggled to control her binge–purge cycle by restricting her food intake. Her cycle manifested itself in the form of binge shopping; she would spend thousands of dollars every week on clothing that she did not need or use, a process that she claimed "calms me down and makes me happy." The purge phase took the form of frequent, random, and undifferentiated clearing out of her closet, returning clothing to stores or giving it away—even items that she loved or had not yet worn. Both activities were compulsions over which she felt she had no control, despite remonstrations from her husband.

Eating Disorders Not Otherwise Specified

The *DSM–IV–TR* describes eating disorders not otherwise specified as a category for disorders of eating that do not meet the criteria for any specific eating disorder. As an example,

> a female who meets all criteria for AN [anorexia nervosa] except the individual has regular menses, or current weight in the normal range; other examples might include where all the criteria for BN [bulimia nervosa] are met except that the binge eating and inappropriate compensatory mechanisms occur at a frequency of less than twice a week or for a duration of less than 3 months; the regular use of inappropriate compensatory behavior by an individual of normal weight after eating small amounts of food; repeated chewing and spitting out, but not swallowing, large amounts of food; and recurrent episodes of binge eating in the absence of the regular use of inappropriate compensatory behaviors characteristic of BN [bulimia nervosa]. (American Psychiatric Association, 2000, pp. 594–595)

Eating disorders not otherwise specified encompass subcategories, including binge eating disorder, activity or exercise disorders, night eating syndrome, diabulimia, orthorexia nervosa, and permarexia, which are discussed later in this section. Perhaps because eating disorders not otherwise specified constitutes the most under-recognized diagnosis by clinicians and the most neglected by researchers (Fairburn et al., 2007), some insurance companies do not recognize it as a diagnosis and have refused coverage.

The classification is reserved for eating disorders that do not follow specific diagnostic standards or that fail to meet established clinical diagnostic criteria with regard to frequency, duration, or juxtaposition with other symptoms. For example, a woman with anorexia symptoms exercised to the point of exhaustion, but she had never gone more than three months without menstruating. Another woman went without eating all day and at 6:00 P.M. began to binge on thousands of calories; she maintained a normal weight by purging infrequently enough to escape a clinical diagnosis. One study documented underweight clients who did not overvalue their shape and weight who would qualify for an eating disorder not otherwise specified diagnosis (Dalle Grave, Calugi, & Marchesini, 2008).

Symptomatology of eating disorders not otherwise specified may be seen in early disease symptoms, in partial recovery, or in symptoms that persist into recovery; clients in partial recovery may have an eating disorder not otherwise specified diagnosis because they meet some, but not all, the criteria of the full syndrome diagnosis. Yet this is also a differential diagnosis within itself. To warrant a separate diagnosis of eating disorder not otherwise specified among women with a history of full-syndrome anorexia or bulimia, more persistent symptomatology may be required (Eddy et al., 2008). Such clients may have the same distinctive attitudes, behaviors, and severity of comorbid psychiatric disorders as do those with anorexia and bulimia (Wilson, 2005). Adolescents with eating disorders not otherwise specified can be expected to present with milder eating disorder symptoms but with greater comorbidity than those with bulimia (Schmidt et al., 2008).

Clients who are diagnosed with an eating disorder not otherwise specified typically describe a sense of relief that their condition does not qualify as anorexia or bulimia. Whether such relief is attributable to denial of the gravity of their condition, the belief that recovery will be easier and timelier, or the feeling of being precisely diagnosed and understood remains to be seen. The important question is whether or not the eating disorder not otherwise specified diagnosis is a liability or an asset in stimulating the self-confidence and motivation required to heal. Like anorexia and bulimia, these conditions involve the genetic predilection to perfectionism, the need for control, and the possible presence of obsessive–compulsive anxiety disorder and/or other forms of anxiety, with food restriction a self-soothing device. Whatever the diagnostic label, it is critical that treatment be comprehensive and team based.

If diagnosing an eating disorder remains an art, eating disorder not otherwise specified—the diagnosis that contains all forms of idiosyncratic or otherwise undefined eating disorders—is the embodiment of the imprecise nature of art. It takes diagnostic acumen and intuition to arrive at an accurate diagnosis within this catchall category. One of my clients provides an example. The young woman, who binged on sweets in bed before sleep, had come home from college with anxiety and a sleep disorder and had lost 20 pounds. Emaciated and wan, she was referred to me for treatment of her "anorexia." It soon became apparent that though she coped with her anxiety about leaving home and transitioning to college by restricting food, she might not be diagnosable as clinically anorexic because of her willingness to regain weight, which she did by restricting food during the day and bingeing on sweets at night; she readily regained two pounds per week within the first month of care. After restoring this initial weight, she began to limit her intake of calories. To achieve a definitive diagnosis of anorexia bingeing type, bulimia restricting type, or eating disorders not otherwise specified with co-occurring anxiety disorder, we needed to wait to see whether and how she would respond to restoring her weight to her body's natural set point.

Even when disorders around eating are subclinical (such as in cases of disordered eating), they remain worthy of attention in the interest of preventing full-blown clinical pathology, reversing potential metabolic dysfunction, and undoing a lifetime of poor eating habits. It is far easier to change disruptive attitudes than it is to dislodge ingrained habits and behaviors.

Binge Eating Disorder

Binge eating disorder, the most commonly recognized category of eating disorder not otherwise specified, applies to individuals who engage in compulsive overeating. Binge eating is defined as eating, in a discrete period of time (such as within any two-hour period), an amount of food that is definitely larger than most people would eat in a similar period of time under similar circumstances or a sense of lack of control overeating during the episode, such as a feeling that one cannot stop eating or control what or how much one is eating (Myers, 2004). More common than anorexia or bulimia, one in five young women reports binge eating, and 40 percent of binge eaters are men and boys. About 2 percent of U.S. adults—as many as 4 million Americans—have binge eating disorder. About 30 percent of individuals seeking medical treatment for obesity and, in some surveys, up to 50 percent of individuals being seen in nonmedical weight reduction programs meet the diagnostic criteria for binge eating disorder. Half of individuals with binge eating disorder also experience major depression (Myers, 2004).

The chaotic quality of eating is a distinctive feature of binge eating disorder (Wilson, 2005). Symptoms include uncontrollable, excessive, and compulsive eating followed by feelings of shame, guilt, depression, disgust, and self-loathing. Individuals with binge eating disorder, who typically eat alone to avoid embarrassment about the quantity that they consume, sometimes eat to the point of extreme discomfort or physical pain; the process can be considered an act of self-injury. A 33-year-old binge eating disorder client described eating so much food at one sitting that her skin hurts from being stretched. Clients with binge eating disorder typically suffer digestive problems, including gas, diarrhea, bloating, cramps, and stomach pain, most of which dissipate after a few months of recovery.

Because binge eaters generally do not purge, they typically attempt to undo binges by intermittent starving or food restriction. In response to a restriction in the intake of calories, the body signals the brain that it needs food, and the individual typically overcompensates by overeating (note that occasional eating binges, indulgences, and food cravings are normal for most men and women). As yo-yo dieters who attempt to control their weight through periods of extended fasting, binge eaters often maintain a weight well within the realm of normal, so their problems are difficult to identify and may be ignored or not taken seriously by caregivers. Being perceived as normal can be trying for the client, who knows she is sick and wants, needs, and requests help but is denied recognition, assistance, and compassion.

A client who had binge eating disorder and was terrified of gaining weight spoke about the excitement she experienced in breaking a $20 bill into $1 bills, giving her unfettered access to vending machines. She spoke of not being able to attend to certain life tasks, such as studying, without having binged first. To satisfy her need to binge without gaining weight, she starved herself all day so she could study at night.

Activity or Exercise Disorders

Activity disorders are eating disorders (bulimia nervosa or eating disorders not otherwise specified) that take the form of compulsive overexercise. The term *anorexia athletica* describes a subcategory of eating disorders not otherwise specified for athletes who engage in at least one unhealthy method of weight control, such as fasting, vomiting, use of diet pills, laxatives or diuretics. Extreme and ritualized exercise is typically a form of purging and an attempt to numb feelings. The excessiveness of their workouts compromises these individuals' quality of daily life and can result in violence or self-injury. A college student with an activity disorder was so torn between the compulsion to exercise and the need to spend time studying for finals that the force of her internal conflict led her to recklessly hurl objects and smash mirrors in her sorority house (Natenshon, 1999).

As many as 80 percent of individuals with anorexia use excessive exercise as a method of purging or reducing anxiety, as compared with 55 percent of individuals with bulimia nervosa. The release of endorphins that comes with excessive exercise can create a reliance on brain chemistry changes that substitutes for effective problem resolution. Exercising to burn off calories in advance of eating in order to establish a "credit" is referred to as "debting."

Certain girls who are active in sports or exercise intensively are at risk for a problem called female athlete triad, a combination of three conditions: disordered eating, amenorrhea, and osteoporosis. When the client uses exercise to purge the body, female athlete triad should be diagnosed as anorexia nervosa to ensure proper treatment. Some believe that this diagnosis was created to offer another, more benign diagnostic option or euphemism that would not require star athletes to be pulled from play.

The disproportionate number of eating disorders in equestrians and gymnasts, as well as runners and other high-powered athletes and performers reflects the combined influence of nature and nurture, of compulsive and perfectionistic temperaments and genetic histories in conjunction with the demands and rigors of achieving excellence, control, and mastery. "In addition to social pressure to be thin, athletes experience extra pressure for increased performance and ranking, making them more cautious of their body shape and size and more susceptible to eating disorders. Research on the risk of athletes for eating disorders, however, remains contradictory and inconclusive" (Plessinger, 2008).

Excessive exercise is associated particularly with the purging subtype of anorexia nervosa, as well as with a constellation of anxious and obsessional temperament and personality characteristics among women with eating disorders (Shroff et al., 2006). When a client is overexercising, the clinician should investigate a diagnosis of anxiety and obsessiveness and vice versa; good treatment will depend on making and investigating such connections.

Night Eating Syndrome

Individuals with night eating syndrome wake frequently at night to eat compulsively in a trancelike state. The core clinical feature appears to be a delay in the circadian timing of food intake; energy intake is reduced during the first half of the day and greatly increased in the second half, such that sleep is disrupted in the service of food intake. For night eaters, a night of fasting may result in insomnia or excruciating hunger pains. Many hold food in their mouths while sleeping, swallowing occasionally through the night, wreaking havoc on their teeth. One young woman awoke every night, unknowingly, to eat; because she stole food from her college roommate, they had to lock up the food that they kept in their dormitory room. The syndrome can be distinguished from bulimia nervosa and binge eating disorder by the lack of associated compensatory behaviors, the timing of food intake, and the fact that the food ingestions are small, amounting to repeated snacks rather than true binges.

According to Stunkard, "Not only is night eating syndrome an eating disorder, but one of mood and sleep as well" (cited in "Night Eating Syndrome," n.d.). "People who fall prey to this syndrome are not simply indulging in a bad habit. They have a real clinical illness, reflected by changes in hormone levels."

Diabulimia

Type 1 diabetes is a disorder in which the body's immune system attacks insulin-producing cells in the pancreas. Producing little or no insulin, these patients must take shots of insulin daily. *Diabulimia* refers to a weight loss method in which people with Type 1 diabetes strategically omit their insulin injections as a caloric purging mechanism; failure to administer insulin places the body in a starvation state, resulting in breakdown of muscle and fat. Studies show that one out of three women with Type 1 diabetes have skipped or reduced the amount of insulin they take to lose weight. Complications may include retinal hemorrhaging, kidney damage, coma, or death. In Type 2 diabetes (more closely linked with obesity), binge eating may become a problem; clients with diabetes invariably struggle with the medical recommendation for dietary restraint (Mathur, 2008).

Orthorexia Nervosa and Permarexia

Orthorexia nervosa is not included in the *DSM–IV–TR*; it was coined by a physician in the late 1990s to refer to an apparent obsession with healthy or "proper" foods. The term *orthorexia* is characterized by an excessive focus on eating healthy foods, which can in rare cases, result in malnutrition or death. It describes a set of symptoms that, in my mind, falls into the diagnostic category of eating disorder not otherwise specified in combination with obsessive–compulsive behaviors and intrusive thoughts. It differs from anorexia in its focus on body purity, or the obsessive drive to overcome chronic illness or improve general health, rather than on weight loss and the drive to be thin. In fact, because the focus of orthorexia is less on weight loss and more on body purity, the odds for the client to feel motivated to recover may become greater. "Healthy" eating habits lead to extreme preoccupations with nutritious foods, detoxification, and fasting. The total elimination of fat can lead to early-onset osteoporosis, compromising health and overall well-being.

Orthorexia describes compulsions that motivate individuals to spend hours each day pondering healthy food choices and planning meals in advance, studying nutritional labels, or feeling guilty when not adhering rigidly to a preplanned eating regimen. People with such food preoccupations typically eat the same things, in the same amounts, at the same time, and in the same order, every day.

A fall from grace typically stimulates acts of penitence, such as ever-stricter diets and fasts. The inner life of a person with orthorexia is dominated by efforts to resist temptation, self-condemnation for lapses, self-praise for success at compliance with the chosen regimen, and feelings of superiority over others who are less pure in their dietary habits. This transference of all of life's value into the act of eating is what makes orthorexia a true disorder. Nutritionists are more apt to be the first to observe and diagnose these problems, as they have an essentially nutritional focus.

With or without the label of a clinical eating disorder, such individuals live tormented lives, fearful and vigilant around food, weight control, and exercise, and they deserve therapeutic attention (similar to that appropriate for standard eating disorders) around their compulsions.

There is a thin line between the diagnosis of orthorexia and anorexia nervosa with a strongly co-occurring component of obsessive–compulsive anxiety disorder. An anorexic 20-year-old man was as compulsively afraid of not eating as he was about eating too much; he refused to take a blood test because of his reluctance to fast ahead of time, fearing his body would "go into shock." He ate regularly but refused to consume enough food and would eat only limited kinds of foods. In eating only "for nourishment," he weighed and precisely measured every morsel of food and fluid that passed his lips, never exceeding the minimum amount required. He would not consider the option of taking medication, as it is an "unnatural substance." Nor would he eat sugar because of its effect on his teeth, dairy products because of their effects on his mucus production, soy products to protect his hormonal balance, or bread unless it was whole grain bread with protein. He experienced genuine grief and mourning at having to limit his daily running routine.

Permarexia is an eating disorder not otherwise specified describing a condition of permanent dieting, though the afflicted individual is not overweight. Although they know they are thin, clients with permarexia will go to any measure to maintain that thinness. Permarexia is a psychologically based disorder and must be treated as such. The risks of dieting in triggering the onset of an eating disorder are well established.

Other Terms

Other terms sometime seen in the popular media include *vigorexia* or *bigorexia*, a muscle dysmorphia obsession about not being large and muscular enough. Those who suffer from muscle dysmorphia are delusional about being "too skinny" or "too small," although they are often above average in musculature. It is not uncommon for these individuals to take potentially dangerous anabolic steroids or to neglect jobs, relationships, or family life to engage in excessive exercising. This condition is sometimes referred to as "reverse anorexia nervosa."

Pregnorexia is an eating disorder not otherwise specified in which the pregnant woman stops eating. A highly anxious anorexic woman sought outpatient treatment from me after having been refused by several outpatient clinic programs that recommended inpatient hospitalization first. She reported being so afraid of being "locked up" and "restrained" in a hospital that she "would rather die than go inpatient." Though never married, in the past, this woman had lost 30 pounds and miscarried at five months with her first pregnancy; became depressed at gaining 14 pounds in a second pregnancy, which ended in a miscarriage; and aborted a third pregnancy. At 5 feet, 6 inches tall, her top weight during pregnancy was 90 pounds. This woman suffered severe mood and Axis II disorders and because of the severity of her eating disorder, anxiety, impulsivity and malnourishment, could not safely be treated on an outpatient basis.

Some women are able to discontinue their dysfunctional eating disordered behaviors, if only temporarily, during childbearing years. A woman who describes herself as having an eating disorder since early childhood was able to remain symptom free for 12 years while pregnant and nursing her first three children. Throughout her fourth pregnancy, however, she indulged in her bulimic behaviors, restricting food intake and continuing to purge

CO-OCCURRING SYNDROMES WITH EATING DISORDERS

Clients with eating disorders typically suffer from other mental health disorders; frequently, the other mental health disorders receive the primary focus, leaving eating disorders undiagnosed and untreated. A substantial number of individuals with anorexia and bulimia present with at least two comorbid psychiatric illnesses at admission to treatment (Weltzin, Weisensel, Cornella-Carlson, Riemann, & Bean, n.d). Diagnosticians need to recognize that the presenting complaint could be just one of many conditions. An unreported eating disorder diagnosis will be more difficult to detect when a client is in a precontemplative stage of change.

Comorbidity among clients with eating disorders presents serious challenges for recovery. Under these circumstances, the eating disorder tends to be more severe and chronic, the medical complications more complex, treatment more resistant, and outcomes less successful. Co-occurring diagnoses make it critical for eating disorder practitioners to be capable of offering a blend of dynamic pharmacological, cognitive–behavioral, and psychodynamic interventions over an extended period of time. Although most people recover from their eating disorder, most will continue to struggle to one degree or another with the co-occurring conditions that first gave rise to it.

Depression in particular, a natural outgrowth of malnourishment and purging, disrupts the treatment progress and must be recognized and treated. When a person struggling with an eating disorder denies feeling depressed, the diagnostician needs to become hypersensitive to the possibility that depression is being masked by self-medicating compulsions.

Dissociative States

While engaging in self-destructive forms of purging or other violence against the self, some bulimic clients report entering trancelike, or dissociative, states during which they are unaccountable for their actions, "involves the inability to recall important personal information, usually of a traumatic or stressful nature, that is too extensive to be explained by normal forgetfulness. The disorder involves a reversible memory impairment in which memories of personal experience cannot be retrieved in a verbal form (or, if temporarily retrieved, cannot be wholly retained in consciousness" (*DSM–IV–TR*; American Psychiatric Association, 2000, p. 520). A 17-year-old client who had been physically and verbally abused by her father when she was younger entered a dissociative state during which she engaged in binge eating (10,000 calories daily after 4:00 P.M.). When her mother tried to limit her excessive intake of food, the client followed her around the house threatening and intimidating her, then tried to break down the bathroom door when her mother attempted to protect herself. Diagnosed with bipolar disorder, this client did not respond to medication and would cry in helpless agony and fear in describing these behaviors, which she felt completely incapable of modifying.

For this young woman, admission to a hospital would provide the opportunity to recognize co-occurring conditions, such as oppositional defiant disorder or a possible Axis II diagnosis, and to obtain neurological testing and genetic consults to rule out metabolic abnormalities that typically manifest at this time of life. An inpatient stay would also allow experimentation with psychotropic medications and exploration of the influence of family dynamics.

Another client, described having such a sense of fear and panic when she ate that she lost the capacity to think and behaved like a "zombie," disconnected from herself. V had been diagnosed with bipolar disorder and anorexia purging type, as a recovering alcoholic and laxative abuser. An employer fired her for her "frantic caged-animal antics" following her return to work after lunch one day. She described engaging in compulsive flagellating self-talk as her inner critic demanded to know, "Why did you eat? You should not have eaten it!" This self-talk sabotaged her work functions, causing her mind to "step outside of her body." V lost a second job when, in a trancelike state, she shoplifted an article of clothing. V's eating disorder diagnosis and recovery became an important point of entry into a complex system of dysfunctions and remediation. The structure of eating three normal meals a day with snacks, planned and ultimately self-determined, provided her the practice she needed to develop the impulse controls necessary to sustain herself successfully within other life contexts.

In bringing V back to herself, I taught her the dialectical and cognitive–behavioral strategies of thought stopping and replacing negative thought processes with self-affirming statements, in combination with requiring a medication re-evaluation. Behavioral techniques such as these capture and encapsulate impulsive urges in redirecting the client's energy to an awareness and presence in the moment; such techniques might include snapping an elastic band on one's wrist, engaging in meditation, deep breathing, and/or bodily techniques such as the Feldenkrais or Anat Baniel Methods.

Body Image Preoccupations and Distortions

As a construct of the brain that is genetically imposed and socioculturally influenced, body image disturbances in anorexia and bulimia are neurologically determined within the brain neurocircuitry (Doidge, 2007, p. 190). Body image concerns involve a compulsive fascination with and inaccurate perception of one's appearance and body parts. For clients with eating disorders and obsessive–compulsive anxiety disorder, these preoccupations, which typically alter from day to day, portend a more difficult and lengthy recovery path. One study found that higher levels of body image disturbance contributed to a risk of relapse in clients with anorexia and bulimia, and worse psychosocial function, suggesting the need for focused body image work during relapse prevention (Keel, Dorer, Franko, Jackson, & Herzog, 2005).

Clients with body image disturbances overevaluate their shape and weight, engage in body checking and body avoidance, and experience sensations of "feeling fat." Body checking is a compulsive behavior characterized by the client's compulsively touching and pinching various body parts after eating in order to monitor what they perceive to be their increase in size. Body avoidance is characterized by the refusal to look in mirrors, by wearing oversized clothing, and so forth. Clients with body image disturbances approach ongoing recovery changes with anxiety, self-hatred, and the fear of a dreaded loss of control in all areas of life. The anxiety level of most clients with anorexia begins to subside as weight is restored, allowing a greater sense of well-being; it is the process of getting to that point that is tough. But for clients with body image distortions (which are usually accompanied by anxiety or obsessive–compulsive disorder, internal pain and anxiety may intensify with weight restoration, requiring the use of anti-anxiety medications and the development of mindfulness and dialectical and cognitive–behavioral coping skills.

One client cried herself to sleep if her weight rose from 101 to 103; she claimed she could discern this gain precisely without the use of a scale. If her thighs "touched," she despised herself and was consumed by anxiety. "Every pound I gain squeezes the confidence further out of me," she reported. Her self-perception, although she believed it to be exquisitely discerning, provided an inaccurate vision of herself that was many times heavier than others perceived her. Another teenager with anorexia claimed that she "doesn't even know what she looks like anymore—even when I look in a mirror, I can't see through my own distortions to know if I am bigger or smaller."

Body Dysmorphic Disorder

Body dysmorphic disorder is an obsession focused less on total body thinness and more on concern that specific body parts are ugly, misshapen, or fat. Preoccupied with imagined or slight defects in appearance that are minimal or undetectable to others, these clients consider their misperceptions to be completely rational. Mirror checking or camouflaging one's body under oversized clothing is a common response, as is social isolation and shame about perceived shortcomings. Mirror checking represents the client's compulsive need to spend substantive amounts of time in front of a mirror to ascertain that she is not becoming fat. One client felt compelled to spend 20 minutes in front of the mirror before school in the morning and another 20 minutes before going to bed at night. She also dawdled in front of store windows on her way home from school so as to monitor the reflections of her body. Body dysmorphic disorder accompanied by severe anxiety disorders can underlie and form the very foundation of an eating disorder. Violence and aggression may be directly correlated with these disorders, and it is typical for men with body dysmorphic disorder not to volunteer their core symptoms to diagnosticians unless directly questioned.

A client with anorexia claimed that with each swallow of food, she actively experienced her chin doubling or tripling in size and her stomach and thighs expanding repulsively. Another teenager with anorexia and obsessive–compulsive anxiety disorder could not get herself to go out and socialize with her friends because of her shame about her nose being misshapen after a fight with her brother, which in fact had left her without any injury or mark.

Current theories conceptualize obesity as a symptom of interactions between genes, metabolism, biochemistry, hormones, and environmental factors. At least 64 percent of U.S. adults and 13 percent of American children are overweight (Gersema, 2003). On the basis of genetics, a study (Myers, 2004) about the incidence of obesity showed that if both parents are obese, the child has an 80 percent chance of becoming obese; if one parents is obese, the child has a 40 percent chance of becoming obese. If neither parent is obese, the child has a 15 percent chance of becoming obese.

The stigma attached to being overweight invariably leads to dieting, which is the most common trigger to the onset of a clinical eating disorder in a genetically susceptible individual. When obesity co-occurs in the company of an eating disorder, it is not the weight itself, rather it is the nature of thinking and behavior behind the weight gain, that determines the existence of the disorder.

Binge eating may be a contributor to the development of obesity in susceptible individuals; comorbid binge eating disorder may result in a less favorable outcome for weight loss (Wilson, 2005). Therapists sometimes lose sight of the fact that when obesity is a result of binge eating disorder, it must be treated as an eating disorder. Although treating the eating disorder without treating obesity may not result in rapid weight loss, it does result in gradual (and more sustainable) weight loss, as well as "decreased weight regain over time" (Yanovski, 2003). Treating bulimia clients solely for weight loss may exacerbate eating disorder symptoms, particularly if therapists fail to convey the consistent message that the goal for treatment, rather than weight loss, is acquiring a healthy eating lifestyle as a way to secure and sustain a healthy body weight.

A previously mentioned obese client who described her past therapist as being harsh and judgmental about her failing attempts at weight loss preferred not to discuss this client's relationship with food but focused solely on general life issues. She failed to involve a nutritionist to sustain and promote the client's past eating and weight management achievements or a medical doctor to monitor the client's physical condition or possible hormonal imbalances. In our work together, this client commented about how helpful the food and eating focus had been for her; in following the structure of a food plan, she began to experience a sense of stability and self-determination in all her life spheres, countering what had been a passive and chaotic existence and creating a newfound sense of self-control and empowerment.

In treating obesity, I believe the answers practitioners seek lie in asking a different set of questions than we are accustomed to ask. When obesity is narrowly construed to be the result of unhealthy eating habits, a sedentary lifestyle, underlying emotional problems or inept parenting, such judgments become indictments that stigmatize and harm, by failing to assess the comprehensive picture of the person as a whole. The task for therapists is to evaluate the etiology of the obese condition, then simultaneously address the behavioral, hormonal, cognitive, and emotional issues underlying it. In determining the existence of an eating disorder in an obese client, the significance of weight loss (as well as gain) is primarily in how the weight reduction occurs, not necessarily in the number of pounds.

With or without an eating disorder, the task for the obese client is to learn to eat differently, not less, developing a more empowered relationship with food, and to live a more active lifestyle. Interventions should focus on modifiable behaviors (e.g., increasing physical activity, lowering intake of sugar-sweetened beverages, handling teasing from others, decreasing time spent watching TV) when there is evidence that such modification will improve a person's health and existence. Weight is not a behavior and therefore not an appropriate target for behavior modification; the aim should be increasing healthy living.

Because bodies come in all sizes, with varying degrees of efficacy in metabolizing and storing fat, the treatment of weight issues needs to be weight neutral, a challenging task for both client and therapist. Even professionals whose careers emphasize research or the clinical management of obesity show very strong weight bias, indicating pervasive and powerful stigma that can be damaging to intervention strategies (Schwartz, Chambliss, Brownell, Blair, & Billington, 2003).

Polycystic Ovary Syndrome

Polycystic ovary syndrome is an endocrine disorder that may result in menstrual irregularity, depression, acne, and excess facial hair. It can also be a common cause of infertility (Seidenfeld & Rickert, 2001). The condition can result in tenacious overweight in girls, who may diet and exercise without perceptible changes. Polycystic ovary syndrome may be associated with restricting, binge eating, obesity, and other forms of disordered eating and mood and body image disturbances. For this reason, women with polycystic ovary syndrome should be screened for disordered eating behaviors (and by an endocrinologist for hormonal disturbances) before beginning dietary intervention. The syndrome responds well to the restoration of a hormonal balance and dietary changes (Scalzo, 2001).

Mood Disorders

Mood disorders, according to the *DSM–IV–TR* (American Psychiatric Association, 2000) feature the categories of mood episodes, depressive disorders, bipolar disorders, and other mood disorders. All of these conditions commonly occur alongside eating disorders, as contributing factors in their onset or exacerbated in their intensity as a consequence of the eating disorder. The treatment of mood disorder comorbidity creates significant clinical challenges; for example, medication interventions for one condition may trigger a negative consequence in another; certain medications for depression may increase the appetite of an anorexic individual who is afraid to gain weight or of a compulsive overeater who is attempting to eat less; certain stimulant medications used to treat attention deficit hyperactivity disorder cause appetite suppression, as a result, becoming contraindicated for the treatment of anorexia and overweight conditions, in which girls might misuse these medicines to encourage weight loss, thereby triggering an eating disorder.

The literature leaves little doubt that bipolar disorder and eating disorders, particularly bulimia nervosa and bipolar II disorder, typically co-occur; there is also a co-occuring relationship between lifetime bulimia and anorexia and cyclothymic and related affective temperaments. Some eating disordered individuals struggle with recovery over the course of years and even decades because a mood disorder has gone unrecognized, was ignored as irrelevant to eating disorder treatment, or was not disclosed in the interest of protecting the client from enduring a "stigmatizing label." As hard as it may be for a young client to carry such a hefty diagnosis, accurate diagnosis is a most critical component in conducting effective treatment.

Mood disorders and their symptoms typically remain dormant or not clearly recognizable until puberty, adolescence, or beyond. Attentional disorders, social phobias, panic attacks, depression, and substance abuse may occur as a temporary byproduct of the eating disorder, only to subside with recovery. It has been my experience in treating these clients over the decades that those with mood disorders may be prone to suffer from seasonal affective disorder, premenstrual syndrome, or postpartum depression, heightened anxiety and depression, and hypersensory sensitivity. A client with a mood disorder might experience a "mixed state"—simultaneously feeling revved up or agitated and depressed. Clients with mood disorders also typically suffer from attention deficit hyperactivity disorder, though this condition may be a temporary side effect of the eating disorder.

A client who had recovered from bulimia had been free of binge and purge behaviors for two years. She began to experience a smattering of occasional and short-lived behavioral regressions during periods of emotional crisis. Having completely recovered from her eating disorder, backsliding incidents were fleeting; she no longer relied upon them to function as primary coping devices for her in the face of adversity. We noticed that these isolated incidents were always precipitated by her menstrual cycle. Recognizing this helped her anticipate and accommodate these hormonal tsunamis ultimately through medication adjustment and alternative coping strategies.

Depressive Disorders

Depression is the most commonly co-occurring psychiatric problem with eating disorders. Between 20 and 98 percent of patients with eating disorders have been diagnosed with some form of depression. Depression can be primary or secondary, arising after the onset of the eating disorder.

Bipolar Disorder

The *DSM–IV–TR* lists two distinct types of bipolar disorder: bipolar disorder types I and II. The manual describes bipolar disorder I as a mood disorder characterized by the occurrence of one or more manic episodes or mixed episodes or one or more major depressive episodes. A shift in polarity is defined as a clinical course in which a major depressive episode evolves into a manic episode or a mixed episode or in which a manic episode or a mixed episode evolves into a major depressive episode. In contrast, a hypomanic episode that evolves into a manic episode or a mixed episode is considered to be a single episode.

Bipolar disorder II is characterized by recurrent major depressive episodes with hypomanic episodes. The presence of a manic or mixed episode precludes the diagnosis of bipolar disorder II. Space does not permit extensive discussion of these diagnoses for which the *DSM–IV–TR* (American Psychiatric Association, 2000) offers a full 10 pages of diagnostic description. I would advise all practitioners to become well acquainted with this discussion.

In one study of 61 adults with bipolar disorder, 13 percent met criteria for binge eating disorder, whereas an additional 25 percent met criteria for a partial binge eating syndrome (Krishnan, 2005).

A psychiatrist who missed a diagnosis of bipolar disorder type II sought to help his client resolve her problems by requesting that she "go through the motions of being a healthy person," implying that through actions alone, feelings and chemistries would change and her compulsions would abate. In not wanting to "saddle" her with a bipolar diagnosis, this physician failed to prescribe the medication required for her to recover from her eating disorder. Mood and bipolar disorders will not self-correct without the intervention of mood-stabilizing drugs to correct cycling mood states. Nor will the eating disorder that co-occurs in tandem with it.

We have noted that manic–depressive polarities are associated with bipolar disorder I and that the presence of mania precludes a bipolar disorder type II diagnosis. Hypomania is characteristic of the bipolar disorder II, which consists of recurrent major depressive episodes and hypomanic episodes. Hypomania is similar to mania but distinctively less severe and less protracted. Characterized by elevated mood, increased activity, decreased need for sleep, racing thoughts, restless energy, and poor judgment, hypomanic behaviors can be seen in impulsive behaviors such as promiscuity or activities with a high potential for painful or pleasurable consequences such as drinking, substance abuse, or dangerous risk taking. Hypomania may also take the form of high levels of achievement and creativity. Unlike mania, hypomania tends not to cause significant distress or impair one's work, family, or social life. As an expression of bipolar disorder, hypomania may cycle into depression and carry an increased risk of suicide.

A bipolar teenager with an eating disorder not otherwise specified engaged in self-destructive behaviors such as drinking mouthwash, compulsively viewing horror movies instead of studying, and rereading horror novels 15 times each, jolting her from her numbness and self-disconnection and making her feel "alive to herself." She binge drank her way through her first semester at college, and without a proper diagnosis of bipolar disorder, she came to consider herself alcoholic. Once she received proper medication for her bipolarity, the drinking abated. When co-occurring with an eating disorder, it is not uncommon for behaviors that appear to be addictions, such as binge drinking or drug abuse, to be the result of co-occurring bipolar hypomanic self-medicating compulsions that respond to mood-stabilizing medications.

It can sometimes be difficult to distinguish between psychotic disorders (e.g., schizoaffective disorder or delusional disorder) and bipolar disorder in clients with eating disorder because both involve delusion in self-perception and fantasy. A woman suffering from bipolar disorder II demanded that her nutritionist refrain from discussing the fact that anorexia can cause heart problems because "it would trigger her obsessive paranoia that she was dying of a heart attack." In discussing her need for medication for her newly diagnosed bipolar disorder, I related my concerns that a common cause of unintentional suicide occurs when a person with bipolar disorder stops taking needed mood stabilizers (or chooses not to start taking them), resulting in risk-taking behaviors that could, in fact, lead to death. Hearing this, she became red in the face and instructed me never to speak of such things again; rather than assuaging her fears of taking medication for her bipolar disorder, she would now obsess about her fear of dying. Weeks later, once she had started on appropriate medication, she confessed that my having offered this information reassured her that I really did care deeply about her, providing hope for her recovery.

Mood swings in women with bipolar disorder may become more intense in response to hormonal changes. During the menstrual cycle, ovulation alternates between ovaries from month to month; charting emotional symptoms during premenstruation may indicate that hormonal levels vary depending upon the egg-producing ovary that may have a predictably greater influence on mood instability. It is helpful for the client to learn to chart and track her own variances, to learn to anticipate swings, and to be prepared with coping mechanisms to deal with them It is also important to remain aware that such reactivity may substantially affect the consistency of recovery changes.

Bipolar disorders require medication with a mood stabilizer or antipsychotic. Selective serotonin reuptake inhibitor antidepressants and antianxiety drugs alone are insufficient to treat eating disorders when they are accompanied by bipolar disorder. In fact, antidepressant medications by themselves could trigger a manic state for the first time in clients with a mood disorder.

Anxiety Disorders

Anxiety disorders lie at the heart of a great many eating disorders. A study showed that 64 percent of clients with eating disorders experience one or more anxiety disorders in their lifetime (Wall & Cumella, 2005; estimated rates among women in the community range from 13 to 31 percent). The relationship between anxiety and eating disorders may indicate a common etiological mechanism with genetic (Wall & Cumella, 2005), neurobiological, and psychosocial features. In fact, eating disorders have been called "anxiety disorders with specific food and weight-related content" (Wall & Cumella, 2005). Most of the participants who reported an anxiety disorder said that it had begun in childhood, before the eating disorder (see also Arehart-Treichel, 2005). Davis, Shuster, Blackmore, and Fox (2004) proposed that family risk factors have a more potent influence on young women who are easily made anxious—perhaps because they are more sensitive to, or more likely to internalize, pressures and expectations to conform to family values.

The most common anxiety disorder among one study's participants was obsessive–compulsive disorder (41 percent) (Wall & Cumella, 2005). It is not unusual for clients with eating disorders to experience obsessive–compulsive anxiety disorder symptoms such as counting compulsions, hand washing, or other checking behaviors (e.g., stove, door locks) to create a sense of control or order. In these clients, the obsessive–compulsive anxiety disorder typically predates the eating disorder. Improvement in one condition is often accompanied by an improvement in the other; a study found that participants whose eating disorders were most improved showed the highest reduction in obsessions and compulsions (Weltzin et al., n.d.)

"When the presence of genetically heritable anxiety gives rise to a genetically heritable eating disorder, the effects of malnutrition on brain chemistries exacerbate preexisting anxiety, making clients with both an eating disorder and anxiety more treatment resistant" (Weltzin et al., n.d.). For some, the urge to binge and purge is a compulsion that may initially have been a tool to ward off anxiety; ultimately, as the compulsion develops a life of its own, it gives rise to additional anxiety. For example, a client with anorexia and high anxiety felt compelled to exercise off every calorie she consumed. If she was unsure exactly how many calories she had ingested, she would overexercise, sometimes until her legs ached, to be certain that she had done the job fully enough. This young woman ran five-mile stretches several times a day.

According to the *DSM–IV–TR*, obsessions are "persistent ideas, thoughts, impulses, or images that are experienced as intrusive and inappropriate and that cause marked anxiety or distress." They function for the client as coping devices, distractions, and control mechanisms. Compulsions are repetitive behaviors designed to reduce anxiety or distress, which the individual feels compelled to perform. Body checking and mirror checking, previously mentioned in conjunction with body image distortions, are a manifestation of obsession and compulsion. These behaviors foster preoccupation and dissatisfaction with shape and weight via selective attention to disliked body parts that magnifies the person's perception of fatness and imperfection (Wilson, 2005). If the person checks and finds herself thin, it motivates her to continue to restrict food to stay thin; if she finds herself fat, it becomes a stronger motivation to restrict food. Because perception tends to be distorted in individuals with an eating disorder, the accuracy of body checking impressions is very low. A young woman with an eating disorder not otherwise specified described the motivation behind her mirror gazing compulsion:

> From certain angles I look like I am not even of the human race. I look weird; my head does not fit my body . . . the two look grotesque together. I am so embarrassed that everybody sees judges, and defines me by my shameful appearance.

Given the potential role of body checking in the etiology and maintenance of eating disorders, clinicians should make a point to inquire about it. By bringing awareness to the behavior as a compulsion and enabling the client to see that body checking is not an accurate or reliable way of measuring one's body, the use of behavioral techniques such as exposure and response prevention can be instrumental in eliminating body checking and avoidance behaviors (Wilson, 2005).

In another example of compulsion, a woman with anorexia and obsessive–compulsive anxiety disorder spoke of having to scratch her face on both sides if she had an itch on one side. By age seven, she described having become obsessed, as the seemingly helpless victim of an abusive and dictatorial peer who controlled her every thought and action, precluding her own decision making and self-determination. Once released from her "peer's" spell anorexia became the tyrannical substitute. An obsessive–compulsive 10-year-old child with anorexia refused to eat the tiny portion of a potato chip that she held between her thumb and forefinger for fear it would make her fat. This same child would not permit foods to touch each other on her plate and would consume only one food at a time. She chewed her food to a liquid "so as to be sure not to choke."

Sometimes, individuals with eating disorders feel compelled to cook and bake to feed others but not themselves, to handle and organize food in others' kitchens, and to handle food ritualistically. Many such individuals turn these compulsions into careers as chefs and bakers. Compulsions may also take the form of hyperfocused binge viewing of pro-anorexia (also called "pro-ana") websites, with the intention of making body comparisons. A young woman with anorexia spoke of spending time watching a new sport called "competitive eating" on MTV. The winner of the contest ingested 54 hot dogs at once to set a world record. This form of personal self-imposed violence and disrespect for the body has apparently become an "athletic event," and viewing it, a form of recreation and entertainment. It is for parents to intervene to monitor, educate, and limit such exposures that are distorting and destructive and that counteract the process of recovery.

Substance Abuse

Alcohol and drug dependency in individuals with anorexia is more common than had been believed and is associated with the presence of bulimic symptomatology (Pinheiro,Thornton, Strober, Kaye, & Bulik, 2008). Twenty-six percent of patients with eating disorder have co-occurring substance use disorders. The first comprehensive examination of the link between substance abuse and eating disorders reveals that up to one half of individuals with eating disorders abuse alcohol or illicit drugs, compared with 9 percent of the general population. Conversely, up to 35 percent of alcohol or illicit drug abusers have eating disorders, compared with 3 percent of the general population (National Center on Alcoholism and Substance Abuse at Columbia University, 2004). Studies have shown that one third to half of people with bulimia have associated drug and alcohol histories in their families (Moss & Von Ranson, 2008). Nicotine addiction has been shown to predict other problematic behaviors and psychopathology in the assessment and treatment of bulimia (Krug et al., 2008), and the evidence shows a positive association between smoking and dieting behaviors (Potter, Pederson, Chan, Aubut, & Koval, 2004). The rule of thumb is to treat the addiction first or at least concurrently with the eating disorder.

Attention Deficit Hyperactivity Disorder

Hyperactivity, inattention, and impulsivity can have multiple causes; restless hyperactivity has long been known as a characteristic of nutritional deprivation in underweight anorexic individuals. It is critical to establish whether the symptoms of attention deficit hyperactivity disorder are the result of malnourishment or if whether preceded the eating disorder. A differential diagnosis of attention deficit hyperactivity disorder requires the case history to show at least some symptoms of either hyperactivity or inattentiveness present before the age of seven years, with impairment present in at least two settings (e.g., at home and at school). An assessment and discontinuation of medication may be appropriate following weight restoration. There is a proven correlation between attention deficit hyperactivity disorder and mood disorders, and there has been preliminary evidence of psychometric and genetic association between bulimia and attention deficit hyperactivity disorder. Girls with attention deficit hyperactivity disorder are more likely to develop an eating disorder; as they get older, their impulsivity makes it difficult for them to maintain healthy eating and a healthy weight, resulting in self-consciousness about their body image, food restriction, and bingeing and purging symptoms. Girls with undiagnosed and untreated attention deficit hyperactivity disorder are at higher risk of eating disorders (Kaplan, Levitan, Yilmar, & Kennedy, 2008).

Suicidality

I have heard anorexia described as a wish for death or a slow form of suicide. However, I see anorexia as an attempt to *survive* the adversities of life to the best of the client's ability. All eating disorder professionals should be proficient at assessing suicide risk, however, as eating disorders typically mask clinical depression. Studies show that clients with eating disorders demonstrate a cumulative risk for suicide attempts beyond that explained by the presence of a mood disorder or other important comorbidity (Lund et al., 2008). "The suicide mortality rate in people with anorexia nervosa is one of the highest of all psychiatric illnesses, with the risk of death by suicide in patients with anorexia nervosa calculated as high as 57 to 58 times the expected rate in similar age and gender populations." Because of this extremely high rate of suicide, suicide is a more likely cause of death in a current anorexia nervosa sufferer than are complications from the disorder.

Individuals with eating disorders should always be asked directly about suicidal ideation or past suicide attempts. If the client confesses to suicidal ideation, the clinician must be prepared to ask whether the client feels depressed currently as well as the last time that she felt suicidal. I generally make it a policy to insist that clients with a history of suicidal ideation or suicide attempts enter a contract with me to notify me and/or call 911 at the first sign of significant consideration of suicidal behaviors or attitudes.

Axis II Diagnoses

On Axis I, eating disorders are coded without respect to personality. Personality disorders, which are common in those with eating disorders, are coded on Axis II. A study showed that the most common Axis II diagnoses for eating disorders are schizotypal, histrionic and borderline disorders, but avoidant and dependent personality features also occurred. Classifying clients with eating disorders by symptoms alone is insufficient to differentiate those who are "highly functioning and self-critical" from those who are "highly disturbed, constricted, avoidant, impulsive or emotionally dysregulated," distinctions that affect prognosis and treatment (Westin & Harbden-Fischer, 2001). Though it is not within the scope of this book to explicate the specifics of treatment of Axis II disorders, it can be assumed that the presence of an Axis II diagnosis calls for clear communication and boundaries on the part of the clinician and consideration of specific kinds of interventions and treatment alternatives (American Psychiatric Association, 2000).

Self-Injurious Behavior

Self-mutilation by cutting, burning, and scratching is often associated with eating disorders. I would include in this category stomach stretching as a result of extreme bingeing or laxative abuse that produces agonizing pain. Such behaviors are intended to make life more bearable by distracting the individual (through physical pain) from the intensity of emotional pain that she knows no other way to dispel. The client who is numb to herself begins to sense herself as the person that she is through such behaviors. Habitual acts of self-mutilation have been described as "a purposeful act of self-help which enables the subject to re-establish contact with the world" (Favazza, as cited in Eberly, 2005). Self-injury can become addictive, with the release in the brain of opioidlike endorphins that result in a natural high and emotional relief. Clients who self-mutilate typically disavow their intention to die, as these behaviors are typically not life-threatening by nature. Though 60 percent of clients who engage in self-injurious behaviors have never had suicidal thoughts, some are at risk for accidental suicide. Treatment must protect the client's safety, in addressing behaviors that sometimes take the form of dissociative pathology and in building affect regulation.

About 15 percent of the general adolescent population and 17 percent of college students have self-injured. One in four meets the criteria of borderline personality disorder. In clients with eating disorders, estimates of those who engage in self-injurious behaviors range from 25 percent to 45 percent. Correspondingly, as many as half of those who injure themselves have a documented history of eating disorders (Eberly, 2005). Cutting behaviors typically co-occur with hypomanic impulsive and risky behaviors that might include excessive drinking and unsafe sex.

Like eating disorders, these behaviors are typically kept secret; they tend to be hidden in places that are covered by clothing such as the belly or upper arms or thighs. At times, signs of cutting may be explained away—for example, "The cat scratched me" or "I keep falling down." Because of the secretive and shameful nature of self-injurious behaviors, most clients who self-injure do not voluntarily offer this information in diagnostic sessions. Diagnosticians should inquire about self-injurious behaviors of every client they assess for an eating disorder.

Sexual Abuse

About 30 percent of individuals with eating disorders were sexually abused in childhood, a figure that is relatively comparable to rates found in the general population (Connors & Morse, 1993). Women who experienced both physical and sexual abuse during childhood are three times as likely to develop eating disorder symptoms and nearly four times as likely to meet *DSM* criteria for an eating disorder as women in the general population. Women who have eating disorders in the context of sexual abuse appear to have higher rates of comorbid psychiatric conditions than other women with eating disorders (Rayworth, Wise, & Harlow, 2004).

CONCLUSION

There is nothing simple or straightforward about recognizing eating disorders. Designed to endure, they remain elusive and camouflaged, cloaked in secrecy, ready to slide beneath the radar of diagnosing professionals, clients, and parents. A substantial percentage of eating disorder cases go unnoticed and undiagnosed, and these individuals may receive no mental health care at all. Effective treatment depends on accurate diagnosis. In all too many cases, when eating disorders are unrelenting or heal only partially, it is because the full and integrative complement of co-occurring diagnoses has not been fully assessed or treated.

5

Diagnosis and Eating Disorders: Seeing the Whole Picture

One sees clearly only with the heart. Anything essential is invisible to the eyes.

—Antoine de Saint-Exupéry

A client of mine had spent three years with a highly regarded psychologist who refused to acknowledge her eating disorder as a pivotal aspect of her personhood or care. He perceived the disorder as tangential, symptomatic, and secondary to other, "more core" co-occurring problems. In terminating with this client, who was about to leave his practice to begin treatment with me, he warned her, "Don't let anyone treat you like an 'eating disorder patient.' You are much more than that."

He was right that her problems ran deep; he was wrong in thinking that an eating disorder diagnosis would preclude accurate diagnosis of co-occurring conditions. In the face of a complex and integrated system of co-occurring diagnoses, managing the dysfunctions around eating-based behaviors represents a "way in," leading to the unmasking and treatment of co-occurring problems.

A mother called seeking a referral to an internist who was knowledgeable and skilled in handling eating disorders. Her 28-year-old son, whom she suspected had anorexia, had seen one medical doctor after another after having lost 20 pounds precipitously. Gastroenterologists prescribed tests and spoke of gluten intolerance, asking him to cut out more foods from his diet. An endocrinologist said his testosterone was too low and ordered a magnetic resonance imaging (MRI) scan to diagnose what he thought might be a brain tumor. When this test was negative, the doctor told him simply to "go home and start eating more." A nutritionist told them that according to the charts, he was not "too thin" so they could "rule out anorexia."

Because preparation to treat an eating disorder falls through the cracks of specialty care, eating disorder diagnosis remains an elusive and slippery task. In this chapter, I describe an approach to diagnosis of eating disorders both when a disorder is hidden and when the diagnosis of an eating disorder may be already suspected. In discussing the nature of the diagnosis of an eating disorder as it evolves, I provide recommendations for the need to take action even before the diagnostic process is complete. Finally, I list some diagnostic red flags that require the therapist's attention.

Diagnosis is not a discrete process in and of itself. It is, in fact, the first and most pivotal treatment intervention. As a treatment tool, diagnosis can be powerful enough to stimulate sufficient self-awareness and learning capable of evoking personal changes even before the start of formal treatment. A well-conducted diagnostic session can become the lure for the resistant client to engage in care, in providing optimism, education, and the motivation it takes to make a run for recovery in the company of a good coach.

WHEN AN EATING DISORDER IS HIDDEN

Professionals who may come face to face with an eating disorder need to develop the capacity to sniff out an existing or potential clinical eating disorder from the larger context of information offered, from the quality of the client's functioning, and by recognizing evidence of the underlying issues that drive these diseases. In making the educated guess, therapists can then read between the lines of conversation. By anticipating what might have gone unstated based on what has been stated, by discerning discussions that require further investigation, and by actively probing impulsive and compulsive behaviors (including non–eating-related behaviors such as self-mutilation, shoplifting, promiscuity, and substance abuse), professionals learn to identify clusters of symptoms that could shine a light on existing, future, or past problems. Identifying an existing problem and addressing it to avoid its becoming worse is called "secondary prevention."

Making an astute eating disorder diagnosis is like observing a disparate grouping of stars and seeing a constellation. E was a 29-year-old woman who came to treatment for her depression and relationship problems. In response to her description of her college days, in which she spoke of herself as a perfectionist, highly compulsive, and depressed, I made a point of wondering aloud if she had ever struggled with an eating disorder or other eating-related issues. "My God!" she responded. "How did you know? I have never told a soul!" By understanding the conditions that frequently co-occur with eating disorders, I was able to intuit the existence of a past eating disorder, and through the knowledge that my hunches were correct, I became more confident about how to understand her treatment needs. The client's sense of trust that she is understood and unconditionally accepted lies at the root of comfort in self-disclosure. The therapist who models openness encourages a mirroring of such openness in the client.

The primary difficulty in the diagnostic process with clients who have eating disorders is that they cover, protect, and hide their symptoms in the interest of securing their emotional survival. Many clients do not know they are sick because they experience their disorder as sustaining and improving their lives. Many do not *want* to know they are sick or to consider the prospect of living life without the protection of the eating disorder, feeling in control and satisfied with their life as it is. Most significantly, clients often feel that they are incapable of recovering, as the disease has decimated their internal resiliency and capacity to fight back. Because clients with bulimia, binge eating disorder/eating disorder not otherwise specified generally maintain normal weight, physically there is little to indicate the existence of pathology, which facilitates keeping the disease hidden indefinitely. Box 5.1 lists clues that can alert the therapist to the possibility of a hidden eating disorder.

A client came for help after having been treated for seven years by a psychiatrist who never knew that she was bulimic and purging as many as 30 times a day. She admitted that she had not confided in him for fear that he would be "grossed out" and would reject her. Had the psychiatrist understood eating disorders in

---

BOX 5.1

Clues to a Hidden Eating Disorder

In diagnosing clients, the following signs should prompt a deeper investigation into the possible presence of an eating disorder:

- preoccupation with the fear of becoming fat, or client claims to "feel fat" even though she is not
- rapid weight loss or gain
- idiosyncratic eating habits, such as limiting food choices, cutting food into small pieces, moving food around plate, spitting out masticated foods, regurgitating, or needing to eat alone
- food restriction through dieting or skipping meals
- commitment to vegetarianism (possible alibi for food restriction)
- signs of anxiety, such as compulsions, perfectionism, or overachieving
- signs of depression, such as social withdrawal, irritability, or difficulty concentrating
- low self-esteem, approval seeking through physical appearance
- body image concerns and preoccupations, such as body checking
- compulsive habits and preoccupations of all types
- need to be in control of all aspects of life, beyond food and weight management
- compulsive exercise
- excessive amounts of time spent in the bathroom
- loss of menstrual period
- swollen salivary glands
- low heart rate or electrolyte imbalance
- high cholesterol levels
- unstable or orthostatic pressure signs
- dizziness, faintness, or fatigue or occasional blackouts
- tendency to shower soon after eating in order to purge down the drain.
- habit of measuring carefully every bit of food to be certain about getting portion size correct

the context of the personality characteristics she presented, her temperament, and her environmental and genetic history, he would not have missed this diagnosis.

Parents may initially miss a child's eating disorder because, in attempts to hide her disease from her family, the child is apt to communicate cryptically with parents. She may speak in "code"—for example, "Does this outfit make me look fat?" Many children leave evidence of body image disturbance in bedrooms scattered with heaps of clothing, tried on and discarded, that did not make them "feel and look thin enough"; others leave their bedrooms strewn with empty diet soda cans or will hide evidence of candy wrappers under cushions. Not many parents are sufficiently educated in the ways of eating disorders to recognize or pursue these warning signs.

Be aware that because of the stigma against mental health problems among certain cultures, evidence of eating dysfunction within these populations may rarely come to light unless specifically probed. In one instance, a social worker, inquiring about a child's falling asleep regularly in the classroom, asked what the child ate for breakfast, only to find that he never ate breakfast at all. When asked about what he ate for lunch, the answer was the same. In investigating why, the child explained that eating meals would make him "big and fat." This child has attitudes typical of eating disorders and that could potentially become clinical disease if there is a genetic propensity. If there is a cultural taboo within his home or community against acknowledging problems or seeking and accepting help for them outside the home, the therapist will need to use powerful antennae to detect such problems.

Whenever a client presents with an eating-related problem that may be subclinical, atypical, or yet undefined, it is wise to consider the potential for a diagnosis of an eating disorder. A mother who contacted me was ambivalent about considering treatment for her son as he did not have a "textbook" eating disorder. "He eats, after all." This opinion was corroborated by his medical doctor, who saw nothing unusual about his weight or his lab tests and expressed no concerns, and by a college counselor who assured him that he was "not eating disordered and not depressed." The more he received reports of normalcy, the more fearful and crazy he felt. In fact, this young man was clearly anorexic and depressed. In a 90-minute telephone session, I diagnosed his eating disorder, determined his immediate risk, and educated him about his disorder and how to heal from it. We created a plan that involved a commitment to treatment twice a week, nutritional counseling once a week, and a visit to a psychiatrist for a medication evaluation. This young man recovered fully within a 6-month period of time.

Practitioners should be aware of the tendency to overlook the possibility of an eating disorder diagnosis in men. Because eating disorders are considered female disorders, men are rarely considered as candidates for an eating disorder; along the same lines, depression in men is often missed, instead being construed as a sign that one is "the strong silent type."

WHEN AN EATING DISORDER IS SUSPECTED

Because indicators and discussion of eating disorders tend not to show up in the doctor's office, the responsibility for initial diagnosis typically falls to parents at home and/or peers at school who, though unequipped for the task, see evidence of disease at kitchen tables, in bathrooms, in school cafeterias, gymnasiums, and health clubs.

Clients with eating disorders may be diagnosed at various stages of disease, treatment, and recovery processes, and with any of various treatment team members on board, including physicians, school counselors, nutritionists, and/or psychotherapists. Nutritionists often find themselves the initial contact in the client's search for "the best way to lose weight more effectively." No matter where and when the client enters the professional care system, the chosen professional is obligated to act as temporary case manager, referring the client for a formal assessment with a qualified eating disorder evaluator if unable to provide it himself or herself. Any individual professional need not be fully knowledgeable about the work of other disciplines within a treatment team, though it is critical that the diagnostician know enough about all spheres of eating disorder pathology to know when referrals are required and to whom. Any practitioner on a case may be held liable for a missed diagnosis, even if that person is not the primary diagnostician and not a specialist in the treatment of eating disorders.

In instances where team resources are not available locally or known to a referring professional, organizations such as the National Eating Disorders Association or the National Association of Anorexia Nervosa and Associated Disorders can act as important referral sources, offering information about how to locate expert eating disorder professionals in one's locality. If a diagnostician determines that a client's life might be in danger, loved ones need to be apprised so as to share the responsibility of procuring the best care wherever those services might be located.

In attending to the whole client, keep your diagnostic eye out for conditions that may appear to be unrelated to the eating disorder but that may be a symptom and function of the disorder. Learning disabilities and brain processing disturbances can contribute to poor self-esteem and powerlessness and to a feeling of lack of control that can ultimately exacerbate an eating disorder (see Chapter 4 for a more complete list of possible co-occurring conditions).

For example, a seemingly oppositional young woman with anorexia who was living at home was unable to keep her room neat, resulting in a strained relationship with her parent. In fact, her obsessive–compulsive anxiety disorder deterred her from finding exactly the "right spot" for each item, creating anxiety so great that she felt "paralyzed" when she attempted to keep her room neat. This young woman had an organizational processing problem, with an overlay of severe perceptual problems that impaired her ability to visualize more than one item at a time, contributing to her confusion, resistance to this task, extreme anxiety and anorexic behaviors.

An eating disorder that does not fit the description of anorexia or bulimia in the *Diagnostic and Statistical Manual of Mental Disorders* (4th ed., Text Revision, [*DSM–IV–TR*]; American Psychiatric Association, 2000) should receive a diagnosis of eating disorder not otherwise specified. We know that this is by far the most often missed and underused diagnostic category of clinical eating disorders. A therapist believed that G's self-loathing and pathological need to be thin could not be caused by an eating disorder because she was of normal weight, "on the robust side." Considering her problem as primarily one of low self-esteem and depression, he and the psychiatrist failed to diagnose eating disorder not otherwise specified/binge eating disorder. Diagnosis of a co-occurring disorders should not preclude the diagnosis of an eating disorder; in fact, the existence of comorbidity explains how and why certain eating disorder cases may be more intractable to healing than others. Similarly, diagnosis of an eating disorder should not preclude attention to co-occurring conditions. G was ultimately diagnosed with co-occurring bipolar disorder type 2, obsessive–compulsive anxiety disorder, and Axis II structural personality dysfunction, and possible ADHD. Until she had a thorough diagnosis, G believed herself to be simply "crazy."

EATING DISORDER DIAGNOSES EVOLVE

Unlike most mental health disorders, which can be determined within the course of a single evaluation session, the eating disorder diagnosis evolves over time, through diverse sources of input from the collaborating team, the family, and the psychopharmacologist. It is not uncommon for a proper initial diagnosis to take six to eight weeks or more, depending on the circumstances of the case. (See the case study at the end of Chapter 6.) The single-session evaluation and consultation, however, can offer lifesaving education and strategies to start the healing process.

It may be difficult at first assessment to differentiate disordered eating from aspects of a clinical eating disorder; a mood disorder or nervous condition (depression or anxiety) from a temporary symptom of anorexic malnourishment; the specific type of eating disorder (distinguishing anorexia purging type from bulimia restrictive type; or eating disorder not otherwise specified from the imminent onset of an eating disorder in the making. Axis II diagnoses will only become discernible over time; even then, they are typically hard to differentiate from the naturally occurring effects of a clinical eating disorder. Presentation and combinations of symptoms will vary from case to case and will undergo dramatic changes throughout the life of any individual recovery process over time. A full and exacting reliance on the *DSM* can become counterproductive in light of the fact that eating disorders do not lend themselves to precise or consistent diagnostic criteria.

Many clients recovering from an eating disorder will have had a previous diagnostic and treatment experience. Eating disorder diagnosticians assess not only pathology but also current strengths that may have evolved out of a past recovery process. In arriving at an accurate diagnosis, it is critical for practitioners to recognize and consider the significance of prior recovery growth and change and to structure new goals for the client around the assessment of those already accrued, if not fully recognized, strengths.

Every treatment session contains a diagnostic element. Eating disorders never stay the same; throughout treatment, practitioners must track their movement, monitoring and shepherding the recovery progress to keep the treatment purposeful, relevant, and paced. Through ongoing assessment, the practitioner gauges the fluctuating nuances of where the client is, where she has come from, and where she is going, ensuring her safety when symptoms become life-threatening. In the diagnostic process, the clinician monitors the pace of compliance with behavioral goals and tasks, always keeping in mind the continued appropriateness of the chosen current therapeutic milieu.

In determining the effectiveness of current and past efforts to heal, in a metaphorical reference to computer uploading data, I typically ask the client, "So, at what point would you say you are, at this moment in time, in terms of your eating disorder recovery?" Collaborative diagnostic monitoring of the client's self-appraisal allows me to compare the client's assessment of herself with my own assessment of her, gauging the accuracy of both perceptions and offering an opportunity for goal redefinition. I generally find that the client's assessments of self and progress coincide very closely, if not exactly, with my own. Box 5.2 lists other questions therapists can ask clients routinely to ensure that the diagnostic process remains current.

The question of when, and how, to disclose a diagnosis of an eating disorder to clients and families is critical. In certain cases, I may not immediately disclose my hunches unless there is a reason to do so. First, it is not always easy to arrive immediately at a full and definitive diagnosis in the initial stages of the process. Second, certain aspects of diagnosis cannot be complete without interventions from other team members. And third, revealing a diagnosis that the client is not yet ready to hear can increase the client's denial and resistance to treatment.

The treatment, however, stays the same, even without a formal diagnosis, with the diagnostician prepared to offer eating disorder care, immediately and proactively. Labeling these disorders is less significant than promoting appropriate action toward recovery. In situations where certain symptoms are not definitively diagnosable as a clinical eating disorder, keep in mind that if it looks like a duck and quacks like a duck, for all practical purposes, it may as well be considered a duck.

When new clients refuse therapy or need leeway and time to process and accept the diagnosis of an eating disorder, I sometimes refer them to my nutritionist partner, who is wise to the ways of eating disorders, giving the client the opportunity to grow into the possibility of accepting a potential diagnosis, even

---

BOX 5.2

Diagnosis Is an Ongoing Process

The process of ongoing diagnosis, by catching regression at its inception, is key to secondary prevention. There is rarely a psychotherapy session where I do not ask such questions as the following:

- So how have your efforts to follow the food plan been going?
- What changes have you been working on?
- What have your efforts to change been like for you this week?
- Where have you had success?
- What did you find to be the most challenging aspects of change making?
- Were you able to be consistent in your attempts to make changes happen?
- Do you notice that the eating patterns around food reflect behavioral or emotional patterns in other life spheres?
- How do you feel about yourself and your recovery after making these efforts?

while addressing and remediating behavioral and nutritional issues. Be aware that the client's own timing for arriving at readiness for change may not parallel her physical needs. Under certain circumstances, the client may need to be pressed to consider more intensive or restrictive treatment care.

TAKING ACTION BEFORE THE DIAGNOSIS IS COMPLETE

It is critical that practitioners inform clients and their families to expect that a complete diagnostic process will take place *over time*. It is common practice to allow the client to first attempt to recover in the least restrictive environment, as an outpatient, and to see if she can prosper within this environment. An initial treatment plan that allows the client to recover at home should always be contingent on the client's physiological safety (as determined by a medical doctor) and the cooperation of family members. The client's ability to initiate and sustain positive change in that milieu will very quickly determine the appropriateness of that choice.

The father of an 11-year-old child at 70 percent of her ideal body weight called to request my services. A preliminary evaluation at a hospital indicated that the child would be an appropriate candidate for hospitalization. But because of the child's age and fear of being separated from home and family, he wondered if outpatient treatment might be an appropriate alternative to try first.

Because it is preferable to keep a very young child at home with family, and because the child was potentially at risk physically, this case was not clear-cut. If these parents could be educated to appropriately feed and provide nourishment for their child under the watchful eye of a doctor, the decision in favor of the outpatient care at this juncture might be appropriate contingent on the child's beginning to restore her weight immediately and continually, with a plan to reevaluate the decision within the first week of care.

At this pivotal point in diagnosis and treatment, the scale becomes a central and determining factor in her care; once this phase is passed, it becomes just one of many factors in tracking the progress of healing. In the case described above, the parents needed to understand that if their efforts did not work out as hoped, they would not have wasted their time in trying; it would have been a legitimate part of the diagnostic process. Determining the severity of this youngster's condition and assessing the appropriate level of care for her entrance into treatment would become a necessary part of a diagnostic process that would need to evolve under the watchful eye of a physician.

In light of the ever-changing, ebbing and flowing process of pathology and wellness, doctors and psychopharmacologists, who tend to see their clients on a less regular basis than do therapists and nutritionists, need to maintain regular contact with the team in readiness to respond to the recovering client's physiological and chemical changes. It is for the therapist (and/or client) to initiate contact with team members and prepare the doctor or psychopharmacist when the need for their services may arise. Physical instability or continual weight fluctuation requires medical monitoring, and it behooves therapists to encourage the doctor's willingness to remain vigilant in continuing to monitor the client's physiological status at appropriate intervals.

In concert with Abraham Maslow's hierarchy of needs theory, physical survival supersedes all other needs; thus, medical monitoring becomes a prerequisite for eating disorder care (Huitt, 2004). The first task of treatment is to rule out physiologically based (i.e. gastroenterological) origins of problems that relate to eating and weight control. Yet, even when the problem is determined to be behaviorally, emotionally, and genetically based, monitoring by an attending physician is critical to ensure the client's physical stability throughout the weight restoration process. The therapist may also initiate the request for the physician to reassess and consider adjusting medication for the client on an as-needed basis. Attending to the body's demands not only may save the client's life but also prepares what has been a malnourished and dysfunctional brain to accept and benefit from the healing process.

DIAGNOSTIC "RED FLAGS"

"I Eat Healthy"

I never miss a single opportunity to discover what "healthy" means in the eyes of the speaker. Most clients and parents assume that healthy means restricting fats, sugars, and carbohydrates. For many, the concept of healthy eating implies that less is more and that skipping meals when not hungry is the best thing you can do for your waistline. In questioning my clients about what, in their opinion, marked the beginning of their disease, about four of five respond, "I just started to eat healthy, and then I just kept on eating healthier and healthier."

"I'm a Vegetarian"

Although no one could love animals more than I, when children as young as age five or six years declare that they will never again eat "anything that has eyes," it gives me pause. In most cases, the young children whom I have observed taking on such orthodox views of eating also have a diagnosis of obsessive–compulsive anxiety disorder and/or other form of anxiety disorder. Many children become self-professed vegetarians during the latency years, a precursor to, or a sign of, anorexia. Vegetarianism legitimizes enforced restriction of various types of foods, in most instances resulting in legitimized weight loss. Ironically, a good number of self-declared vegetarians refuse to eat vegetables, confining their eating to chicken nuggets and white carbohydrates, such as pasta and French fries. Some clients have reported how their "vegetarianism" helped them avoid arguments at the dinner table: "It sure beats having to whine and be forced to eat something that's off limits in my book."

In some instances, sympathetic parents have argued that the vegetarian choice demonstrates integrity and that animal fats are unhealthy anyway; these same parents can benefit from a reminder to make it their business to see that their child is getting adequate protein and fats, which they need to grow and develop healthfully. In distinguishing appropriate from inappropriate vegetarianism, I typically will investigate whether the vegetarian child (or her parents) is fully prepared to shop and responsibly prepare foods that represent all the food groups. It takes a real and conscientious effort to commit to healthful vegetarian food preparation. Many parents with vegetarian children simply expect the child to "find substitutes in the refrigerator" in the form of peanut butter or cottage cheese when the family dinner served does not meet their child's requirements, a strategy that can enable picky eating syndrome (see Chapter 7).

Clinicians should assess the origins and intentions of vegetarianism, remembering that vegetables are good and nutritious foods and should be eaten in quantity. You can anticipate that therapeutic discussions about vegetarianism tend to be highly charged; those who follow its tenets tend to be deeply committed to the orthodoxy of its requirements and to the defenses it affords. A client may be considered an appropriate vegetarian if she has grown up in a vegetarian family and was vegetarian before the onset of the eating disorder.

"I Get My Period Regularly"

Many girls who are on birth control pills to regulate their period will offer an affirmative answer to the question, "Do you have a regular period?" But this answer derails the intention of the question. Assessing the history of the function of the client's menstrual cycle may be as important as assessing her current function; did she *ever* have a normal period and if so, when did she lose it?

A 22-year-old client, a talented athlete for an Ivy League team, had gotten her period for the first time in a long time, most likely because she had gained weight as her binge eating disorder spiraled out of control. What she failed to mention was that for the first nine years of her cycle, her period was never regular because of her extreme athleticism and a lifestyle of compulsive workouts, an important diagnostic indicator of an activity disorder. An interruption in menses occurs when anorexia or activity disorders mark a loss of fat cells significant enough to compromise the store of estrogen needed to fuel a functioning reproductive system. Clients need to be aware that even if they do have a "regular" period (one that is not induced by hormone replacement with birth control pills), the regularity and flow will be indicators of the quality of hormonal function. A few days only of a very light flow may or may not indicate "normal" function.

"I'm Doing Better"

Clients may use the concept of "doing better" as a device to deflect continual recovery progress and placate parents and treaters. "I ate edamame beans for protein and squash for carbs" may reveal a client's not-yet-normalized relationship with food and need to upgrade her comfort with eating a greater variety of foods. Weight gain in the absence of a genuinely healthy eating lifestyle represents the start of something very good, but goals for continuing improvement must be kept clearly in sight.

In reporting how "wonderfully" her recovery went at a vacation resort, an emaciated client with anorexia spoke of eating blueberries for the first time, calling them her "nightly dessert." She proclaimed that she missed her aerobic exercise once, in order to watch a friend's tennis match, "something she never would have done before," yet she participated in aerobic exercise the six other days. She reported that she didn't "fly up" the strenuous mountain climb every morning as she had done in years past, but walked slower; still, she climbed the mountain daily before breakfast. She never stopped exercising. She clearly remained in denial.

It is important to respect the legitimacy of the client's need to pace her recovery and, intermittently, to reduce the pace of progress to allow for acclimatization to current changes if necessary. When pacing (and not resistance to recovery) becomes the issue, it should be defined and recognized as such so as not to risk collusion with the eating disorder by expecting and accepting less from the client than recovery demands. It is up to practitioners to retain the vision of what truly healthy eating looks like.

Beware of what may appear to be immediate and total compliance, though the client's capacity to eat better and to tolerate weight gain by adopting a healthy eating lifestyle immediately is a strongly positive prognostic indicator. Remember, that eating disorders do not heal overnight; in some instances, inpatient anorexic patients may choose to gain weight precipitously to qualify for discharge with the intention of losing it immediately afterwards. It is critical to help the client keep her weight goals realistic, gain weight through healthy and balanced eating, and anticipate that anxiety will intensify, if only temporarily, as recovery evolves through weight gain as well as through other means.

"But I Ate Dessert With Dinner"

The claim of having eaten dessert may camouflage or deflect what is true and actual. My response is, "That's great! So tell me, what did you eat? how much did you eat? And how was it for you?" "A taste" or "two bites" is better than eating none at all, though it is clearly not "eating dessert."

I also inquire about the size and quality of the meal that this dessert followed. How much had the client eaten during the earlier part of the day leading up to this meal? Recovery from an eating disorder is about developing a healthy, fearless, and balanced relationship with food, consistently, over the course of a day, week, month, and year.

CONCLUSION

The eating disorder therapist arrives at diagnosis through knowledge and sensing. As the point of entry into the disease and into family, treatment, and recovery systems, diagnostic assessment is the first and most potent intervention; if not effectively executed, it could be the last opportunity for client and family to avail themselves of professional care. The quality and nature of the evaluation process sets the stage for establishing trust in the therapeutic connection, in the client's trust in her capacity to change, in the treatment process, and in the potential for successful outcomes. Because eating-related problems are neurological, physical, nutritional, behavioral, chemical, emotional, developmental, psychological, and relational, all conditions need to be considered and assessed; behavioral abuses of food may represent only the tip of the diagnostic iceberg.

6

Getting Started: Structuring the Diagnostic Process

The important thing is not to stop questioning.

—Albert Einstein

The diagnostic assessment process begins with the initial telephone inquiry. The phone rings, you pick up the call, and the diagnosis has begun, and so has the highly pivotal education process—the start of relationship building and the action plan that is the benchmark of eating disorder treatment. The caller, whether the potential client or family member, will have varying experience, knowledge, and acceptance of the disease; it is a given that emotions at the other end of the line will run high. The call may represent the first public acknowledgment, on the part of the individual and the family, that they are facing a potentially life-threatening problem. The caller may be seeking first-time treatment, a change from past treatment, or professional consultation about having become stuck in a static or failing treatment process. The caller needs to be advised about what the next step should be and how long it might take before progress can begin to happen. In wading out to join forces with the client or the parent in whatever state she might be, you can be sure that your words during that conversation constitute a form of crisis intervention.

At the same time, the professional needs to respond to the caller's agenda, questions, and needs. In cases where the pathology is advanced, the client may require an immediate referral to a more restrictive treatment milieu. Through this first contact, the client or family member develops a feel for what may be in store, and the professional gleans a sense of the nature and quality of the human resources that reside within the family system. Box 6.1 lists topics that should be covered in the initial phone call with a potential client or family member.

BOX 6.1

Getting Started: The Initial Contact

Prospective therapists should assist callers in learning what they need to know. It is appropriate to let the caller lead in requesting the information that she needs and wants to hear. Be prepared to share your background, treatment philosophy, how you work, and instructions for the client (e.g., contacting the insurance company for authorization, seeing a medical doctor).

The client or family member needs to know the following about you:

- that you are a fully knowledgeable and experienced practitioner in the area of eating disorders
- that you really care about her concerns and are willing and ready to teach her what she needs to know about eating disorders and the process of healing
- that you value the input of parents and families
- whether it is realistic to consider evaluation for outpatient care
- how you work—define your philosophy of care and understanding of recovery.

The client or family member needs to know what will happen next:

- the next steps in their effort to heal or help their child
- the need to get prior authorization from their insurance company
- if appropriate, suggestions for what to say to their child to influence him or her to attend the diagnostic session
- options for who should attend the first session, a decision based on the age, life stage, and preference of the child client and of the parent.

When speaking to a potential client or family member who has met with a less than successful treatment experience in the past, make it clear that you are prepared to offer a therapy experience different from what she has known previously. This time, the client deserves to see change, as that is what this work is about.

SETTING THE STAGE FOR TREATMENT

When the identified client is a child living at home, the wider family system will also need attention. One mother's initial phone conversation revealed that the father was more resistant to therapy than their 16-year-old daughter; the mother revealed her fears about how this might affect the girl's willingness to attend a therapeutic evaluation for anorexia. By first attending to her own pain and gathering knowledge for herself so that she could bring it home to her daughter and husband, this mother temporarily became the identified patient. She attended several preliminary consultation sessions with me to learn how to handle her family's resistance to care as well as the pediatrician's lack of responsiveness. At this point, it would be left to her to assume responsibility for facilitating the child's recovery environment within the home. In light of the daughter's conviction that she was "just fine," we scheduled the initial evaluation with mother and daughter together.

When parents do not see eye to eye with each other about their child's problem or need for care, it can be most efficient initially to work with them apart from the child in an effort to diminish the discrepancy in how they approach the situation, to bring them closer to providing a united front in enhancing their child's recovery.

ASSESSMENT STRATEGIES

First Diagnostic Session

The initial diagnostic session has many of the characteristics of brief, time-limited therapies that combine psychodynamic process with crisis intervention. In a concentrated effort to solve the immediate and most pressing problems, the work of the first session needs to be comprehensive and encompassing, to include education, trust building, relationship building, and problem solving; it may include task assignment, specific requirements (such as seeing a medical doctor for a physical evaluation), commitments, and contingency contracts. At this time, personality problems are put aside in favor of prioritizing the most real and pressing issues of the moment . . . determining the client's safety and making the proper referrals.

As with crisis intervention, the most critical consequence of the first diagnostic session is the establishment of an action plan. This plan explains how the assessment process will proceed in continuing to seek a comprehensive diagnosis and an evolving, collaborative treatment plan. The initial session includes referrals to other prospective members of the treatment team, with instructions for clients and families to initiate contact with them and embark on an integrative treatment process before the next meeting or as soon as possible.

The initial session needs to deal with the immediacy of the client's negative, positive, and ambivalent feelings about seeking help and the triggers prompting her motivation to seek help now. The professional should assess the client's current emotional and physical states and eating lifestyle to ascertain the need for a timely (or immediate) referral to a restrictive level of care. The session includes information gathering and giving, including some history taking when relevant, with a greater emphasis at this juncture on where the client is now in her disease and recovery process. History gathering at this point needs to have clear relevance to the agenda of understanding the client's current needs.

Do not agree to treat a client on an outpatient basis if you believe it may not be sufficiently intense to heal the client—for example, if she is in physiological or emotional danger or is not simultaneously under the watchful eye of a physician to check vital signs, blood levels, brain function, weight, and so forth. The provider's liability becomes heightened if appropriate medical intervention is not part of the treatment plan and team function.

Who attends the initial sessions? It is generally the parent who makes the initial contact and appointment for a child client's first session. Clearly, there is no formula to follow about who should be seen in any particular session or in the course of a series of sessions. Decisions about who comes to treatment and when are largely determined by the process of treatment and the needs of the recovering child and family. Invariably, the child who comes to your door will be accompanied by an adult driver. For the child under 12 years it is often helpful for parents to be present throughout the session to listen, understand, absorb, and interpret much of what is said to the child, who is too young to take it all in and comprehend it by herself. Depending on the age of the child, I invite parents to attend the first session if the child is willing, because once parents have gotten their child to treatment, it is imperative that they learn how to support her recovery and tenure in treatment. Particularly with young children, parents can be instrumental in "telling the story" and providing important diagnostic information as observers to the disease process.

If the child begins treatment individually, which is appropriate for older adolescents and young adults, I welcome parental and family input on a regular or ad hoc basis and generally attempt to schedule a conjoint session as soon after treatment engagement as the client might agree to it. If the family initiates a request for a meeting to learn how best to support their adult child, such a meeting requires the consent of the client. Under certain circumstances, with the consent of the client, parents and family members may choose to meet with the client's therapist for family treatment in her absence.

If an adolescent or young adult client initially chooses to be treated separately (remember, that the child may have been the keeper of dark secrets until now), I will typically invite parents to come in for 10 to 15 minutes toward the end of the first session to fill them in on what to expect in the upcoming treatment process and to answer questions, always being careful not to disclose confidences. I generally request that the second or third session include family members throughout its entirety and invite the family to meet for family therapy at regular intervals to be determined by need. If the child demonstrates a reluctance to include parents, this becomes a fertile therapeutic issue that demands address. Be certain to allot sufficient time (perhaps a double session) for the evaluation session, particularly if several family members are present who will require time and attention. Box 6.2 lists possible treatment goals that may be held by the different attendees in conjoint sessions.

The dynamic of the initial session is one of give and take; the clinician engages clients and families actively in dialogue, educating, inquiring about their needs, and seeking their contributions, while establishing their connection to the treating professional and to the process. In making an accurate diagnosis, it is critical that the practitioner knows what to ask, when, what to listen for, and how to interpret what is heard, picking up on cues about spoken, as well as unspoken, concerns and issues. Box 6.2 provides guidelines to shepherd this process.

During the initial session, it is wise to query the client about what she liked best and least about her past therapist and therapy experience in order to achieve important insights into past learning, current expectations of treatment, and her view of herself in the context of human relationships and her recovery. If the client has displayed a history of noncommitment to the treatment process, notice how it

---

BOX 6.2

Navigating Diverse Treatment Goals

The personal agendas the practitioner faces in early conjoint sessions will be diverse, wide-ranging, and most likely in some ways contradictory. The practitioner must hear, address, and legitimize the goals of all parties in a limited time. Clients and families alike must leave each session with the trust that they have the capacity to attain their goals and that the therapist can facilitate this process.

The client's agenda typically involves the following elements:

- She knows she cannot exist without her eating disorder, which gives her a sense of security and well-being.
- She wants to remain thin and to become even thinner in an effort to sustain a secure sense of predictability and safety and a rock-solid sense of control over herself and her world.

The parents' agenda typically involves the following elements:

- They know this disease could kill their child and that the child they knew has vanished.
- The stranger who has taken her place in the family sustains a stronger allegiance to the eating disorder than to the family.
- They want their child back.
- They wish to help their child and family survive this crisis.
- They hope to see change and see it now.
- They want to do the right thing for their child.
- They would like to resolve their own feelings of guilt.
- They long to reconnect with the child through the healing process.

The therapist's agenda typically includes the following elements:

- The therapist knows that by restoring the client to herself, to healthy functioning and self-care, he or she will restore healthy connections between client and family.
- The therapist wants to address the diversity of client and family agendas, legitimizing and validating all of them, simultaneously and immediately, within this first treatment session. The therapist seeks to assess medical risk, engage the client in the healing process, offer a plan of action, and provide referrals that will stimulate recovery.

---

manifested itself in the past and anticipate how the two of you might avoid history repeating itself in the course of the current treatment. Awareness and learning come with the potential for the choice to do things differently.

Formal Intake

Social service agencies and care milieus generally have separate intake departments with clinicians whose sole role it is to handle the initial evaluation session, then refer the client to in-house treating clinicians. In the best of all worlds, the intake worker is a highly skilled and experienced practitioner in fulfilling this most critical function. All too often, however, diagnosticians tend to be less experienced in treatment protocols, such as dealing with resistance, which is typically a pivotal dynamic of the first session. Some practitioners are required to interview prospective clients solely through the use of pre-programmed questioning and formal questionnaires. Even if the questionnaire defines the format of a diagnostic session, the professional's responsiveness and capacity for connection are critical. In these instances, the client needs to be informed at the outset that the intake evaluator will see her only for evaluation.

The use of diagnostic surveys and evaluation forms can be useful in prescreening and establishing diagnosis, eligibility, and appropriateness for treatment. Requiring a client's self-assessment and offering a thorough summary of findings, has been found to be helpful in building motivation and strengthening commitment for change (Miller & Rollnick, 1991, p. 89). Most treatment facilities make use of pretreatment surveys. If offered at regular intervals throughout care, such surveys can also be useful tools for measuring ongoing recovery outcomes. This type of homework, when combined with other behavioral tools, allows the client to accrue confidence and independence, encouraging accountability in better recognizing her own progress.

The Eating Disorder Examination (Ed.16.0D) and the Eating Disorder Examination Questionnaire (EDE-Q 6.0) are offered in their entirety in *Cognitive Behavioral Therapy and Eating Disorders* (Fairburn, 2008). The Eating Disorders Quality of Life survey is another increasingly important instrument appropriate for use in research with clinical and subclinical anorexic, bulimic, and binge eating clients (Engel et al., 2006).

In my early years as a professional working in agencies and hospitals, I recall being required to follow unbendingly the history-taking form in intake interviews. Invariably, these forms were chronological, starting with the client's early history, regardless of whether it had any bearing on the specific demands of the moment. There is a time and a place for chronological history taking, particularly when a review of the past has relevance in the present in helping a client better understand herself and her disease. But if intake rituals or questionnaires preclude attention to the pressing needs of all attendees during those pivotal first moments of care, they are likely to interfere with an effective start to the critical process of human connections. The presence of an eating disorder within the family system represents a crisis of intense emotions. Data gathering is less important than the intervention of relationship building and the process that occurs alongside it. Obtaining information can wait; relationships and empathy cannot. One of the most important goals of the first session is to motivate the client to return for a second session.

At the end of the first session and at other significant points in treatment, it is useful to recapitulate the essence of what has transpired, reflecting back what the client has said. Offer a useful plan of action for her to take away with her. This technique can inspire motivation in resistant clients. I generally create a can-do momentum and hail the potential for a successful prognosis where one becomes evident.

First Session Checklist

- Agree on goals of treatment, staying aware of goal diversity while pointing out where goals coincide.
- Educate clients about disease and treatment. Dispel myths.
- Gather information about the client, explaining your motives and intentions in seeking this information. This sets the stage for honesty, clarity, and trust.
- Refuse to work with a client who will not be monitored regularly by a physician. This is a critical condition for continued care.
- Offer a tentative diagnosis, and explain the process through which the team will arrive at a full diagnosis.
- Are you able to tell that within the process of the first session, you have won the client's confidence in herself, in you, and in the process?
- Offer a concrete action plan, helping the client envision what lies ahead in treatment.
- Offer referrals to the treatment team.
- Specify ground rules for care. I suggest specifying that clients are not expected to be able to accomplish all attempted tasks but merely to begin the process of initiating self-care and internal self-monitoring. In addition, families need to be given boundaries, as well as permission, in becoming involved in supporting their loved one's care.
- Illustrate for family members, using examples from the session, that they are capable of communicating effectively with each other. Seeing is believing.
- Respond to questions, hopes, and fears as they arise, with a sense of immediacy. No question should go unanswered.
- Offer as much clarity as is possible; acknowledge that ambiguity simply "comes with the territory" when recovering from an eating disorder.

USE OF SELF IN DIAGNOSIS

The client's feelings in the first session typically run the gamut from fear, guilt, shame, anger, and sadness to relief and hope. Inevitably, the young person has felt domineered by limit-setting parents, a tyrannical disease, and potentially by your own presence now as a professional caretaker with the power to recommend treatment and, scarier still, hospitalization. Effective practitioners are aware, present, knowledgeable, spontaneous, and opportunistic, and they need to seize the diagnostic moment provided by the heightened emotions of the initial sessions.

Highlighting the Client's Strengths

In the face of the client's potential discomfort, hostility, or reluctance to bring difficult concerns to light, the therapist's capacity to probe with tact and genuine caring is one of the greatest challenges and skills of eating disorder treatment. To push or not to push—that is the question. The determination of how soon, how much, and in what manner to confront the client challenges the very process of creating the trust that is required to accomplish this. There is a thin line between soft pedaling a request and making a demand; that line is drawn through a careful

BOX 6.3

Getting to Know the Client

The therapist formulates a diagnosis on the basis of information offered as well as withheld, discerned through knowledge as well as intuition. The questions in Box 6.3 are meant to provide a starting point from which to diverge; practitioners need to take generous liberties in what to ask, when, and how, although the most important dynamic is in how the diagnostician listens and hears.

Topic	Questions
The moment	What is it like for you to be here at this evaluation today? Are you aware of thoughts, fears, hopes, and goals you might have for the session? Do you feel comfortable sharing them?
Behaviors	Eating disorder symptoms their etiology, evolution and change. Are you aware of what might have triggered these behaviors and for how long they have been going on? How would you describe the difference between the nature of the problem when it first began and what it is today? What impact has your previous therapy had on the problem?
	Have you ever abused diet pills, diuretics, ipecac, or laxatives?
	Have you ever engaged in compulsive overexercise?
	Have you ever engaged in substance abuse? Have you ever used drugs? What about cigarettes? Compulsions in lifestyle that extends beyond the context of food and eating, including shopping? Shoplifting? Sexuality/promiscuity? Obsessive–compulsive symptoms? Viewing pro-anorexic websites?
	There is much to be gleaned about the client's impulsivity, judgment, and personality structure from her responses to a discussion about acting-out behaviors, their intention, and their impact on her life. The diagnostic session, however, may not be the optimal time to engage in an appropriately in-depth discussion, if it is to the exclusion of other diagnostic goals that require accomplishing. You need to keep the larger agenda and time frame in mind throughout the evaluation.
Moods and emotions	On a scale of 1 to 10, how anxious do you feel? On a scale of 1 to 10, how depressed do you feel?
	Determine the risk for suicidality, suicidal ideations. Make a contract around immediate contact in case of suicidal thoughts. Have you ever thought about killing yourself? When was the last time you thought about it? Have you ever harmed yourself intentionally, such as by cutting yourself? What led you to cut yourself? How recently did you last cut yourself? What is the experience like for you? How does it help you? Might there be other ways to accomplish the same goals?
Treatment history	Have you engaged in psychotherapy in the past? Around what issues?
	Have you ever been hospitalized? Have you ever been treated for an eating disorder?
	Have you ever taken medication? How do you feel about possibly taking medication? Are you currently taking medication?

	Have your periods always come regularly? Are you on hormone replacement therapy?
Related experiences	Have you ever been raped or experienced other abuse?
	Did you have problems managing your weight as a child?
	Were you ever bullied or teased as a child? What for? Do you remember how it made you feel and what you did in response?
Genetic history	Do you have a family member who has been an alcoholic? How about other addictions? How about bipolar disorder? depression? obsessive–compulsive disorder? anxiety? Has any one in your family member had an eating disorder? What was that like for you?
History of eating disorders	Do you remember what might have inspired you in dieting? Purging? What do you consider to be healthy eating?
	Are you a vegetarian? Are you able to eat in a balanced and varied manner as a vegetarian? Describe.
Eating lifestyle	What do you eat on a typical day? Do you eat three meals a day and at least one snack? Is there anything you won't eat? Do you ever overeat? What do you consider overeating? Can you give me a "ballpark" figure about how many calories you consume in a day? Would it be closer to 500, 1,800?, 2,200?
	Have you dieted or restricted your food intake in the past? Investigate eating quirks: limited food choices, picky eating history, eating rituals. Do eating requirements restrict life function? Night eating?
	Purging? Different forms. Can you describe your experience of bingeing? When, how often, and on what foods? Have you ever tried to stop? With what outcome? Why do you wish to stop now?
	Do you ever preview restaurant menus to pick out the least fattening meal?
	Do you ever carry your own food to social events?
	Do you avoid family gatherings where there is food? Do you typically eat dinner with your family?
Ego functioning	Have you ever *felt* fat? Have you ever *been* fat?
	How do you cope with negative events? How do you solve problems?
	Do you feel there are distortions in the way you view yourself?
	In the portion sizes of food that you choose? Can you give me an example? (A scoop of potato may seem like "a room-full.")
	Describe the quality of your relationship with family members.
In conclusion	What else would you like to know about me or the treatment process?
	Is there anything you might like to ask?
	Are their any unique symptoms or behavioral patterns you would like to share?
	What do you suppose your thoughts and feelings will be as you walk out the door today?
	The practitioner lays the ground rules for care; the most important single requirement is that the client takes responsibility for consistently attending therapy sessions.

reading of the moment, the client, the requirements for engagement, and the assurance of the client's physical safety.

U came to the assessment session prepared with a "script" about what she would say. She knew it by heart from having spoken it so many times during other evaluations. Seemingly relaxed and in control, she came across as happy, energized and ready to make a swift and strong recovery start before returning to college for her senior year. During the second session, now more in touch with her vulnerabilities, she wept, feeling unprepared, out of control, and frightened. It took until the third session for her to feel more comfortable, connected, and grounded and more able to accept the challenges she faced. She confessed to feeling that she had been caught red-handed in the act of pretending initially to be strong and invincible; I was happy to reframe the positive implications of her having relied on her defenses to carry her through the hardest times and on her capacity now for honest self-appraisal and sharing, as she assumes a more reality-based, moderate, and problem-solving stance. This positive reframing inspired her trust in herself and foreshadowed how the treatment process might unfold.

Many professionals believe that it is not their responsibility or ethical right to "go to a place" where the client has not specifically asked to go or to intuit, extrapolate, approximate, and investigate diagnostic hypotheses that may, or may not, turn out to be true. Because an eating disorder can render a client incapable of engaging in sound judgment and decision making, and of initiating self-care, I believe that it is very much our responsibility as practitioners to do so, particularly at the start of treatment. Diagnostically astute questions are entirely appropriate, even if pointed or leading, if the informed professional is listening carefully to the process, with clarity of boundaries. "Leading" a client is not equivalent to telling her what to do or how to think. Like the physician who inquires, "Where does it hurt? Does it hurt here? Here?" the process is about directing the client to learn about herself in honest self-appraisal and problem solving. If an assumption fits, go with it; if not relevant, let it go and investigate another line of reasoning.

D, an athlete with anorexia who exercised compulsively, had dropped 20 pounds in two months. She came with her parents to the initial session; tears readily sprang to her eyes at the realities spoken and the expectations required for her recovery. She was certain her parents were wrong in thinking she had a problem. Her beloved former therapist, who was also an athlete, had assured her that her exercise compulsion was "natural for athletes" and "not of concern." Sensing D's emotional strength and internal resiliency, I chose not to mince words. After reflecting the strengths I perceived in her and my sense that she was up to the challenge that faced her, I confronted her with the reality of the danger she was in, her need to change, and the consequences of not doing so. She did not call back immediately to set up a next appointment, so I called her after 12 days to inquire about her response to our session and the nature of her plans.

D chose to begin treatment with me and made a speedy recovery within three months. As she ultimately prepared to terminate treatment, just before moving away to a new city, a new life, and a new career and to be near her boyfriend, I asked her to rethink that first session aloud with me and to confide what the tough love experience had been like for her. Would she have preferred my being less forthright with her? Her response to the dynamic of that rigorous first session was

> Wow! This person really means business. This time it could really be different for me. If I want to get help, I suppose she might be the one to help me. If I am ever going to get better, it might as well be now.

"My gymnastics coach was the same way," she went on. "I hated the high expectations, yet it really helped motivate me to perform." She expressed her gratitude for my follow-up call, which provided the incentive she needed to proceed with this work.

Be aware that this forthright and presumptive stance is highly atypical for a first session, but in assessing this young woman who had been in treatment previously, it appeared to me that she was ripe for change. A sensitive practitioner who is able to pick up on such nuance puts the client at a great advantage . . . unless of course, the client decides not to return to treatment. Courage and reality-based risk taking are the name of game if the goal is to secure positive outcomes.

DIAGNOSTIC DECISIONS: "HANGING TOUGH"

The sensitivity of the eating disorder practitioner in the assessment and engagement stage of diagnosis and treatment is like that of the skilled angler standing hip deep in the rapids, reeling in and letting out the fish on the line, playing with its resistance, alternating between tough love and tender loving care, both accomplishing the same task of luring the client into a productive engagement in treatment.

Vulnerable and at risk for suicide, N clearly required inpatient services. This young adult purged all but a small breakfast, self-injured, and had attempted suicide in the past while undergoing physical abuse by her boyfriend. Her parents were unable to convince her to enter inpatient care. During the initial evaluation, I was clear, honest and firm with her. Though at risk, she could save herself by embracing the right kind of care. Kindly, informatively, I explained that there would be no alternative for her but to participate in a program first if she were to eventually seek outpatient treatment with me. I took the initiative to contact the intake department of a program nearby during the session to set up an appointment for an immediate evaluation to ensure that action resulted from the momentum of the session. N chose to reject the recommendation for inpatient care, and her mother begged me to see her again. Would I have enabled her denial by allowing her to return to my outpatient care? If I were to deny her now, would I be leaving a very needy young woman without any care at all? I chose to allow her to return for one more session with the goal of bringing her closer to acceptance of inpatient care. My message in this session was quite clear: She was in serious physical danger, and I would put her at greater risk by agreeing to treat her as an outpatient. This time, her mother called to say she was still refusing more restrictive care but that my direct approach was "too harsh." N felt I had "done nothing to help her get better."

I explained to N's mother that were I to be any less harsh now, she would soon be beyond help; that the path to recovery doesn't always feel helpful; and in fact, that path typically feels more painful than does the disease. I explained my intentions in saying what I did to her daughter and advised this mother to help her daughter recognize that her angry words were the voice of her eating disorder. I educated N's mother about her responsibility to take charge of N during this time when she was incapable of taking care of herself I set her up with a psychopharmacological referral and offered her information about interventions and hospital commitment, ideas that have saved others in the same situation.

When to refuse to treat and when to continue offering support to an intractable client who cannot overcome fear and move forward in recovery is an ambiguous and pivotal judgment. Your educated judgment and reliance on your own good instincts are generally sufficient indicators, along with a heightened awareness of the criticality of physiological risk. If a client's life is in danger, it is important that a medical doctor is in a position to monitor her condition closely.

ESTABLISHING MINDFUL CONNECTIONS

In the diagnostic interview, the therapist speaks to the client's core self, defines it, and calls its sustaining qualities out of the closet, where it has been imprisoned by the impenetrable armor of the disorder. "Keeping an open mind is key to a thorough diagnosis that will pave the way to lasting healing: Holding our concepts and theories lightly allows us to make a journey of co-discovery with the patient. Diagnosis is a collaboration in which our thoughts about treatment are deemphasized in favor of the 'felt sense' of the connection" (Germer, Siegel, & Fulton, 2005, p. 204).

A healthy therapeutic relationship taps the deepest inner sanctum of all parties, creating the compelling, empathic dynamism of the "hook" of connectedness, the right-brained energy that is largely responsible for the give-and-take dynamism of the growth-producing human connection. The well-boundaried and empathic therapist can and does experience a sense of well-being or healing within the presence of his or her clients. There are days when I feel depleted or blue but find myself uplifted and more relaxed, with a greater sense of self and well-being, after conducting a psychotherapy session for someone else. And following particularly tough sessions that don't feel so good while they are happening, there is no greater pleasure for both client and therapist than to work through the process in search of reconnection and learning, after the fact.

Therapeutic connection in diagnosis is based on the same loving use of self to provide motivation, encouragement, and hope as one does in treatment. During the first session, the interviewer attempts to convey unconditional acceptance of the client by making clear that he or she understands her, her disease, and the motivations behind it. The professional can reassure the client by letting her know that the team and her family seek the same things for her that she seeks for herself—happiness, acceptance, appreciation, competence, and security in navigating her life on her own. Each party's means to that end may diverge, but the goals and intentions of all are perfectly aligned.

When realistic and possible, a main component of my early work with a client, becomes the inspiration of the client's self-trust by pointing out the strengths that have become apparent to me immediately during the diagnostic process. I do not hesitate to offer positive prognostic hunches where appropriate. Evidence of a client's healthy core, including their intention, motivation, capacity for insight, capacity for making changes, forthright and honest communication, and/or the support of a loving family system, justifies the prediction of a successful outcome.

The diagnostic process stimulates supportive connections not only between the client and her self, but between members of the treatment team as well. I take great comfort in working with committed and deeply caring team members (some of whom I have never met personally, but with whom I communicate often) who are passionate about healing our mutual clients and about learning through our discourse. Parents, as partners on the team, provide an incomparable boon to diagnosticians and the child clients they treat.

ANATOMY OF AN EVOLVING DIAGNOSIS

The following case study illustrates the following principles of diagnosis:

- Eating disorder diagnosis and treatment are the warp and weft of the same fabric, in some ways virtually inextricable, one from the other.
- The eating disorder diagnosis process is ambiguous and unpredictable.
- A versatile use of self and a multifaceted team effort are essential in establishing an accurate diagnosis and viable treatment plan.
- Parental input is an invaluable asset to the treatment team.
- The comprehensive eating disorder diagnosis rarely happens within a single session; a full diagnosis tends to be a functional and dynamic phenomenon based on what the client is able to accomplish in the way of integrating changes over time.

K is a young woman who returned home from boarding school to recover from her eating disorder, having been asked to take a leave of absence in light of her sudden weight loss. At home with her mother for a six-week "recovery break," she came to see me for short-term treatment, her goal being to become healthy enough to return to school. We met typically twice a week for the duration, sometimes in conjunction with her family; she also saw a nutritionist weekly. By the end of our time together, she had a diagnosis that took fully six weeks to establish and she had become genuinely engaged in both treatment and healing.

Session 1

K attended Session 1 with her mother. K did not see herself as being sick, despite her compulsion to restrict calories and carbohydrates, her pathological fear of being fat, and her rapid weight loss of 23 pounds. She claimed that she "eats" and is "perfectly able" to gain back the weight at will and therefore that she did not have anorexia. In this session, she vowed to lose any restored weight once she returned to college. With a significant history of addiction, bulimia, and Axis II and mood disorders in her extended family, her genetics had surely "loaded the gun," and her "environment had apparently pulled the trigger." K had become a vegetarian during her semi-starvation mode. During this session, I gathered history, made referrals to the treatment team, and established an initial plan of action that would ultimately determine just how "fine" she really was.

Session 2

One week later, K attended Session 2 alone. During the preceding week, K was to have met with the nutritionist and to have started to implement the food plan, with the results leading us closer to understanding the degree of K's pathology. According to the scale, she had gained six pounds during this first week of care by "following her food plan." This quick weight gain might have suggested that there was no pathology here, just choice, and that K was indeed able to determine her own fate at will. However, six pounds seemed an inordinate amount of weight to gain in one week by following a pre-set food plan, and her attitude toward weight gain led me to wonder if she had water-loaded or carried rocks in her pockets before her weigh in. Fluid shifts (edema) are most probably responsible for such rapid weight changes.

Having established that she was "fine," she now began to manipulate the food contract, lobbying for halving her grain intake, still another diagnostic indicator that she sought to eat less, pointing to a possible diagnosis of anorexia. K chose not to take advantage of the privilege of exercising that came with increasing her caloric intake. "Why should I exercise if it will not result in weight loss!?" another potential diagnostic indicator of her single-mindedness about losing weight (anorexia?) and the weight-loss agenda of her previous use of exercise (bulimia or eating disorder not otherwise specified?).

Session 3

K's mother and stepfather attended the session seeking parent consultation; the client refused to join them. The mother reported discovering diet pills hidden in K's drawer. In the interest of "slowing down" the rate of her weight gain, and denied the liberty to reduce her carbohydrate intake, K chose to compensate by abusing diet pills. Fearful that the pills would represent the start of an addiction, K's mother favored reducing her food plan intake. In this session, the goals were twofold: to seek a more definitive diagnosis and to resolve the parental crisis at hand. Taking the parents into my confidence as valued treatment team members, I disclosed all the factors that my nutritionist partner and I would consider in structuring K's plan.

The use of diet pills could mark a proneness to addiction; that K had not disclosed it indicated a pattern of secrecy and deception. We discussed the logistics of the small window of time available before K would return to school and the question of whether her return to school was possible. (Her parents discussed their readiness to encourage her to remain at home to recover.) Considering the time constraints of this recovery, I recommended taking the hard line—setting firm limits on K's controlling demands and requiring that she enter a treatment program for the weeks before school resumed.

This session raised a number of difficult questions. Would K consider a calorie reduction a reward for diet pill abuse or an encouragement to assume a greater degree of self-regulation and self-control? In an effort not to create a split within the treatment team and to benefit from our resources, I advised that we confer with the nutritionist for her perspective about adjusting the food plan. K's mother voiced her concerns about her own appropriateness in having "breached K's privacy" in coming across the pills. Was she being intrusive or reality oriented in her attempt to define and resolve problems? I counseled her that if she had reason to believe that her child was in danger, it was her responsibility to protect K, particularly while she was not equipped to protect herself.

In seeing parents in the absence of the child, the therapist does well to confirm the boundaries of confidentiality, for the child as well as the parents. If issues surface that demand communication among all parties, this can be best accomplished through conjoint family treatment to avoid breaching privacy issues.

Out of this session came a plan: K would decide her own fate, assuming full responsibility for the consequences of her actions, with weight restoration noncompliance resulting in her missing a semester of school. She would be given the freedom to succeed or to fail, with the scale alone determining her destiny. Through this process we would move closer to a diagnosis to be determined by her capacity for compliance.

Session 4

K attended Session 4 by herself. In this session, she revealed her plan to hire a personal trainer to "work her out daily" if she were to agree to eat as many calories as she was asked to consume. K's fear of weight gain, her frenzied machinations, her determination to lose weight once she returned to school, her abuse of diet pills all now pointed to a diagnosis of anorexia or possibly bulimia, restricting type. Other information emerging about her impulsive nature, including her physicality (hitting and pushing) with her sister and discovery of her father's potentially heritable Axis II characteristics, would have supported that diagnosis. K was still desperately fighting a diagnosis, if not the disease. I explained to her that the goal of diagnosis is not to apply a label but to help her fulfill her own dream to return to school. With or without an eating disorder label, the treatment would be the same.

Session 5

K attended Session 5 alone. At this juncture, K's chief concern was her mother's self-appointed role as food police. Because a responsible and vigilant professional team was in place, I agreed that it was time for her mother to be released from this duty so that K could become an increasingly autonomous player in determining her own fate. K responded well to this incentive.

Session 6

K attended Session 6 alone. Now halfway through the process, she experienced a resurgence of ambivalence, fretting in anticipation of being monitored for weight at school and insisting that she was not and never had been sick. With an increasing anxiety and resistance to weight gain, she would continue to find a diagnosis of anorexia unacceptable.

Session 7

The whole family came for treatment, including K's mother, stepfather, and sister. I offered the family the opportunity to explore the dynamics of the blended family, and evidence emerged of K's overly powerful and oppositional role in the family system, in contexts beyond food and eating. Family dynamics revealed her abuse of her younger sister and her role as go-between with her divorced parents in an attempt to micromanage family feelings and her attempts to deflect the inflammatory behaviors of her volatile father.

I took bold personal risks in using myself within the family system, modeling for parents how to confront an intimidating and overly powerful K. I used myself to reflect back K's intolerance of and defensiveness around her sister in the effort to help her assume accountability and responsibility for her own behaviors and attitudes. I fostered a new balance within the system, initiating a voice for the voiceless sister and supporting a highly appropriate but unappreciated mother.

Anticipating that K at first would feel affronted, judged, and even ganged up on, I spoke directly and with immediacy to such feelings, stating my intention not to be critical but to help her better know herself so she could better choose how she would like to behave. By the end of the session, K began to respond positively to a learning process that left her feeling relieved to have been honestly seen and reined in.

During this session, I assigned the family some communication tasks that they collaborated in creating. In this session, the severity, persistence, and frenzy of K's reaction to her sister (and her father) having called her "fat" (in light of her sister's frustration at being excluded from the family "secret" about K's condition), further confirmed the eating disorder diagnosis. I encouraged her to take ownership and control of aspects of her eating behaviors that she could choose to change of her own accord that might change the quality of her life, health, and well-being.

Session 8

I opened this mother—daughter session by asking, "So how have things been going, and where might we begin today?" K's answer to the first question was "Fine"; to the second, "Nowhere special." Mother chuckled and revealed that K had complained all the way to my office about how unnecessary the sessions were because she was "not sick, after all." She simply "felt better eating less and worse eating more" and wanted everyone to leave her alone to make her own decisions. K's resistant tirade during this session about the unfairness of having to gain weight and be monitored for weight at school after her return was a significant diagnostic indicator of the resistance of her eating disorder, as she remained entrenched in the pre-contemplative stage of treatment (see Chapter 13).

Team Involvement

The dean of K's school, a still unknown but pivotal member of this treatment team and its choices, phoned to discuss my opinion about this client's readiness to return to school. She had spoken with K's mother, who was very positive about K's progress in gaining weight and preparedness to come back to school and to eat "normally." According to her mother, K had "turned the corner." My question was, which corner? Was it the corner of weight restoration, eating lifestyle, attitude, coping capacities, self-awareness? K had made some changes during the start of treatment—she had gained weight and essentially had returned to her pre-anorexic eating habits (which were disordered at best). K claimed to no longer seek a "dieting lifestyle," to feel more energetic, and to understand that she could "eat healthy" without becoming fat. She had learned how to put together a balanced meal and even began to eat chicken in a new post-vegetarian mode.

This progress, in combination with the changes she had made in her capacity for self-awareness, in assuming responsibility for her actions within the family system, and now demonstrating uncharacteristic new strengths, led me to recommend that K could return to school with the stipulation that she be monitored closely for weight stability and gain during the next three months, that she continue to speak with a therapist and nutritionist there, and that she have regular medical check-ups. At this point, to do otherwise would be negligent, given the risk of her backsliding and losing ground. I explained to the dean that aftercare is an essential component of good care, though in this case, follow-up could hardly be considered "aftercare" after only six weeks into the recovery process. Her return to school would mark the end of the *beginning* of treatment, rather than the end of the treatment process. An eating disorder cannot be "fixed" within six weeks. Healing requires the establishment of a new and healthy eating lifestyle, which requires time and the emotional and neurological capacity to integrate changes.

The dean and I spoke about how to deal with the potential for K's continuing resistance to accepting monitoring at school. I suggested that the dean reinforce the school's position in the face of these potentially life-threatening problems; my sense was that K would now appreciate and be responsive to clear boundary setting and consequences. I applauded the school on its flexibility in considering this young woman to be at risk.

Session 9

K was sick in bed for the ninth session, which her mother attended by herself. This individual session provided a healing opportunity for her to better understand how her own family history of intimidation and conflict avoidance might be playing itself out in her parenting. She left feeling strengthened in better understanding herself and her increased capacity for self-awareness, assertiveness, and flexibility in response to K's tantrums. She would soon be called upon to exercise this new empowerment in further dealing with K's disorder.

Session 10

Our last session was a family session, conducted in the family's home. Seeing the family within the culture of their own home environment to discuss feelings and actions that take place there proved a superb opportunity. Through my support of the mother's intentions in dealing with her children, she became increasingly capable of overcoming her own conflict avoidance in caring for them. In the eyes of her children, this enhanced her respect and role legitimacy, leaving them feeling safer and more contained.

The legacy practitioners leave in the wake of empowered treatment is empowered parents. Therapists provide role modeling for parents in how to communicate openly, set limits, and know their rights and obligations. This is a critical function for practitioners, who act as therapists for 45 minutes a week for a limited period of time; parents remain parents forever.

Termination

As she prepared to leave for school, K and I discussed a tentative diagnosis of eating disorder not otherwise specified/permarexia (an addiction to sustaining a diet permanently; although they are not overweight, these individuals will go to any measure to maintain thinness). The validity of this diagnosis (as opposed to anorexia nervosa) would depend on the client's capacity to continue compliance with recovery protocols at school when she was functioning independently. In the eating disorder not otherwise specified/permarexia diagnosis, K understood that though she suffered with an eating disorder, she felt she had more control of her illness than she would with anorexia. It was an important distinction for her (though not so much for me, as the treatment would be just the same), and she was proud and grateful.

Would this diagnosis feed her denial or inspire her self-confidence . . . or both? This case study shows how professional decision making is full of nuances and viable alternatives to be based on professional judgment and the weighing of priorities, the needs of the client, and the therapeutic moment. Whether the diagnosis would become bulimia, restrictive type would remain to be seen; K was now emotionally prepared to consider the possibility of recovery and to accept care as she needed it. All bases were covered.

Diagnostic labels can be significant for clients in how they view themselves. One of my clients who suffered with a "stigmatizing" diagnosis of bulimia expressed her envy of those with the "good fortune" to demonstrate the self-discipline of a "respectable" diagnosis of anorexia. She never realized that her own true diagnosis was in fact anorexia, purging type.

A Diagnostic Postscript

Several hours before the trip to the airport for K's return to school, her mother called in tears to say she had discovered laxatives in her daughter's carry-on bag. K had taken 50 pills within the past two weeks. We confronted what would become the final diagnosis—bulimia, restrictive type—and its implications, in a telephone conference call between me, K, and her mother. That the school would accept her back was most likely out of the question. This did not negate the good progress she had made, though this discovery felt like a benchmark of failure to her and her family; rather, it elucidated the confounding nature of the disease and of its recovery.

K confided in her mother that she felt ready now to stay home to recover, that she had many things that she needed to discuss with me about concerns that superseded eating and weight, which included very real family issues. She acknowledged that the eating disorder had been a mask covering up her real feelings, and she was prepared now to endure the pain of unearthing them. K may also have had an Axis II diagnosis, to be determined.

CONCLUSION

Expert professional consultation in eating disorder care, offered to clients, parents, and other professionals, is essentially a diagnostic process that takes on some characteristics of crisis intervention. I receive calls from all over the country (and the world) from clients, parents, and other professionals, such as lawyers and dentists, seeking expertise or a second opinion about the effectiveness of current treatment. The tasks of consultation include assessment of the client's current condition and potential for growth, the quality of current care, the need and urgency for change in treatment, and specific options for change and alternative plans for carrying out these changes. When the change process has begun to stagnate, when the current team is running out of ideas, when parents or professionals cannot contain their own frustration and confusion about what needs to happen next, they seek consultation. Parents need to understand how best to support the child and her treatment and how to confront and work with professional providers, who may be loath to include them in effectively responding to their needs.

7

Diagnosing and Managing Eating Disorders, Feeding Disorders, and Picky Eating Syndrome in Young Children

Animal crackers and cocoa to drink, that is the finest of suppers I think; when I am grown up and can have what I please, I think I shall always insist upon these.

—Christopher Morley

Entertaining preferences about the way foods look, feel, smell, and taste is normal The restricted eating that characterizes eating dysfunctions in children must be distinguished from normal individual likes and dislikes. If a child eats peanut butter and jelly sandwiches for lunch every day because he loves the taste, there is little cause for concern, except for a lack of nutritional variation in his diet. It may well be a cause for concern if he eats only peanut butter and jelly because he is afraid that something bad might happen to him if he were to eat different foods; if he cannot tolerate change; if he fears he might gag on varying textures; or if he insists that he eat no more than a single spoonful of peanut butter on his bread. (Natenshon, 1999).

This chapter addresses the unique aspects of treating young children who have clinical eating disorders and those with two little-known and related syndromes that disrupt of the lives of children and their families: feeding disorders and a subcategory of feeding disorders called picky eating syndrome, pervasive feeding disorder, or selective eating. Selective eating is also considered a childhood eating disorder. It is often seen as a phase that the child will outgrow, though frequently, the more severely involved child does not grow out of it, and the feeding disorder is carried into the adult years. Eating disorder practitioners need to become familiar with these syndromes. When pediatricians predictably miss these diagnoses, it falls to eating disorder therapists and nutritionists to recognize them and to make appropriate referrals for care.

EATING DISORDERS IN YOUNG CHILDREN

At one point in a therapy session, a seven-year-old child jumped off my couch, raised her shirt, and pinched the flesh around her thin little waist between her thumb and forefinger to illustrate to me and her mother "just how fat I really am!" Diagnosing and treating young children with eating disorders is a process unique and apart, even within the specialized protocols applicable to eating disorder practice. Child psychiatrists have begun to recognize increasing numbers of children with childhood anorexia (McCune & Walford, 1991). It has been noted that by the age of 10 years, 81 percent of girls have already been on a diet; in addition, dieting can become an environmental trigger to an eating disorder in a child who has genetic susceptibilities. Children can develop anorexia nervosa from around the age of 8 years onwards. Anorexia nervosa will be associated with an accompanying depression in a significant number of children and with clear obsessive–compulsive symptomatolgy (Lask & Bryant-Waugh, 2000).

The clinical presentation of anorexia nervosa in childhood is similar to that in adulthood, though very young children are challenging to diagnose, as only 38 percent meet the criteria for anorexia nervosa. For example, children with poor growth in height as a result of malnutrition may have an "expected" weight that is falsely low; amenorrhea as a criterion for anorexia obviously does not apply to very young girls or boys. In addition, such young children have not yet achieved the developmental milestones and emotional maturity to enable them to regain autonomous self-determination in the face of an eating disorder. Younger clients present at a lower percentage of ideal body weight and lose weight more rapidly. "During childhood, bones need to thicken and lengthen, hearts need to become stronger, brains are adding mass and laying down neuronal pathways. All these functions become reversed for the starving child" (Tyre, 2005).

Lask and Bryant-Waugh (2000) proposed an alternative classification for childhood eating disorders called the "Great Ormond Street" (GOS) criteria (Katzman, Morris, & Pinhas, n.d.). The diagnoses within this classification are anorexia nervosa, food avoidant emotional disorder, selective eating, functional dysphagia, bulimia nervosa, and pervasive refusal syndrome. The overriding feature of all of these eating disorders is the "excessive preoccupation with weight or shape and/or food intake." An early age of onset for anorexia nervosa has been associated with a poor recovery outcome (Halmi, Heebink, & Sunday, 1995). More specifically, for anorexia, the prognosis is less optimistic for disease onset younger than age 11 years (Bernstein, n.d.). Very young children with anorexia frequently suffer from anxiety and obsessive–compulsive anxiety disorder, as well as other genetic susceptibilities (Lucka, 2006).

A study that revealed a prevalence of anxiety disorders and obsessive–compulsive disorder in adults with anorexia nervosa and bulimia nervosa stated that anxiety disorders commonly have their onset in childhood before the onset of an eating disorder, which supports the possibility that they might be a vulnerability factor for the development of anorexia and bulimia (Kaye et al., 2004). Physical and sexual abuse can trigger the onset of childhood eating disorders, as do other predisposing life events and the modeling of a less-than-ideal eating lifestyle in the home. A five-year-old child who had anxiety and anorexia jogged around her bedroom and schoolyard incessantly to lose weight. This child's mother and grandmother were overweight and only drank liquid diet supplements rather than consuming real food. The combination of this child's genetics, along with environmental factors, created her susceptibility to a childhood eating disorder. It is a myth that there is an "epidemic" of childhood eating disorders and that eating disorder sufferers are becoming ever younger. Neither is true. There is, however, a general increase in weight sensitivity and youthful dieting behavior, however, which can trigger an eating disordr in the genetically susceptible child (Lask & Bryant-Waugh, 2000, p. 29).

Triggers of Eating Disorder Onset in Young Children

Trauma can result in behaviors that may eventually lead to an eating disorder in susceptible children. V, age 6, had a 10-year-old sibling with anorexia. V stopped eating soon after her sister began her recovery, refusing meals and eating only potato chips when she was hungry. Her parents were convinced that she was modeling after her sister, who attracted a great deal of attention around meals. V had become violently ill from food poisoning just before her food refusal began, which was a far more likely trigger. V's food restriction, in combination with her genetics and anxiety, might foreshadow the imminent risk of a clinical eating disorder.

Trauma can produce temporary and fully curable anorexia in children who have no genetic predisposition to developing an eating disorder. A 10-year-old boy heard about a child who died from choking. He began to refuse to eat solids and lost a great deal of weight, putting him at risk for anorexia, although he experienced no wish to be thin. With psychotherapy and medication, he eventually outgrew this phobia and easily regained all of his weight. With no genetic susceptibility to developing an eating disorder, he became a normal, healthfully developing young man.

Another trigger to the onset of anorexia in children is an illness called PANDAS (pediatric autoimmune neuropsychiatric disorders associated with streptococcal infection), an early childhood condition that is worth diagnostic investigation. "Children with PANDAS develop obsessive–compulsive disorder, potentially a precursor to anorexia, often accompanied by tics or Tourette's syndrome, following a strep infection. Antibodies attacking strep bacteria may mistakenly attack the basal ganglia of the brain, causing the onset of obsessive–compulsive disorder and potentially anorexia in the genetically susceptible child" (Pukley, Midtsund, Losif, & Lask, 2007, p. 15). A recent study corroborated the connection between anorexia and bulimia, on one hand, and infection and altered autoantibodies, on the other (Fetissov et al., 2005).

Peer influence, in combination with genetic susceptibility and environmental influences, can be a potent trigger to disease as well. Children learn from each other, inadvertently causing adverse consequences, either from lack of knowledge or in an effort to calm their own anxieties. When L's elementary school changed its lunch menu to exclude "unhealthy" foods (french fries, ice cream, and pizza), her friends stopped eating lunch. L, a recovering anorexic, described feeling like a "pig, shamed and embarrassed" as she was the only one of her peers who ate the sack lunch her mother made for her daily as part of her recovery.

E, an anorexic 11-year-old, claimed that on a weekend away with her choral group, "the only thing the girls discussed was weight loss and dieting." She believed that her own views about food restriction could not be "extreme or distorted" because so many of her peers thought the same way. N, at age 10, learned about the importance of reading nutritional labels from spending time with friends. Her mother discovered her obsessing over the sugar content in her daily vitamins one morning.

Dieting can be a pernicious trigger to the onset of overweight and eating disorders. Children's self-established diets have been shown to lead to binge eating and weight gain (Field et al., 2003). Studies have shown that adolescent girls with pronounced body dissatisfaction had a higher body mass index (BMI) at eight years old and that their BMI increased relatively more in the following four years, illustrating that a negative body image in adolescence might have its roots in childhood overweight conditions (Mertens & Vandereycken, 1998). Body image dissatisfaction and dieting go hand in hand. "The effect of peer bullying and teasing for being overweight may also be a risk factor for disordered eating that can play a part in the development of a child's negative self-image and commitment to dieting" (Suisman, Bart, & Klump, 2008).

Signs of Eating Disorders in Young Children

The symptoms of eating disorders in children may be different from those in adults. Thus, the criteria for diagnosing children may also be different. In children, loss of control over eating may be a more important factor than eating an objectively large amount of food. Also, dieting may not be consistently associated with binge eating in children (Andersen, 2004b). Other signs include

- food seeking in the absence of hunger
- a sense of lack of control over eating
- food seeking in response to negative emotions,
- food seeking as reward
- sneaking or hiding of food (Andersen, 2004b).

Children may not have the facility to verbally express distress concerning body shape and self-perception but may instead experience and describe somatic symptoms, such as abdominal pain or discomfort or feelings of fullness, nausea, or loss of appetite. Individuals with childhood gastrointestinal complaints and other risk factors have been found to be at greater risk of developing a more severe eating disorder at an earlier age (Gendall, Joyce, Carter, McIntosh, & Bulik, 2005). (Clinicians need to rule out gastroenterological and other functional problems of the body before reaching a diagnosis of anorexia.)

Play Therapy

To enter the child's immediate and intimate space (of play), therapists must be willing to abandon their logical, linear, and verbal modes of thought and expression; within the forgotten world of childhood—immediate and spontaneous and as immersed in the here and now as it is—resides a kind of mindfulness training for our adult minds (Germer et al., 2005). "The mindful practice alternative, with its non-judgmental acceptance, creates a necessary atmosphere of emotional safety in the therapy room, enhancing nonverbal awareness in children. Most of life experience involves deep, preconceptual and preverbal (child-like) awareness; we learn to abide calmly in that domain during mindfulness practice which counters the adult tendency to foreclose a child's experience by offering verbal explanations or solutions" (Germer et al., 2005).

Because children tend to be less verbal and in many cases less capable of personal insight, play therapy can increase familiarity and trust in the practitioner and process. Most significantly, it uncovers and speaks to the child's underlying issues via metaphor, within a context that the child is most capable of understanding and integrating. Play therapy can be an important element in a treatment situation where a child is resistant to healing and to attending sessions. I have used play therapy successfully to capture the child's interest and trust initially, preparing the stage for bringing up the issues that need to be discussed. During a session with a 10-year-old withdrawn child with anorexia, a card drawn in the board game called *The Talking, Feeling, and Doing Game* (Gardiner, 1973) helped her to express a part of herself that had been beyond her conscious awareness. The card read, "You found a bottle with a note in it on the seashore. What did the note say?" The child replied, "I am hidden under the sand; you will never find me," revealing her sense of being invisible, unheard, disconnected, and unreachable at home and at school, with peers and family alike. The discussion took us into productive tangents that stimulated the client's personal growth, trust in herself, and trust in the change process. My own personal responses to my own cards allowed me to model awareness of feelings and honesty in confronting otherwise uncomfortable situations, thereby developing trust and familiarity with the child.

Case Study

The mother of R, an eight-year-old boy, was worried about a change in his eating habits and called me for consultation. In describing her son, she said he had "a healthy appetite, loved to eat, and did not appear depressed, but he would eat dessert only after trying to defecate first. He had several small bowel movements a day but wasn't vomiting or taking laxatives. Once in a while, he mentioned calories in foods and had asked to weigh himself twice. He weighed 70 pounds and was less than 5 feet tall, but he thought he weighed too much."

R first started talking about fat in foods after a nutrition class at school. R's mother observed that he was very much a "rule follower," taking things people say very much to heart. His parents thought the teacher's advice to avoid fats during this class triggered R's behavior. R's parents tried to talk with him, but he was defensive. They talked with his pediatrician, but she was uncertain how to address the problem. R's parents wanted to correct any misperceptions as soon as possible, without blowing things out of proportion.

I agreed with R's mother that vigilance at this point could prevent a clinical eating disorder in her son. His condition could not yet be considered a clinical eating disorder, because he continued to eat nutritious foods in the form of healthy meals and did not use laxatives or other substances or engage in self-destructive behaviors such as purging. But a change in eating patterns, such as restricting sweets, could be significant. In addition, his concern about fats in food could indicate a fixation on fat as leading to an overweight state, and he might have been using toileting as a purging device. Most importantly, his temperament, which included inflexible rule following and food rituals, seemed to lean toward compulsivity.

I suggested that R's mother seek to positively influence her son with an intentional and directed course of action as prescribed by an eating disorder therapist who could educate him about healthy eating, discuss his understanding of why things were changing, what his concerns might be, and so on. In addition, the plan might include their consulting a nutritionist; R needed to understand that fats are essential for his brain development and healthy body functioning and that dieting and food restriction are the least efficient way to lose weight.

I encouraged R's mother to stay alert to possible changes in any other of her son's life spheres, to seek help for herself, and to attend therapy sessions with R to facilitate her dialogue with him and help reduce his anxiety.

Picky Eating Syndrome

Of the hundreds of e-mails I receive every week through my website www.empoweredparents.com, a large percentage come from parents of infants, toddlers, and latency-age children who are picky eaters. These parents have been unable to find help (or diagnosis) for their children, as the vast majority of therapists, pediatricians, and nutritionists are unacquainted with these conditions and incapable of making accurate diagnoses or referrals. Parents who fail to obtain the information they seek from the child's pediatrician are likely to turn to an eating disorder practitioner. In fact, some picky eaters are treated in eating disorder units in hospitals, an inappropriate milieu, as picky eating behaviors are not associated with the distorted body image, fear of eating fat or becoming fat, or identity issues that characterize clinical eating disorders.

The few academic texts that deal with childhood eating disorders offer only a few pages on what is known as selective eating, (also known as picky eating) but the bottom line is that these widely occurring problems remain unrecognized, confusing in their nomenclature, and virtually ignored by the professional community. The current medical model stance in response to picky eating is that these behavioral patterns do not signify pathology as long as the child's weight remains in the realm of normal on the weight charts and if the child continues to grow and function normally. Pediatricians invariably tell parents that these problems represent a passing phase that the child will outgrow and that parents are "not to be concerned." In failing to recognize eating and feeding problems for what they are, early on, physicians enable these problems by failing to direct and refer parents to early and effective prevention and care.

In fact, these conditions are of tremendous concern; children who fail to take in important nutrients cannot mature normally and suffer stunted growth, poor bone development, and functional problems. Without proper nutrition, the brain and heart will ultimately be affected, along with all of the vital organs. Picky eating behaviors limit taste preferences, precluding the development of a healthy eating lifestyle. Picky eaters are intolerant of new foods and sensations, and they may also have difficulty adapting to novelty and change in other life spheres.

The following are signs of picky eating:

- Picky eaters have a severely limited food repertoire; many will only eat pasta and white foods, peanut butter, hot dogs, chicken nuggets, pizza, and sugary soft drinks. When a child only eats foods from one category or only a few foods in each category, he or she is considered a picky eater.
- Parents of picky eaters, assuming it is normal for kids to have restricted palates, typically tend to reduce the variety of foods offered, exacerbating the problem.
- What differentiates benign food preferences from these compulsions is the *extreme* nature of picky eating behaviors, which preclude a healthy eating lifestyle. Picky eaters rarely eat more than 30 foods. Normal preferences do not interfere with one's intake of a healthy balanced and well-rounded diet.
- Picky eating children tend to be underweight, but because of erratic and unbalanced eating behaviors and damage to the metabolism, they tend to become overweight adults.
- Picky eaters often display symptoms of obsessive–compulsive anxiety disorder.

Families with picky eaters may experience crisis at mealtimes, which puts undue stress on marriages and siblings. The picky eater may become conditioned to using food as a device to attract attention and exert control, in some cases providing distractions from other more relevant or highly volatile issues within the family system. Siblings often fail to learn healthy eating patterns as a result of deregulated meals. Many picky eaters, frail and underdeveloped, find themselves the butt of peer ridicule, unable to enjoy normal socialization because of their limited capacity to eat what, when, and where others are eating. The child feels like a pariah, pushed, controlled, criticized, frightened, and misunderstood. Picky eating syndrome may transform into clinical eating disorders in individuals with a genetic susceptibility.

A 10-year-old picky eater began life as a colicky child who could not be soothed and who never smiled and did not sleep. She fought nursing, refusing to attach to the breast, and was uncomfortable being embraced or touched. She would eat only "white foods"—pasta, rice, bread, pizza, french fries, and chicken nuggets—and was highly discerning of textural differences in foods. To this day, she is not comfortable with change of any kind; she may eventually be diagnosed with a nonverbal learning disability or some form of autistic spectrum problem.

It is a commonly held notion that if children are hungry enough, they will eat and that children will not intentionally starve themselves. Although this theory may be true for 96 percent of children, it does not apply to the 4 percent of kids with feeding problems who are, in fact, capable of inadvertently starving themselves. Dr. Kay Toomey, one of the nation's leading specialists in treating problem feeders, refuted the idea that eating is completely instinctual:

> Instincts only start the process, and only then if they are not interfered with by premature birth or a physical disorder. Eating is, in reality, a learned behavior. Just as children learn to eat, so children can be taught to not eat by the circumstances of their lives. (Natenshon, 2005)

FEEDING DISORDERS

Feeding problems often occur with children who are developmentally disabled. Parents of children with autistic spectrum disorders commonly report that their children have feeding problems. With the rise in the incidence of autism today, feeding problems are also on the increase (Ledford & Gast, 2006). Feeding disorders describe conditions where the child is unable or refuses to eat or has physical difficulty eating, which can result in failure to grow and even death. This childhood eating disorder is not to be confused with eating disorders, such as anorexia or bulimia. Feeding disorders include food refusal, taking too long to eat, choking, gagging, vomiting when eating, real or imagined difficulty swallowing, inappropriate mealtime behavior, and picky eating according to food type and texture. To varying degrees, picky eaters and children with feeding disorders experience similar physical effects, but these effects are more severe and noticeable in children with feeding disorders, particularly at younger ages (Penn State Hershey, Milton S. Hershey Medical Center, 2008).

On a spectrum of severity, picky eaters tolerate new foods on the plate, usually will touch or taste a new food, and will eat at least one food from most food texture groups. Children with feeding disorders, however, will cry and act out when presented with new foods, refusing entire categories of food textures. These distinctions remain unrecognized by or inconsequential to most pediatricians, who typically assume that problems of childhood eating that do not adversely affect weight, be they feeding problems or picky eating syndrome, represent benign preference or immaturity to be outgrown, and require no early interventions. Parents of children with feeding disorders often discover that what they assumed to be a child's benign food preferences becomes an enormous and intractable impairment in a child's and family's existence. Children with feeding disorders (as well as picky eaters to a lesser degree) tend to demonstrate clusters of traits that indicate a broader, more pervasive, neurologically based dysfunction, such as sensory integration disorder, Asperger syndrome, nonverbal learning disability, or pervasive developmental disorder. A study investigating the contribution of genetics and environment to childhood neophobia (fear of trying a new food) reported that this characteristic is 78 percent genetic and 22 percent environmental (Severson, 2007). Feeding disorders occur within a reported incidence of between 25 percent and 35 percent in normal children. The more severe feeding problems are observed in 40 percent to 70 percent of infants born prematurely (and were intubated) or children with chronic medical conditions (Rudolph & Link, 2002). The latter problems do not sort themselves out through development; if not treated, they are certain to result in nutritional, interpersonal, behavioral, and developmental effects, altering the sense of self and self-esteem, family relations, and sociability, as well as academic and professional performance.

Children with feeding disorders typically demonstrate tactile and oral defensiveness and an overactive gag reflex and experience hypersensitivity to certain or all senses, such as discomfort with bright lights and loud noises. One youngster was so sensitive to noise that she could not tolerate the sound of her feces hitting the bowl during potty training. Some children cannot tolerate being touched by another person or by certain types of fabrics. Others feel discomfort with textural variations in the mouth and on the tongue, the temperature and feel of various foods, or the sound of crunchy foods between the teeth. The smell of spicy foods may trigger the gag reflex, indicating sensory integration problems.

For children with childhood feeding disorders, food smells, textures, and feeding can literally "hurt," and no amount of hunger will overcome that fact. Through their efforts to protect themselves from this pain, eventually the appetite becomes suppressed, and in time, such children no longer respond correctly to appetite as a cue to eat. Innately sensitive taste buds help explain why some children are so staunchly opposed to eating vegetables. Scientists have identified a gene, dubbed TAS2R38, that controls a receptor for bitter flavors. Children with certain variations of that gene are particularly sensitive tasters. One of my clients who was a picky-eating child and who became a picky-eating-adult–turned bulimic reports "a metallic taste in her mouth" from eating most vegetables, another reflection of the genetic and chemical basis of these problems. Early diagnosis and treatment benefit children with feeding disorders and picky eaters by taking advantage of the highly plastic brain which is so characteristic of the early years. Without a proper diagnosis and treatment, feeding problems, along with their related disorders, cannot be adequately treated and will not be outgrown.

Signs of early childhood feeding disorders include the following:

- ongoing poor weight gain
- gagging during meals
- history of eating and breathing coordination problems (which might cause problems with nursing)
- inability to transition to baby food purees by 10 months
- inability to transition to baby food solids by 12 months of age
- inability to transition from breast or bottle to a cup by 16 months of age
- crying and arching the back and neck at meals
- food smell and texture intolerance
- parental history of an eating disorder
- in older children, chewing and spitting, pica, counting calories, inappropriate vegetarianism, fear foods, water loading, excessive gum chewing.

In seeking a diagnosis, it is critical first to investigate organic digestive problems such as gastroesophageal reflux disease, gastric emptying delays, or dysphagia (difficulty in performing the mechanics of swallowing) that could lie at the root of the feeding problems. Parents need help to discern whether their child may have food allergies or oral motor skill problems that act as feeding deterrents.

Without a comprehensive diagnosis, feeding problems and the full spectrum of their related disorders cannot be adequately understood or treated. Parents will tend to get blamed for their child's "headstrong" behaviors, and children will be scolded and punished; schools will not offer the feeding disordered child the special attention or accommodation she requires, failing to see the correlation between a child's capacity to be well nourished and his or her capacity to learn.

Through the decades, a handful of parents have approached me for consultation about Prader–Willi syndrome, a very rare genetic disorder. This syndrome is frequently associated with feeding problems and poor weight gain in infancy; extreme hunger, overeating, and obsession with food after infancy; there is extensive weight gain between one and six years of age, ultimately leading to morbid obesity. Medication and diet supervision can help control this condition.

ORIGINS OF EARLY CHILDHOOD EATING DISORDERS AND DYSFUNCTIONS

Like eating disorders in adults, eating dysfunctions in children originate in nature as well as nurture, with genetically based traits and propensities carried in the DNA (nature). These conditions can also result from physiological conditions such as cystic fibrosis, cerebral palsy, autistic spectrum disorders, low muscle tone, sensory integration disorders, allergies, early intubation, and genetic disorders.

Environmental factors (nurture) may include a parent's own unresolved eating problems and finicky practices in handling, cooking, and eating foods with the family. By not offering a full complement of nutritious foods, parents forfeit the opportunity to develop healthy taste and textual preferences in their children during the most critical developmental years. Children with parents who have difficulty setting appropriate limits for the child may learn to use eating behaviors as manipulations. There is even evidence that maternal eating habits during pregnancy may affect the fetus, as "the presence or absence of different hormones at different times changes the way the brain gets wired up" (Judson, 2008).

TREATMENT ISSUES

When feeding disorders go undiagnosed, they are typically considered willful opposition or obstinacy. Problems of the central nervous system are hardly benign quirks. The professional team needs to be integrative to meet the needs of the whole child as well as the family. Diverse team disciplines may include occupational therapists, speech therapists, psychotherapists, pediatricians, and in the best of all worlds, even a Feldenkrais method or Anat Baniel method practitioner, as well as a gastroenterologist. A behavioral orientation may be helpful in handling these cases, although research shows that only 12 percent of feeding disorders are purely behavioral in nature (Fraker, Walbert, Cox, Fishbein, & Barker, 2007).

Some teams make home visits around mealtimes to better assess and treat the family dynamics around eating.

Parental Involvement in the Treatment of Young Children

The younger the child with an eating dysfunction, the greater the need for active parental intervention and involvement. Because responsibility for participation in the day-to-day process of bringing about change in a child's eating lifestyle falls largely to parents, residential placements separating children from parents should be avoided for young children at all costs. In fact, when possible, recovery for children of all ages (but particularly for very young children) is best achieved within the context of outpatient treatment—at home, and in the context of family and natural course of daily living. Box 7.1 summarizes the role of parents in treating eating dysfunctions.

Parents require assistance to fulfill their role in addressing their child's eating disorder diagnosis. Most parents become their child's diagnostician by default, unprepared as they are to assume this responsibility, and it is for them to handle the ongoing daily trauma for the child vis-à-vis food and eating. Enlightened parents are clearly the young child's greatest asset in making an empowered recovery.

BOX 7.1

Parents' Role in Treatment of Children with Eating and Feeding Disorders

- Parents require the advice and counsel of the child's therapist simultaneously with the child's exposure to treatment. Knowledgeable parents facilitate the child's capacity and readiness to engage in treatment and to heal, avoiding regressions that could lead to premature treatment termination. Parents have a great deal to give and a lot to learn.
- Those who seem unconcerned because their child is not yet "dangerously thin" need to understand that their child is "dangerously restricting food."
- Parents need to understand that though it is commendable that an anorexic child eats a full and balanced dinner, healthy meal needs to be surrounded by other healthy meals, preceding and subsequent to it, on a regular basis, every single day to learn a healthy eating lifestyle.
- Parents need help to recognize and speak to what they see, feel, and know, even if at times painful, and to speak the language of truth, which is the language of support and recovery.
- Parents' feelings are inviolate, valid, and irrefutable, simply because they exist. Feelings need to be shared as vessels of learning and support. Parents need to confront their own feelings in preparation to confront their child's. Parents need to stand together as a united front to enforce compliance, out of love. Honest confrontation is as loving a form of connection as a hug or a compliment.

Clinicians need to recognize the enormity of the parent's responsibility and support the courage and fortitude it takes for parents to confront the eating or feeding disorder as well as their struggling child. One mother describes "crying all the time," arguing with her husband about what to do in response, and feeling guilt that she cannot fix the problem, as he expects her to. Parents need guidance from the referring practitioner in order to know how and what to observe, how to find an effective treatment team, what information and questions to bring to the treatment situation, and how best to support their child (and themselves) in sustaining the recovery process at home. The treatment team should applaud what parents provide appropriate interventions, suggest alternatives when they are at a loss, and steel them when they need strength to stay firm. If a child enters an inpatient facility, outpatient team members act as liaisons and facilitators, helping parents improve communications with their child's (inpatient) milieu staff when necessary.

Though genetic and neurologically based problems may not be preventable, they can be ameliorated by enlightened parents or exacerbated by parents who are not "with the program." Secondary prevention comes in the form of a response to behaviors within a child's environment designed to turn an existing problem around. The culture of the family with regard to cooking and eating can do a great deal to contribute to a healthy eating lifestyle of any child. Parents' presence by itself at dinnertime appears to influence their children's eating habits for the better; "The less often kids have dinner with their families, the less nutritiously they eat" ("Family dinners," 2000). Less than 50 percent of parents eat dinner on a daily basis with their children ("Family dinners," 2000). Practically speaking, the time and energy it takes to plan, shop, cook, serve, and clean up after meals is an increasingly rare commodity. Parents work, and children are busy with organized sports, music lessons, and many other activities. But mealtimes need to become a priority if children are to become healthy eaters. Mealtimes offer children a connection to loved ones and a time for sharing and being nurtured, as well as a start to developing a truly healthy relationship with food. A client with anorexia found it insulting that her mother did not set a place for her at the Thanksgiving table, though she had consistently refused to join her family at meals. She admitted to needing and wanting prodding and limit setting from her mother about joining the family, which to her would feel like love and provide a sense of relief.

A young couple and their 20-month-old toddler were invited to dinner by a friend who inquired as to what kind of food their child would eat. The mother answered that he would eat a smaller quantity of whatever the adults were eating. "No, really—what can I make for him?" the friend continued. A little surprised, this mother assured the hostess that that is what he eats and not to prepare anything special for him. The toddler ate a wonderful dinner that night of soup and salad, herbal chicken with a wine and garlic sauce, cooked greens, and fruit. The hostess's own child missed out on this delicious meal, eating chicken fingers and frozen peas defrosted in the microwave oven.

"Kid-friendly" restaurant menus reinforce a child's limited palette and the belief that kids eat differently from adults. Child menus offer peanut butter and jelly sandwiches, chicken nuggets, macaroni and cheese, hamburgers, hot dogs, french fries, chips and cookies, and juice boxes. Many of the parents of children who eat these foods are highly health aware and committed to healthy eating and workout regimens for themselves. By feeding children the same limited foods over and over again, parents may inadvertently trigger a possible susceptibility to eating dysfunction. Children need to be exposed to a wide variety of different tastes and oral textures by the time they are two years old in order to become and remain open to developing a taste for good food throughout their lives.

Professional Treatment Techniques

An occupational therapist with expertise in feeding disorders used her creativity to make food attractive to youngsters—for example, by placing white bread in a rabbit mold, then adding peanut butter and raisins to create the bunny's face and ears. A therapist treating a child with an eating disorder increased the child's exposure to condiments, sauces, and spreads by using them as "finger paints" for art projects, easing his fears (Fraker et al., 2007). Techniques for stimulating and exercising the tongue diminish the gag reflex. The side of the tongue, rather than the tip, is less sensitive to strange new tastes and provides the best place to introduce new foods. The Feldenkrais and Anat Baniel Methods in particular offer specific training for tongue-use facilitation.

Food chaining (Fraker et al., 2007) is a therapy developed to treat children who have or are at risk to develop a feeding disorder or picky eating. The technique involves identifying nutritious foods the child is willing to eat and making slight modifications to those foods by gradually adding new ingredients, resulting in an expanding "chain" of foods the child will eat (Fraker et al., 2007). For example, if pizza is an accepted food, it can be used to gradually start a chain of changes that might include putting cheese mozzarella cheese on a slice of bread and finally, dipping it in tomato sauce.

The Anat Baniel Method for Children, based on the work of Moshe Feldenkrais, can be used to treat problem feeders. Well adapted for work with the very young, the work is movement based and nonverbal, bypassing a reliance on language to facilitate learning. Children engage in play and pleasurable movement in one-on-one work with a skilled practitioner (Baniel, 2009). This mind–body approach to treatment reorganizes and integrates the central nervous system, creating new sensory pathways and increased receptivity to change in malleable young brains.

WHEN PICKY EATING EXTENDS BEYOND CHILDHOOD AND ADOLESCENCE

Picky eating children who are untreated grow up to be picky eating adults. Many picky eating children with sensory integration disorder become increasingly selective about what they eat as they grow and mature. Picky eating adults, suffer as their eating problems interfere with professional and personal lives. The fear of food and a reluctance to try new foods generalizes to a fear of experiencing change and uncertainty in life and taking risks in other spheres of life. Options of all kinds become limited to the picky eater, making problem solving and judgment ineffective. Many find themselves isolated socially, rejected by potential life partners because of rigidity that precludes normal dating and professional socialization around food. Rather than challenging themselves to experience risk and deal with it, picky eaters choose to avoid risk altogether. Manipulating one's environment in lieu of making emotional demands on the self for coping is a modus operandi that picky eaters share with individuals who have anorexia. A helpful resource for picky eating adults is the website www.pickyeatingadults.com, which offers an active and supportive listserv and blog.

CONCLUSION

The role of the eating disorder therapist in the face of feeding and picky eating disorders is pivotal, though limited. As the diagnostician most likely to come face to face with these problems, the eating disorder therapist needs to be familiar with these diseases, what they are, and how they must be treated. The eating disorder practitioner's role is to provide individual and family consultation and make appropriate referrals for treatment of the eating and feeding disorders, as well as behavioral therapy for anxiety reduction and desensitization, if needed.

CONSULTATION/COACHING TIPS FOR PARENTS OF PICKY EATERS

- Parents are wise to use nutritional supplements and daily vitamins to achieve maximum nutritional balance.
- Parents benefit from learning that appropriate, healthy food choices including all the food groups need to be offered at mealtimes, limiting snacking until the child learns to eat at meals. Keep expectations realistic.
- Turn off the TV to make mealtimes a calming, sociable time; families need to eat together and talk together at mealtime, without threatening the child or forcing foods.
- Reoffer new foods that the reluctant child initially refuses. It takes an average of 10 exposures to a new food, paired with positive reinforcement, before a child will consistently accept the food (Fraker et al. 2007).
- Parents need to be reminded that it is their responsibility to cook for their child. Therapists need to investigate what parents eat and whether parents know how to cook. If not, parents need to learn and to consider changing their own eating patterns.

SECTION 3

TAPPING TREATMENT RESOURCES

8

The Therapist's Unique Use
of Self in Treatment

The difference between good and bad mothers [and practitioners] *is not in the commission of errors, it is in what they do with them.*
—D. W. Winnicott

W hat goes on, face to face, in the context of the healing dynamics that make up the 45-minute treatment hour? This chapter spotlights unique aspects of eating disorder care in light of the unique requirements of the therapist's use of self.

HEALING HAPPENS EYE TO EYE, SOUL TO SOUL

Clearly, the most challenging task in approaching the writing of this book has been to capture the essence of what needs to happen within the thousands of sessions that heal hundreds of clients throughout tens of thousands of unique moments in time. Because eating disorders are relationship-based disorders, a fully evolved and versatile therapeutic connection between the therapist and client ultimately becomes the medium through which the professional transmits the integration of his or her knowledge, acumen, technical skills, and personhood and through which the client gains access to her own authentic self to resolve problems, build self-trust, and heal. The healthy treatment relationship becomes the prototype for all other healthy relationships.

The impact of the treatment relationship has been, and will continue to be, discussed in many contexts throughout this book. Both clinical and empirical research indicates the crucial importance of the treatment relationship within the context of skilled case management, with a recent shift from a neutral, analytic style of psychotherapy to more intersubjective, relational approaches. Studies have found that "most forms of treatment work as well as most other forms of treatment; the model of therapy simply does not make much difference in therapy outcome" (Germer et al., 2005, p. 56). In addition, empathy may be even more influential in intervention-based treatment than in relational-based therapy. It might be said that the therapis–client relationship *is* the treatment (Germer et al., 2005).

> Given that there is little empirical evidence that (treatment) effectiveness improves with experience, continuing education, licensing, professional degree, clinical supervision, or any other marker of professionalism, and given the importance of the therapeutic relationship, the larger challenge is to find a way to help cultivate the qualities of excellent therapists. (Germer et al., 2005, p. 57)

How fortunate we are to refer to psychotherapy, the art and act of mindful connection to self and other, as our "work." Offering the very best of what it means to be quintessentially human, the mindful connection integrates and overrides (but does not exclude) treatment skills.

MAKING MINDFUL TREATMENT CONNECTIONS

"Accurate empathy involves skillful reflective listening that clarifies and amplifies the client's own experiencing and meaning without imposing the therapist's own material" (Miller & Rollnick, 1991, p. 5). Even the best therapist can remain mindful only intermittently; therapists' minds are absorbed in associations that at times provide meaningful clues to what is occurring during the session (Germer et al., 2005). "As the therapist learns to identify and disentangle his or own thoughts and feelings, the client may discover the same skills" (Germer et al., 2005 p. 12). Sharing a common ground, therapist and client experience and discover each other from a position of equality.

> The treatment relationship has been called an intervention itself, rather than a context or support for therapeutic work. . . . The intention of therapy is to work through the effects of isolation and disconnection, as they play out in life and in therapy, toward the goal of reconnection and restoration of mutual connection; this results in a greater capacity to act, increased clarity, enhanced self-worth, and the desire for more connection, while remaining present and accessible in his or her shared humanity. (Germer et al., 2005, pp. 92–93)

Mindfulness may well be the essential ingredient that explains why and how dissimilar forms of psychotherapy work. Mindfulness training may prove to become a tangible and eminently teachable means for building empirically supported relationship skills, offering the potential to bridge the clinician–researcher gap (Germer et al., 2005, p. 4).

EATING DISORDER TREATMENT IS A LABOR OF LOVE

It takes a strong therapist to persevere in treating an eating disorder. The concept of strength is not in power, as we know it, but instead in flexibility and in openness in the use of self—in other words, in one's own mature emotional development. We cannot offer our clients a critical understanding of themselves without having first mastered a critical understanding of ourselves. Perhaps the most critical capacity in approaching clients with eating disorders is curiosity and facility in discovering parts of herself that she can connect with and learn to love.

The therapist needs to approach the client with humility and acceptance of her own life as she experiences it, with an eagerness to meet the client at the place "where she is at" at any given moment. It is from that place that the therapist and client join and discover a way forward together. Therapists need to learn from their clients as their clients strive to learn from them. It is this constant learning that makes this work so exciting; it is the courage to keep on learning that makes this work so challenging.

In 40 years of practice, I can recall few clients whom I did not actively enjoy working with, for a variety of reasons. I find myself feeling energized, invigorated, and whole after a full day of work, in spite of the reputation of this client population and their families as sources of professional burnout. I enormously admire and respect my clients' intelligence, perseverance, and drive toward excellence (in disease if not in recovery); for the humanness of their frailties; and for their passionate, fearless commitment to a cause, misguided as this one may be. I delight in working with bright and loving families (most are) and in entering family systems to facilitate change within them.

THE TREATMENT PROCESS FROM THE CLIENT'S PERSPECTIVE

Between 20 percent and 57 percent of clients do not return after their initial session with a generalist psychotherapist, and another 37 percent to 45 percent attend therapy only twice (April & Nicholas, 1996). The fact that most therapists have no idea why clients terminate is testimony to why and how clients lose confidence in the therapist's ability and feel uncomfortable in talking with their therapist. Learning to engage and motivate clients with eating disorders is the first and most important relational task of the eating disorder practitioner. The client needs to feel understood and "felt," first and foremost.

During the 20-year history of her bulimia, M worked with four separate therapists before beginning work with me. She described three of these therapy experiences as "a bust." The first two dealt with emotional and relationship issues solely, offering no assistance with and for the behaviors and compulsions of the eating disorder. Neither practitioner had "a clue as to what to do about the disorder," she explained. The third, a behavioral therapist, instructed me to "purge until I exhausted myself in an effort to expose and then extinguish the urges, thus breaking the habit." Fortunately, the fourth and most effective therapist addressed the eating disorder directly, "helping me consider the role food plays in my life as a tool for understanding myself better. This practitioner welcomed discussions about this client's distorted body image, offering cognitive and behavioral guidelines from week to week and making demands in an effort to effect change. Like money in the bank, the work of this therapist became the foundation of the timely progress the client would accomplish in her work with me years later.

What does it take to become competent as an eating disorder therapist? An inverse correlation has been found between therapist experience and dropout rates (Mahaffey & Granello, 2007). Skill and professional experience ("treatment mileage") in accruing know-how must be accompanied by the courage and confidence to execute, augment, bend and be creative in using it. Practitioners who treat eating disorders need to be made of special stuff; like the fruit of a cactus plant, they need to be at once tough and sweet—and always highly resilient.

The eating disorder practitioner needs to be a jack-of-all-trades and, to some degree, a master of all. Mastering this work is an intensively integrative process. Driving a racecar is an apt metaphor for therapy. Anybody who knows how to drive a car can get into a quality racecar and drive it, but not every driver can achieve an optimal level of performance from even the finest automobile. What separates the average racer from a talented racer are the same qualities that separate the underskilled and the masterful eating disorder practitioner. Efficacy lies in the performer's capacity to integrate skill with resources, intuition with reflexes, and a spontaneous responsiveness with the demands of the moment. Over the years, I have enjoyed observing my husband's friend and partner in racing vintage automobiles, a task far more complex than it might first appear. This driver is endowed not only with skills but with the capacity and commitment to augment and optimize them.

- *Skill development:* As a highly functioning athlete, he is in superb physical and mental shape to operate a vehicle that has likewise been readied for optimal performance.
- *Experience:* He has had diverse, related personal experiences that have provided skill development behind the wheel—for example, as a past national champion motorcycle racer and the driver of a schoolbus (which he parallel parks "just for the fun of it").
- *The capacity to use resources:* He can repair a car and tune it to various track conditions with as much facility as he can drive one, and he seeks out the services of teams of automotive experts for consultation on upkeep and repairs.
- *The capacity to take charge:* Although his timing and reflexes are exquisitely developed, there has never been a racecourse that he has not walked before the actual race; by creating mind maps that offer an element of control and predictability, he methodically readies himself to handle the less predictable risks and hazards of every moment of the race.
- *Flexibility and responsiveness:* Alert to changes in weather, course conditions, and competing drivers, he remains responsive to the perpetual feedback loop

that exists between car, driver, and environment, fine-tuning adjustments to optimize the performance of his car throughout the course of the race.

Recovery from an eating disorder is a unique race of its own. Therapist, clients, and families join forces to overtake a forward-driving disease that is never at rest, ultimately to leave it in the dust. Recovery from an eating disorder is a race against time and loss—of the client's health, relationships, emotional and personal development, life quality, and sometimes life itself. The race with an eating disorder is a race that must be won.

SIX BASIC TENETS OF USING THE SELF IN APPLYING TREATMENT PRINCIPLES

The acronym VIABLE provides a model for the therapist's use of self in eating disorder treatment: The practitioner needs to be Versatile, Integrative, Action oriented, outcome Based, Loving, and Educative. This acronym summarizes the qualities that set this work apart from other therapies and that distinguish the eating disorder practitioner from generalist practitioners.

Versatile Use of Self

A versatile and emotionally flexible personality is a fully differentiated and integrated personality. In recovery from an eating disorder, clients learn versatility in functioning, adapting, and adjusting to the demands of life. Practitioners seek to encourage in their clients the same emotional differentiation and integration that enhances their own emotional and mental agility, as well as their comfort in taking therapeutic risks and in handling the ambiguity and unpredictability so characteristic of this recovery. Moshe Feldenkrais defined emotional maturity as "emotional flexibility," which creates adaptive "response-ability," or the capacity and freedom to change directions with seamless agility (Feldenkrais, 1972). A lion after her prey moves in any direction with perfect integration of precision and agility. Likewise, the effective clinician needs the know-how, creativity, and capacity to use the self with a degree of flexibility that matches the unpredictable and fluid requirements of the therapeutic moment. Every treatment plan needs to be custom tailored and upgraded continually to match the ever-changing requirements of progress within each unique case.

As in life itself, approximation in eating disorder treatment takes the place of predictable prescription. Strict rule following does not lend itself to life in the real world. Author Anna Quindlen (2007) said it best: Life is messy; and its vagaries go down hardest with those who fool themselves into thinking they can keep it neat.

Clients learn through what clinicians say and, most significantly, through what they do in role modeling. A practitioner's inflexible need to follow rules by exerting rigid control not only will fail to meet the immediate needs of the client, but in so doing, will fail to model flexibility in coming up with realistic and workable coping solutions. For example, a therapist at an outpatient treatment center refused to see a client who was two pounds below the limit for "safe" weight, claiming that the client first needed to attend an inpatient or partial program for "complete" weight restoration. Although this client was motivated to begin recovery, she was left on her own either to find an inpatient hospital program, which she would not be able to afford, or to remain unsupported in her efforts to restore the weight required to qualify for outpatient care. She needed therapeutic support to refeed herself and floundered without any treatment at all. This professional's diagnostic assessment needed to take into account the client's readiness for recovery, her financial constraints, and her medical doctor's permission to proceed in outpatient care. A short-term weekly contract for weight gain would have been an appropriate and workable alternative.

Versatility in Confronting Ambiguity

Change is about learning. Learning is about the capacity to tolerate novelty and the unpredictability that is so distasteful to the anorexic individual. In that respect, change can be scary and exhausting. For the therapist, it takes courage to stand up to the disease process and to the rigors of eating disorder recovery. For the client, it takes courage to let go of the eating disorder, to adhere to a healthy eating food plan, to try, and to fail, all significant aspects of the learning process. It is through a generous sharing of self that the clinician lends his or her ego (as well as vulnerability). The therapist models the vision of strength as it exists alongside weakness, as therapist and client anticipate and prepare to meet the unknown side by side.

It also takes courage to confront the fairly constant fielding of manipulations, resistance, and denial that characterizes this treatment; to enter and alter a family system in crisis in the attempt to rectify imbalances for the moment and for perpetuity; and to stimulate emotional and behavioral options for clients and family in the form of learning. It takes courage for the practitioner to internalize diverse and free-floating emotions as the "lightning rod" that he or she is, remaining mindfully and subjectively open to the experience. It is the excitement of standing at the mountain's peak before skiing down into unknown challenges and feeling confident that you will figure out how to navigate that jagged slope as you go.

The husband of a bulimic woman chose his bride when she was in the throes of severe purging anorexia. Though he had little tolerance for her illness, he clearly enjoyed its fruits, and their implicit marital contract required that she remain thin to keep him happy (and to keep him at all). Their marriage counselor recognized this dynamic, though she chose not to deal with the eating disorder and its impact on their marriage in their sessions; instead, she confided her concerns separately to my client, admitting that she felt "intimidated by a certain power about your husband." By backing down and submitting to his will, this practitioner failed to realize one of the major tenets of therapy relationships: Although in many ways the therapy relationship mimics other personal relationships, the therapy relationship needs to be unique in offering something new and different within that relationship to promote change. By failing to muster the courage to stand up to the intimidating spouse, this therapist missed a poignant opportunity to impact my client's eating disorder recovery as well as her marital system.

To create "enlightened discomfort" in the client takes courage. Skilled eating disorder practitioners need to flex and bend through mutually coexisting polarities of leniency and limit setting, authoritative assertiveness and cutting slack, reality-based confrontation and self-esteem building. A client described our relationship as being a combination of "tough thought and warmth," referring to my respectful but relentless determination to face the "unmentionable."

It takes confidence and courage (as well as a resilient therapy relationship)

- to take on, welcome, interpret, and use the client's resistance as an invaluable treatment and learning tool
- to "make waves" within marital systems, potentially evoking anger that might be turned against you or the spouse
- to enter and influence family systems while remaining enough outside the system to keep boundaries clearly defined, well honed, and seamless
- to join with client and family in whatever emotional space they currently inhabit to follow one's instincts in deciding which treatment protocol to use, when, and with whom, to decisively change one's course of action at any moment
- to initiate and act on one's convictions and intentions, prepared to accept the client's rejection of a plan or interpretation in the knowledge that one may have planted a seed that will germinate in the future
- to confront the patient with non-negotiable limits and demands when it comes to her physical safety, despite her resistance and hostility.

If an interpretation of mine misses the mark, I encourage the client to try to find her own words to more precisely define the experience as she knows it. The best teaching for therapists occurs during the client's self-discovery. Professionals need the courage and curiosity to listen to client feedback that may be difficult to hear. This ability is particularly important in the field of eating disorders, as therapists model for clients and parents what it takes to listen effectively. The following example shows the value of encouraging parental self-expression, even when the message for the therapist may be critical, hurtful, or otherwise confrontational. As with all countertransference, self-awareness and honest intention are the therapist's parachute.

After a conjoint mother–daughter session for an 11-year-old girl with anorexia, the mother never called to schedule a second appointment. I contacted her and discovered her ambivalence about returning. She said, "You seemed tired during our session. You yawned twice." Here was my opportunity to listen, to educate, and to connect. I began my response by reinforcing the fact that her attention and concern were signs of proactive, committed parenting, foreshadowing constructive parental input and successful outcomes for the child. I offered to help guide her assessment of what she needed to look for in a therapist.

I asked, "What did my yawning say to you? Might you have thought I was disinterested? Didn't care?" I stated my intentions and goals for that session, speaking honestly to this mother about my observations about the session and how I envisioned the child's future goals. I applauded her attention to detail, curiosity, and assertiveness in demanding the best for her child. This conversation led to a trusting treatment relationship, in which I became a mentor to this anorexic mother.

Vulnerability is the benchmark of humanity. One's openness to hearing, learning, and accepting responsibility for oneself and one's own behaviors, foibles, and choices is the best and most poignant of all role modeling. Professionals, who are faced with emotional risk and challenges within the context of this treatment, must do what they counsel clients to do—to take control where they have it and then develop confidence in rolling with the rest of life's punches, relying on their own (and their clients') resourcefulness to pull solutions out of a hat. In exploring ambiguous moments, I typically say, "You know, you've just said a mouthful—so many things that we could talk about today. Where might be the best and most appropriate place for us to begin, in your opinion?" Or I might ask for clarification: "I'm not sure I fully understand what you are trying to convey. Tell me more." At difficult moments, "And what else beyond that?" models a message of courageous acceptance. By modeling the process of active listening—listening to hear and inform the client about her own underlying feelings—practitioners provide living proof that faults and failures are the raw material of learning, change, and breakthroughs. Professionals do with parents what parents need to learn to do with their children.

How we practice emerges out of who we are as people, how we live our lives, and what values and belief systems we espouse. To stay vulnerable is to stay real. Vulnerability requires transparency; admitting to our own shortcomings and mistakes not only models effective problem solving but also dispels the seduction of therapist idealization, challenging the brittle superego structure of clients with eating disorders, who long for perfection in others as they do in themselves. This approach also promotes healthier identification, engendering a sense of self-cohesion and separateness imperative to the healing process. Through appropriate and well-chosen personal sharing, professionals teach clients to learn from their mistakes and to remain a perpetual student in solving life's problems.

One of my young adult anorexic clients was an elementary school teacher in training. Highly rigid, perfectionistic, and uncompromising in her expectations and demands of herself, her responses to food, to life, and to her teaching were limited and without spontaneity. I recounted to her one of the most poignant learning experiences of my own life when, many years ago as a student teacher for a third-grade class, my supervisor came to school to observe and evaluate my accruing skills. I created a pristine lesson plan and executed it through conscientious preparation. The only element I had neglected to consider was the response of the students to the novelty of the supervisor's presence in the classroom and my own nervousness and distractibility in the face of the student's uncooperativeness. I plowed through the plan as constructed, teaching as though the children were listening and learning. My supervisor later advised me that a more effective lesson would have involved a more mindful attention to the requirements of the moment Her recommendation for that day was to ditch my initial lesson plan, focusing instead on having the children do structured board or desk work, as they were clearly unreceptive to more conceptual teaching and learning.

The versatile therapist offers the client a most reassuring life view—of "one foot in front of the other," of biting off small and manageable pieces as we move forward with the assurance that none of us is perfect, because as human beings we are not meant to be. Clients need to know that therapists live what they speak so that they can learn to do the same.

Integrative Style of Thinking and Functioning

Integrative disorders demand an integrative system of best practice approaches. Eating disorders demand an integrative perspective and the practitioner's capacity to multitask in thought and behavior. They require the integration of skills with instinct, of intention with flexibility, and of the demands of the treatment moment with the therapist's own personality as the therapist exercises varied roles in the context of varied treatment styles. Integrative multidisciplinary teams bring together traditional techniques with innovative 21st-century strategies.

As integrationists, therapists hold the big picture of disease and recovery even while attending to the small details of behavioral change that accrue to bring healing. With eating disorders, small changes are the stuff of vast transformation. Eating disorder therapists need to be myopic visionaries.

Integrative practitioners piece together the disparate facets of the client's personality to foster the re-creation of the client's true and authentic self. In uncovering, discovering, differentiating, reorganizing, and reintegrating all parts of the client's exiled self, disclosed and undisclosed, systematically and intentionally, the 1,000-piece puzzle of the client's holistic self slowly assembles itself through the recovery process. Integrative practitioners also play diverse roles in the lives of clients with eating disorders—as teacher, mentor, cheerleader, confidant, case manager, and "parent," in supporting and containing the client until the latter is ready for solo flight as an autonomous, independently functioning, self-determining, and problem-solving human being.

Eating disorders require an expansive peripheral perspective. Keeping all balls in the air, the practitioner juggles the potential options for care to match the needs, financial expectations, and other logistics of treatment requirements, facilitating the transition into and out of the available outpatient and inpatient milieu alternatives. An insular treatment perspective is simply not viable in treating eating disorders; overlapping spheres of dysfunction demand simultaneous attention from the full complement of specialists who comprise the treatment team.

As an example, the assessment and monitoring of psychopharmacological medications is typically considered to be the sole responsibility of the psychopharmacologist. Once a medication regimen is working consistently, the doctor generally assumes that it will remain effective and constant, and he or she will not see the client again unless the client initiates contact for prescription refills or re-evaluation. The client with an eating disorder in proactive care undergoes a great many changes that occur relatively quickly; the start of recovery and normalized food intake predictably marks increasing anxiety about the possibility of becoming fat. Because it is the therapist who has the most frequent and consistent access to the client and her changing needs, it becomes the responsibility of that clinician to recognize if and when the option for medication becomes appropriate and requires a referral, or when a re-evaluation of medication becomes appropriate and necessary.

The treachery of these disorders demands the therapist's constant vigilance in assessing the progress of both disease and recovery to avoid the worsening of pathology. Therapists need to hold the vision of wider goals, thinking globally even while acting locally to integrate available recovery resources that include families, collaborating team professionals, and milieus representing more restrictive and higher levels of care. The capacity to move freely within and among multiple levels of care becomes necessary when outpatient care renders recovery progress out of reach or when the client is in danger or at risk for self-harm. Using day programs and other restrictive intensive care facilities intermittently within the treatment process can "unstick" a stagnating recovery process, facilitate refeeding, improve and stabilize a worsening or at-risk orthostatic physiological condition, and support the cognitive and behavioral messages of the outpatient work.

Action-Oriented, Directive Treatment Style

With a moving target, you can't afford to take your hands off the wheel. Eating disorders wait for no one; diagnosis demands a call to action. In seeking and demanding changes, the eating disorder clinician moves and motivates people in an effort to move and motivate the healing process. The therapist redirects the forward momentum of a focused and forward-moving disease to the client's advantage into healing and sustaining the vision of possibility. Being directive is not synonymous with imposing control, judgments, projections, or intrusions on the client, which would replicate the role of the eating disorder. *Authoritative* is not synonymous with *authoritarian*. Soft power is always a preferred alternative. "So it is obvious that your husband is abusing you—you need to get a divorce" would be a less appropriate intervention than "Do you see how your husband is being abusive to you? Is this the way you would feel most comfortable living out the rest of your life? Do you see that there may be alternative solutions for you?"

As case manager, the therapist is the great connector, bringing personalities, needs, professional services, and support resources together and determining how, when, and why to use them all. The effective eating disorder clinician interprets the needs, requirements, and dynamics of the therapeutic moment to the client in an effort to promote change, the treatment process, and her reconnection to herself.

The physical health of a client with an eating disorder is potentially at risk throughout the entire journey to cure. Once a person is under a therapist's care, risk assessment and management is primarily up to the therapist. The team shares collective responsibility for the child's health with the medical doctor, who generally has limited access to the client and therefore limited opportunity to stay abreast of the changing status of disease. It is up to the team to be proactive in keeping the physician up to speed.

In an example of team partnership and effective care, a school social worker took it upon herself to contact the pediatrician before her anorexic student's physical examination, which would determine her eligibility to attend a three-day outdoor class retreat. Lab tests and weight would not tell the whole story for this doctor, who had not seen the child recently; the social worker described the recent history of this child's eating disorder, fainting, refusal to increase caloric intake, and parental resistance to bring her to medical care with appropriate frequency. This child would ultimately not be allowed to attend the retreat.

Action brings about learning and change. Eating disorder treatment demands change; change requires practitioner and client to take action through behaviors. E's treatment team decided to medicate her depression, then "wait to see what happens," hoping the eating would "pick up on its own." The extent of their demands was to make a suggestion that she add nutrition bars to her daily food regimen. Their advice to parents was, "Ask E, 'Do you want to eat something?' If she bristles, ask her to please try to eat more." Not surprisingly, the weight loss continued; these tentative treatment techniques did not inspire or require change.

Whether immediate or delayed, invisible to the naked eye, or clearly observable, change must be ongoing as part of a definitive action plan; if change of one sort or another is not happening, it is incumbent on the practitioner to seek and find it through another route. Though the journey may be varied and irregular, the destination must be clearly etched in the practitioner's mind. Interviewing techniques need to be purposeful and directive, leaving little leeway for random or nonspecific care. A young woman with bulimia began treatment with me during Thanksgiving break while she was home from college. On her return to school, she began therapy with a woman whom she described as "reluctant to probe" about her eating challenges, choosing instead to focus solely on emotional issues and things that occurred in the past.

> She would wait for me to bring up the eating, and of course I didn't, so not much got done. She's pretty passive . . . doesn't initiate discussions, doesn't offer feedback. I always know I can steer clear of discussing the eating disorder if I bring up my relationship with my boyfriend.

During our first session together during this young woman's four-week Christmas break, I set up a temporary food plan with her, referred her to a nutritionist, and set up preliminary plans for possible entry into a day program if she did not make significant progress within a week's time. Through family therapy, I renewed a dialogue between her and her family and referred her to a psychopharmacologist for a medication evaluation. I also expressed my excitement at noticing already significant changes in her behaviors since our work together during

Thanksgiving break. Her response to the infusion of energy into her care was to completely curtail her exercising for the first time in many years and to start integrating new challenge foods into her diet. Best of all, she began to eat three meals a day.

Therapists who are passive, nondirective, and more like a friend than a therapist dodge their responsibility to address the tough issues. By colluding with the client's denial and resistance, these therapists enable the disorder. Less weighty topics might be reserved for warm-up conversations, session openers, and breaking the ice, particularly with young child clients who may be ill at ease. Though it is important for the client to initiate the tenor and direction of the session on the basis of her current needs and issues, most discussions will ultimately lend themselves to a segue into behaviorally based "eating disorder housekeeping" tasks; that is, "So how is the eating going? What's "a typical 'eating day' like for you these days?" How were things different this week from weeks past? And how does it feel to have incorporated those changes? The client learns that there will be ongoing clear and realistic expectations for ongoing changes, that mindful awareness and accountability are both intrinsic parts of healing.

In seeking changes, the next biggest challenge for professionals is to learn to recognize, reframe, and celebrate change in all of its varied and disguised forms. Evidence of positive changes may be ephemeral or even take the form of regression. No matter, change is what we are after. J returned from college with a sad confession. She had begun to slide back into her purging patterns. "I'm a failure" was her conclusion, clear and simple. Her doctor and nutritionist had both read her the riot act. Her lesson from me was not about how to eat better or become more disciplined, but about how to become more assertive and forthcoming with her doctor and nutritionist to help them understand what seemed to me to be a benign and normal part of recovery. "So," I began, "Let's take a look at what *has* changed!" I helped her see that she had become more ready to be honest with herself and with others and more acutely aware of the precipitants to her regressions. Her digressions had become more contained; now isolated incidents, they no longer led to extended patterns of dysfunction. General problem solving in other life spheres had improved, as had her relationships with others. Increasingly aware of her needs and feelings, she was becoming assertive in communicating those needs within and outside of the treatment session. Eating disorder recovery is about personhood, as much as it is about stopping self-destructive behaviors.

Because change in eating disorder recovery is typically camouflaged, elusive, hard-to-read, and sometimes disguised as regression and failure, clinicians must be prepared to decipher the codes, recognizing them for what they are. All recovery changes deserve to be considered and applauded. Change making provides a foundation on which the client can build her own treatment mileage, confidence, and self-esteem.

Measures that evidence positive change include the following:

- increased willingness to attend sessions
- behavioral changes around eating and purging

- increasing honesty and openness in communication with others
- greater awareness and acceptance of self and feelings
- increased weight (in the case of food restrictors)
- healthier attitudes toward a healthy eating lifestyle
- increasing confidence.

The proactive practitioner is bound to encounter conflict, hostility, denial, anxiety, and other emotional landmines in taking risks that support change. Active professionals model the willingness to take risks by making tough demands, knowing when to back off, and never failing to build on the client's strengths.

When Change Occurs in the Wrong Direction

After years of a successful relationship that resulted in what I considered to be a 93 percent recovery of a client from anorexia (i.e., not healed enough), F dropped out of care and stayed away for 18 months. She returned seeking help when her weight, once again, began to seriously slip. She called it a relapse; I called it not having kept her nose to the grindstone long enough during her first recovery effort. At the time she terminated, she had restored most of her weight. She could not explain why she felt the need to terminate in the untimely way that she did: It was becoming increasingly clear that she could not face life without her eating disorder.

The odds seemed good that she would be able to regain her footing, having already accrued recovery mileage. Much to everyone's surprise, she was unable to catch herself and suffered a second severe bout of anorexia that would not be healed on an outpatient basis. Following an intervention session with her parents, during which it was determined that she would begin residential care within two weeks, she chose not to return to me for treatment care. If there is ever a choice about whether to take action to connect with clients, I always choose to do so. It remains her right not to reciprocate. I sent the following e-mail:

> I am thinking of you and hoping that you are not feeling abandoned by me or that I have sided with your parents against you. I want you to know that I deeply care about you and I am doing what I believe needs to happen now in insisting that you receive a more intense level of treatment. Please keep me in the loop and let me know how things proceed. You always know you are welcome to come here to talk anytime, day or night. Please contact me.

Readers might wonder where my boundaries are in reaching out and in making myself available "day and night." If a client of mine goes to the emergency room at 3:00 A.M., I want to be woken up to participate in any way that I can in emergency care. These instances will be few and far between, "boundaried" by the reality of circumstances. I am also aware that my caring for these clients is genuine enough to be in no way conditional. Having said that, if my availability were to be abused, it would become a therapeutic issue and withdrawn.

The Proactive Therapist Demands Pro-Action from the Patient

If I had to pinpoint one element that most separates the work of eating disor-der therapy from other psychologically based therapies, it would be the need within every psychotherapy session to keep the focus clearly on *behavioral* require-ments for flexibility and change for both therapist and client. During a family ses-sion, a teenager said to her parents, "Back off now . . . I know what has to be done, and I can do this on my own." My response to this proclamation was,

> Great! Can you tell your parents something about your plan of action to carry out your intentions? What might they look for and expect to see, and in what window of time? Do you have suggestions for them about how to conduct themselves regarding your disorder until your plans begin to bear fruit? And if your plan does not work as you envision it, have you thought about a backup plan? OK . . . so what are you planning to do differently between now and when you come in again this week?

In another instance, a client spoke of her ambivalence about picking up the phone to contact a nutritionist. After discussing the significance of this dynamic in session, I picked up the phone receiver and handed it to her. She felt relieved and grateful to have been given the push she required to set up that first appoint-ment. Eventually, the capacity to initiate such behaviors on her own would become second nature to her.

A 12-year-old declared, "I want to do this myself!" "I'm all for that plan," I replied. "In fact, you must do this [recovery] yourself. I am basically here as coach, cheerleader, and collaborator. So why not make a start according to your own plans this week, and let's talk next time about how things went."

In seeking to encourage experimentation with new behaviors, the therapist and patient together look forward to the time when the client can use self-directed initiative to achieve them. The following is an example of a youngster coming up with her own creative solutions as co-manager of her case. Z, a per-fectionist and compulsive anorexic teenager spent seven hours a night doing homework because of her compulsion to rewrite all her class notes in the tiniest, most painstaking, and most perfect lettering possible. This compulsion, along with after-school soccer practice and games, allowed for no more than five to six hours of sleep a night. Z ultimately left the soccer team and came up with her own creative solution to the problem of her compulsive note copying: She would ask her teachers to demand that her writing get bigger and freer, or else they should "give her a bad grade."

Action Through Intention and Role Modeling

Intentional and purposeful clinicians are those who can anticipate what hap-pens next so as to be best prepared to field the inevitable curveballs of eating dis-order recovery. Therapists need to do whatever it takes to bring their clients through the race against disease and time and over the finish line to cure. The use of self needs always to be intentional; therapists need to know why they have cho-sen a certain course of action and what they hope will come of it. In sharing their intention with their clients, therapists inspire trust in the process and model problem solving and decision making. In some cases, intention might involve initiating action; in others, when clients need to learn to exercise self-determination, it might involve withholding action. Like parents with their children, professionals need to determine when it is appropriate to remind a client of what she already knows, and when certain things are better left unsaid in the interest of allowing the recovering child to rely on her own newly developing instincts.

For the eating disorder therapist, goal-oriented intention may at times involve picking up the phone to initiate contact with a client or parent who has begun to miss appointments, or it may be seen in the practitioner's choice not to reach out, but to wait to see if a pattern of behavior might begin to emerge that will become further grist for the therapy mill. Such a decision would be based on the stage of recovery, the quality of the relationship, and the quality of the client's engagement in treatment.

Action-Based Responses to Premature Termination

When clients with attachment issues terminate treatment prematurely and without closure, I will either wait for the client to choose to resume contact on her own initiative or actively follow up with the client by phone or by letter. I will typically urge the client to attend one last session to review the process of their treatment, their growth, and future directions. In so doing, I provide a model for accountability and proactive problem solving, demonstrating appropriate responsiveness to separations, offering the client an additional opportunity to learn and grow, even in an absence from treatment.

For those clients who terminate treatment because they feel recovered and ready to leave, I have found that simply inviting them to return if they ever have additional problems is a less effective relapse prevention technique than pre-scheduling one or two visits at intervals that take the patient into the next couple of months, a plan that helps to ensure their readiness for self-care even while offering a safety net. Studies indicate that follow-up contact is effective in preventing treatment dropout and relapse. In one study, a personalized follow-up letter reduced dropout from 96 percent to 66 percent, and a personal phone call reduced dropout from 92 percent to 60 percent (Miller & Rollnick, 1991, p. 88).

N failed to call to schedule an appointment after spring break, as she had promised. After waiting for some time, I contacted her and helped her to understand that even if she felt she had made sufficient progress in recovery and it was time for her to stop treatment, informing me of her plans and intentions could have offered an opportunity for closure and additional learning. In helping her assess whether just "walking away" from a situation was a coping pattern in her life, in the end, my call prompted her to admit to herself and to me that she had stayed away because her eating disorder symptoms had returned.

T, a client with advanced anorexia, stormed out of my office in a rage after I confronted her with her breach of contract with the team in promising to gain weight if she was to continue to be treated on an outpatient basis. Her rage was provoked by the feelings of abandonment caused by my asking her to take responsibility for her actions. I left several voice mail messages for her over the next two weeks. Ultimately, she returned to treatment, having recognized that my demanding follow-through was an expression of my genuine concern about her well-being. She told me, "I suppose it would have been easier for you to be complacent and just let me be. Your belief in what I can do surely surpasses my own faith in myself; I have to admit, it both scares and delights me to think about that."

The proactive psychotherapist models thought processes, attitudes, approaches to problem solving, and openness in communications for the purpose of preparing and encouraging the client and family to do the same. W came for an emergency session with her family in response to a binge drinking episode and alcohol poisoning that could have killed her. After instructing W and her parents to obtain emergency room treatment in the future for such a potentially lethal episode, I informed them that I saw an emerging pattern of W's "self-medicating" through her impulsive (hypomanic) and excessive behaviors, including binge drinking, excessive exercise, compulsive dieting, and lying. In helping her to understand the risks of her behaviors and the possibility of an underlying mood disorder, I recommended that she make an appointment with a psychiatrist for a medication evaluation. W then confessed a fear that she is so out of control that she might overdose and kill herself, further indication of a yet to be revealed co-occurring diagnosis. I made it clear that I felt it was not safe for her to remain in outpatient treatment without further action and that I would not be able to continue treating her unless she was willing to see a psychiatrist. Her choice was to leave my care.

Recognizing passivity on the part of the eating disorder treatment plan is the first step toward avoiding it. A university-based team chose not to inform a student with anorexia that if she lost any more weight, the university would ask her to leave school for a year to avoid "burdening her with more pressure before exams. Instead, the team passively asked the client what she would feel comfortable doing to increase her weight, rather than informing her that 1,800 calories was not nearly enough calories to enable her to gain enough weight to stay at school. The team also "recommended" that she stop exercising. They essentially left her to her own discretion. She continued to lose weight and was taken by surprise when the university required her to take an extended leave of absence to recover.

Another action-oriented strategy is to ask the client to become aware of life scripts, therapeutic issues that impact her life, and significant events and feelings that take place between sessions. Besides being a sign of commitment to treatment, between-session interventions stimulate and reinforce self-awareness that lead to internal controls. As with any other skill, practice makes perfect. Devising collaborative behavioral techniques for the client to practice at home is reflective of the professional's personal creativity. Journaling, food logging, raising awareness of self-destructive behaviors, and deciding to act on one particular behavioral challenge each week are all devices that reinforce learning.

L was so frightened to attend a Christmas buffet that she considered staying home in bed. In stimulating a mindful approach to the experience, we decided together exactly how she would behave in choosing her food, predetermining what and how much she would put on her plate, and in what order. Feeling confident and in control, she had a successful evening.

F, diagnosed with binge eating disorder, became obese but had made a good start in integrating a healthier eating lifestyle. The first time she allowed herself a "treat," a frozen fruit pop, she ate it in front of the television and submitted to her urge to immediately have a second one. In an effort to create mindfulness around this act, I asked her to do the following:

- consider whether she had eaten enough over the course of the day
- keep in mind that it's easy to eat compulsively in front of the television
- cut the first fruit bar into six smaller pieces; if she still wanted more, cut the second into six pieces and become aware of her hunger cues in determining how much of the second bar to eat.

Doing something differently, no matter what one does, makes that act a mindful one. Mindfulness offers the alternative of choice.

Outcome-Based Treatment

The eating disorder therapist seeks change in whatever form in the interest of achieving recovery outcomes. With eating disorders, every treatment moment presents a precious opportunity to seek desired outcomes.

At times I have been Machiavellian in seeking outcomes. If a client cannot eat lunch, I consider conducting the next session at my kitchen table. Another of my clients felt so emotionally paralyzed during a therapy session that she was barely able to breathe or to speak. As a Feldenkrais and Anat Baniel therapist, I responded to her emotional inaccessibility by offering to give her a Feldenkrais lesson then and there, unplanned, as an adjunct treatment, freeing her up to reconnect with herself emotionally and physically. Within 30 minutes, she felt transformed by the work, as was seen in her mood, her breathing, the release of tension from her body, and her increased sense of self. (For further discussion of this case, see Chapter 14.)

Adjunct treatment techniques of all sorts that bring clients closer to outcomes they seek should be considered as viable resources. Though my work with this client was hands-on (I am also trained as a certified Feldenkrais practitioner), Awareness through Movement© classes that offer this method communally are increasingly available throughout the country for clients who seek to become more profoundly in touch with themselves. Other useful adjunct treatments include meditation and breathing techniques, yoga, martial arts, and other body–mind classes such as Nia (see www.nianow.com). When a client chooses to participate in such an activity, it is important for the therapist to help the client understand the relationship between the resulting bodily sensations . . . which create feelings of freedom, empowerment, and alternative options for movement and thinking . . . to the treatment goals of the psychotherapy process, maximizing recovery outcomes.

It is for the client to guide the dynamic of the therapy moment; it is for the therapist to guide outcomes. T was a 12-year-old beginning treatment for anorexia. At the start of her third session, she sat in the cold car, crying. Her mother, who had attended the first two sessions with her, rang my doorbell to ask what to do. I instructed her to return to the car and speak with her daughter, setting clear limits and making clear demands: Either T could come into the session to continue her outpatient work, or she would need to enter a day program, which would involve missing school. Treatment would be her only alternative in light of her misery.

T's mother arrived back at my door without T, who remained in the cold car, wailing loudly. I put on my boots and jacket and started the session standing by the car. I told her how optimistic I felt in seeing that she was finally beginning to get in touch with her real feelings, which would make her so much more open to accepting the help she so richly deserved. After reframing her feelings and joining her where she was, literally and figuratively, I credited her for her integrity and courage in standing up for herself, a prelude to her standing up to her eating disorder. T felt cared for by this intervention and began to experience hope and a sense of relief. She followed me into my office, where we had a breakthrough session.

Loving Connections: Expressions of Empathy

Through a loving therapeutic connection, the seeds of successful outcomes become fertile and alive; trust in the therapist and the therapy process ultimately leads to the client's capacity to trust in herself. It helps to love your clients and be excited by the core eating disorder treatment dynamics of relationship and change. Eating disorder treatment requires a genuine, enduring, and tenacious commitment to being in it together for the long haul. Professionals demonstrate caring and concern about the well-being of clients and families by being readily accessible, always within the confines of exquisitely honed boundaries. I typically send clients home with the instruction, "It's been a particularly trying time for you. You know, you don't need to hesitate to pick up the phone and call me if and when times get tough for you between sessions—no need to stand on ceremony." When a parent feels in distress about a recovering child or a family in crisis, he or she should not be required to wait until the next session for assistance. I make it a point to offer weekend hours to increase accessibility to families otherwise unavailable during weekdays, and I never leave town without setting up professional coverage and offering my cell phone number. When parents discover vomit around the toilet bowl or diet pills or laxatives in a child's dresser drawer or if a client is having an adverse reaction to medication, I make every effort to be readily available. I was happy to drive one client home from her session in a torrential thunderstorm the afternoon her mother was working, and I am open to sliding fees for clients in need who are unable to afford care.

A client must feel cared for, valued, and fully understood as a prerequisite to your asking for changes that could otherwise incur her distrust and discomfort. The young woman who struggled with binge eating disorder and obesity, upon doing better, began to think back about what had not worked for her in her previous therapy. She said, "I had the feeling that the therapist didn't like me as she didn't seem to enjoy being with me." She felt this in the woman's harsh, judgmental attitudes about her obesity and difficulty in establishing control over her eating.

In speaking about establishing a loving relationship, I do not use the word *loving* lightly. Ten years after leaving treatment with me, a recovered client described her memories of how safe she had felt in my office. She wrote,

> Even today, in closing my eyes, I can picture the crocheted afghan on the floor next to my chair, where your little poodle Harpo would curl up and sleep for the duration, raising his head for an occasional pat or scratch behind the ear.

She remembered how we threw stadium blankets across our laps in winter, warming our hands on cups of hot tea in my draughty old office, and she recalled feeling safe and taken care of as we drank together. "I needed to be pushed and directed in those days," she recalls "it is far easier to accept demands, limit setting, and direction when you know the other person cares. Now, when I feel frazzled, I return to these memories and to my own little dog to comfort me."

The most powerful form of loving acceptance begins by recognizing and addressing the learner's strengths and by understanding that the eating disorder represents the client's only currently recognized means for coping and survival in her highly vulnerable state. By validating her noble motivation and intention, the therapist creates and reinforces trust and confidence in her capacity to know, to learn, and to change. Hidden though they may be, strengths become obvious for those who know how to look and what to see.

With or without an eating disorder, we all go through life seeking surrogate mothers in other human beings, hungry as we are for wisdom, guidance, advisement, and nurturance for our soul. Author Clarissa Pincola Estes observed, "You are born to one mother, but if you are lucky, you will have more than one. And among them all, you will find most of what you need" (Estes, 1992). The luckiest of us may discover such precious influences in our lives, be it in the form of a therapist, a friend, a teacher, a spouse, or our grown children, who are capable of opening our minds to new ways of thinking and behaving. It is a gift and a privilege to be able to play this role for many of my clients.

I am always happy to see my ex-clients for an as-needed treatment session now and then or to go out for an occasional lunch with them years later to "catch up" when they return to town. It is critical that the nature of the intermittent post-treatment relationship, be it over lunch or in my office, maintain appropriate client–therapist boundaries so as not to preclude the potential for future treatment. No matter how close, loving, and long term a relationship might be, the therapy relationship is just, and only, that: The client who is "like a daughter" must never be led to believe in any respect that she is or must behave like one. As with our own children, the best any parent can do is to hold on with an open hand (Ginott, 1969) in preparation for them to eventually fly the nest.

In acknowledging strengths, remain sensitive to the possibility that when you see beyond a client's weaknesses, she may lose faith that you are being honest with her; she may also believe she has duped you or may experience guilt and embarrassment at feeling falsely praised. Compliments counter the negative self-view that keeps her bound to her eating disorder. By addressing this dynamic, you can resolve it. I generally disarm this fuse by offering the observation that she might predictably respond with such feelings, and if so, that would be under-standable. All the same, recognizing one's strengths is as necessary to the healing process as is reality-based acceptance of pathology.

In the course of a discussion, my client said, "I know you probably think I am full of shit, but this is how I think." After a substantive dialogue about the issues at hand, I revisited her throw-away comment about what she assumed I thought of her. "Let's talk more about what you think I think," I began. I made it clear that contrary to her thinking, I believed she was a highly introspective and sensitive person who had been nothing short of courageous in expressing herself as truthfully as she had about her feelings and thoughts. Even those ideas that she recognized as distortions were as subjectively real and genuine to her as were the more "objective" truths perceived by others. I pointed out that it was proba-bly difficult for her to hear positive things about herself, which presented still another therapeutic issue full of potential for learning.

Empathy Provides Connection

Empathy is a heightened sensibility or "sixth sense"—call it intuition, call it diagnostic acuity, call it the capacity to connect—that signifies one's capacity to really see, to really hear, to really read the moment and the client and to walk in that person's shoes, traveling her path with her. Through empathy, the therapist understands and accepts both expressed and underlying feelings, conveying this acceptance verbally and nonverbally. The empathic sense helps individuals forge relationships with one another as the glue that binds healing relationships. Stud-ies of brain structure show an overlap in the regions that process personal pain and the pain of others; empathy is learned by developing the mental flexibility to put oneself in another's shoes (Gibson, 2006).

P returned to treatment with me 15 years after she had recovered from bulimia and panic attacks. Now married and the mother of two children, she came to discuss her moodiness and concerns about aspects of her marriage. At the start of our second session, I asked her, "So how was it for you, returning here after all these years and all that living?" She replied that before coming, she felt nervous and uneasy. Who was I and who was she, and would we still know each other? Her mother had died when she was an infant, and she knew what it felt like to be left by women who were dear to her. When our eyes met, we fell into a mutual hug, and she said it was as if she had never left, as if no time had passed. The con-nection was as firm and steady, as complete and as bonded as it ever had been. We hit the ground running with her treatment, as if she hadn't missed a beat of the rhythm of therapy. It is through the empathic connection that the practitioner inspires the client's choice to heal, optimizing her capability and desire to change and grow.

How Do People Develop Empathy?

Through evolution, humans have acquired a capacity to connect deeply with other human beings. We learn to read others and relate to their feelings through collections of special cells in the brain called mirror neurons. Recent empirical evidence shows that our brains are capable of mirroring the deepest aspects of the minds of others at the fine-grained level of a single brain cell (Iacoboni, 2008). Detecting intention and inferences, and located in many regions of the brain, mirror neurons explain our instinct to imitate one another—to synchronize our bodies, our actions, even the way we speak to one another, a synchrony that often enjoys an emotion component (Iacoboni, 2008). I am acutely aware of my own neural empathy network connections in my vulnerability to crying at sad movies and my aversion to exposure to violence and horror in movies, in my emotional attachment to fictional characters richly drawn in great books, and in the phenomenon of my voice inflections and gestures so like that of a close friend of 30 years that we are often mistaken for one another.

I am fascinated by the strength of empathic therapeutic connection within the process of a treatment session. In the throes of deep conversation, I often find the client (or myself) unconsciously mimicking behaviors of the other—brushing aside a wisp of hair, crossing a leg, touching a foot, crossing arms across the chest, adjusting one's glasses, scratching one's head—body language that is unconsciously initiated or mirrored by therapist and/or client. This phenomenon is testimony to the profundity of human connections, the unmitigated depth of the unconscious hookup between individuals whose inner selves are intertwined in the act of disclosure, revelation, learning, and growth. This unconscious phenomenon was documented in the discussion of neurolinguistic programming long before the advent of brain plasticity research; neurolinguistic programming is a unique model of how people learn, motivate themselves, and change their behavior based on the work of psychiatrist Milton Erickson. For this reason, the better in touch with themselves therapists are, the better in touch they are able to be with their clients.

Mindful Practice Evokes Empathy

Our capacity for mental attunement to others depends on our ability to keep our minds open and present in the immediate moment.

> Mindfulness is a state of being; by itself, it cannot be captured or evoked predictably through any singular technique. Mindfulness is elusive, with the act of meditation merely a prop to facilitate it. Awakening to our own lives and sustaining a consistent pattern of wakefulness with acceptance requires considerable intention and effort. It is a lifelong endeavor that we undertake for ourselves and share with our clients. (Germer et al., 2005, p. 172)

Practitioners are listeners first; in listening to the client, they permit the client to establish her own voice and to hear herself. To best hear what is spoken, as well as what yet remains unsaid, therapists must mindfully quiet their own internal voices, even while keeping one ear open to their own core self. Quieting a voice is quite different from silencing it altogether; a therapist who silences any connection with his or her authentic self or stuffs away feelings and risks the loss of connection with the client and the therapeutic moment. By staying open to the reality of themselves, therapists mirror what they want their clients to learn.

Clients develop their own potential for empathy and self-love by mirroring the empathy and acceptance they have experienced within the context of the therapeutic relationship. Empathy is a nature–nurture phenomenon, the product both of heredity as it affects brain formation and of learning through our environment. As an example, children of alcoholics develop codependent "survival tactics" in growing up with a surfeit of anger, depression, abuse, and addiction. By developing empathy to the requirements of addiction at the core of a family system, children learn to protect themselves, the family system, the addiction, and their parents' marriages, soothing the angry beast before it rears up to bite them.

Educating Clients

Eating disorders are brain dysfunctions that produce cognitive distortions. Practitioners need to anticipate and address cognitive distortions in clients who make logical arguments based on illogical assumptions. Throughout the treatment process, therapists need to be reality testers, prepared to educate clients by actively correcting misinformed core belief systems.

Recognizing, Understanding, and Correcting Belief Systems About Eating Disorders

The therapist must communicate acceptance of the client while refuting such fallacious ideas as the following, which are typical of clients with eating disorders:

- People I depend on always abandon me. I can never trust anyone but my eating disorder.
- Lower weight and body fat lead to better athletic performance.
- Teenagers are too old to be told what to do by their parents.
- It's nobody's business what another person eats.
- Laxatives cause weight loss by purging the body of waste and fluids.
- A person can gain 10 pounds by eating 50 calories.
- People require only 500 calories a day.
- Movie stars don't eat more than 1,200 calories a day.
- It's normal not to eat breakfast.
- You should never eat unless you are hungry.
- I can recover by myself without the help of others.
- An eating disorder represents a character flaw, a weakness.
- My eating disorder will be part of my life forever.
- Gaining weight signifies recovery.

Education Is About Learning and Teaching

There is a great deal that the client and family need to learn about the pivotal subject of weight and weight management. The role of weight in the diagnosis and treatment of eating disorders is perhaps the most misleading of all the commonly held misunderstandings about eating disorders and how they work. A patient's weight is not a predictable criterion for diagnosis or recovery. With eating disorders, weight is significant in diagnosis, though is not by itself indicative of a diagnosis. Body weight, even if abnormal, does not, by itself, indicate sickness; similarly, weight restoration by itself does not indicate recovery (from anorexia nervosa), as most people assume. Normalized weight and vital signs are an indication of improved brain function, marking the patient's ability to recover cognitively, emotionally, and physically. A person's weight, by itself, is but one parameter amongst many that help us to determine physical status.

An important aim of treatment is to help the patient gain control over her eating, rather than of her weight. Be clear with the client that weight gain is not what she is after; rather, what she seeks is normalized, healthy eating, to replace fearful, dysfunctional eating.

When patients wonder why they can't just "grab" something for breakfast and run out the door, I would help them to differentiate that if they grab a granola bar and call it breakfast, it won't suffice: "Grabbing" a large chocolate muffin, a banana, a carton or two of milk or yogurt and a couple of cheese sticks might be a different story.

Weight gain needs to be differentiated from weight restoration. Neither is a benchmark for eating disorder recovery. Recovery in the absence of full weight restoration will remain partial and temporary. Most patients, parents, and all too many professionals believe that the only required medical rehabilitation is to bring the patient out of immediate danger of death. This is not so. A person with an eating disorder needs to recover her total weight so as to make a total recovery from the eating disorder.

Weighing "Blind" or "Unblind"

Though changing one's thinking cannot be measured by the numbers on the scale, one's capacity to overcome compulsions and develop a more structured and less erratic eating lifestyle can be. Weighing in is an important accountability tool. An 11-year-old anorexic girl insisted that she be told her weight so that she could gauge "exactly what to eat" so as not to go above or below her "prescribed ideal weight." To go above that weight would bring on the growing fear of obesity; to go below would mean she was headed for re-entry into the hospital. Her singular goal was to achieve and sustain the lowest weight possible in order to remain in outpatient status. I "called her" on her intention to use the information to sabotage her recovery and explained that therefore, for now, that information would be withheld.

How a patient chooses to be weighed depends on timing and readiness. "Blind" weigh-ins protect the patient from the wrath of her eating disorder. Early in recovery, weight gain may increase the patient's depression and anxiety, interfering with her motivation for change. When a compulsive eating disorder patient weighs herself, she is in danger of doing so compulsively, multiple times a day, leading to anxiety and the urge to purge. Some patients feel they can't bear the anxiety of seeing weight gain, which could inspire restricting; others feel they can't bear the anxiety of seeing weight loss, of feeling that their efforts are failing, and the thought of the potential for milieu change as a consequence. Some patients may feel compelled to respond to further weight loss by the compulsion to "do more of a good thing." Because of the anxiety aroused by weight acknowledgment, most recovering patients choose to stand backwards on the scale to avoid the havoc of dealing with the emotionally loaded outcome of the week's efforts.

Proponents of cognitive–behavioral therapy believe that the patient needs to accept responsibility for weighing herself and dealing with whatever the emotional consequences may be. In using a more integrated approach to care, I have found that, eventually, patients who are well into recovery, having been able to achieve and sustain a measure of self-determination and accountability, may benefit from knowing their weight as an indicator of realistic next steps and goal refinement. This is an illustration that in striving to "do what works," all rules for performance are nuanced depending on the patient's ongoing, ever-changing needs and capacities.

Tip: It is counterproductive for clinicians to consider or seek the concept of an "ideal weight." Beware of the tendency to offer anorexic patients the "carrot" of reaching a specific "target weight" as their goal. No one—not a nutritionist, not the patient, not a physician—can set a goal weight arbitrarily and expect it to lead to recovery. When a nutritionist or doctor says, "It is important for you to gain another five pounds to reach the low end of normal on the charts," the patient hears, "Five pounds is all I need to gain in order to get everybody off my back; five pounds will let me stay skinny without being called 'sick.'"

The body itself is the only accurate determiner of appropriate weight; any weight less than the body's set point weight is a distraction to complete recovery. Each person has a set point weight to which the person naturally gravitates; the range might span from 5 to 10 or 20 pounds, but it becomes difficult to go beyond that natural weight range (Kolata, 2007). Attaining one's set point weight marks full weight restoration, a normalized internal function of brain and body, and the reversal of amenorrhea. With the restoration of healthy metabolic function at set point, a healthy eating lifestyle can be counted upon to sustain weight homeostasis. The set point counteracts the commonly held misconception that the more one eats, the more weight one gains; that food is fattening; and that when it comes to food, less is more.

Strategy: I explain the set point weight as being like an ocean's tide. When the moon is new, gravitational forces may not pull the body of water as high as it comes in when the moon is full. The rising tide, be it slightly higher or lower, always approaches (but does not exceed), a certain point on the shore, with the exception of hurricanes or other natural forces. So is the set point equally consistent, expected to fluctuate ever so slightly, but always hovering close to the water line.

Strategy: A pediatrician, in being briefed with background information about a 12-year-old highly resistant anorexic girl whom she was about to evaluate, asked, "But how can I recommend inpatient care when she has not lost weight lately and if her vital signs are good?" I explained that what qualified this child for more restrictive care was not weight loss per se but her continuing failure to make sufficient progress in outpatient care.

Food for Thought: Particularly during the pre-contemplative stage of care (See Chapter 11), anorexic patients require hard-core education about extreme weight loss and its consequences for the human body as a way to motivate such patients to understand the need for weight restoration. One of the most important advancements in the understanding of eating disorders is the recognition that severe and prolonged dietary restriction can lead to serious physical and psychological complications (Garner, 1997). Many of the symptoms once thought to be primary features of anorexia nervosa are actually symptoms of starvation. A powerful illustration of the effects of semistarvation and weight loss on behavior is an experimental study that took place during the 1930s with conscientious objectors to World War II. These men endured starvation to determine the influence of malnutrition. The psychological and behavioral changes documented in these previously healthy individuals paralleled those within the restricting anorexia nervosa population. Their symptoms included increased obsessions with food and eating, increased depression and anxiety, the desire to isolate, decreased libido, and bizarre food rituals. Some began sneaking out of the experimental environment to binge on foods and then began purging in response to their guilt for having broken the experimental rules. The men showed poor concentration, compromised judgment, and problem-solving, neurological symptoms such as tingling in their extremities, and gastroenterological functioning problems, including constipation and bloating (Attia & Walsh, 2009).

Tip: In response to the question, "When a person lives for three or more years in a state of virtual starvation, does that permanently affect brain functioning and impair a person's response to a drug?" Allan Kaplan says, "So far, we just don't know" (Graham, 2006, p. 6).

The Family's Eating Culture

In educating parents and families, help them to become aware of their own family's culture—that is, assumptions and rituals—of eating. For example,

- Some families do not cook at all.
- Some do not serve meals during summer months.
- Some believe in eating only half of what is on one's plate in a restaurant and make it a policy to share dinners ordered.
- Some believe that one should always have left food on the plate at the end of a meal.
- Many families "aren't breakfast families."
- Some make it a practice to criticize others for their physical appearance.
- Some consider exercise to be the only way to burn calories.
- Some families leave it to the child to forage for meals on her own.
- Some eat dinner in front of the television set.
- Some foster such a "healthiness" focus that compulsive children or those who are black-and-white thinkers begin to fear and restrict foods that are not considered "health" foods.

T, a young woman with anorexia and obsessive–compulsive anxiety disorder was very resistant to care. Firmly entrenched in the pre-contemplative stage, her resistance, denial, and distortions prevented her from engaging in treatment. In response, I invited her parents to become a significant part of the treatment process early on so that they could become effective team players at home. This case would require all the parental support the professional team could muster.

Intelligent and loving individuals, these parents were eager to find a timely and efficient solution as their financial resources were limited. Because the culture of the family centered on holistic and natural healing, they were unreceptive to a day program alternative and to the medication that T badly needed to jump start the girl's progress. In their attempt to promote good health, they had enabled their child to engage in extreme restricting behaviors. T's mother, finding it hard to watch her daughter grieve the loss of exercise, encouraged her to walk their dog numerous times a day and recommended acupressure on the soles of her feet to stimulate the endorphins that running had evoked. Her loving nature prevented her from making the demands on T that recovery would require. Because these parents were clearly the most important members of this team, I worked extensively with them to help them see that the messages their daughter was receiving at home might inadvertently be countering the recovery they sought. I offered ample education, suggested changes in behaviors, and provided insight into the nuances of their communications. In raising awareness about the parent's own attitudes that could inadvertently sabotage care, I hoped to inspire them to become powerful advocates for the young woman's recovery. Would they be able to do so, T might be able to heal while living at home as an outpatient.

For many clients, learning to erect appropriate boundaries around a self that has been violated by an eating disorder (and sometimes other people) becomes an essential skill. A college graduate who engaged in binge eating, food restriction, and purging came to treatment seeking to lose 25 pounds in two months. Her parents, both compulsive runners, wanted her to become thin as proof that she was "ready to manage her new life as a working girl." They were dismayed to discover, as our treatment progressed, that rather than seeking to lose the weight, their daughter had developed a new and different goal: to learn to eat healthfully, three balanced and diverse meals a day plus snacks. Previously she had hid her bingeing from them, but now she felt the need to hide her new and fully healthy eating lifestyle. This client learned to appreciate her parents' good intentions but then to put up emotional boundaries between herself and the pressure they brought to bear on her to go hungry. Her recovery gave rise to feelings of empowerment that allowed her to sustain her growing integrity at home.

In another instance, a 40-year-old woman with anorexia described being barraged by painful messages about weight by her mother and father. Their first question after her son's return from overnight camp was, "Did he gain weight?" Although this woman was emaciated, she heard such comments as her mother's indictment that she was "fat." I asked her to imagine building a semipermeable, invisible plastic shield that would define and protect her personal space, deflecting stinging darts, insults, and indiscretions from her otherwise beloved parents. Being semipermeable, the shield would filter out some, but not all, of her parents' influences, at her discretion, while permitting newly forming positive perceptions of her self and her body as she recovered.

In some respects, it is as appropriate for a client to maintain boundaries with the therapist, as it is fitting for the therapist to do the same with their clients. One client with whom I had worked for close to a decade lived in the same neighborhood as I, and we frequented the same supermarket, health club, and hairdresser. Hugging and physical contact had been implicitly off limits in sessions, at least largely the result of my response to her needs for separateness. It was only when we found each other by surprise one day, in a place where neither of us expected to see the other, that the relaxing of boundaries felt comfortable and a spontaneous hug erupted, initiated by her.

9

Partnering for Success: Multidisciplinary Treatment Teamwork

A single individual cannot whistle a symphony; even a full orchestra cannot make music together if they are all playing out of tune.
—Bryan Lask

When team members support each other, they keep the healing work on track and moving forward. This chapter explains not only what each team member needs to know and do but also clarifies what each of the other members knows and does. Treatment teams exist within the context of inpatient and outpatient milieus; my focus in this chapter is on the more prevalent outpatient team, whose challenges are easily the most widespread and the most rigorous because of the inherent reality of members not functioning under the same roof. Outpatient teams essentially simulate the work of inpatient teams in a less intense, less restrictive environment that costs less and allows clients the benefits of healing within the context of their daily lives.

IT TAKES A VILLAGE TO HEAL AN EATING DISORDER

Diverse and integrative disorders demand the input of an integrative group of professionals practicing their diverse disciplines. Professionals treating eating disorders cannot afford to be strangers to one another. They need to make their way together. Nowhere is the expression "on the same page" as pertinent and meaningful as with the team approach in the treatment of eating disorders. For team professionals to function in isolation would be equivalent to a football coach telling the players not to bother with the huddle, but to each pick a play they like and do their own thing.

As important as it is for eating disorder practitioners to be effective multi-taskers, no amount of multitasking on the part of any singular practitioner, no matter how experienced or skilled, is sufficient to manage the complex emotional, behavioral, and physical problems presented by an eating disorder. Particularly in the face of a shortage of trained eating disorder practitioners, the need becomes even greater for each clinician to assess and address such clients holistically. Collaborative work is like a tightly knit fabric of care, with the "right hand" not only knowing what the "left hand" is doing but each enhancing the actions of the other.

It is critical that members of the treatment team speak in an informed and unified voice both with clients and among themselves. Psychotherapists need to be sufficiently knowledgeable about the work of the nutritionist to tap into the refeeding process as a mechanism for evoking emotional change. Nutritionists must tailor their own goals and tasks to those of the therapy arm of treatment to direct and optimize the client's progress. Psychotherapists must know enough about the need for and the benefits of psychotropic medications to make appropriate and timely referrals to medicating psychiatrists. Psychopharmacologists must remain in synchronicity with the rhythm, pace, direction, and progress of their client's psychotherapeutic work to accommodate the recovering client's ever-changing needs. Medical doctors must be capable of speaking about the significance of maintaining a healthy eating lifestyle rather than solely managing the symptoms of pathology or the numbers on the scale.

The conductor of an orchestra must know every instrument's score; each instrument is enhanced by the presence of the other instruments. With eating disorder treatment, the baton belongs in the hands of whatever team member has ideas, insights, and observations to report. Particularly when the full complement of team participants is not available, the responsibility for vigilance must be assumed by whichever professionals *are* present. It is incumbent upon team members to discover points of mutual intersection, both vertical and horizontal, that enhance connections within themselves, among their colleagues, and with their clients. Figure 9.1 illustrates the interconnections in communication among members of the eating disorder treatment team.

PUTTING THE TEAM TOGETHER

The first question on the minds of many parents of child clients is, "Who can afford to hire all of those people?" The appropriate response is that putting an experienced and knowledgeable team in place around the treatment of an eating disorder is the best investment clients and families can make in their child's healing, producing dividends that never stop paying off.

Many parents, new to the process, find themselves initially acting as impromptu case managers, both in bringing the team together and in replacing members who are ineffective or unworkable. Parents need professional help to find the best professional help for their child.

The Patient's Reintegrated Self

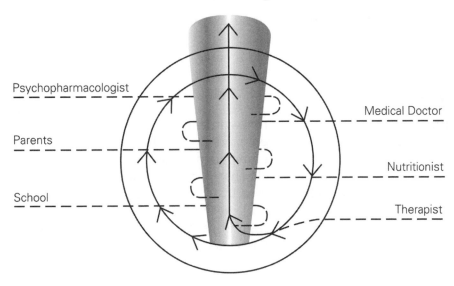

Figure 9.1. The role of the treatment team in promoting recovery from an eating disorder. The outer circle represents the treatment team; the inner circle represents the fluid communication patterns among team members. The treatment team creates a dynamic, integrative, and collaborative system for coalescing ideas, goals, and actions. All treatment goals need to be considered and applied by all members of the team all the time in their efforts to embrace, contain, and sustain the client in achieving her autonomous, reorganized, and integrated self. The psychotherapist, through a versatile use of self and skills, becomes the temporary virtual backbone of the recovering client.

The logistics of creating teams are beyond the control of practitioners and clients in many instances. For people who live in rural communities, there may be distances of hundreds of miles between the client and the nearest eating disorders expert. The bare-bones team of professionals needs to include three professionals: the therapist, the nutritionist, and the medical doctor. Additional team members will come on board depending on the needs of the individual client.

The Psychotherapist

In building the core of the professional team, note that the psychotherapist may be a social worker, a psychologist, or a psychiatrist, representing three levels of degrees, including master's or PhD/PsyD and MD. Preferably, the person who treats the identified patient will also be proficient in treating families. Because there is a dearth of eating disorder training for all levels of professionals in the field, the formal education a therapist has received will have little bearing on the quality of his or her work with individuals recovering from eating disorders. I have found that a professional's training and academic background are less significant indicators of how a person works than are his or her interests, capacity for self-awareness and empathy, and life experience (Natenshon, 1999, p. 141). The individual therapist could also treat the family, or not, depending on the therapist's skills and the preference of therapist and client. It is essential that the family therapist be knowledgeable about the systemic nature of eating disorders as they pervade family life and the role of families in their healing.

The Nutritionist

The nutritionist plays a significant role within the team as the chief educator about food and eating, monitoring the client's progress in developing a healthy relationship with food. It is important that the patient be accountable to someone in carrying out pivotal nutritionally based behavioral tasks that will eventually enhance her emotional status. It is left to the nutritionist to do the weigh-ins and to be capable of handling emotionally loaded issues with all the sensitivity and skill of a therapist. The nutritionist's role is significant at each stage of treatment, as weight fluctuations and changes in eating habits take on different meaning as they impact every stage of treatment.

The Medical Doctor

The medical doctor plays a pivotal role in monitoring the physiological effects of the eating disorder and determining the client's level of risk. Though the phycisian sees the patient less frequently than does the therapist or the nutritionist, the doctor needs to be apprised of the status of patients dealing with these most lethal of all mental health disorders. It is for the medical doctor to make the referral to a hospital or a recommendation for entry into a more restrictive level of care. By demanding change of the patient, the doctor can sometimes act as a protector for the more fragile patient–parent or patient–therapist relationships.

Clients may enter the treatment system anywhere. The process may originate in school counseling offices, homes, nutritional offices, or other settings, in any sequence and with any combination of caregivers, at any one of diverse stages in the evolution of each individual's disease and recovery. It does not matter where and how treatment gets started, who takes charge, and when, as long as someone cares enough to direct the client to a course of action that will result in healing. The eating disorder recovery ship needs a captain at the helm, even if different crew members temporarily take turns at the wheel.

Whoever happens to be solicited first at the outset of help seeking temporarily becomes the acting case manager. The school social worker may remain the person in charge until a successful referral to a medical doctor and therapist can be made. A screening doctor may make referrals and monitor the case until the team comes together. Within the treatment team, it generally makes the most sense for the psychotherapist to manage the conduct and process of the case. It is the psychotherapist who sees the client most frequently and who is responsible for creating and sustaining motivation for healing, the relationship with family, the ongoing and collaborative planning toward recovery, and the close partnership with a nutritionist who can actualize cognitive and behavioral goals.

WHO IS ON THE TEAM?

The treatment process typically begins and ends many times within the course of an extended recovery. Any unique case may involve numerous therapists, doctors, and other treating professionals over an expanse of years or even decades. In treating eating disorders, professionals may find themselves partnering with strangers whom they may or may not know.

The diverse nature of eating disorders demands diversity within the treatment team. Every eating disorder treatment team should include professional partners who function alongside patients and families. The latter need to be included as part of the team, as collaborators in decision making and problem solving. In considering the wider and more inclusive team membership, the following:

- the client, who needs to be seen as a collaborative partner
- parents and families, as mentors and advocates of the client and the therapy process
- the medical doctor, whose presence on the team is compulsory from the start of treatment and ongoing. No psychotherapist should consider treating a client with an eating disorder unless she is being monitored by a medical doctor, and no medical doctor should consider treating these cases unless the client is also being seen by a psychotherapist.
- the individual psychotherapist, who, in the best of all worlds, is not only an expert on eating disorders, but also an experienced family therapist capable of addressing the intertwining systems of client, disease, and family in treatment
- the nutritionist, who provides structure, accountability, and behavioral goals and tasks to support cognitive learning and to instill a healthy eating lifestyle
- the psychopharmacologist, who is needed where co-occurring conditions require the use of medications (the vast majority of eating disorder cases)
- educators, including teachers, administrators, school social workers, school guidance counselors, nurses, and coaches, who are significant in helping the individual transition back into daily life after having spent time in residential or inpatient care. Schools may also provide tutors to teach students privately while they are inpatients. Other potential team members include professionals in residential or hospital programs, therapy group facilitators, and therapists treating other family members.

In describing the dynamic of a well-oiled "team machine," I provide each section with the intention of guiding the therapist's collaborative interaction with teammates. (Because so much of this book is dedicated to the work of the individual psychotherapist, I omit an in-depth discussion of this professional's role here.) Box 9.1 lists resources that may be of use to teams.

Parents and Families

The therapeutic goal for parents whose child has temporarily lost control over her life is to take charge until the disordered child is able once again, through recovery and refeeding, to resume a responsible degree of self-determination. When parents do begin to curtail their interventions, the pull-back needs to be responsive to the developing strengths of the child.

BOX 9.1

Resources for Treatment Teams

For schools	National Association of Anorexia Nervosa and Associated Disorders. *ANAD School Guidelines Program.* Highland Park, IL: Author. (Available at www.anad.org)
	The Go Girls! program of the National Eating Disorders Association engages high school girls and boys to advocate for positive body images of youth in advertising, the media, and major retailers. (Available at www.myneda.org)
For physicians	Campbell, A., McGilley, B., & Tyson, E. (n.d.) *Eating disorders: Medical protocol inpatient admission orders for eating disorders.* (Available at www.healingpathfoundation.org)
	Mehler, P. S., & Andersen, A. E. (1999). *Eating disorders: A guide to medical care and complications.* Baltimore: Johns Hopkins University Press.
For pediatricians	The Society for Adolescent Medicine, the American Academy of Pediatrics, and the Canadian Pediatric Society offer position papers with guidelines on medical complications and criteria for hospitalization.
For dentists	Hurst, P. S., Lacey, J. H., & Crisp, A. H. (1977). Teeth, vomiting and diet: A study of the dental characteristics of seventeen anorexia nervosa patients. *Postgraduate Medical Journal, 53,* 298–305.
For nutritionists	Setnick, J. (2005). *The eating disorders clinical pocket guide: Quick reference for healthcare providers.* Dallas, TX: Snack Time Press.
For the whole team	The Kartini Foundation received a grant from the American Legion Child Welfare Fund to develop a DVD specifically to educate physicians and other health-care providers about childhood anorexia nervosa and related eating disorders. The DVD, called *Spotting the Tiger,* was created by Steve Nemirow and Mark Magee, with voiceover done by Jamie Lee Curtis solely for the love of children. The DVD is available free at help@kartiniclinic.com.

Too many parents feel pressured by professionals not to "interfere" in their child's treatment. Instead, they need professionals' permission to be true to themselves, to their child, and to the healing process. The involvement of family members is the best way to infuse life into a recovery process. By upgrading the nature and quality of parental support to accommodate the changing needs of the recovering child, the therapist preserves the ever-changing homeostasis of the family system in the face of the child's changes, securing and sustaining the client's progress.

There is an inverse correlation between the child's age, his or her developmental and internal resources, and the extent of need for parental participation, though family therapy remains a potent change mechanism for clients of all ages and life stages. With married clients, spouses should be invited into treatment. As a rule of thumb, when an individual with an eating disorder becomes more capable of independent and responsible compliance with self-care, family members may become less engaged.

In first meeting with a family transferring to my care from that of another therapist, one of my first questions is, "In your past experience, what did you learn about what eating disorders are, and how would you describe their implications for your child and for your family?" In probing for insights about what has and has not worked best for clients and families, I am investigating current needs and agendas, learning what voids still need to be filled, and setting the stage for understanding projections and attitudes that clients bring with them to the new treatment process. When therapy has not been successful for children, I find that their parents have invariably been excluded from the treatment and recovery processes and are unprepared, frightened, and clueless about what eating disorders are, what treatment does, and how treatment works. They are clear about their own experience; the lessons they learned were all negative. One parent spoke of being invited by a child's therapist to take "a three-year vacation" from parenting and described the experience as devastating, nightmarish, and guilt-laden.

When it comes to healing and dealing with these disorders, parental love is necessary but, unfortunately, will not suffice if not accompanied by knowledge, strategies, confidence, support, and tenacity to survive on the recovery "firing line" seven days a week, 24 hours a day. Practitioners must take responsibility for preparing parents for these challenges.

Parents as Advocates

The parents of a prospective teenage client who was purging and cutting herself called to speak not only of their concerns about their daughter and their eroding parent–child relationship but also of having felt mishandled and undermined by the girl's previous helping professionals. Although they lived with their daughter "seven days a week, minus one hour," these parent had been told to "trust" the team's work, even while they were systematically excluded from the process and while watching the girl continue to lose weight. The pediatrician commented that the girl's "labs were beautiful" and that she was "perfectly fine" at her weight, "provided she didn't lose any more," giving her increased ammunition against her parents' concerns. These parents needed guidance and permission to be effective advocates for their daughter.

Another parent wrote to me about her 18-year-old son who was away at college and who had just admitted to his girlfriend and to his parents that he was a bulimic, at the stage of coughing up blood and blacking out. "In an effort to placate him and his stress," writes this mother,

> I've tried to accommodate his wishes. He doesn't want to talk to us or about this at all, so I have sent e-mails about how much we love him, telling him that we want to be there to help. He is furious with us that we want to go up to school and bring him to a doctor. We are afraid to push him, thinking it will make matters worse, though we dread getting still another doctor who demeans us, as the one did last year who implied I was overreacting and that "nothing was wrong." Should we "force" him to go for help? I keep hearing that he has to *want* the help and until he makes that decision, it won't help. I'm so lost!

In response, I wrote,

> You need to ignore the advice of doctors who don't understand (easier said than done) and continue your search until you find one who is knowledgeable about eating disorders. You might want to begin your networking with your local hospital. Be clear with your son that you will not take no for an answer, that he is sick with a life-threatening illness, and that you will not stand by and watch him fail. Call it "force," if you will, but with an eating disorder, a person is temporarily incapable of making sound decisions, and as parents, you need to take over the executive function for him now, at least until he can resume responsible self-control and self-care. You've loved and cared for him his whole life. This is hardly the time to stop doing so, despite all of his protestations.

Parents can become powerful advocates for the professional team in the following ways:

- When called in to examine a treatment process that has become stuck or gone awry, parents bring balance and a sense of focus, restoring stability to the work.
- Parents ease the child's transitioning from one level of care to another.
- Parents act as observers and informers in instances where children are too young, too frightened, or too sick to understand, express, or reveal what is happening to them.
- Parents are food police, facilitators, and projective self-objects ready to absorb the feelings and judgments of a child newly in touch with uncomfortable feelings and requirements.
- Parents are role models in fearlessly defining and confronting problems and in coping with adversity.
- Parents can act as a stabilizing and rectifying force when a child seeks premature termination or manipulates the team and recovery process.

- Parents act as teachers, chauffeurs, "cooks and bottle washers," shoppers, and, most of all, sources of constant love and support.
- Parents are fierce advocates of the treatment and recovery processes, of the child, and of the therapist and the therapy.

The mother of a teen with anorexia reported that her daughter had complained about something I had said in a therapy session. The hurtful aspect of my comment had been in its interpretation, not in my intention. This mother's comment to her child was,

> Hmm . . . that doesn't sound like something Abbie would have said or meant to say. I wonder if you might have misinterpreted what she was trying to communicate. Why not tell her how you feel next time you see her and get the story directly from the horse's mouth?

The client returned, we discussed the miscommunication, and in so doing we expanded the breadth and depth of our relationship and the client's understanding of herself. In taking this initiative, she enjoyed a breakthrough opportunity to problem solve and practice self-care, to take initiative and use herself creatively. She learned that humans are all vulnerable to making mistakes. This young woman ultimately became a clinical psychologist. A parent who was less trusting and less part of a united front with the team might have split the recovery effort by aligning with the child's ambivalence, encouraging a hasty and ill-considered withdrawal from both treatment and the opportunity to learn.

Parents as Cotherapists

I offered a nine-year-old client with anorexia the opportunity to decide what she would like to talk about one day. As she did not know where to begin, her mother chimed in, "Do you remember what happened Friday night when you disappeared when it was time to eat cake at your brother's party?" "No," was the child's response. "So you are forgetting something very important. Let me jog your memory." In another instance, the mother offered, "Do you remember how you were able to play your violin in your school concert without becoming overly nervous?"

This gave me the opportunity to reinforce past teachings about stress reduction and problem solving. I asked, "So when you were performing, were you aware of your feelings and what you were saying to yourself in your head? Might you let yourself say those same things again, experiencing and remembering that same sense of empowerment and self-composure?" By laying the groundwork for the child's self-awareness, ownership of the process, and recognition of her strengths, she would become prepared to independently call up these facilities in the future.

Parents as Nutrition Supervisors

The spectrum of parental support provision ranges from stocking pantries with easily available nutritional staples to cooking, eating together, and monitoring the child's eating and weight fluctuations. The nature and amount of support required from parents of recovering children varies from case to case and moment to moment, depending on the life stage of the child, the status of recovery, and the emotional capacity of the parents.

An adolescent with anorexia felt supported and reassured early in her recovery when her mother made her lunches for her. Later, she would appreciate her mother's suggestion that she include a glass of milk or an extra slice of cheese or turkey on her sandwich as she prepared her lunch. As she became increasingly capable of making her own good choices, she began to see her mother's input as unwelcome. Parents need to take cues from the child verbally and nonverbally and respond accordingly; the nature of parental support needs to change to accommodate the recovering child's changing needs; the quality of support remains ever constant.

Helping Parents Participate in Treatment

Professionals need to become advocates for parents, facilitating their capacity to become advocates for their children. Parents need to be taught about eating disorders, healthy eating, and how to use their parental authority. Therapists need to be careful not to feed the misconceived "lie of separation," the notion that parents must step out of their child's life entirely in order to stimulate the child's emotional autonomy. In reality, the healthiest separations come of successful parent–child bonding and rapport, not from an untimely and wrenching separation. If a child were stricken with diabetes or cancer, the appropriate, proactive, and indeed obligatory parental response would be unquestioned involvement. The same expectation should apply to dysfunctional eating, weight management, and the serious consequences that they imply.

The mother of K, the young woman attending boarding school whom we discussed in Chapter 6, e-mailed the doctor who was in charge of her case after she returned to school to ensure that the girl was engaged in treatment and that the pace of healing was timely. The only response she received was from her daughter, who questioned why the mother was being "so aggressive" in approaching the doctor, apparently using the doctor's own derogatory term. In my mind, this mother was aggressive only in her advocacy for her daughter and for herself as a learner in her efforts to be supportive; her intervention was appropriate and intelligent, and she deserved to have a conversation with the physician. It takes a secure professional to invite and welcome such interest from parents; parental intervention has the potential to keep a team on its toes by keeping treatment goals explicit and refreshed.

Professionals can help parents by teaching and modeling therapeutic behaviors. It is never too late for a parent to begin to convey a more forceful and enlightened message to their child in need. A 12-year-old girl with anorexia whose brittle bones were already starting to break required hospitalization. I confronted her with an ultimatum about the options she faced if she were to refuse to accept more restrictive treatment. The message, firmly rooted in reality, was clearly uncomfortable for her to hear. Her mother's response was to question her daughter: "Is this plan OK with you? Do you think you could do what she asks?" The more appropriate parental response would have been as follows:

> Here is what needs to happen next, and here's why. There is really no alternative at this point, because your life and life quality are in danger. Dad and I are behind you every step of the way. We simply will not sit by and let this disease get the best of all of us. You can do this—we can all do it together.

Therapists also teach parents how to enhance healthy eating habits. It is a child's inalienable right to be provided with three nutritious meals and snacks a day by their parents, simply by virtue of being children. It is also their right to eat in the company of their loved ones.

The kitchen of a healthfully eating household is an active and heavily used place, stocked with readily available proteins such as precooked chicken and turkey breast, hummus, yogurt, cheese, milk, fish or chicken salads, hard-boiled eggs, washed lettuce, and peanut butter. I hesitate to include protein bars in this list, as these too readily become meal substitutes. Ease of preparation enhances food consumption; oversized pots of soup that can be frozen and defrosted, nuts, dried fruit, breads, noodles, cottage cheese, fresh fruits, melons, berries, and potatoes ready for microwaving all need to be replenished when current stocks are depleted. These food choices should be available apart from hot cooked meals, the latter preferably prepared and eaten together with the entire family. The therapist or the nutritionist must uncover any deterrents to healthy food provision in a family; if parents have their own issues about eating or weight control or do not want to or know how to cook, for example, these issues need to be addressed.

Parents typically do not feel entitled to ask for help for themselves. They need to learn how to use the team, how to plug into the resources it can provide, using them to their own and their child's advantage. They need encouragement and education about how, when, and why to use the child's therapist as a resource. For example, Y had a meltdown before school about what she was wearing and how she looked in her clothes. She began to hit her mother, who called 911. An ambulance brought her to a local hospital. The hospital social worker who saw Y in the emergency room called to ask for my advice. This mother would have done well to contact me first. Y's parents had failed to have her evaluated for medication according to my previous recommendations. I contacted them and offered to facilitate a psychopharmacological evaluation immediately for the child, potentially avoiding the need for hospitalization.

A seemingly intrusive parent is typically a parent without the know-how to more effectively approach her child's team; she may need guidance to learn how to communicate her needs more gracefully. The mother of a client contacted me to say, "My daughter has been very depressed this week. Would you please speak to her about this?" She appeared to be telling me how to run her child's treatment. Realizing otherwise, I helped her to reframe and restate what she really needed: "It sounds to me as though you are deeply concerned about your daughter's depression, about your own role in possibly causing it, and possibly about dealing with it productively at home." I invited her to voice her concerns together with her husband and daughter in a conjoint session. She was relieved and grateful to have been so understood and well attended to.

When Parents Have Eating Disorders of Their Own

The mother of a 10-year-old with anorexia struggled with her own continuing food issues from early childhood; she refused to cook, eat with the family, or set limits for the child's acting out or eating behaviors. In response to her daughter's decision to become vegetarian and the team's refusal to allow this option, the mother staunchly defended the child's choice by stating that she, too, had become a vegetarian as a youngster. She attributed the "lean and lanky look" to her daughter's recent growth spurt. This child faced a double hurdle in her recovery; one battle was with the disorder, and the other was with her mother, who had an investment in the child's remaining sick.

A 43-year-old mother of four admitted that her life was spent thinking about food and her inability to feel safe around it. She came to treatment when her teenage daughter began to show symptoms of anorexia. To this mother, it did not seem right to offer guidance to her child about healthy eating when she was so confused about what healthy eating was and because thoughts and words about food and eating come from "a part of me that is sick and obsessive." By offering guidance to her child, she feared she would inflict her own problems, possibly uncovering and revealing painful secrets of her own inner life.

It became apparent that this mother needed counseling for herself if she was to be able to support her daughter. It is up to the child's therapist in a case like this to help the mother overcome her own ambivalence about accepting care and to refer her to a therapist of her own. Having done so, it would remain an appropriate option for her to participate in her daughter's therapy through family sessions and/or consultation, either with or without her husband, about living side by side with a recovering child. We have seen that all too often, those who suffer with an eating disorder fail to receive appropriate care; it is never too late. Parents have an obligation to themselves, as well as to their children, to get help from eating disorder experts. Consider the next example.

N, who currently struggles with bulimia, is the mother of a young adult with anorexia. N struggles to sustain her self-esteem in the context of her relationship with her daughter. She feels that she cannot trust herself to make parenting decisions wisely, set realistic limits, or offer comfort or support to her daughter. "In my situation, who am *I* to tell *her* anything about who and how she needs to be?" She went on to say, "I so completely understand and feel for her impulsivity and lack of control that I am left with absolutely no objectivity about her suffering." Here, this parent projected her feelings of helplessness in the face of her own disease.

Not surprisingly, N's daughter had a different perspective. She was enraged with her mother for not fulfilling her parenting role, as well as terrified that her eating disorder would similarly follow her throughout her life. She felt that her mother didn't take her (daughter's) restrictive anorexic behaviors seriously because they weren't as pernicious or serious, in her mother's eyes, as were her own destructive purging behaviors."

Over the course of three decades, N had never found appropriate treatment to help her improve her limited access to her feelings and ability to make decisions for herself and her family. N clearly had a co-occurring mood disorder that was never accurately diagnosed or treated. Confirming her worst fears about herself, one therapist castigated her for being inappropriately "parental" with her daughter when she attempted to set a limit in suggesting that her sick child not spend her next college semester abroad in Europe. Her therapist demanded that she stop trying to "control" her daughter. "You are the *last* one who can help her get well!" Both mother and daughter required individual care, but conjoint sessions would also be essential to help them secure, and then differentiate, the relationship that would liberate the daughter to begin healing.

With very few exceptions, in the many hundreds of cases I have treated, I have found parents to be emotionally balanced and healthy individuals who love their child and who would give their right arm to help their child in any way they could. The truth is that most parents who suffer from personal issues that impair their ability to respond appropriately to their child's recovery would do the same to help their child. In the abovementioned case, because the mother was already involved with her own psychopharmacologist and therapist, the team was limited in bringing about change for her. The emphasis of the work would need to be exclusively with the young adult client.

Physicians

A physical examination by a medical doctor is the most important prerequisite for both inpatient and outpatient care. The doctor's examination is pivotal in determining the appropriate treatment milieu and whether emergency action or a more restrictive environment is required. The physician needs to establish and record a baseline reading of vital signs and electrolyte levels, to investigate heart function and bone density, and to initially rule out organic causes for weight loss. A physician need not be an eating disorders specialist to treat a child with these diseases as long as he or she is willing to coordinate the management of these clients with the treatment team. Medical management of eating disorders needs to be appropriate to the specific requirements for the client's care. I would urge medical doctors to attend training workshops geared to physicians who treat eating disorders, as these disorders demand specialized knowledge.

Although most teams rely on medical doctors to understand the unique demands of eating disorder treatment, the reality is that too many doctors are unaware of potential medical problems, both in managing these disorders and with their treatment. In whatever way he or she can, the therapist should inform and educate team members, physicians included, in instances where the therapist's knowledge about the specific requirement of eating disorder care may surpass theirs. Physicians need to be kept up to speed on the patient's progress in recovery. The following paragraphs outline some issues to look out for.

As team members, physicians fulfill a vital function as "weight police," in this way protecting and supporting the client–therapist relationship. It is the medical doctor who assumes responsibility for hospitalizing the client. Frequency of visits to the doctor vary according to the client's physical condition and needs, as well as the interest, prompting, and vigilance of the doctor. Psychotherapists need to respond immediately to any physical changes that a client may report, requiring that the client sees the doctor on an as needed basis. The frequency of monitoring should ultimately be determined by the physician, but with the ongoing input of the therapist, who is in the best position to keep a watchful eye on physical changes.

In addition to internists and pediatricians, consulting physicians may include endocrinologists, who treat disturbed growth patterns; gynecologists, who treat reproductive problems and amenorrhea; orthopedists, who diagnose bone density problems; cardiologists, who assess and treat heart dysfunction, arrhythmias, and circulatory abnormalities; gastroenterologists, who diagnose and treat a vast array of stomach and digestive problems, including reflux, edema, and regurgitation; neurologists, who diagnose numbness, tingling, and perceptual dysfunction; psychiatrists, who diagnose and treat mood disturbances; and dentists, who treat compromised tooth enamel and jawbone abnormalities.

Inpatient physicians need to be particularly vigilant in managing a serious adverse side effect that can be associated with the treatment of clients with anorexia nervosa: Refeeding syndrome is a potentially life-threatening condition characterized by shifts in fluids, electrolytes, and minerals, along with alterations in nutrient metabolism and other related changes (Attia & Walsh, 2009).

> Refeeding syndrome can cause sudden death in those who are malnourished or even those who have had rapid weight loss. Biochemical features of the syndrome include hypophosphatemia, hypomagnesemia, hypokalemia, glucose intolerance, fluid overload, and thiamine deficiency. These conditions may lead to congestive heart failure, cardiac arrhythmias, skeletal muscular weakness, respiratory failure, metabolic acidosis, ataxia, seizures, and encephalopathy. (Attia & Walsh, 2009, p. 504)

Too many physicians and emergency room doctors are unaware of the precise medical requirements that a severely malnourished anorexic client needs when being re-feed to prevent edema and to keep electrolytes safely balanced. All hospitalized clients undergoing behavioral therapy should be regularly monitored with physical exams and biochemical testing (especially of phosphate, magnesium, potassium and glucose), and a clinician with expertise in managing refeeding syndrome should be involved during nutritional rehabilitation (Attia & Walsh, 2009).

Pitfalls for Physicians

Medical doctors find themselves at a disadvantage in diagnosing and treating eating disorders. Trained to diagnose and treat pathology and constrained by limited time for client education and consults, medical doctors are likely to miss symptoms of eating disorders that may be disguised as signs of self-discipline and self-care. Medical laboratory tests fail to show abnormalities until the disease is highly progressed and in its most dire stages; even though one young woman with anorexia had a BMI of 12.89, her electrolytes, chloride, sodium, and potassium readings were still normal. A clean bill of health from laboratory tests typically gives clients license to engage more rigorously in disordered behaviors, reinforcing disease denial and laissez-faire attitudes about regular monitoring.

Similarly, cardiac monitoring can be misleading. It is critical that physicians not fall into the trap of considering an anorexic heart to be an "athletic heart." A low pulse rate can be a sign of an athletic, well-conditioned heart, but it may also indicate lost weight or a chronic underweight state (starvation bradycardia). A pulse that runs lower that the 50s may be insufficient to effectively deliver oxygen to cells during exercise. A 14-year-old track athlete with anorexia saw a cardiologist for a low heart rate of 40, which the doctor described as within"normal range for an athlete like you." Calling the girl's condition "fine," he set her eating disorder recovery back substantially. Specialized cardiac assessment in clients with eating disorders is generally not required unless abnormalities have been discovered. Be aware that although an electrocardiogram is an important diagnostic tool, it cannot be counted on to confirm an eating disorder diagnosis.

The greatest pitfall for physicians may be attitudinal. Many medical doctors are so uncomfortable handling eating disorders and weight issues that they ignore the root of the problem, attending only to the medical symptoms or consequences and failing to make referrals to professionals required to treat other aspects of the illness. Also, medical doctors are accustomed to seeing visible outcomes relatively quickly. Because "quick" is a concept foreign to the treatment of diseases that do not lend themselves to formulaic treatment or surgical removal, many physicians understandably lose patience with resistant clients.

Because early care is the best defense, medical doctors need to become better informed not only about recognizing eating disorders (e.g., what they are, how they present, risks and outcomes, basic assessments) but also about managing the more complex manifestations (refeeding syndrome, gastroparesis, severe metabolic acidosis, electrolyte abnormalities). Family doctors are in an ideal position to discover problems in patients who may be either unaware of an eating disorder or determined not to disclose it; they tend to be the first person consulted by parents and families. Every pediatric office would do well to appoint a liaison patient educator to accommodate the special needs of parents seeking information about eating problems and solutions to avert the crisis of a clinical eating disorder.

Nutritionists

Individuals seeking to learn effective weight loss techniques typically call a nutritionist first. Treatment success hinges on this professional's capacity to diagnose an eating disorder and refer and treat the case in conjunction with a therapist and medical doctor. Suggesting a potential eating disorder diagnosis is a delicate issue, particularly when the client remains unaware or resistant to considering the existence of a problem. In such a case, the nutritionist must be sufficiently knowledgeable about these disorders to challenge the client who seeks to enhance her "wellness."

Assessment of nutrition and eating can be a "way in" to begin the change process for the client, revealing undisclosed fears and unearthing long camouflaged anxieties. The nutrition assessment is as much about self-awareness, self-determi-nation, and self-care as it is about weight management. To a child's comment "I am feeling fat," my nutritionist partner will reply, "You know, that is a tip off that you are actually feeling something else. Are you aware of what that feeling might be?" (Natenshon, 1999).

Contributions of the Nutritionist to the Team

The role of the nutritionist is to offer sound advice about healthy eating. Healthy eating represents regular, balanced, joyful, fearless eating that takes place during regular meals and snacks and that includes realistic portion sizes and all food groups at every meal.

The food plan is the centerpiece of the nutritionist's contribution, providing structure, realistic expectations, accountability, and limit setting. In teaching the client self-awareness and self-determination, nutritional interventions provide opportunities for her to develop and practice self-controls and a healthy eating lifestyle that will endure for the rest of her life.

Eating disorder nutritionists create and vary their food plans around exchanges rather than caloric intake. *Exchanges* refer to a specific portion of food within a food group. Through a meal plan, a person is expected to consume a certain number of exchanges for each food group, including grains, fruits, vegetables, dairy, protein, and fats/oils. The difference between an exchange plan and a calorie-directed plan is that the exchange directive will assure a more balanced approach to eating. In the exchange plan, the amount of exchanges is determined by the needed calories, so the exchange plan can be used for any well balanced plan . . . for weight loss, weight gain, or maintenance. Created collaboratively with the client, the plan may be for-mulaic and definitive, detailing specific foods in specific amounts to be eaten at a specific meal, or it may be a more skeletal framework of ideas or exchange require-ments. The plan will vary according to the client's taste preferences and readiness to make changes. The client must adhere to the plan closely at first, but a great mar-gin for error must be allowed. For growth to be sustained, the client must slowly and gradually develop behavioral consistency. As the recovery process unfolds, and as self-trust increases, the behaviors may become more instinctive, with the leeway for approximation and intuition growing exponentially.

Although it is counterproductive for nutritionists to prioritize caloric intake as the focus of the food plan, they should be aware, even if the client is not, of ulti-mately ensuring an appropriate caloric range daily. That range will vary with age, height, health conditions, athleticism and exercise, and so forth. The dietitian must be careful to start out slowly, gradually increasing caloric intake from what the person has become accustomed to eating, as asking too much too soon, can jeop-ardize compliance. The nutritional demands must be made clear and the dietitian needs to be creative in finding ways to help her client adhere to them. A person requires an intake of 3,500 calories to gain a pound. It takes 1,200 calories to sus-tain weight in a bedridden (i.e., totally immobile) person. Michael Phelps con-sumed 12,000 calories a day in training for the Olympics, and Lance Armstrong needed 26,000 calories a day to bicycle the Tour de France. It is up to the dietitian to request that the client restrict exercise if she is not consuming sufficient calories.

At least initially, the nutritionist handles the weigh-in process. Weigh-ins provide accountability, reality testing, and an indication that recovery has begun. (See a more in-depth discussion of weigh-ins in Chapter 8.)

Some nutritionists offer a food plan and the instructions to "call if there are questions or problems in following it." This strategy precludes accountability, the opportunity to teach, guide, support, and provide caring attention and problem solving. The message from the nutritionist to a client with an eating disorder needs to be, "You are not alone. I'm with you, joining, watching, caring, listening, and supporting you. Lean on me until you can establish your own balance. No one is expecting perfection here. In fact, overcoming perfection will become a mark of your recovery." The process of moving from dependency to accountability will be based on the client's developing self-sufficiency.

The fear of becoming obsessive about counting calories and compulsive in fulfilling the requirements of the food plan with precision is the most common reason a client with an eating disorder and obsessive–compulsive disorder will avoid nutritional counseling. Although this fear is a valid concern, the need for nutritional counseling remains paramount, and such clients might consider seeing a psychopharmacologist to obtain anti-anxiety medication to help them face the fear of consuming required calories.

Another reason individuals with an eating disorder may refuse to obtain treatment from a nutritionist is that they believe they know as much as the professional does about healthy eating. This belief is a most insidious form of resistance to recovery. In response to such a situation, it is up to the other team members to dispel the many myths and misconceptions a client may harbor about eating and weight management, in the way of encouraging nutritional treatment. The list of some typically misconceived notions provided in the following section can become a helpful guide for practitioners.

Pitfalls for the Nutritionist

As discussed in Chapter 1, a person's healthy goal weight is the sustainable set point weight determined by the body itself—not by the client, the weight chart, or the nutritionist. A nutritionist I have worked with reported that our mutual client was "doing very well" with her eating, for she had gained nine pounds in a month. The client, however, refused to offer a written accounting of her food use. I suggested that the nutritionist be sure to investigate the nature of this client's eating patterns and to monitor what she was eating, when, and why. It turned out that the client was restricting food during the day, then bingeing on sweets compulsively at night. Her weight alone was not sufficient to disclose extreme and unusual habits. Identifying such habits is one of the many benefits attached to food logging.

The following are other pitfalls nutritionists should listen for and address with clients:

- Avoid the notion of a "target weight." If the client attains such a weight, she may cease to continue working on recovery.
- There are no "good foods" and "bad foods."

- Gaining weight healthfully is not about having an ice-cream soda every day. Losing weight healthfully is not about dieting. Both tasks require a change in eating lifestyle.
- Fitness should not be equated with thinness.
- Athletes who exercise excessively or compulsively are disordered.
- Determine whether the client has been accountable to her nutritional promises from week to week. Promises are easier to make than to fulfill.
- Though many clients find portion sizes challenging to discern, beware of requiring precise food measurement. Measuring reinforces the concept of consuming minimum amounts. It also feeds a client's perfectionism and obsessiveness.

There is no room for extremism or lack of variety in healthy eating. A nutritionist treated a client of mine who had bulimia and engaged in yo-yo dieting. This nutritionist recommended that the client restrict yeast, dairy, and sugar for the summer, then loaded her up with dietary supplements and warnings about gluten intolerance in preparation to help her lose 25 pounds. This professional stressed the importance of self-deprivation—"no pain, no gain"—advice that encouraged perfectionism, fear, and extreme behaviors in this client.

My suggestions for this young woman were to see a nutritionist with experience in treating eating disorders and to learn to eat healthfully instead, losing weight gradually and differently from any time before. This nutritionist could show her how to develop a healthy eating lifestyle and relationship with food so that the client could avoid having to diet for the rest of her life. The nutritionist who ultimately worked with her normalized her eating plan by adding dairy, fruit, more protein, some oil, and a few grain servings (the client was already eating lots of vegetables). Under the original plan, the client was eating only protein and vegetables "until she couldn't stand it, and then binged on cookies and other forbidden foods." Her treatment that summer led to the beginning of self-acceptance and self-esteem and to the dissolution of the "skinny equals happy" myth and her lifelong preoccupation with dieting.

Nutritionists should beware of offering too much nutritional self-determination too soon, before a client is ready to assume it responsibly. A college student with anorexia worked with me for a short time before leaving for college. Upon returning home, she reported what had become of her recovery once she left for college: "Once I gained five pounds, the nutritionist asked me what I wanted to do. I said I wanted to stop coming. She said, 'Your weight is good, so that's fine.'" This nutritionist blocked the client's progress toward recovery by failing to communicate what the client knew but wanted to forget: that recovery is not about gaining five pounds, unless those pounds were gained as a result of adopting a healthy eating lifestyle arising out of change that is self-determined.

The Psychopharmacologist

The services of a psychopharmacologist are critical for evaluating and mediating the client's chemical imbalances. Psychotropic medications foster emotional and attitudinal improvements that promote behavioral changes; the latter, in turn, enhance feelings of well-being and improved self-esteem, leading to changed brain chemistry and function, healing, and ultimately, the potential for a diminished need for the use of medications.

Psychopharmacologists work primarily with teams in inpatient treatment centers, where structural amenities such as regular staffings, all under one roof, reinforce team communication. The challenges of involving psychopharmacologists in the treatment of outpatient clients are dramatically greater. Medication check appointments are typically scheduled at 15-to-20 minute intervals, which may not be adequate time to meet the rigorous and ongoing requirements of the eating disorder assessment. Doctors typically schedule medication check-ups in three-week, three-month, or six-month intervals, depending on how well the medication of choice works. Clients in recovery from eating disorders and co-occurring conditions will typically need more frequent and closely monitored medication follow-up.

The therapist, in close touch with the changes occurring throughout treatment, educates the client about aspects of medication use and keeps the doctor abreast of the need for ad hoc medication reassessment. Recovery invariably causes increased anxiety and unearths underlying previously undisclosed emotions and moods, making the input of the psychopharmacologist pivotal in many cases. For clients who are too young, too sick, too resistant, or too ambivalent to contact the psychopharmacologist themselves, greater initiative may need to be taken by the therapist to procure this mode of treatment, through educating families, providing referrals, communicating with the medicating doctor, and so forth. Therapists can actively prepare clients for their psychopharmacological visits by creating lists of items the client needs to bring to the doctor's attention and questions that require answers. This preparation is useful for the doctor as well and will optimize the client's benefits from the visit. If necessary, the therapist can talk with medicating doctors before a client's appointment to alert him or her to special circumstances or issues.

A common problem is the scarcity of psychopharmacologists who treat patients under the age of 18 years. Those who do treat young children often have lengthy waiting lists. Time and again, I have watched clients' conditions deteriorate while waiting four to six weeks for an appointment, sometimes resulting in hospitalization. After being released from a hospital day program, a client of mine sustained her weight but continued to suffer terribly from obsessive–compulsive anxiety disorder, body image distortions, and frequent outbursts of violent rage at her parents. The child's medicating psychiatrist could not fit her into his busy schedule for a month. Other doctors contacted would not return the mother's call. As the therapist in the team, I called the doctor of choice to inform him of the time sensitivity of this case and to personally ask that he fit this child into his schedule as a priority.

In my experience, it is a rare psychopharmacologist who takes the time to fully discuss potential side effects of medications with their patients. Knowing what to expect can reduce the client's anxiety about the unknown and the unpredictable, always a highly charged issue for clients with eating disorders. It is often left to therapists to take on this task, particularly for the more commonly prescribed selective serotonin reuptake inhibitor antidepressants.

Educators

The level of services that schools will provide for students with eating disorders varies on the basis of the interest, knowledge, and internal resources of their staff. Though it clearly is not the responsibility of the school to diagnose or heal a child, it *is* the responsibility of the school to foster learning, which requires the student to sustain recovery changes. A child with an eating disorder is not a learning child, as learning requires concentration and a nourished brain. Many children experience effects of the disease that resemble ADHD, becoming too distracted by perseverative thinking about food and calories to concentrate in school. As much as 80 percent of an eating disorder patient's mental focus can be involved with perseverative thoughts about what they have eaten and what they will eat. The treatment team should work with the school to address such problems.

School staffs are in a prime position to identify when the child's learning capacity, work quality, or physical or social adjustment may be affected by an eating disorder. For example, the school nurse who reports a child's frequent visits to her office for fainting, headaches, dizziness, or fatigue may be identifying a small piece of a wider diagnostic picture. The nurse might also assess whether the student seeks the comfort of her couch to avoid the discomfort of eating in the lunchroom and/or if malnourishment is at the root of her physical fatigue. Likewise, knowledgeable and responsible fitness instructors find themselves in an ideal position to detect activity disorders in individuals who may be struggling with an eating disorder (Manley, O'Brien, & Samuels, 2008). The obligation of trainers and health club staff to confront these individuals remains debatable, but less so in a school or university environment where the welfare of their students is their interest and responsibility.

It has been my experience that when school staff cooperates willingly with the outpatient team, the child is at a distinct advantage in sustaining recovery gains. A school social worker who treated a client of mine periodically called me to coordinate services and keep recovery goals in symmetry. She also took initiative in contacting other team members when necessary. Her efforts were highly instrumental in moving this child toward recovery.

In a case previously discussed about the anorexic child who was not allowed to attend a three-day field trip with her class, formulating a plan of action represented a collaborative effort. The school social worker contacted me for guidance before she met with the parents. I suggested that this might be a timely opportunity to motivate the parents' incentive to demand that the child finish each meal and gain weight in preparation for the trip. The child's strict compliance would, in essence, determine her readiness to join her class in this adventure. I also suggested that the parents obtain a full menu from the cafeteria where the children would be eating so that the child might anticipate and prepare herself to eat every meal responsibly, precluding spontaneous and irresponsible decision making. In the end, the child lost weight before the field trip, and her physician declared her unfit for the experience. Children who receive inpatient care have the right to tutorial help provided by the public schools to keep a child abreast of current work and prepare her for the transition back to school. It is critical for parents to contact the school about the child's treatment plan and possible need for an extended absence.

Upon the child's return to school, parents and child need to work with teachers and counselors to enable a seamless transition back to the classroom and to address peer issues that may inevitably arise. If there are human resources available, the school might consider providing limits and seeking compliance for nutritional accountability in the cafeteria. In addition, a 504 plan may be appropriate in making classroom accommodations to alleviate stressors. Examples of accommodations include allowing the child to eat snacks and lunch in the nurse's office, seeing the school social worker on a regular or ad hoc basis, and omitting gym class from the child's daily program if she is underweight. The child previously discussed who had a compulsion to write and rewrite class notes perfectly was allowed to bring a laptop computer to school for note taking. Another accommodation involved communication with her teachers to reduce the pressure and amount of homework assigned, which she would otherwise work on until very late at night.

WORKING AS A TEAM

Diversified teams need to work with synchronicity as well as individuality. Each professional in the therapy team becomes a representative of the wider healing process, a coach and counsel capable of addressing issues that apply to all participating disciplines. Team members need to understand and "understudy" each other's parts, learning essentially to speak each other's lines as needed, fluently, throughout the course of treatment. Eating disorder symptoms need to be recognized and managed by whichever team professional happens to be present until appropriate referral can be made or the specializing team member can be consulted. As we have noted, the therapist, who generally has the most frequent and substantive access to the client and her changing needs, needs to develop a sense about when medication may be indicated, when it is working, and when it may have lost effectiveness so as to refer the client for evaluation or re-evaluation by the medicating physician. Nutritonists need to be able to deal with body image distortions and mounting anxiety in the face of weight restoration in anorexic clients. Good communication is also critical in providing continuity of services when treating professionals are unavailable. The client should know whom to contact so that any emergency is covered.

It is important for each team member to keep conscientious professional records supporting the individual goals of treatment, the responsibility they have assumed for they client, contacts they have made within the team, and recommendations for care. Record keeping generally takes the form of official recordings or personal notes. If a client demands to see her records, the provider is not required to share them but may write a summary (edited and interpreted) containing relevant materials instead. Professionals can ensure the protection of the client's right to privacy by keeping highly confidential information as "personal notes," which can be legitimately withheld from courts or other potential forms of privacy invasion. In making such determinations, the practitioner's overriding priority must be the client's welfare.

Sustaining Motivation for Team and Client

In an effort to move and motivate the healing process, the eating disorder practitioner's task is to move and motivate not just clients and families but themselves and their colleagues. In the treatment of P, a young woman with anorexia, the nutritionist and I together were able to motivate the client through motivating each other. M had had a substantive working therapy relationship with me for over a year before she left treatment feeling discouraged with her inability to make change.

Several months after terminating treatment, she lost 10 pounds; at that point, she decided to begin work again, this time solely with a nutritionist. This sensitive, smart, and caring professional made clear nutritional demands, starting with what P could tolerate, then gradually adding food challenges. P gained 15 pounds in 6 months on 1,600 calories a day. The nutritionist's goal was to help the patient gain enough weight so that she could become emotionally available for psychotherapy once again. At that juncture, she encouraged P to restart her work with me. P returned for care at a point where she felt she had become "stuck" once more in her recovery. At the point when she returned to my care, in light of the client's rising frustration, the nutritionist had begun to backpedal in her demands for change. I encouraged the nutritionist to keep her eye on the goal, suggesting regular caloric upgrades and the addition of weekly food challenges, which could also be addressed in her treatment with me. Together, we ushered the client back into the action stage of recovery.

COMMUNICATION AMONG TEAM MEMBERS

Eating disorder issues are complex and run deep, and it is only natural for intended meanings to sometimes miss their mark, requiring clarification, interpretation, and collaboration. In the case of ambiguities and contradictory messages communicated by other teammates, therapists and nutritionists may be called on to clarify the clients' misunderstandings or to otherwise enlighten the process; in cases, where a team member may not be an eating disorders expert, the therapist may even need to correct erroneous information. Such interventions need to be carried out with delicacy to avoid undermining or splitting the team.

The team becomes a consultation and support system for collaborating professionals as well as for clients and their families. In a case previously mentioned, a teen client of mine entered a day program, in which she reported a reluctance to participate in groups. For various reasons, the group leader chose to respect her choice to remain silent. Knowing her capabilities, and wishing to maximize her experience in the program, I discussed this dynamic with the client privately and then, with her permission, contacted her case manager at the facility to recommend that the group facilitator call the young woman to task, not allowing her to sit back and coast in group therapy when her purpose there was to learn and to change. The change in dynamic enabled my client to benefit from group therapy by confronting, not avoiding, her discomfort.

When a client is referred from another professional or agency, the new treatment professional might find it beneficial to engage in consensual dialogue with former treatment professionals as part of a healthy transition, but not without a signed release of information form. To facilitate regular teamwide communications, team members may consider using a simple one-sheet checklist to communicate pertinent information about the client's goals and progress toward meeting them, monthly, weekly, or on an ad hoc basis, inviting team responses and commentary. Team members must remain keenly aware of confidentiality issues in communicating between offices via fax and e-mail.

The following are excerpts from e-mails describing issues that require sharing among team members:

- *Nutritionist to therapist:* I discovered yesterday upon speaking to P alone that her parents have not brought her to the pediatrician regularly to check her vital signs, as you requested. Was wondering if you are aware of that. . . .
- *Therapist to nutritionist:* S feels "full" almost immediately after eating. If she's suffering from delayed stomach emptying, as she claims she might be, I wonder if she might be better off eating five or six small meals rather than the three bigger meals accompanied by snacks?
- *Therapist to school social worker:* If B begins staying at school for lunch, could it be arranged for her to eat in the nurse's office, under a watchful eye?
- *Therapist to school social worker:* Z reports that she is distractible and having a hard time concentrating in class. Has the school noticed a drop in her performance that could possibly be the result of malnutrition?

Privacy and Confidentiality in Team Treatment

An implicit contract that clients earn simply by virtue of becoming clients is their right to privacy and confidentiality about information shared. Protecting the confidentiality of a child with an eating disorder can be challenging, as the parent or guardian has a legal right to all information the minor reveals; at the same time, the sharing of confidences with parents can undermine trust and create barriers in the therapeutic relationship with the child. Conjoint family therapy provides the best solution to this potential obstacle by allowing everyone to communicate directly with each other without putting the therapist in the position of go-between.

Protecting the rights of any client with an eating disorder is challenging because of all the professional disciplines involved in offering care. The following are some guidelines for maintaining confidences:

- Clients need to be made aware of their confidentiality rights and the limitations of these rights. If I believe a resistant client is at serious risk, I make it a policy to be immediately in touch with next of kin or significant other, informing the client that I intend to do so.

- The practitioner is obligated not to disclose confidential material without the consent of the client. When the client's life is in danger, however, the therapist may inform others without having a signed consent form.
- In disclosing information to other team professionals, team members may offer only the information that is relevant for that individual and required to enhance services to the client. Professionals should advise the client that the information she shares will be relayed to the team as needed, with her written consent.
- Be particularly careful in communicating confidential information electronically. If there is a possibility that someone else will see it, avoid disclosing identifying information about the client.
- The burden of handling a client whose life is at risk should be communicated immediately with those in a better position to enforce compliance with medical advice. For clients at risk, a psychiatrist and a medical doctor need to be on board as available resources ready to tap.
- Before a professional can release information in legal proceedings, the client or (if the client is incompetent or a minor) the parent or guardian must sign a waiver for release (Association for Advanced Training in the Behavioral Sciences, 2008).

TROUBLESHOOTING PROBLEMS IN TEAMS

When teams don't work together effectively, they can become a liability to the healing process. Whenever personalities come together, some incompatibility is natural. Personality styles, priorities, biases, approaches to practice, attitudes toward parents, flexibility in thinking and action, and understanding of issues involved with eating disorders and their recovery all vary from professional to professional, potentially creating discord or within-team resistance. Countertransference issues, so likely to exist between professionals and their clients, affect relationships between professional team members as well. Dealing with professionals' egos can also muddy the treatment waters.

For example, on more than one occasion, I have discovered that an eating disordered psychotherapy client of mine was being seen simultaneously by a behavioral therapist hired specifically to treat the obsessive–compulsive disorder and phobias. Although obsessive–compulsive anxiety disorder can be a significant factor in the onset and evolution of an eating disorder, specialized obsessive–compulsive anxiety disorder therapy involving exposure, flooding, and desensitization fails to address the myriad of emotional, social, physiological, and relational issues central to the eating disorder. The behaviorist is not equipped to treat the eating disorder aspect of such a client's care, though the eating disorder therapist should be prepared and capable of treating obsessive–compulsive and other anxiety disorders. When an obsessive–compulsive anxiety disorder therapist is on the scene to stay, it may behoove the eating disorder therapist to attempt to integrate that professional's skills into the wider eating disorder treatment goals. I once suggested to a client that she speak with her behavioral therapist about organizing some of her weekly behavioral tasks to focus on increasing food diversity and caloric intake. (Aspects of eating disorder therapy may be considered behavioral "exposure therapy" that occurs at every meal.) Interestingly, this behaviorist chose to "steer clear" of tasks that threatened the client's vulnerability around eating and weight management issues.

When team functioning goes awry, the quality of the client's care becomes threatened. Divided and incompatible opinions are unavoidable in the face of a disease as complex as eating disorders, but they can be managed. C, an athlete with anorexia, came to her first session reporting that her internist told her that she had to increase her weight to "at least 105 pounds," leading her to believe that once she reached this target weight, she could stop recovering and never go beyond that weight. Her nutritionist, who was also an athlete, told her that 110 would be her ideal weight for making the fastest running times on the track team. Speaking on behalf of reality and recovery, I explained to her that her anorexia would be with her to stay until her *body* determined her best weight (its set point weight) It was not up to her internist or her nutritionist to make that determination.

It is not uncommon to find professional biases on the part of some team members about working with certain other disciplines. I have known physicians and insurance companies to place less value on social work treatment, though social workers typically bring the most inclusive integrative and community-based perspective to their work, so vital to the treatment of eating disorders; in addition, by virtue of their choice of professional training, social workers tend to be highly empathic human beings, another characteristic vital to the treatment of eating disorders.

Competition to decide who ultimately manages the case can result in dissent and even battles for control within teams. A doctor worked with a client of mine who had anorexia. This client was dancing 24 hours a week in preparation for a school dance show. I suggested that this excessive exercise was counterproductive to her recovery, but this doctor, perhaps in an effort to secure the girls' trust or in response to her own personal priorities and agenda, told the client, "But you have to prepare for your school dance show! Disregard what the therapist said." This doctor's role was unboundaried and overly controlling in her refusal to concede to the concerns and realities of this case as seen by other team members.

Team members may vary in their level of commitment to these cases, displaying unevenness in their tolerance to deal with the vicissitudes of client motivation and to communicate with team members and families. One pediatrician referred all his eating disorder patients out of his practice as he "hadn't the patience to listen to parents and hold their hands." A medical doctor who prided herself on working with clients with eating disorders, when asked to participate actively in a team effort to monitor and rein in a 23-year-old client with anorexia who was rapidly losing weight, claimed that her treatment style and personal belief system precluded her from demanding closer vigilance. "I'm not going to babysit her," was her comment. "It's not my style."

Client "snatching" can become a problem when members of the team are not team players. One psychopharmacologist I have worked with has, on several occasions, accepted my referral of a client, then referred these individuals to other psychotherapists, generally to behaviorists (anxiety specialists), because he believes such specialists are better suited to handle the anxiety that accompanies eating disorder.

Uncooperative team members may be "inherited" from other teams in the case of transferring clients. A 16-year-old girl with anorexia, obsessive–compulsive anxiety disorder, and body dysmorphic disorder began to improve with the medication her psychiatrist prescribed. Ambivalent about committing to psychotherapy to treat her anorexia, she asked this doctor if it would be OK for her to continue the medication and discontinue psychotherapy. "Sure, that'll be fine," was his reply. He suggested that a behavioral therapist might be a better fit for her, as she had regained some weight, and "Abbie is only about eating, anyway." He failed to refer the client back to me to discuss this pivotal therapeutic choice. Instead, he independently split the team, enabled the disease, and fed this young client's resistance to healing.

Client advocacy should always supersede loyalties among team members. V changed therapists and started work with me, but she decided to remain with her former nutritionist. The client then asked the nutritionist for shorter and more task-oriented sessions, for weekly concrete assignments, and for more self-determination. This nutritionist was offended and told V, "You are no longer making your work with me a priority. You're running away." In response to V's predicament, I asked, "Can we talk about what prompted you to request these changes, why now, and what they mean to you?" In our discussion, V articulated that by seeking smaller, more concrete steps, she was attempting to assume greater responsibility for her malnourished body; her requests signified progress, not resistance.

Because I believed the nutritionist had failed to notice this client's evidence of growth, I helped V better understand her own needs and the nutritionist's good intentions so that she could help the nutritionist understand that what she sought was increased self-advocacy. The nutritionist might have interpreted my response as potentially divisive, but my loyalty lay with the client's health and with her mature, flexible, and courageous use of self, neither of which should have excluded team consensus.

The most common response to conflict or differing opinions among team members is to avoid communication. The preferred response is to acknowledge, confront, and resolve problems as they arise. If a client relays concerns or displeasure to one member of the team about another member of the team, it is for the first member to encourage the client to directly confront the practitioner in question, offering alternative solutions to approach a potentially sticky subject. Taking such action holds great potential for teaching and reinforcing important interpersonal and communication skills. In instances where the client is yet unable to advocate for herself in confronting another team member, the therapist may agree to intervene on her behalf or alongside her.

At times, we are all guilty of miscommunication; in addition, all too frequently, clients with eating disorders misinterpret information that is properly communicated. When this happens, team members in the know may need to become informers to other team members. A client of mine with anorexia told her nutritionist that I thought she needed 3,000 calories a day and that she should weigh 130 pounds. The nutritionist e-mailed me to say that the client was on 1,600 calories a day and was doing well at 86 pounds. I responded to her as follows:

> I don't know how P came up with 3,000 calories. I believe that gradual weight gain becomes lasting gain; somewhere around 2,000 calories is what I would have imagined for her. As far as 130 pounds, I did not say that I felt *she* should be that, but that the average weight for a person 5′ 6″ tall is 130 conservatively. I meant to offer her some leeway in her perspective for weight gain and to diminish her fears about her current gains. I thank you for informing me so I can clarify all of this with her. It is wonderful of you to share these insights as she might never have shared them with me herself.

The time required for communication is a precious commodity for busy professionals. Some lack the interest or sense of responsibility to the team to devote adequate time for consultation and coordination with other professionals. When team members sense problems brewing in areas that fall to other treatment disciplines, they need to remain committed to communicating with appropriate team members actively if clients do not speak for themselves.

Sometimes, a simple awareness of potential problems can be sufficient to prevent and manage problems. A nutritionist told my client, "Don't worry. I'm not going to ask you to eat *pizza* for dinner! There are better and healthier ways to gain weight." This client left the nutritionist's office frightened that all of her fears about foods being destructive and toxic were true, that healthy eating is restrictive eating, and that one can never be thin if one eats fats and cheese. I informed this professional—delicately—that the client's misinterpretation of her statement perpetuated her disordered beliefs about food. A tone of respect is the key—*how* one approaches a fellow team member and how one says what one has to say can be more important than *what* one has to say.

Parents can also be responsible for splitting team efforts through intentional or inadvertent manipulations, potentially creating a loss of focus, momentum, and direction in the work and contributing to burnout in clients as well as professionals. The mother of a child with anorexia disregarded the recommendations of the treatment team and changed pediatricians several times, seeking one who would confirm that her son did not suffer from an eating disorder and that all he needed was a zinc supplement to restore his eating and weight. In another instance, a child who returned for treatment for anorexia after a year-long break left treatment precipitously once again because her parents were ambivalent about dealing with the child's unhappiness in confronting her eating disorder.

THE TEAM AT WORK: CASE STUDY

D, an 11-year-old boy, struggled with an intractable eating disorder. The team arrived at a consensus that if the boy could not begin to gain weight he would need to enter an inpatient milieu for more intensive care. D's mother insisted that he was of low but normal weight according to the growth charts and that the team was responsible for making him feel pressured and sick; D's father was in favor of more intensified care. It was clear that the child, caught between his two parents, was not in a position to recover.

It was also clear that something different needed to happen at this point in the recovery effort. I spoke with the team about considering a time-limited plan of complying with the mother's and child's agenda, leaving him to "recover on his own," as his mother had suggested. The plan would involve the stipulation that the client gain weight and remain under the watchful eye of his pediatrician, whom the family had been dodging for months; if he lost weight, it would provide evidence that he needed to enter a local day program.

I spoke with the child's pediatrician to ensure that she was on board with the team in preparation for the boy's upcoming physical exam, helping her to mentally and emotionally prepare for the assessment. She needed to be aware of the rift in the family's recovery dynamics and to understand that by assessing the child's physiological health, she could help the team choose from among various strategies under consideration. D's mother also wanted the boy to be allowed to attend gym class at school to improve his self-esteem, another consideration that would depend on the doctor's assessment. As the doctor found the boy to be in a stable physiological condition, the team decided that if physical education would be an incentive for him to feel better about himself and to recover, this could be allowed; this decision was reached with the stipulation that his current health remain stable enough to tolerate the activity, that he continue to gain weight, and that he remain under the care of the doctor until stabilized. Feeling appeased, D's mother recognized that because of his fearful relationship with food, her son did, in fact, have anorexia, despite his "normal" weight; she ultimately committed herself to continuing to monitor his food intake at home.

Following the exam, mother was triumphant that her will had prevailed and that the boy was found to be healthy enough to attend gym class and now could "feel and act normal at school." D's father called me, feeling helpless that his son's progress had been "placed at risk" by the doctor's findings. I explained that in having carefully and intentionally prepared the doctor ahead of time, I felt confident that she was synchronized with the goals of the team. I suggested that he reiterate to both mother and son that this was not the time to regress but to meet these new challenges with resolve and gratitude.

I had previously spoken with each team member separately about possibly offering a change of intervention in light of how stuck this recovery seemed to be. In communicating with the team now about the status of the case, I felt hopeful. We needed change; we got it. D's mother was on board once again, feeling heard and having her needs met. She conceded that her son was sick and did not relent in monitoring his food. The school was relinquished of assuming responsibility for the boy's health in physical education classes now, having gotten the green light from the doctor. We had the family's assurance that the child would continue to be monitored medically. The boy gained three pounds during the first week of this new plan and began to be less withdrawn socially. The corner had been turned.

ANATOMY OF A PARTNERSHIP THAT WORKS

An eating disorder treatment partnership is like a marriage in that each partner's function is maximized through a collaborative relationship. Lynn Freedman, my nutritionist partner in our practice, called Eating Disorder Specialists of Illinois: A Clinic Without Walls, and I have gathered around us skilled and talented physicians and resources to co-treat our clients. Together we have parented and healed our clients, as well as each other, as each other's best supporters, teachers, and sounding boards. We sincerely respect the other's work and judgment, use of self, and the quality of understanding and sensitivity that each consistently extends to clients and families. We do not practice under the same roof and don't talk endlessly or routinely about cases, though our e-mails back and forth are constant and always supply timely and relevant information about the clients we share. We also enjoy an occasional lunch together to catch up on and delve into the personal issues about professional life or client-centered crises as needed. Since the dissolution of my previous long-term peer consultation group, my nutritionist partner has consistently been a rich source of guidance and support. As the superb listener that she is, she is a master at reflecting back to me the formulation of my own thoughts. Our mutual clients agree to, and are grateful for, our ongoing dialogue about their progress.

As an example of effective treatment collaboration between us, a client of mine, F, had decided that she was "OK enough" to discontinue the therapy work and to "wing it" for the time being. F's mother told Lynn, "I guess there were problems with scheduling. Abbie was too hard to reach." Lynn responded, "Abbie always makes herself accessible to her clients. My guess is that your daughter's decision to discontinue the work is based purely on her own wishes. You may want to pursue this further with Abbie if it is a concern to you." The support that Lynn and I offer to each other not only benefits each other in our own professional performance but enriches the quality of treatment we provide our clients and their families as well.

Lynn regularly includes parents in her sessions with clients who have eating disorders, in the interest of educating them as the food providers in the family and preparing them to best support their child's recovery efforts. Although her style and sensitivity with clients takes on the feel of psychotherapy in some instances, I never feel threatened that she is taking over my job or concerned that she might be overstepping boundaries. Instead, I trust the ameliorative effects of her reiterating in her own words and reinforcing from her own perspective the same messages I offer my clients. There is always room for collaborative "parenting," particularly when professionals present a clearly united front. Lynn will hear out a client's problems that are unrelated to food but will ultimately relate them back to aspects of the client's life that parallel her use of food and her feelings toward her eating disorder. She directs the client to speak of therapeutic issues with me and informs me of emotional issues that may be of significance in my own work with the client.

In some instances, she will recommend that clients who have terminated treatment return to therapy if she sees the need. A 12-year-old client was released from a hospital day program and felt ready to discontinue her individual outpatient therapy. According to her mother, she was at a "safe enough" weight to try her hand at self-regulation with some nutritional support. When the client's progress began to backslide, upon Lynn's urging, she returned to my care.

It is typical for the nutritionist to play the role of the "bad cop" in physically weighing the client and making demands around food and eating so that the therapist can enjoy being the "good cop" with an unfettered connection. If I believe a nutritionist may not be making rigorous enough demands of the client, that is something we discuss together. In what may appear to be a role reversal, in my fully sharing the burden of making stringent demands on the client to secure her nutritional progress and physical safety, I do not hesitate to simultaneously share with the client my views about her need to rethink her eating behaviors. The therapist needs to juggle her ongoing acceptance of the client, with an ongoing and firm rejection of eating disordered practices.

A client of mine, O, suffered from anorexia and high generalized anxiety and obsessive–compulsive anxiety disorder. Although O continued to lose weight steadily, her nutritionist failed to make her aware that she would need more intensive care if she continued to lose weight; instead, the nutritionist sympathized with O, who was "trying so hard." As the client's weight slipped week after week, the job was left to me as the therapist to communicate the urgent need to turn her eating around. Her medical doctor discovered a thyroid imbalance, so the family chose to assume that the weight loss was not about O's restricting food, but about her thyroid problem. O accused me of not appreciating or understanding her, unlike her nutritionist whom she considered to be "kind and better to work with."

It is a stroke of good fortune when professionals find other professionals who are skilled, amiable, and compatible enough in their attitudes, values, and behavioral outlook to enhance and reinforce each other's work. No matter how conscientious the efforts of clients or parents to search out the most suitable care for their child, it takes similar good fortune for a client or parents to find themselves in the hands of an eating disorder therapist and team that are skilled, adroit, and compatible enough to meet their needs optimally. This favor goes both ways; enlightened and involved parents hold the potential to become the professional team's most important asset.

10

Treatment Modalities and Milieus: Integrating Diverse Resources

If a man will begin with certainties, he shall end in doubts; but if he will be content to begin with doubts, he shall end in certainties.

—Francis Bacon

S kill diversity and the capacity to select the most effective modalities and milieus enable eating disorder professionals to enrich and enhance the treatment process.

OUTPATIENT TREATMENT MODALITIES

Outpatient treatment modalities for eating disorders include brief interventions, family therapy, self-help therapies, and psychopharmacological interventions. (Because therapy with the individual client is discussed throughout this book, it is not discussed in this chapter.) Adjunctive therapies are discussed in greater depth in Chapter 12.

Brief Interventions

It seems impossible to think of treating eating disorders, which in some cases develop over decades, in the context of short-term or even single-session interventions. In reality, however, because of client resistance to care and other factors, eating disorder specialists need to treat every session as if it were the last. Brief interventions include crisis intervention, consultation, and treatment for out-of-town clients. In addition, for clients who simply cannot afford long-term care, I may offer to perform brief work that is heavily based on cognitive–behavioral therapy, requiring homework tasks, and that prepares the person for the end of treatment even while first introducing her to care. I don't think it is unrealistic for clients to expect to leave each and every session, no matter how time-limited the therapy, having gained substantive insights and having felt touched in some way through a connection with the therapist and with themselves.

Crisis Intervention

For clients who need, but refuse, appropriate care for their eating disorder, interventions that include the client's family, friends, and loved ones and sometimes critical members of the treatment team can be an effective mode of persuasion. In a crisis intervention, participants demonstrate their love and caring and mobilize the enormity of the energy behind it to arrive at a plan of action that will save their loved one's life. The goals of the intervention are rudimentary: to convince the client that she deserves to stay alive, that recovery and a renewed life is within her reach, and to move her from the pre-contemplation stage to a stage where change becomes possible (see Chapter 11 for further discussion).

Therapists may be invited to facilitate a family intervention or to prepare families to conduct their own interventions. During an intervention, the therapist helps the client's family members evoke and sustain an active dialogue about real and honest ideas and feelings. Parents need to be made ready to counter and supersede "conversation stoppers" that may serve as distractions, such as "I've heard all this before" so as to remain undaunted by the client's attempts to manipulate the moment, resist, or intimidate. Such interventions help family members know, that no matter what else may happen, they have responsibly exercised every possible option to save the life of their loved one.

Consultation for Parents

With no preparation or training, parents are typically called upon to serve as their child's case managers, at least until they can find consistently reliable professional services. Especially in localities where resources are scarce, they need the instinct, courage, know-how, and tenacity to stay with the project until successful resolution. Time wasted enables disease. In seeking consultation, parents deserve a willing and enlightened source of education, support, and motivation for themselves and for their child.

When the change process has begun to stagnate, when the current team is running out of ideas, or when parents or professionals cannot contain their own frustration and confusion about what needs to happen next, they will do well to seek consultation. Many parents choose to consult with an eating disorder therapist in the hopes of learning what to say to persuade their child to enter treatment. *When Your Child Has an Eating Disorder: A Step-by-Step Workbook for Parents and Other Caregivers* (Natenshon, 1999) offers a sample script of just such a discussion.

In considering the idea of using one's knowledge about eating disorders for purposes of consulting with clients and parents, it is a common misconception that only a few of the most experienced experts in the field would ever be tapped as consultant resources. My sense is that every professional who has knowledge about eating disorders and their treatment qualifies as a critical resource for the less informed. Every time a clinician picks up the phone, he or she becomes a consultant about a topic that requires exposition. The world needs and seeks education about eating disorders; a consultation is essentially an information dissemination process designed to determine a course of action.

Consultation, like any short-term informational contact around eating disorders, should be goal oriented and outcome driven. Clients and families need to learn not only about the disease but also about what action needs to be taken next. Professional consultation can enable a client or parent in crisis to become his or her own most effective case manager, providing the foundation of all the care that follows.

Consultation in eating disorder care is essentially a diagnostic process with some characteristics of crisis intervention. Tasks include assessment of the client's current condition and potential for growth, the quality of current care, the need and urgency for change in treatment, and specific options for change and alternative plans for carrying out these changes. Parents need to learn how to best support the child and her treatment and how to confront and work with professional providers who may be unwilling to include them in treatment or otherwise fail to respond to their needs.

The goals of a consultation session with parents include the evaluation of:

- the client's strengths, pathology, and risk factors
- the quality of current care
- the client's current progress in recovery
- the family's utilization of resources
- the resource utilization of parents.

By the end of the session, the therapist should:

- offer client and family a definitive plan of action
- suggest ways for parents and child to improve their relationship and communications with each other
- educate the family about symptoms of eating disorders, their effects on the client, and treatment options
- create and optimize motivation to change and heal.

Throughout the consultation with parents, therapists should remain highly supportive, reinforcing what the parents have done right and well and acknowledging their good intentions, the bonded and loving quality of their family life in general, and the difficulty of coping with the child's pathology. Such motivation building enhances problem solving and commitment to change.

Parents typically ask certain questions in consultations, and there are others that they typically do not know enough to formulate but that also need answers. Even when parents don't ask, I make it a policy to tell. For example, most parents do not know that 80 percent of eating disorders are curable fully, completely, and lastingly. For parents who are not certain if their child suffers from a "true" eating disorder, I help them see that if it looks and acts like an eating disorder, they should not miss an opportunity to intervene, either for prevention or for cure. Box 10.1 lists common questions asked by parents and effective answers.

At the conclusion of the consultation with a parent, the therapist may want to reiterate a few points:

- The child must see a medical doctor regularly for monitoring of vital signs, electrolyte imbalances, and heart function.
- Parents should talk with their child about what they learned through the consultation, making it clear that it is critical that she obtain help.
- Parents should encourage the child to contact the professional directly for input if she wishes.
- The family must act now because eating disorders are a threat to life and life quality; because if an eating disorder is not getting better, it is getting worse; because for a person to become and remain thin, she must eat healthfully and regularly; because the client deserves a better life; and because she is causing irreparable damage to her bones and body.
- Parents should employ a therapist who will work with them as well as with their child.
- Parents should work with their child's nutritionist; they may need coaching as the provider of the child's food and meals.

If parents or clients ask a consultant to provide consultation to members of their child's team, the therapist should be prepared to deal with the possibility of defensiveness or resistance. The therapist should point out that there are no "wrong" choices and highlight positive team dynamics and evidence of best eating disorder practices. In offering nonthreatening guidance, the therapist can note that even the best rules of practice are effective dependent on the timing of their use.

Treatment of Out-of-Town Clients

Because of the long-term nature of disease and recovery from an eating disorder, clients sometimes move out of geographic reach of their treatment team. The client and family need to decide whether it suits them best to continue across-the-miles treatment by telephone with intermittent face-to-face appointments where possible or to find a new on-location therapist and team. If telephone contact is the client's choice, the capacity to benefit optimally from such contact depends on the client's preference, skill, motivation, and capacity for auditory learning. I have frequently worked successfully with people whom I have never met personally, establishing constructive phone relationships purely by voice, through what is said, and how it is said. Regular calls depend on the client's willingness to assume the discipline it takes to remember to keep appointment times. In some cases, out of sight means out of mind. Phone clients need to abide by the same requirements for medical vigilance and accountability to the team as all other clients.

BOX 10.1

Questions Commonly Asked by Parents

Q. How can I determine the quality of my daughter's treatment when her therapist excludes me from care?

A. You need to request to become involved in treatment. If the therapist tells you that you cannot be included in order to protect your child's privacy and confidentiality rights, request to become involved in family treatment sessions, where you can offer your perspectives, state your concerns, and ask your questions face to face, without fear of speaking behind your child's back.

Q. What can I do if my child's therapist forbids me to discuss food and eating with her at home? How should I respond to the accusation that this is "none of my business," when I am forced to stand by helplessly watching her become worse?

A. As the parent, your child's health and welfare are very much your business. You are seeking to support her, not to interfere with her developing autonomy. Explain that it is your understanding that when an eating disorder controls your child's body and mind, she will be temporarily unable to make responsible decisions for herself; you seek to step in with the awareness that your active participation in her treatment would be time limited until the child can navigate her life and decisions safely on her own. You can also seek family therapy as a venue in which to speak with your child about how best to support her efforts. In fact, if she does not need assistance at this point, it would be reassuring for you to learn this from her in a family session.

Q. How can I know when it is time to seek a change in my child's treatment?

A. Follow your instincts. If your child is not actively changing for the better (in all fairness, a process that is sometimes imperceptible to outside observers), be assured she is becoming sicker. You need to communicate substantively with her team for the purposes of providing and procuring information and seeking change. Though progress can be slow, it should not be imperceptible. The bottom line for care is that change . . . whether in thinking, action, emotion, self-perception, eating lifestyle, and weight attitudes . . . must be continual.

Q. How can we know if our daughter needs a higher level of care?

A. Start with the least restrictive care environment. If recovery changes are not ongoing, consider moving to a greater intensity of care. Seek the team's feedback about the current status of recovery. If team members are reticent about communicating with you, as the parent and financially responsible party you may want to consider replacing them. If your child is an adult and responsible for her own care, all you can do is educate her as best as you can, seeking to inspire change in what you believe to be counterproductive choices.

   Your child's milieu options will be determined partly by the realities of circumstance—by the constraints of time, geography, financial resources, and your child's readiness to heal. A day program, if available nearby, will intensify the experience of eating and learning, promising to move your child's recovery forward. If not available, you may consider sending your child out of town to a residential program.

Q. What can and should I expect, and demand, in terms of weight change?

A. For individuals with anorexia, keep in mind that eating disorders are not principally about weight gain, although recovery cannot happen without weight restoration. In the absence of weight gain, therapy for anorexia can have minimal effect.

For clients with anorexia and bulimia, recovery depends on the development of a healthy eating lifestyle and the cessation of self-destructive behaviors.

Small incremental changes in your child's eating lifestyle are often hard to see. Though weight change can be slow, efforts toward it need to be appreciable and constant until your child achieves her set point weight. For clients with anorexia, protracted plateaus may occur in the weight restoration process. In outpatient work, healthy weight gain should approximate a pound a week.

Q. What can I do to help my child gain weight or stop purging?

A. Parental support comes in all forms and can be expected to change substantially in nature and process (but never in quality) during the course of treatment and recovery. Take your cues from your child about how active to be in her efforts to heal. One of the most important functions of family therapy is to help you stay apprised of your child's changing needs with regard to family support throughout the healing process. You also need to provide a healthy culture of eating in the home for the recovering child. That means that breakfast, lunch, and dinner become a guaranteed perk of being part of your family, along with the expectation that all family members will eat together as often as possible. When not together, families need to provide for healthy meals through lunch money or a sack lunch.

Q. What must I look for in seeking a therapist for my child?

A. Find a person who is knowledgeable and who cares about you enough to spend time listening and responding to you. Interview that person; find out his or her philosophy of treatment. This person should integrate cognitive–behavioral techniques with a focus on the therapy relationship, within the context of a family systems frame of reference, and in collaboration with a collegial team. This person should be intent upon learning what you need, answering your questions, and educating you sufficiently, giving you an immediate direction and plan to follow in mentoring your child's recovery. This person should also direct you to engage with a medical doctor if you haven't already done so.

Q. What if my child is not showing improvement but doesn't want to change therapists?

A. Speak to your child realistically about the potential danger she might be in and how essential it is to treat the eating disorder as soon as possible. Her good relationship with the therapist should work in your favor in providing incentive for the therapist to become more flexible in working with you, as well as your child, to seek better solutions. Be aware that your child's attachment to her therapist may have to do with what she might sense as an implicit contract between her and the therapist to allow the eating disorder to remain in place.

Q. Do my own eating issues influence my child's? Must I change my ways?

A. Your child has an eating disorder not because of anything you did, except for contributing to her gene pool. But although you are not the cause of her eating disorder, you could exacerbate one that exists or contribute to its resistance to healing by things you do and say. Be sensitive to her issues, refrain from being critical of yourself or others about weight issues, and although you need not curtail your own excessive exercising or fully change unhealthy eating habits, it helps if you can offer positive role modeling.

Q. What do I say when she says "No!" to treatment that she desperately needs?

A. Don't forget who you are. As a parent, it is your responsibility to get her the care she needs, whether she agrees or not. Use whatever leverage, reason, and persuasion it takes. Explain to her that if she feels she can cure herself on her own, she is welcome to try, as long as there are specific goals and a predetermined time parameter and she is under a doctor's care. Make certain that you don't lose your advantage by getting caught up in her illusion that she can stop this behavior when she chooses to or when she says, "I'll eat dinner out with my friends" or "I just ate, I'm not hungry." Keep the dialogue going until you have said what you want to say and she has heard it.

Q. Why can't she just stop? How do I handle my own feelings of anger and frustration?

A. An eating disorder is an indicator that otherwise controllable behaviors have become out of control. Your child cannot stop her behaviors on her own, and it is important for you to recognize this. To quote one client, "If I could stop, I would have done so a long time ago!" It is critical to her recovery that you understand her struggle and her disorder, with all of its implications.

One of my clients, H, came home from college to spend an entire semester devoted to recovery from her anorexia, anxiety, and depression. She saw me four times a week for five months, along with a medical doctor, psychopharmacologist, and nutritionist. Her family was involved in her treatment on an as-needed basis. By the time she returned to school, she had fully regained her weight and was prepared to continue her work with me once a week by phone and with the nutritionist through e-mailing her food logs. She was weighed weekly by a clinic nurse, who e-mailed the nutritionist, who in turn communicated with me. After graduation, this young woman remained in telephone treatment for the next few years on an ad hoc basis. She stabilized her weight and sustained her full recovery and came in to see me whenever she returned to Chicago. As a fully and lastingly recovered individual, the aftercare work we did together involved more precisely defining and resolving underlying emotional and interpersonal issues that had been uncovered during recovery and that warranted attention.

For those who must travel distances to seek treatment or consultation, I typically schedule coordinated "marathon" treatment segments. Clients and families typically stay in a nearby hotel and attend extended sessions daily, sometimes twice a day. The intensified focus for client and family adds an element of potency and dynamism to the process of self-awareness and change, as well as providing a vibrant laboratory for experimentation with new behaviors. Many of these clients follow up such therapy sessions by phone. Family therapy by phone across the country (and around the world, for that matter) is a potent way to educate, motivate change, reassess and redefine problems, and encourage dialogue between parents and children, in securing a recovery path.

Case Study

K's family drove four hours from a neighboring state to seek a family coaching and consultation session. For two years, K, who was 17 years old and had bulimia, had undergone emergency room visits and tube feedings, outpatient treatment, day program participation, and a three-month residency at two extended care treatment settings. The cost for the latter two programs alone was conservatively

$125,000, and continuing care would require the liquidation of her parents' remaining assets, including car, a boat, siblings' college funds, and a pension fund. K's mother had been forced to leave her job to support her daughter's travel and participation in programs around the country. The family sought help to ensure that this time around, their treatment choices would meet with success, as they were running out of time and resources. K's health was deteriorating, her weight was plummeting, her electrolytes were depleted, and she was becoming more socially isolated as her bingeing and purging spiraled out of control.

K was unable to formulate any of her own goals, stating, "I don't know what I need . . . I can hardly think straight anymore." Although her previous treatment experience taught her some good recovery skills, she found herself unable to sustain the motivation to retrieve and use these skills in the context of daily living. In establishing goals to support her strengths, I recognized the existence of past gains and suggested that together, this day, we needed to uncover and acknowledge the many skills she had accrued in her past treatment experiences. In so doing, we would recreate and reinforce her motivation for recovering her life as she'd known it.

K had developed bulimia at age 15 years, though she claimed to have known she had a problem since the first grade, when she began to skip meals, exercise excessively, and try to make herself purge. She hated what she saw in her dance class mirrors and informed her 7-year-old peers that she was pregnant to explain why, when she sat down, a small roll of flesh would appear around her middle. She envied extremely thin friends and engaged in weight-losing competitions with them. By seventh grade, K had become a practicing vegetarian to legitimize her food restriction. K had made three suicide attempts in the past, including a prescription drug overdose of 250 pills, a rope around her neck, and ingestion of laundry bleach, though she claimed not to want to die at this juncture. Her pediatrician's solution was, "You need to start eating."

Recently, K had begun the healing process at a 60-day residential program. After only 19 days of this successful start, the family's insurance company denied further coverage, leaving the parents financially responsible for the remaining 41 days of care plus the much needed transitional care that would have ensured a sustained outcome. K left treatment prematurely and lost her footing after returning home.

The only food K currently ingested was in the form of two protracted (two-hour) binges per day, followed by purging. The family's grocery bill exceeded $1,000 per week. During the binge–purge states, she went into a dissociated state, beyond the reach of self- and parental control. K commented, "I don't mean to do it; I don't know why I do it."

As a result of bingeing and purging, K's potassium, sodium, and chloride levels were dangerously low; she suffered from dizziness, lightheadedness, and blackouts during which she became momentarily blind. She currently was unable to drive or attend school. Although she had been told she was dangerously close to death, she felt she was "still living" and therefore felt invincible. She refused to take her potassium supplement regularly but instead "crammed" for her blood tests by taking three at a time so that her test would appear normal. She had taken herself off all medication three months previously.

Through the course of her illness, K's symptoms included hypomania and impulsive acting out as seen through the abuse of alcohol, marijuana, laxatives, and diet pills. She became involved with the police on several occasions for running away from home and shoplifting. She also admitted to using promiscuous sexual activity as a device to "burn calories." All of her previous treatment professionals and psychological evaluators had failed to diagnose her cycling moods, and what appeared to be bipolar disorder II. (Upon investigating, I learned that K's father's brother also had bipolar disorder.) None of the 10 different medications prescribed over the years to handle K's "racing" thoughts, attention-deficit hyperactivity disorder, obsessive–compulsive disorder, oppositional defiance disorder, esophagitis, potassium imbalance, acne, menstrual problems, and constipation would address the bipolar disorder. I explained to K that the most common cause of accidental suicide is medication refusal or failure to prescribe medication for undiagnosed bipolar disorder.

K was currently being treated by a psychologist who was reported to be the only "eating disorders expert" in town. K's therapist had agreed to go along with K's refusal to discuss food and eating-related behaviors in sessions, claiming that by making such challenging demands, she would be in danger of jeopardizing the treatment relationship and losing her client. She instructed K's parents to "back off" and not discuss food or eating with their daughter. Despite the lack of judgment and self-control that arose out of a malnourished brain, K was free to self-determine her food management. The therapist advised the parents to provide all the diet soft drinks her daughter would drink if that was all she would consume.

K's father said, "My instincts told me not to trust her advice, but what alternative did we have? *She* was the expert. . . . We knew nothing, and we dared not cross her." Their own medical doctor claimed that he was only a general practitioner and declared that it was up to the parents and eating disorder experts to come up with their own plan for what would happen next.

K was currently working with a medicating psychiatrist who dismissed her from his care on two separate occasions following suicide attempts, saying he was "off her case until she could walk herself into a hospital for care." Again, her parents were told that it was up to them to take responsibility for her care. The team members, by refusing to communicate with each other and leaving the task of researching appropriate treatment programs to K's parents, left them feeling "totally abandoned."

During the course of this single evaluation and consultation session, I educated K and her parents about how electrolyte imbalances threaten heart function; I explained that to expect cardiac "electricity" to work without balanced electrolytes is "like pulling an electrical plug out of a light socket and expecting the lamp to light anyway." I validated their efforts, accomplishments, and feelings, including K's accrued (though yet underused skills) and her parents' frustrations and fears. I foresaw optimistic outcomes with proper diagnosis, treatment, and medication on the basis of signs of K's current motivation and the support of this loving and emotionally healthy family. I helped evaluate their current treatment options. I assessed K's current motivation to change, as well as the logistical limitations of financial and geographic realities. Lastly, I outlined the following plan of action:

- K's parents needed to procure a physician's referral to a hospital for tube feeding. K had admitted that she was unable to "get my hand to move toward my mouth" and could not make herself chew or swallow.
- K's parents needed to determine whether hospital staff were familiar with the protocols for refeeding starving eating disorder clients in the event that they might be unaware that too rapid a pace of refeeding can be dangerous, uncomfortable, and even lethal; potassium needs to be administered in the right dilution as well to avoid patient discomfort.
- K needed to be regularly monitored by a medical doctor for vital signs and weight monitoring.
- K needed to see a new psychopharmacologist for a more complete Axis II and/or mood disorder diagnosis and appropriate medication, including a mood stabilizer. I also suggested that they speak to the doctor about using an anti-anxiety drug before meals to facilitate her eating.
- K was to consider participating in an Overeaters Anonymous group and engaging the help of sponsors and the wider community.
- K was to strive to recognize and revisit learned skills and recovery strategies, integrating them into a framework of current behavioral changes.
- K was to get help in discontinuing her marijuana abuse immediately, which contributed to already severe brain chemistry imbalances and structural brain changes.
- K was to work with a nutritionist whom she could trust to give her a food plan in which she had confidence and that would provide for a gradual increase in calories and weight restoration.

Following this session, K and her parents expressed relief and gratitude. This family's experience was unfortunately not atypical, particularly for folks residing in small rural communities away from institutions of learning and medical facilities.

Family Therapy

According to systems theory, homeostasis and equilibrium are achieved when systemic change occurs through the interaction of the parts that make up the whole of an organism or unit; changes in any part of a system will affect every element of that system. Systems theory provides a substantial argument in favor of family treatment for children, particularly teens and young adults who live at home. Eating disorder treatment techniques require the treating professional to join with the family; in evaluating the family structure, the therapist deliberately highlights roles and imbalances within the family system as a motivation for families to discover alternative behavioral patterns in seeking a newly configured homeostasis. Family treatment teaches a moderate expression of emotion, improves communication, and is responsive to inappropriate alliances, undue conflict or conflict avoidance, and suppression of individuation. It also provides the ideal venue to teach parents and children to heal alongside each other, protecting integrity, and creating opportunities for open communications and sharing that override the risk of confidentiality breaches, while fostering well-being.

By addressing dysfunctional family patterns, the treatment professional releases the child who exhibits symptoms or engages in eating disordered behaviors to protect the family system at large (e.g., to save a marriage) of this charge. In helping to reframe or relabel negative behaviors in positive ways, the therapist reinforces intrinsic strengths, empowering the entire system to work toward change. Through modeling values and communication styles, therapists liberate the expression of feelings, and parents learn to parent more effectively, filling in developmental voids that may have been missed in the child's upbringing and shifting the focus from the pathological child to the growing health of the entire family system.

Through work with nine-year-old J and his family, it came to light that at six years of age, his relationship with his mother had become estranged for an unknown reason, leaving him feeling suddenly unloved and rejected. His anorexia appeared to be at least partially a bid for attention in an attempt to recharge and repair the disconnections within the family unit. J's mother, who also had an eating disorder as child, revealed a similar dissolution of her own family of origin at age six, when a sibling died and her parents divorced.

Before R's parents came to see me for consultation, they suggested that the session might be more effective if R joined them to shed light on her own thoughts about her condition. She came to the session feeling controlled and angry. I was clear with her that if she felt it would be counterproductive for her parents see me, we could talk by ourselves, though I would be interested to know the reason for her reluctance. I shared my sense that from what I had seen and heard of their behavior, it seemed that her parents had acted as a loving and supportive force throughout her recovery, well intentioned and eager to learn what kind of support would be best at this juncture. I invited her to explain otherwise. R chose to continue with the session together with her parents, as well as subsequent sessions, and moved significantly forward in her recovery.

Through family therapy, parents and other family members gain permission and the wherewithal to become assets to each other and to the recovery process. Family therapy provides infinite opportunities to structure the moment in ways that are respectful of the feelings and agendas of child and parents alike. In the majority of cases, parental involvement at the start of treatment contributes to accurate diagnosis and the child's engagement In treatment. Later on in treatment and recovery, the decision in favor of parental involvement varies according to the needs of the child in recovery, her age, and life stage. Parents' involvement may take the form of cheerleading and hand holding, monitoring or policing food consumption, shopping and cooking, providing and sharing meals, carpooling to sessions and attending appointments, and remaining substantively connected to the child and the process of recovery.

One mother, early in her daughter's treatment for anorexia, left work every day at lunchtime to go to her daughter's high school and eat with her in the cafeteria. The external structure she initially provided was necessary to reinforce the child's lack of internal regulation early in treatment. Through therapy with her daughter, and as the teenager progressed, she learned to trust her child and the change process sufficiently to change the nature of her support to the advantage of both of them.

She learned to trust that her daughter would not only prepare her own healthful lunch, but remember to bring it to school and eat it among friends. Her daughter's success in self-monitoring would ultimately be determined by the numbers on the scale that continued to move in the right direction.

Group Therapy

Group therapy is the primary mode of treatment for clients in intensive outpatient day programs and inpatient or residential care, and it is sometimes available as a form of outpatient therapy. The benefits of group psychotherapy are many for clients who are ready to benefit from this treatment mode. Particularly because so many individuals with eating disorders have kept their disease hidden and experience feelings of loneliness and isolation, exposure to others who share similar symptoms in varying stages of recovery can be eye-opening and profoundly reassuring. For clients who have difficulty recognizing and accessing feelings, listening to and learning vicariously from others' feelings can augment their own self-perception. As with individual therapy, confidentiality is a basic tenet of group practice, and the facilitator should bring up this requirement at the start of every session for groups whose membership changes from session to session.

Exposure to others might evoke its own share of problems, too, for those who feel competitive about thinness or who remain impressionable and susceptible to experimenting with newly discovered eating disordered practices. Readiness for group participation demands a level of self-awareness, an incentive to heal, and appropriate and realizable goals for group participation. A woman with bulimia contacted me to inquire about becoming part of an outpatient group I was forming. As she began her inquiry, I began mine: What was she struggling with? for how long? Had she received appropriate treatment previously? What prompted her to seek a group at this point? It became apparent that she wished to join because she had not found successful treatment to date; her neediness for individual attention and lack of knowledge about what it takes to heal would render her unprepared at the moment to benefit maximally in a shared communal learning situation. I suggested that she obtain some individual help first to become involved in the healing and recovery process, develop some degree of self-awareness and personal goals, and hone a readiness to benefit from the unique opportunities that group dynamics offer.

The client who has had the benefit of individual treatment is at an advantage in knowing what she needs and drawing that from the group experience to further her recovery. Individuals who have little awareness of themselves may be at risk to become monopolizers, withdrawn and nonparticipatory, or use the group to feed the eating disorder and its distortions. Group work, though essentially a communal experience, offers the potential for learning that is highly individualized, as it sharpens the individual's socialization skills, self-determination, and self-sufficiency. Therapists should prepare their clients for what to expect and how to conduct themselves within a group format to maximize positive outcomes and minimize anxiety.

For the group-shy client, I typically ask that she imagine herself speaking out and then process with her what that felt like for her. I may urge a client to share with the group just how difficult it is for her to participate. If a client of mine participates in a group elsewhere, I will typically ask permission to contact the group therapist to share some background, impressions, and my perceived goals for that client.

Multifamily groups are a highly beneficial subcategory of aftercare groups generally provided by milieus that treat eating disorders. Individuals with eating disorders in various stages of recovery and their parents and/or families come together to further communication both within and between families, learning and sharing on many levels and in diverse contexts. These groups foster the knowledge that solutions to problems do exist, that communication has great power to heal, and that the act of sharing with supportive others is a healing process by itself. Educative, supportive, and motivational, multifamily groups tend to be drop-in groups, with a revolving membership from week to week; in that respect, these groups tend to be more educative and supportive than they are psychodynamic. Multifamily groups are an excellent resource for clients seeking to prevent relapse and for families who might otherwise find themselves to be helpless and uninformed onlookers to their loved ones' recovery efforts with a sense of powerlessness in not having learned how to be of support.

There is no ideal state of preparedness for participation in drop-in educative support groups. Such groups serve as a guided self-help support mechanism, as an incentive to heal and seek professional help, and as an invaluable learning tool. Typically peer led, such groups can be highly beneficial supplements to professional care. The National Association for Anorexia Nervosa and Associated Disorders is a volunteer-based organization that provides and sponsors access to free eating disorders support groups throughout the country.

Most groups offer clients a combination of intrapersonal and interpersonal communication skills, self-awareness, and education; others offer nontraditional interventions as well. As an example, combining traditional group psychotherapy with inspired and inspiring body movement techniques can evoke fascinating and relevant outcomes that augment the healing process. (Chapter 11 describes such a treatment experience in more detail.)

From my own personal experience working as part of an intensive outpatient facility for many years, I discovered psychodrama groups to be consistently the most popular of all treatment experiences offered by the community hospital eating disorder day program. In psychodrama groups, through role playing, the client gains access to the power of her own personal dialogue between herself and her disorder. Clients act out and resolve their issues and conflicts with their eating disorders and with other individuals in front of a sympathetic and supportive audience of peers. The scenario includes the client, an empty chair, and the facilitator, who acts as producer and director. Art classes and dance and movement groups similarly help clients regain internal controls and choices through enjoyable and effective self-expression.

Overeaters Anonymous and Anorexics and Bulimics Anonymous groups are workable venues for certain binge eaters and bulimics (Johnson & Sansone, 1993). Offering accountability, human connections, self-reflection, and personal sponsorship or mentoring, this form of care is most effective as an adjunct to professional care for some clients with eating disorders. Overeaters Anonymous required food plan, which restricts foods with flour and sugar, can be a boon to those who require limits and structure to contain their eating lifestyle; however, these same protocols could stimulate disordered eating excesses in clients whose response to deprivation is gorging. Overeaters Anonymous 12-step model differs from those of other 12-step groups because food, not being a noxious or addictive substance, requires management, not abstention, which is invariably a greater challenge.

Overeaters Anonymous does not officially sponsor a fully balanced and self-determined food plan, which could potentially lead to restricting behaviors. Group members are asked to see a medical doctor or a registered nutritionist to obtain a food plan and commit to it with their sponsor. Though groups vary from location to location, the right fit can be a real bonus to the client with co-occurring substance abuse when used as an adjunct to psychotherapy and nutritional therapy.

A full understanding of the 12-step approach takes a group participant far beyond the expectation for abstinence from self-destructive behaviors, offering psychological, physical, and spiritual enrichment. There is growing evidence that faith and spirituality can serve as healing influences for women with eating disorders. Spiritual exploration and growth during treatment have been positively associated with better treatment outcomes (Richards & O'Grady, 2008). According to Johnson and Sansone (1993), "The role of spirituality in the recovery process offers a control-and-surrender need to help patients clarify what they have control over and what they don't. A relationship with a 'Higher Power' can help manage the terror of uncertainty" (pp. 121–134).

The appeal to a higher power may be a liability to those who are not religiously oriented, particularly if not Christian. My sense is that much of the power of 12-step groups lies in the base of community support and that the "higher" energy lies in horizontal energy—a palpable human connectedness. Overeaters Anonymous at best, will stabilize a person's condition but not heal it where eating disorders underlie the overeating dynamic. Anorexics and Bulimics Anonymous is a Fellowship of individuals whose primary purpose is to find and maintain "sobriety" in eating practices. Not a replacement for professional therapy, the program uses the 12 steps adapted from Alcoholics Anonymous to address the mental, emotional, and spiritual components of anorexia nervosa and bulimia nervosa. Compulsive overeaters in particular find the program, which connects individuals to a Higher Power, to be helpful.

Self-Help Interventions

The National Institute for Health and Clinical Excellence guidelines recommend that people with bulimia follow an evidence-based self-help program while on a waiting list for care or as an adjunct form of eating disorder treatment. One study found that unguided self-help produced outcomes similar to those of being on a waiting list for care, but that guided self-help, with health-care professionals providing direct encouragement and support, was significantly more effective than delayed treatment, producing clinically impressive improvement that was maintained at a 6-month follow-up (Wilson, 2005). Several innovative online self-help programs are currently under investigation and may ultimately be recommended in the absence of alternative treatments. Moreover, as the Internet becomes increasingly accessible, it has the potential to enable widespread education and interaction via online groups (Zabinski, 2001).

Medication: The Treatment Facilitator

As integrationists treating the whole person, social workers, psychologists, and other counselors treating mental health disorders understand that any genetic, chemical, or emotional issue that goes unrecognized, misunderstood, or un-addressed can interfere with successful treatment outcomes. The issue of medication becomes a central element of care for a disease whose symptoms arise out of brain and body chemical imbalances. Patients who require medication but who choose not to avail themselves of it inevitably, and adversely, affect their prognosis for recovery from an eating disorder. Though managing medication is the domain of medical doctors, the potential significance of medication must remain on the radar screen for all members of the treatment team, all of the time.

As we have observed, the psychotherapist may be in the best position to observe the client's ever-changing pharmacological needs and requirements and to refer the client to the medicating doctor for re-evaluation when necessary. Every brain is as unique as a thumbprint, and its chemical requirements are equally unique and ever changing. If a certain medication does not work effectively for a client, she may need to be prescribed another, perhaps in combination with others or in different dosages. In addition, certain medications require periodic dosage increments to counteract the normal diminishing of effectiveness after sustained use.

Medication does not "cure" eating disorders; it treats and stabilizes sabotaging mood states and diminishes self-destructive drives, thus enabling the client to benefit from the treatment process. "A study reported that 80 percent of clients get better when they use mindful practices in psychotherapy in combination with medication" (Germer et al., 2005, p. 22). Anti-anxiety medications can enhance a client's capacity to accept hospitalization and/or to eat meals, ultimately allowing food itself to be accepted as the very best medicine of all.

SSRI Antidepressants

The development of selective serotonin reuptake inhibitor (SSRI) antidepressants has had a profound influence in increasing life quality. SSRIs render the brain more receptive to fulfilling treatment tasks and therefore reaching recovery outcomes. These drugs interrupt the absorption of the neurochemical serotonin into the brain, leaving more of it on the surface of the brain where it needs to be to function optimally in regulating mood. SSRIs in combination with psychotherapy are widely used in treating clients with eating disorders and may also success-fully address comorbid psychopathology, such as depression, persistent anxiety, or obsessive–compulsive symptoms. SSRIs in specific dosages have also helped to reduce bulimic symptoms in weight-restored individuals.

Fluoxetine (Prozac) has been successful in reducing the urge to purge and in enhancing self-control; 60 mg of fluoxetine has been shown to result in a 67 percent reduction in binge eating and a 56 percent reduction in vomiting (Wandler & Lee, 2007). A client of mine found that fluoxetine allowed her to reduce purging from three times a day to once a day or not at all while diminishing her compulsion to eat. Without the medication, she felt "unable to harness herself; it all just happens too fast." The hope is that eventually her remediated behaviors would become self-perpetuating and empowering, diminishing her need for reliance on the medication.

Psychopharmacological medications treat symptoms and functions, not spe-cific diagnoses. Medication, in some respects, functions like training wheels on a bike, allowing one's own natural sources of balance and self-sufficient empower-ment to surface. It is critical that an accurate and complete diagnosis precedes the prescription of medication. Where a co-occurring mood disorder has been missed, SSRIs by themselves cannot be counted on to alleviate these problems and, in fact, can sometimes exaggerate their ill effects.

Clients need to understand that SSRI medications do not change personality or erase pain; their effects can be better described as "lowering the volume" on feelings and affect experienced by the client. The effects of SSRIs tend to be subtle and may go unnoticed initially; the client may notice, upon looking back on some behavior or attitude, that things have in fact been subtly changing for her, that she feels better and behaves with a greater sense of control. It was not until a client with anorexia had begun to take an SSRI that she became aware that she had pre-viously been burdened by a "dull ache in a heavy heart" and a "constant, under-lying drone of anxiety every waking moment." Now she was aware that there was an alternative way to feel.

Systemic by nature, it takes approximately three weeks for SSRI medications to accrue a sufficient concentration in the blood stream to notice positive change. For the most part, the side effects of SSRIs tend to be minor and transient, as these drugs do not technically add a chemical to one's system, but simply reinforce the existence of the client's own naturally occurring neurotransmitter. Most adverse side effects can be expected to disappear within the first week or so of taking the drug and may include slight queasiness if not taken with food, sleeplessness or night waking, and headaches that can be treated with over-the-counter remedies. More long-term side effects may include fatigue, diminished sexual drive, weight gain or loss, irritability, and agitation. If the client feels fidgety, is unable to sit still, or experiences trembling, it may be an indication that another SSRI should be considered.

In 2003, the U.S. Food and Drug Administration issued a special warning about the risk of suicidal thinking and behavior with antidepressant use in chil-dren and teenagers. Anti-depressant medication appears to increase the risk of suicidal behaviors in children and teenagers. Clinical studies conducted on Prozac and suicide show that it is difficult to know if it is the medication that actually causes suicidal thoughts and behaviors; certain people may be at higher risk for suicidal behaviors while taking antidepressants, including those with bipolar disorder or those who have attempted suicide in the past. Medication must be appropriately monitored by the prescribing doctor, and the psychotherapist must remain vigilant of the client's mood and behaviors in order to identify suicidal behaviors and thoughts and be ready to intervene if necessary. No medication should be taken without consistent and responsible medical monitoring. Antidepressant drugs are often taken in conjunction with other drugs and require a doctor's prescription.

Research results on SSRI use by clients with eating disorders have been mixed. In 2006, it was reported that fluoxetine "works no better than dummy pills in preventing recurrence in young women who have recovered from [anorexia]" (Carey, 2006, p. xxx). Dr. Walter Kaye, a researcher at the University of Pittsburgh, published a small study in 2001 suggesting that fluoxetine did help some young women who had recovered from anorexia to "hold onto their restored weight," preventing relapse (Tiemeyer, 2008). More research is needed on the effectiveness of medication in treating eating disorders, but for now its use by these clients is widespread.

Resistance to Taking Medication

Referring therapists and medical doctors may need to address the clients' and parents' initial resistance to considering evaluation for or the use of medication. Some clients are afraid that medicine will alter their personality (which has in fact already been altered by the eating disorder), robbing them of their already compromised identity. Others claim that to take medication is unnatural, a form of "cheating," or of "taking the easy way out." Others are reluctant to coming closer to overcoming a disease they are not ready to give up. Some clients fear the side effect of weight gain. They may also erroneously assume that if one particular medication does not work effectively, none will. Some overly anxious clients consider medication to be a bodily contaminant. Clients need to be informed. Preparing the client for all eventualities, including expected benefits and side effects, will allow her to muster the courage to give medication a try, and will provide an incentive for the client to give the medication every chance to work. Discussing the benefits of medication is an indicator to the client that the therapist cares about her as a whole person, and sincerely wants her to become well.

Hormone Replacement Therapy

Although birth control pills remain the prevailing treatment of choice for anorexic teens with amenorrhea, data suggest that estrogen replacement, even in combination with nutritional supplementation, does not correct the loss of bone density in these individuals (Seidenfeld & Rickert, 2001). This therapy, however, "is unfortunately followed 75 to 80 percent of the time by practitioners caring for females with anorexia" (Mehler & MacKenzie, cited in Kartini Clinic, n.d.). In fact, by inducing monthly menstrual bleeding, hormone replacement therapy contributes to the client's denial of the need to gain further weight to protect her bones. "Studies also show no evidence of improvement using bisphosphonates either, despite being useful in the treatment of osteoporosis in menopausal women" (Mehler & MacKenzie, 2009).

Rather than offering estrogen to youngsters with anorexia, efforts should be made to encourage such clients to increase weight and achieve resumption of normal menses through behavioral, nutritional, and psychological therapy. "Doing better" is not good enough when it comes to weight restoration unless the individual has begun to menstruate naturally.

I have seen numerous young women with mood disorders plunge into severe and immobilizing depression through the interaction of hormone replacement therapy with their naturally occurring hormonal shifts. It is important for gynecologists and internists (as well as psychotherapists) to investigate the possible presence of a mood disorder if the client experiences extreme swings in mood around the time of menstruation.

About half of adolescents with bulimia have hypothalamic dysfunction and oligomenorrhea or irregular menses. Generally, such abnormalities do not impact bone density and can be regulated with interval dosing of progesterone or regular use of oral contraceptives (Seidenfeld & Rickert, 2001).

Medication Contraindications

Pharmacological research has highlighted the uncomfortable 21st-century reality that a good drug may not be good for everyone (Weisberg, Hayden, & Pontes, 2009). Professionals treating eating disorders should be aware of the following:

- An inaccurate diagnosis may lead to inappropriate medication protocols. SSRIs are not the medication of choice for bipolar disorder and could actually trigger the onset of symptoms (Monson & Schoenstadt, 2007); individuals with bipolar disorder and other untreated mood disorders require mood stabilizing medication.
- Clients prone to abusing medication may not be appropriate medication candidates, though a carefully followed regimen of mood stabilizing drugs might diminish self-destructive impulses that would lead to such abuses.
- Clients with bulimia are sometimes deprived of medications for attentional problems that accompany mood disorders because these medications can act as appetite stimulants, increasing the impulse to binge.
- Bupropion (Wellbutrin) is contraindicated for clients with bulimia purging type and anorexia purging type because it may cause seizures.

INPATIENT TREATMENT MILIEUS

Care within the different treatment environments, or milieus, provides an invaluable resource for outpatients and treating professionals and may maximize the client's capacity to achieve a complete and timely recovery. The best place for clients to heal is within the least restrictive environment; young children in particular need to remain in the loving developmental environment of home and family as they heal. More intensive milieu therapy offers an opportunity to energize a stalled recovery process.

The mother of a 12-year-old was advised not to bother with outpatient treatment at the start of her daughter's care but rather to save time and money by putting her directly into a treatment program. This unsound advice falsely implied that more restrictive environments are more beneficial than those that allow recovery to happen in the course of daily living, at school and at home and that all individuals and all recoveries are alike. Only when outpatient treatment proves unworkable or the child's condition deteriorates should she be transitioned to the next level of care. With eating disorders, when it works, less intensity of care is more. Therapists should advise clients who begin in outpatient treatment with the contingency for more restrictive care in the event that outpatient treatment does not enable an effective and timely recovery. In setting up a workable and practical treatment plan, practitioners need clarity, foresight, and freedom to deviate from established plans, to improvise, to approximate, to anticipate, and to accommodate the unique and changing needs of the client in recovery. It is critically important for therapists to keep clients and parents apprised of changing needs and realistic expectations as the case moves forward, explaining how, why, and when decisions are made; what they signify; and the potential consequences of their outcomes. Decisions need to be collaborative whenever possible.

After two weeks of outpatient care, it was determined that a 10-year-old client with anorexia needed a more intensive milieu in order to contain her disorder, and she entered a day program. The parents believed that I had "duped" them into trying what turned out to be the wrong initial approach, causing them to lose time and money. Diagnostically, the plan was appropriate and made good sense in its attempt to give the youngster the chance to make changes in the least restrictive environment first. This plan would have been most comfortable for the child, least expensive for the parents, and most significantly, part of a rational assessment of the nature of the disorder, the child's personality, and her internal resources and capacities to change. It was, under the vigilance of her medical doctor, worth giving it a try. In hindsight, these parents had not understood that the initial plan was a contingency plan.

Carried out by a team of professionals who function together in the institutional environment, milieu treatment provides interventions that are integrated throughout the treatment day into mealtimes, in corridors, and while lounging during breaks. I refer approximately 30 percent of my clients for multilevel care at some point during the course of their recovery. Human connections are an important factor in the success of specialized eating disorder centers. The relational benefits that come with a communal experience is evident in a survey of inpatient clients that found that they valued the communication skills of professionals, the therapist–client working alliance, the contact with peers, and the focus of treatment on both eating disorder symptoms and underlying issues (de la Rie et al., 2006). While attending a program, clients and families may or may not choose to continue the connection with their outpatient therapist whose input could potentially enhance the quality of changes happening within the milieu.

Logistical considerations, such as geographic availability and financial constraints may heavily influence the client's determination to consider treatment within an intensive care milieu. Before a client commits to any form of care, it behooves her to investigate the nature of her insurance coverage, as some companies may be more amenable to covering the costs of inpatient, rather than outpatient, care. In communities where intensive care facilities or day programs are not readily or conveniently available, and in situations where insurance coverage restrictions and financial limitations deter entry into such programs or limit days of care, opportunities for complete and timely recovery may become limited.

Intensive Outpatient Programs

One level up from the outpatient level of care is the intensive outpatient program or day program. These programs offer the client the two most critical aspects of care: (1) refeeding and (2) full immersion in the task of recovery at the least cost, as clients return home after their day of care for dinner and sleep, to return the following day to process the events of the night before. Aside from providing meals and the opportunity to process the experience of consuming them, day programs offer educative and skill acquisition groups to augment the client's treatment experience, as well as medical and nutritional care. Intensive experiences offer the client the unique opportunity to practice what she has learned and to remain immersed in introspection and healing throughout the day.

Most day programs operate from early morning (including breakfast) to midafternoon (after snack), and some extend into the evening. Programs geared to adults may begin after work hours at 4:00 P.M. and last until 9:00 or 10:00 P.M., including snacks and dinner. The provision of regular meals is an invaluable boon for clients with restrictive and impulsive eating behaviors. The specific goals of the treatment program for clients with anorexia include interruption of disordered eating behaviors, the reintroduction of 'feared foods,' and practice in normal eating along with psychotherapy and family therapy (Attia & Walsh, 2009). The continued access to the uninterrupted structure of one's daily life at work, school or home enhances the benefits of the day program. The primary indications for referral to a structured day program includes insufficient progress or weight gain through less intensive treatment approaches, the development of physiological risk factors, or the need to quicken the pace of healing because of the realities of life contingencies such as leaving town to return to college.

D, who had anorexia, began a summer-long day program before leaving for college that accomplished in two months what might have taken six months to a year had she chosen once-weekly outpatient work. Combining outpatient treatment with day program care enabled her to make a healthier and more secure transition to college, offering her greater confidence in her ability to care for herself and optimizing her capacity to sustain her recovery changes.

Hospitalization

Hospitalization may be appropriate when outpatient treatment teams have offered coordinated and timely treatment without achieving desired outcomes or when the client is at risk, physiologically or emotionally. The following are commonly used criteria for hospitalization:

- The client's vital signs are unstable, reflected in a low heart rate (in the 40s), low blood pressure, electrolyte imbalances, low body temperature, dehydration, an abnormal EKG, and osteopenia or osteoporosis.
- The client is depressed to the point where she ceases to function in normative life roles.

The client is not capable of making recovery progress through outpatient treatment alone.

Hospitals save lives, but they do not cure eating disorders. The role of the hospital is to stabilize the client's physical condition by restoring weight and internal organ and system function, preparing her to continue treatment effectively in a less restrictive environment. Hospitalized clients benefit by receiving a complete diagnostic assessment to determine the need for medication or to adjust current medications.

When a client is unable to eat for whatever reason, hospital care can provide involuntary feeding methods, including tube feeding, stomach shunt, or tracheal intubation. It is critical that hospital staff understands the complexities of the refeeding syndrome (see Chapter 9). If blood chemistries are not kept in balance, refeeding can result in painful edema and potentially lethal side effects. Refeeding through normal food intake should take place gently, starting with 1,200 to 1,500 calories daily, with regular increases. The goal for weight restoration should be one to three pounds per week in hospital.

Hospitalization should never be used as a threat but rather as a solution to a problem that the client has been unable to fix through outpatient care. In determining the appropriate level of care, the question is how much support the client needs in order to practice effective self-care. Because weight restoration alone does not signify recovery from an eating disorder, outpatient treatment following hospitalization is necessary to further the client's efforts to achieve recovery goals and to sustain the goals she has accomplished.

Sometimes clients need to be hospitalized involuntarily. When an adult with an eating disorder is faced with making potentially life-saving decisions but is deprived of the capacity to do so by her disease, it is up to the next of kin, in conjunction with health professionals, to see to it that she gets the attention she requires. For the noncompliant adult child older than 18 who refuses life-saving care, parents may need to hire a lawyer and take over legal guardianship in order to commit the child to an appropriate venue. In other instances, the state can take over guardianship and demand involuntary hospitalization in cases where there is clear and convincing evidence that a person is a danger to self or others. Clients are required by law to be admitted to the least restrictive treatment environment and can release themselves after a brief stay. Fortunately, many clients who are involuntarily hospitalized learn and change enough in the first days of care to become more willing and motivated to continue with treatment (Guarda et al., 2007).

The strength of the parent–child relationship in most healthy families often negates the need for draconian legal measures to persuade an adult family member to enter a facility. The parents' responsive, determined, and loving commitment to care is usually all that a client needs to agree to submit to residential or hospital care. By taking action to follow through on their commitment to do right by their child, parents need to mean what they say, and say what they mean, as responsible and loving parents. In one instance, parents surprised their 18-year-old bulimic daughter by waking her at 4:00 A.M. and presenting her with a packed suitcase and the reality that a cab would be in the driveway in 20 minutes to take them to the airport to fly to a residential care facility in Oklahoma. She later claimed that their ambush-style tactic, though heavy handed, had saved her life. Therapists can be helpful in providing guidance and alternatives for action to parents and family members who are considering committing their child to hospitalization or long-term care.

Residential Facilities and Halfway Housing

Intensive and long-term immersion in residential care provides the client with the opportunity to integrate her accruing recovery skills. However, recovery changes need to be practiced and solidified within the context of daily living to secure sustainability. The transition to the realities and stressors of the "real world" can be jarring for the client who has been sequestered in the rarefied environment of a residential facility, throwing a recovering individual off balance and increasing the likelihood of relapse.

Halfway houses provide the most affordable and least intensive form of residential care. The client seeking a longer-term tenure than a hospital can provide may consider placement in a residential facility. Based on the peer support model and providing living accommodations (small apartments) geared for clients with a history of recidivism following recovery gains, these facilities extend the period of active recovery by offering clients limited therapy and supervision as they assume the responsibilities of normalized living. Participants go to work every day, return "home" (to the halfway house) to eat dinner with peers, and join support groups led by professionals to process the dynamics of their daily life. The consistent therapeutic support helps clients retain their gains and handle regressions quickly and effectively to prevent relapse. Most are covered by insurance, and some even offer scholarships (Poppink, 2006).

Transitions Between Milieus

Healthy communications between outpatient and inpatient venues can be instrumental in helping clients make productive transitions into and out of intensive care, providing treating professionals with the opportunity to share impressions about the patient's changing needs and status in coordinating best practice and team function. The outpatient therapist's feedback can become an invaluable tool to guide the provision of inpatient care and vice versa. As an example, an intensive outpatient program put a patient's dietary plan "on maintenance" (rather than asking the patient to continue gaining weight toward achieving her set point goal). This action fed the patient's denial that she had to fully restore her weight, inadvertently negating the outpatient team philosophy and sabotaging her recovery efforts. Professional communication rectified the situation to the benefit of the client.

Strategy: For best results, transitions can be made smoother if the outpatient therapist prepares the patient for what she can expect upon entry into an inpatient program, and if inpatient professionals prepare the patient with coping techniques in anticipating and readying herself for life on the outside

At what point is it appropriate to release an inpatient or day program participant back to outpatient treatment?

Case study: A divorcing couple contacted me to consult about when their child would be ready to transition from inpatient care to outpatient care. The program apparently had not offered guidelines about termination, which had become particularly critical at that point in light of the insurance company's refusal to pay the $1,000 per day costs. In their preparation to fight for continued coverage for inpatient services, these parents had been under the misconception that patients are supposed to fully "recover" in inpatient care, which had not yet happened for their daughter. They were confused about how she could leave there if so many of her underlying issues yet remained unresolved. During her 60 days of inpatient care, she had ceased purging and had resumed a normal eating lifestyle, gained back much of the weight she had lost, and in fact, had become a likely candidate to transition to outpatient care; her readiness to leave the facility would depend on four questions:

1. Had she achieved sufficient physical safety and stability to allow her to recover in outpatient care?
2. Had she developed sufficient motivation to heal, coping tools, and recovery skills to continue her recovery in the context of daily living?
3. Would the insurance company make her continued stay at the facility a viable reality?
4. Should she be released into a day program prior to being sent home for outpatient care?

Realistically, only time, experience and "therapy mileage" ensures a complete and sustained recovery for any patient. These parents, along with their child, needed to begin to prepare themselves for the child's transition home and into the outside world, where her recovery would be a more individual endeavor. It would be up to the parents to find an outpatient therapist facile in treating families as well as individuals, which was particularly critical in light of the parents' current separation and impending divorce. These parents would need to learn to present a clearly united front to the child about her recovery efforts and learn how best to support her efforts to sustain her current gains. Having achieved weight restoration and physiological stabilization, patients need to "own" their own preparedness to return their child to an outpatient aftercare situation.

SELECTING THE APPROPRIATE PROGRAM

Beware of commonly held myths about eating disorder treatment milieus, which can act as decoys blocking understanding and effective and rational responses to care. A doctor told the mother of a youth with an eating disorder, "Don't waste time with outpatient treatment. Just put her directly into a program and get the problem fixed." Some parents report being told by their pediatricians that children need to "hit bottom first " making them eligible for the hospitalization that will "cure" them.

A mother of a child with an eating disorder described having contacted close to 10 facilities; after careful interviewing and assessment, she came to the conclusion that "everyone has a winning description to share. What I learned is that this will cost a great deal of money and will have a tremendous impact on my daughter's life . . . there is little room for error, here, as the money source is finite. Whatever we choose had just better be the right place."

It behooves clinicians to advise patients about the quality of care in alternative programs, though in most circumstances, the decision about placement will be made by the patient and parents in dialogue with milieu staff. In seeking optimal care in guiding patients and parents, several issues need to be considered and shared:

- There are many fine and well-reputed residential facilitates across the country to choose from. Unfortunately, it has been my experience that even the best of places may not be a perfect fit for every patient who enters and participates.
- Any program is only as effective as the professionals and administrator running it. Patients are offered no guarantees of recovery. I have known some patients to have productive experiences and others to have "disastrous" experiences, even within the context of the same residential facility. It is left to families and outpatient therapists to intervene on behalf of the child patient to customize and upgrade the quality of an experience that seems less than ideal.
- Local, smaller community facilities, usually hospital-based, frequently offer multilevel options for care that can be counted on to provide predictably high-level services. Such versatile near-home facilities, in allowing the patient the diversity of a recovery within the more normalized milieu of home, school, work, friends, and family . . . may offer a preferable option to "away from home" resources. It takes initiative on the part of professionals, patients, and parents to investigate these options.
- In order to provide the best advice and counsel to prospective inpatients, it is helpful for practitioners to visit inpatient facilities to become as familiar as possible with the quality of treatment and routine practices, as well as the knowledge of the staff.

Tip: In determining a choice of milieus, it is best for there to be a number of patients participating on the ED unit for patients to derive the best group-based care. Group dynamics are central to the effectiveness of communally-based ED facilities. In an ideal situation, therapy groups are best if segregated according to age/life stage.

Tip: The amount of time spent at a milieu, by itself, will not ensure recovery. Quality of care, in combination with the patient's motivation and readiness to heal, along with the availability of support resources, will provide more accurate determiners of successful outcomes.

In some cases, a likely alternative to failed outpatient care might simply require a change or changes in the outpatient team with the hope of finding professionals with a greater level of expertise and experience. If upgrading the level of expertise of treating professions could make progress more accessible, enhancing outpatient care in this way could potentially negate the need for clients to enter, or re-enter, an intensified treatment milieu.

The parents of an anorexic young woman sought help in finding a long-term residential facility for their daughter after having discovered that she was continuing to lose weight despite having been treated for an eating disorder at college. Though this young woman had been under the care of three separate therapists, two nutritionists, and two outpatient hospital-based day programs in the course of her three-year recovery journey, her parents described the nature of all of these past treatment as "unsuccessful" and "random," with uncoordinated or non-existent treatment team efforts.

In light of the youngster's less than successful past care, my prescription was to evaluate her current situation to assess her accrued progress and strengths, which might more consistently be called up through the functioning of a more effective outpatient team at this juncture. These parents had been operating under the misconceptions that residential care would be necessary to provide the " final fix" for their daughter, that the quality of all outpatient treatment is equal, and that patients come away from "unsuccessful" treatment experiences having gained little or nothing at all. None of these assumptions are correct.

Troubleshooting Within the Context of Milieu Care

Program staff need to be particularly sensitive to the needs of the individual as she plays a part in the wider residential group community. A patient who attended a day program complained that the "one-size-fits-all" program was not individualized enough in its capacity to listen and attend to her unique needs. As a robust athlete, she described wolfing down her food at meals and being left to sit and watch the emaciated anorexic patients surrounding her struggle for extended periods of time over every meal; as a result, she found herself starting to obsess about food, which made her feel like a pariah and surely an unlikely candidate to prosper at that program. No one offered to process that dynamic with her. "As a binge eater, they told me the same thing they told the anorexic patients: 'You have to gain weight' rather than 'You owe it to yourself to learn to eat without fear and care for yourself to the point where you *want* to nourish your body healthfully,'" she reported.

Tip: One of the greatest deterrents for patients entering a milieu setting is how to explain their absence from school to peers should they prefer to keep their condition private. Adult eating disorder patients may seek to keep their participation in day programs hidden from their spouse, children, extended family, and so forth. The issue of whether to lie or tell the truth is a therapeutic decision, concerning the individual's shame versus acceptance of her disease and recovery.

SECTION 4

THE EATING DISORDERS
TREATMENT TOOLBOX

11

As the Brain Learns, People
Change: Innovative Treatment
Approaches That Work

*Psychotherapy works by going deep into the brain and its neurons and
changing their structure by turning on the right genes.*
—Norman Doidge

THE LEARNING BRAIN

The vertical multi-mile sheering of rock by the passage of wind and water from
the beginning of time continues to carve its own unique signature in the creation
of the Grand Canyon. The continuing forces of nature that have created the depth
and age of these canyons make structural changes in the Canyon slow to evolve.
The human nervous system has been described as a learning system; the brain is
trainable and expandable in recruiting other pathways in the brain that lie fallow.
As Norman Doidge has described in *The Brain That Changes Itself*, within the
human brain, the formation of neuronal pathways carved from deeply rutted
habituated behaviors is in some respects similar, though happily, the results are
far more malleable in developing rich networks of neuronal tributaries, estuaries,
tide pools, and puddles. These are capable of altering the direction, speed, and
flow of ever-changing cognitions and behaviors within the human experience,
which in turn, direct the formation of new neuronal pathways. Like a beaver
building a dam to change the distribution of water in the aftermath of natural
forces, the patient who rejects an obsessive focus of the past to rethink and re-
create the course and flow of the present, has a hand in creating a far-reaching
influence on her brain to affect the future.

The human nervous system is a learning system; the brain is trainable and expandable, able to create and recruit alternative pathways for use when others lie fallow. The mind develops across the lifespan as the genetically programmed maturation of the nervous system is shaped by ongoing experience. Genes, in combination with experience, shape our neural connections, creating intelligence and instinct. The trillions of synaptic linkages in our brains are created by both genes and experience. In the book, *The Brain That Changes Itself*, Norman Doidge speaks of the experience (of movement and behavior) as creating neuronal networks from the "outside, in."

I learned to play tennis in my mid-20s. For decades I took ineffectual lessons taught by ineffective teachers and was content to play tennis with mediocrity, injuring elbows, knees, heels, and so forth. One day three years ago, at close to age 60, I stood transfixed, watching a pro who had been a Davis Cup champion hit a ball back and forth with his student at my tennis club in a way that I had never seen (or heard) before. I decided then and there that I, too, wanted to learn to hit a tennis ball "so that it knows it's been hit." It's not easy to unlearn bad habits, particularly for an aging person who is hardly a natural athlete. But for two years, I enjoyed my struggle to input this brilliant new information into my old brain and body, experiencing only intermittent successes even under these most ideal situations. My efforts were interrupted by an 18-month break because of an Achilles tendon injury that required surgery and rehab.

To my amazement, when I was able to first pick up a tennis racket again, I discovered that the new neuronal pathways I had developed gradually and painstakingly during those two years of learning and practice were happily still gracing me with their presence. My teacher began to laugh after hitting shots to my backhand, which I returned deftly, two handed. I had forgotten (but he and my brain had not) that my 30 previous years of hitting one-handed backhands had been superseded by a new network of dynamite neurons; his two-handed backhand techniques had become my new default.

"Maintaining improvement and making a skill permanent requires slow, steady work in forming new connections" (Doidge, 2007, p. 199). "Shaping" or "incremental" training molds a behavior in very small steps (Doidge, 2007), allowing the brain to recover from atrophy, to relearn lost or missing functions (or to replace old learning) step by step, through approximation, slowly, and with attention. Sustained practice solidifies learning (Doidge, 2007, p. 200), although as Feldenkrais put it, so smart is the brain, when we permit it, even after doing something a million times the wrong way, doing it right even one time feels so good that the brain–body system recognizes it immediately as right (Feldenkrais, 1949).

EARLY RESEARCH ON EATING DISORDERS AND THE BRAIN

During the early 1970s in England, psychotherapist John Hevesi, in conjunction with the Anorexic Aid Society of Great Britain and mathematician Christopher Zeeman, used a mathematical model called "catastrophe theory" to describe the progression of anorexia and the benefits of using trance inducement (a sleep state) to stimulate structural brain changes; this therapy had resulted in complete recovery for 80 percent of Hevesi's clients (Zeeman, 1976, p. 61).

The work of these researchers provided early evidence of the importance of plasticity in brain structure and function in eating disorder treatment. Zeeman (1976) observed that "the mathematics was insisting that we ought to look at the underlying neurology as well as the psychology even if only implicitly, in order to locate the dynamic" (p. 70).

Hevesi and Zeeman observed that typically, "after two years of commitment to anorexic food restriction, the person finds herself alternately fasting and gorging, which these researchers called bimodal behaviors, bringing about the onset of bulimia and entrapment in a "catastrophic jumping between two abnormal extremes." The person is denied access to the normal person's rhythm of eating and satiety, which represents a "continuous smooth cycle of unimodal behavior" (Zeeman, 1976, p. 47). Zeeman explained anorexia "not as the complicated behavior of a perverse neurotic, but as the logical outcome of the structure of brain changes where the limbic brain jumps from one set of states to the other, denying the person access to the normal states in between" (Zeeman, 1976, p. 47). He recommended connecting the extreme behaviors through "opening up a new pathway back to normality" by creating a third abnormal behavioral mode through a trance state, during which the person's insecurity could be treated with reassurance, causing a catastrophic collapse of the abnormal attitudes" (Zeeman, 1976, p. 52).

With our current understanding of brain plasticity, today we would conclude that these researchers sought to create access to new options for behavior and attitudes by creating new neuronal pathways. In inducing a trance state in clients, they sought the potential for normalcy in the "twilight zone between waking and sleeping" and "between dreaming and perceiving" typical of the trancelike states of people with anorexia, who typically suffer disturbed sleep patterns (Zeeman, 1976, p. 54).

Hevesi's therapy technique was similar to current attempts to evoke the mindful state. He suggested to participants, "We don't need to talk about food," reducing the somatic input, and "Take a look inside yourself; let your mind drift," reducing the cerebral input. . . . "Thus, the mind is cleared of food and scheming and becomes free to look at itself" (Zeeman, 1976, pp. 54, 56).

> By suspending the threats, the rules, the resistance and the hunger, the trance offers temporary freedom from anxiety. The patient becomes better able to inspect the products of her own mind, contemplating its images and memories; in this state she remains open to reassurance and becomes able to work out her own reassurance. (Zeeman, 1976, p. 56)

"In the trance or mindful state, the 'real self' observes the other selves (or parts) within; ultimately, the participant emerges with renewed access to the unified normal self, capable of eating again without fear of gorging" (Zeeman, 1976, p. 60).

"The trance Hevesi induced was not a hypnotic state, but rather a state of mind (a mindful state) induced by the participant's own self, through the intensity and depth of her own internal focus, that puts her into a contemplative state of internal clarity: "When a person goes into trance, the reduction of sensory input causes a shift in focus, from the close-up to the long-distance, from the immediacy of mood and behavior to the long-term perspective of personality and insight" (Zeeman, 1976, p. 60). Thus, this research foreshadowed mindfulness in psychotherapy.

THE NEUROPLASTIC BRAIN: THE NEW FRONTIER FOR EATING DISORDER TREATMENT

As biopsychosocial disorders, eating disorders are diseases of the brain. Until the mid-20th century, scientists believed that the brain was hardwired and unchanging and that people are born with predestined potential and limitations. Neuroplasticity research that began in the late 1960s, however, showed that the brain changes its very structure with each different activity it performs, continually "perfecting its circuits to be better suited to the task at hand. If parts 'fail,' than other parts take over; if brain cells die, they can at times be replaced or other parts recruited to take over their function" (Doidge, 2007, p. xv).

The neuroscientist Michael Merzenich argued that practicing a new skill, "under the right conditions, can change hundreds of millions and possibly billions of connections among the nerve cells" (Doidge, 2007, pp. 46, 47) in our brain's maps, continuing into adulthood. Merzenich found that "the maps of normal body parts change every few weeks" (Doidge, 2007, pp. 61, 62) "through reorganization that occurs within and across brain sectors"(Doidge, 2007, p. 161). He hypothesized that "neurons in brain maps develop strong connections to one another when activated at the same time and that new maps can be formed by getting healthy neurons to fire together and wire together" (Doidge, 2007, p. 63).

The Neurobiology of Relationship

Although I have referred to establishing the relationship in eating disorder treatment as an art, the healing therapeutic connection enjoys its own foundation in brain physiology. Neuroimaging studies of structural brain changes associated with the process of relationship within psychotherapy demonstrate that relational experiences in psychotherapeutic treatment result in detectable changes in the brain (Doidge, 2007, p. 233). "The aim of talking cure . . . from the neurobiological point of view [is] to extend the functional sphere of influence of the prefrontal lobes" (Doidge, 2007, p. 233).

> The emotions and the patterns people display in relationships are part of the procedural memory system. When such patterns are triggered in therapy, it gives the client a chance to look at them and change them. When clients relive a trauma, for example, and have flashbacks and uncontrollable emotions, blood flow decreases to the prefrontal and frontal lobes, which help regulate behavior, and the more primitive areas of the brain take over, resulting in impulsive behaviors. (Doidge, 2007, p. 233)

Siegel (2006) developed an approach to psychotherapy called "interpersonal neurobiology" in which "the objective domains of science and the subjective domains of human knowing find a common home" (Siegel, 2006, p. 1). Siegel defined *mind* as "an embodied process that regulates the flow of energy and information"; he described regulation as "being at the heart of mental life." He stated that "energy and information can flow within one brain, or between brains, and that relationships profoundly shape the flow of energy and information within and between people." (Siegel, 2006, p. 1)

In describing the interdependence between nature and nurture, Siegel demonstrated that "heritable factors that were once seen as immutable are alterable through different forms of environmental stimulation and learning, resulting in the creation of newly forming neural pathways in an ever-changing brain. Synaptic linkages, created by genes and by experience, shape new connections among neurons depending on how genes are activated, proteins are produced, and interconnections are established within the neural system." (Siegel, 2006, p. 2)

Siegel (2006) summarized the newly evolving understanding of the potential for brain plasticity to facilitate and enhance psychotherapeutic learning:

Being emphatic with patients may be more than just something that helps them "feel better"—it may create a new state of neural activation with coherence in the moment, the possibility for interpersonal attunement to initiate a new form of awareness that makes intrapersonal attunement possible, improving the capacity for self-regulation" (p. 3)

Such interactive experiences, which allow the client to "feel felt" and understood by the therapist, also may establish new neural network firing patterns that can lead to neural plastic changes. The "mirror neuron mindfulness hypothesis" proposes that the focusing of one's nonjudgmental attention on the internal state of intention, affect, thought, and bodily function may be one way in which the brain focuses inward to evoke well-being. . . . Ultimately lasting effects of psychotherapy must harness such experiences that promote the growth of new synaptic connections so that more adaptive capacities for self-regulation and well-being can be established. (Siegel, 2006, p. 2)

Psychotherapy and Brain Structure

Psychiatrist Norman Doidge (2007), in his fascinating and readable book, *The Brain That Changes Itself: Stories of Personal Triumph From the Frontiers of Brain Science*, confirmed that "thinking, learning, and acting can turn our genes on or off, thus shaping our brain anatomy and behavior. When we learn, our minds influence which genes in our neurons are transcribed. Thus we can shape our genes, which in turn shape our brain's microscopic anatomy" (p. xv). In his book, Doidge (2007) recounted neurologist Álvaro Pascual-Leone's description of brain change:

The plastic brain is perpetually altered by every encounter, every interaction. . . . The plastic brain is like a snowy hill in winter. Aspects of that hill—the slopes, the rocks, the consistency of the snow—are, like our genes . . . a given.

> When we slide down on a sled, we can steer it and will end up at the bottom of the hill by following a path determined both by how we steer and the characteristics of the hill. Where exactly we will end up is hard to predict because there are so many factors in play. The second time you take the slope down, it won't be exactly that path, but it will be closer to that one than any other. And if you spend your entire afternoon sledding down, walking up, sledding down, at the end you will have some paths that have been used a lot, some that have been used very little . . . and there will be tracks that you have created, and it is very difficult now to get out of those tracks. And those tracks are not genetically determined anymore. (p. 209)

Is it possible, once "tracks" or neural pathways have been laid down, to get out of these paths and onto different ones? Yes, according to Pascual-Leone, but it is difficult because once we have created these tracks, they become "really speedy" and very efficient at guiding the sled down the hill. To take a different path becomes increasingly difficult. A roadblock of some kind is necessary to help us change direction (Doidge, 2007).

In 1895, Freud began the "Project for a Scientific Psychology," one of the first comprehensive neuroscientific models to integrate brain and mind and propose neuroplastic ideas. In this work, Freud described the "synapse" several years before Sir Charles Sherrington, who bears the credit, and he offered a description of how synapses might be changed by what we learn (Doidge, 2007, p. 223). Freud discovered that transferences of early traumatic scenes could often be altered if he pointed out to his patient what was happening when the transference was activated and the patient was paying close attention. Thus, the underlying neuronal networks, and the associated memories, would be retranscribed and changed (Doidge, 2007, p. 225). Freud argued that to be changed, memories had to become the focus of conscious attention, as neuroscientists has since shown. Regression in analysis at a neuronal level may be an instance of unmasking older neuronal paths and thought, one of the chief ways the brain reorganizes itself (Doidge, 2007, p. 235). As the "father of psychology," Freud was prophetic in ascribing changes that occur through the psychoanalytic process as being related to organic brain changes. In his conceptualization of regression, Freud foresaw what now might be considered mindfulness in psychotherapy, the importance of paying close attention, as a process that Doidge believes takes place on a neurological level and precedes psychological reorganization.

Brain Integration and Learning

Separate areas of the brain are linked in an integrated system that is a flexible, adaptive, coherent, energized, and stable whole. described integration and coherence as the flow of a river that is banked on one side by rigidity and on the other by chaos (Siegel, 2006). The process of differentiation precedes the brain's capacity to reorganize and integrate new learning; the brain learns through variation and through the capacity to sense differences.

My 2-year-old grandson was making a racket at the dinner table one night, kicking his shoes against his highchair, entertained by the joy of his own discovery and attention from the family. I suggested that he kick the chair as loudly and as fast and hard as he possible could. He enjoyed this experiment immensely. Then I suggested that he kick the chair as slowly and as softly as he possibly could, seeing if he could make it so soft that no one else at the table would know that he was even moving his feet. This activity was not only an exercise in loud and soft, fast and slow, hard and gentle and the potential for variation in the way he uses himself, but it created an action for him that became empowering in offering self-control, self-determination, self-satisfaction, and yet another "can-do" self-esteem builder.

Any therapeutic experience that moves an individual toward well-being promotes integration (Siegel, 2006). Siegel claimed that "being empathic with the client through the mirror neuron system may be more than just something that helps her "feel felt and feel better"; it may create a new state of neural activation with coherence in the moment that improves the capacity for self-regulation" (Siegel, 2006, p. 11). Siegel spoke of nine domains of brain integration that move the brain toward well-being; I will comment in the paragraphs that follow on three of these—integration of consciousness, vertical integration, and interpersonal integration—which address brain function in therapeutic change through eating disorder treatment.

The integration of consciousness (mindful awareness) enables new patterns of neural activation to occur (Siegel, 2006, p. 3).

> Where attention goes, neural firing occurs, and where neurons fire, new connections can be made. In this manner, learning a new way to pay attention within the integration of consciousness enables the client with an open receptive mind to catalyze the integration of new combinations of previously isolated segments of his or her mental reality. (Siegel, 2006, p. 4)

Vertical integration "links the basic somatic regulatory functions of the brain stem with the limbic circuit's generation of affective states, motivational drives, attachment, and appraisal of meaning. Mirror neurons reveal the fundamental integration within the brain of the perceptual and motor systems with limbic and somatic regulatory functions. In other words, "the mind is embodied, built in part from its roots in somatic reality" (Siegel, 2006, p. 4). I believe this concept goes far to explain the impact of techniques involving body movement, with attention on eliciting change in emotions and cognition.

Interpersonal integration involves the mirror neuron system, which enhances empathy, where "resonance," or perceptions of another's affective expressions, may alter our own somatic and limbic states. Being open to one's own bodily states as a therapist is a crucial step in establishing the interpersonal attunement and understanding that are at the heart of interpersonal integration. Countertransference represents a way in which the therapist's own nonverbal shifts in brain state offers a direct glimpse into the internal world of the patient" (Siegel, 2006, p. 10). As the therapist attempts to achieve an open, receptive state of awareness toward the client's internal state changes and the interpersonal signals sent, the client's mind is offered important social experiences to create a similar state of awareness.

When the therapist is sensitive to the client's signals and also has made sense of his or her own life, the state of brain activation in the therapist serves as a vital source of resonance that can profoundly alter the ways in which the client's brain is activated in the moment-to-moment experiences within therapy.

Neuronal Incentives to Take Action

Brain research has showed that people become aware of the intention to act after the brain has readied itself to act and before motor activity begins. The fact that one's intention to act is formulated in the brain before one becomes aware of it suggests that people may be able to change the brain through mindfulness practice and psychotherapy and that the individual has an opportunity to better control behavior by increasing mindful awareness of brain activity. Once a client learns to better control behavior through mindful awareness, the next step is to help the client recall such awareness as needed (Germer et al., 2005).

As the deadline grew closer for submitting the first draft of this book last winter, I began to experience a familiar dread; in the face of this huge, linear organizational task, my paralyzing thought was, "This will never come together on time." On that dreary Chicago winter's eve, my neurons were firing along those frightful old pathways when my husband returned from a flea market carrying an armload of evergreen branches to decorate the seasonal planter in front of our home, a task long overdue. It took some doing, including boiling water and screwdrivers to ferret through the frozen soil. Just as the snow began to fall, the planting came together, swiftly and beautifully. I felt elated, as the planting project recalled and accessed other neural pathways that had been laid down for me through past Herculean organizational challenges (such as planning my daughter's weddings, celebrating bar mitzvahs, and writing my first book), timely reminders of my capacity to pull things together under the wire and with quality. The holiday decorating inspired a burst of motivated writing for me, as the draft began to come together. A glance through my window every now and again at the snowy greens triggered the unmasking of my own occasionally hidden "success" neurons, reassuring me of the resiliency I knew I could, and would, muster for the task

Words and the Power of the Brain

Verbalizing the brain's capacity to change motivates optimism and the power to act. Simple words of explanation can enlighten an extraordinary process and can promote and place change clearly within reach. V, a woman with binge eating disorder, experienced a repetitive cycle of creating charts to structure her day and her actions; finding herself unable to achieve perfection in following a daily schedule, she would abandon all efforts and function in total chaos. The internalized voice of her mother, who had emotionally suffocated and abandoned her, effectively stifled her permission to herself to act with moderation in any context.

I helped V conceptualize these charts as a mere approximation of an ideal; I then invited her to consider if, and how, her black-and-white thinking might affect her own mothering. In fact, her sensitive nurturing and caretaking of her own children indicated the existence of adjunctive neuronal capacities quite capable of tolerance, acceptance, and flexibility. A newly adjusted goal now would be for her to access and use *these* connections in caretaking *herself* as she does her children. "You are right, you are right, you are right," she repeated, carefully turning this idea over in her mind with an accruing sense of empowerment. Through recall and awareness she would need to learn to access these extant and more tempered and moderate pathways in order to show the same tolerance, forgiveness, and nurturance toward herself. V left our session that day with a genuine sense of hope and possibility.

Brain Plasticity and Obsessive–Compulsive Anxiety Disorder

Obsessive–compulsive anxiety disorder worsens over time, gradually altering the structure of the brain" (Doidge, 2007, p. 165). "Clients with OCD worry compulsively as a form of temporary relief to diminish anxiety, and in so doing, they insure that the obsessive thoughts and compulsive urges will worsen" (Doidge, 2007, p. 168). "Brain scans show that talk therapy can change the brain even in severe OCD brain lock" (Doidge, 2007, p. 169). Psychiatrist Jeffrey Schwartz theorized, then proved, that people could "shift the brain "manually" by paying constant, effortful attention and actively focusing on something besides the worry, such as a pleasurable activity. Recognizing that each moment they spend thinking of the symptoms deepens the obsessive circuit, he found that by bypassing it, they are on the road to losing it" (Doidge, 2007, p. 173).

"Replacing bad habits with better ones 'grows' new brain circuits that give pleasure and trigger dopamine release, rewarding the new activity and consolidating and growing new neurons" (Doidge, 2007, p. 170). When Schwartz scanned the brains of people whose obsessive–compulsive anxiety disorder had improved, he found that, in time, the manual gearshift got more automatic and that the three involved parts of the brain that were locked (firing together hyperactively) had begun to fire separately in a normal way. Eighty percent of Schwartz's patients got better when they used his method in combination with medicine. Chapter 14 describes strategies to treat obsessive–compulsive anxiety disorder in clients with eating disorders in greater detail.

ADJUNCTIVE TREATMENT MODES

We have seen that enriching the life of the brain increases neuronal networks and the number of branches among neurons, leading to increased brain weight, volume, and thickness. Anorexia represents the antithesis of learning. Its effect on the brain over time is to shrink its size, diminishing its structure and function. Techniques designed to improve brain plasticity have the potential to enhance the structure and function of the eating disordered individual's brain, bringing the client closer to healing.

Research has shown that inflexibility of thinking with anorexia is related to the severity of the presenting psychopathology and interferes with the client's everyday functioning and biopsychosocial adaptation. Bulimia has also been associated with deficits in memory and executive planning, perseverative thinking, and interference and latency in selective attention. The more areas of the brain that can be engaged in learning, the greater the potential to organize and balance opportunities to integrate knowledge and personal growth. Enhanced and varied opportunities for learning create more rapid changes and increase the odds for better retrieval. Recognizing and approaching a problem from multiple angles also affects related deficits.

Enhancing the Brain by Enhancing Learning

Neurodevelopmental and neurocognitive techniques are capable of augmenting the brain's capacity to learn. Doidge describes Merzenich's Fast ForWord program (Scientific Learning, Oakland, CA), developed to benefit children with language impairments and learning disability, as a kind of cerebral cross-training. Donalee Markus's (2003) neurocognitive restructuring therapy program offers context-free graphic puzzles to increase intelligence and change the brain so that the participant can build a tolerance for ambiguity and develop alternative thinking through differentiation and integration. When used as adjunct treatment techniques with clients who have eating disorders, such techniques offer unique opportunities to facilitate behavioral change through cognitive restructuring. This treatment protocol can also be used to address distortions of body image and distortions in perception of the self.

According to Markus (2003), the more neural connections there are and the stronger those connections become, the more likely a patient is to recover (an optimized) functional capacity—provided that the therapy is progressively organized with intention.

U, a 15-year-old client with anorexia, felt unworthy and defective and became hostile and withdrawn from her family. She was unable to connect with me in treatment; her affect was low and inappropriate; and she refused to make eye contact. She experienced difficulty and headaches while reading and was unable to concentrate on her studies; although she studied compulsively, she failed to score well on tests, augmenting her sense of shame and defectiveness. My sense was that her problems were the result of an integration of factors, including her anorexia, anxiety, perfectionism, obsessiveness, attention-deficit hyperactivity disorder, and perceptual and learning problems.

I referred U for evaluation by Dr. Markus and by a developmental optometrist, both of whom diagnosed and treated U's perceptual dysfunction. As a result, her reading improved so dramatically that her narrow, compulsive studying lifestyle was transformed, her anxiety abated, freeing her up to begin the process of recovery from her eating disorder. The individual is a whole person; the whole person must be cared for. Changes in any part of the brain, be they problematic or ameliorative, will not be contained within a single sphere.

Although the neglect of intensive learning as we age diminishes the systems in the brain that modulate, regulate, and control plasticity, remediated brain experiences that require highly focused attention, discernment, differentiation, and integration can reverse decline and dysfunction in multiple spheres. Learning new physical activities that require concentration, solving challenging puzzles, making a career change, or learning a new language will gradually upgrade global brain function (Doidge, 2007, p. 87).

Movement Therapy

The Feldenkrais and Anat Baniel methods are not about body movement as much as they are about brain training. The Feldenkrais and Anat Baniel methods have certain goals in common with eating disorder psychotherapy: Through both disciplines, practitioners help clients create new options for using the self creatively and with novelty, for discovering alternative problem solutions, increasing self-awareness, creating differentiation, and developing integration. Clients who use the Feldenkrais and Baniel techniques access these intrinsic aspects of eating disorder heal on deeper and more visceral levels, bypassing the use of language alone. Movement, combined with attention, is the language of the brain.

"By optimizing our skeletal structure and neurological function in movement within our own gravitational field, we create and re-create who we are, facilitating empowerment and an esteemed sense of well being and optimistic possibility. Movement, the language of the brain, hones the potency of the connection between mind and body, upgrading physical posture and brain function, structure, chemical composition, and mood; it functions as an agent of change in attention, perception, and differentiation of movement variations. (Russell, 2004), stimulating alternative thinking, feeling, moving and behaving. According to Feldenkrais, the more completely a person accesses and uses his entire muscular apparatus, the more the brain will become activated, with the activated regions further stimulating adjacent areas.

The best learning happens through doing. The Feldenkrais and Anat Baniel methods, through gentle and pleasurable bodily movements, can help a client access and inform a brain that is hungry to learn and that thrives on stimulation and novelty. Clients who have eating disorders experience the biological malfunctions giving rise to the disorder, a nervous system battered by malnourishment, co-occurring diseases, and genetic and environmental influences that place them at risk; these clients' disconnection from the embodied self goes far beyond poor self-esteem. The Feldenkrais and Anat Baniel methods teach clients a continuing process of autonomous shifting out of old habits and into useful new ones, helping them create and re-create images of self and empowered confidence. Studies have shown significant benefits of this method for clients with eating disorders. The latter study indicated the development of "a felt sense of self, self-confidence and a general process of maturation of the whole personality."

Self-Image and Body Image Healing

"Because we see (perceive) with our brains and not with our eyes, the plastic brain becomes capable of reorganizing its sensory–perceptual system and with it, potentially, our body image. We perceive ourselves—what we look like and feel like—with a perception that exceeds vision" (Doidge, 2007, pp. 15, 16). Doidge noted that "people with distorted body image and body dysmorphic disorder typically seek plastic surgery but still feel misshapen. He suggested that they really need 'neuroplastic surgery' to change their body image" (p. 188).

When dysfunctional habits and patterns occur over a period of years or even decades, as they do with people with eating disorders, the structure of the brain changes to incorporate these habits and patterns, so the brain does not move on or "turn the page" (Doidge, 2007, p. 169). The representation or image of the self is one such pattern; the brains of individuals with eating disorders have become committed to extreme neuronal pathways that have temporarily obliterated use of more adaptive pathways.

There is a tremendous capacity for self-correction built into the human nervous system. The Feldenkrais method and Anat Baniel method are effective means by which to re-access that potential at any age (Reed, 1993). "In the 1930s, Austrian psychiatrist Paul Schilder observed that a healthy sense of being and a 'stable' body image are related to one's vestibular sense; people with distorted body images report feeling unbalanced, rootless, and ungrounded—all vestibular terms" (Doidge, 2007, p. 2). Moshe Feldenkrais realized the value in systematically exploring and reorganizing the sensory–motor aspects of self-image as well as on the verbal–narrative aspects of self-image (Feldenkrais, 1972).

The Feldenkrais and Anat Baniel Methods in Eating Disorder Practice

In the process of my own training with Anat Baniel (see Baniel, 2009, for a description of her techniques), I began to see the potential of the work to make whole the distorted, truncated, or otherwise misconceived bodily perceptions that plague clients with eating disorders. I use these methods as an adjunct treatment to ongoing psychotherapy, and as a result my clients have become more acutely, mindfully, and intentionally self-aware, differentiated, and reintegrated in their perception of self, bringing disjointed parts of their body into connection to create whole and complete human beings. Therapists need not have training in the Feldenkrais or Anat Baniel methods for their clients to benefit from movement therapy, as Awareness through Movement© or Transformational Movement© classes, which are based on these methods, are affordable and increasingly available worldwide, and provide relevant learning for eating disorder clients.

As a practitioner of both methods as well as a psychiatric social worker, I offer treatment groups that combine traditional group therapy for people with eating disorders with the Feldenkrais and Anat Baniel methods, for the purpose of enhancing the brain and learning. Generally, group participants spend an hour in talk therapy and group process and an hour on the floor on mats, where they move gently and pleasurably to my verbal instructions, increasing self- and body-awareness. The following is a description of a typical session of group movement therapy.

Group members lay on mats before me, taking stock of how their spine and body make contact with the floor. This day, I choose to make the clients aware of their pelvis and instruct each member to gently and slowly move the right side of her pelvis in a downward motion. The next set of instructions remind the student that she is to move as slowly as possible, perhaps at a quarter of the rate she initially thought to be slow. Very slow movement allows for increased awareness of previously unrecognized body parts in motion and an enhanced connection with skeletal and neurological systems, focusing participants' attention on the aspects of self and being.

I ask a series of questions to direct their attention. What might be happening in the participant's rib cage as she moves her pelvis? Is she even aware that she has a rib cage, and if so, that it needs to "join the party" in moving along with the pelvis? Can she initiate the movement now from her softening rib cage, now from her pelvis, now from her heel? Through successive movements, does the participant notice that connections become easier and more comfortable, differentiated, and fluid? Does she become aware of additional body parts becoming involved? Of using herself differently? Of accessing options for herself that she never knew she had? Does her head begin to become part of that larger connection? Are there new alternatives available for the use of self?

I ask participants to revisit how they notice themselves making contact with the floor now. Invariably, they find themselves lying flatter, with more parts of their spine and body touching the floor as their skeleton becomes organized and integrated through movement and their muscles release the tensions that contort them. When participants stand up, the feet, the posture, the sense of well-being, the function of breathing, and the excitement of change all provide evidence that learning, manifested in the body, has taken place in the brain.

For those who have experienced my work one to one, the issues of trust, boundaries, and transference are particularly relevant as the client must give herself over passively to lie on a treatment table to be gently moved by the practitioner. Not every one of my psychotherapy clients is a candidate for my offering this body work; each must be deeply committed to wellness and to a trusting and well-established therapeutic relationship with me. Most clients are reluctant to do this work in conjunction with their psychotherapy because they feel shame and fear that any form of touching would reveal "just how fat they really are." Clients may fear "failure," though there is no such standard for judgment of this work, or they may fear any form of unpredictability that relates to the body, particularly in light of past abuses. For others, it may be hard to accept what feels like nurturance from another human being.

As with meditation practice, the Feldenkrais and Baniel methods may have "an adverse effect on more fragile clients, who may decompensate when cognitive controls are loosened" (Doidge, 2007, p. 128). One impulsive, acting-out client chose to stop having Feldenkrais "lessons" because she could not tolerate the feeling of relaxed calm that she experienced afterward. It frightened her, and left her feeling unprotected in being so in touch with her real self. For many clients, the effects of this work are transformational.

E was a 33-year-old woman who had had anorexia and bulimia for close to 20 years. In addition, she had struggled with addictions to cocaine and prescription drugs and had been physically abused by men she had dated. She came to therapy one day feeling massively anxious and depressed and unable to make eye contact. It was a hot summer day, yet she clutched her jacket fast to her chest, self-protected and bundled tightly. As she spoke about her anxiety in her agitated, dissociated state, her talk was perseverative and compulsive, and talk therapy appeared not to be an option. "How about lying down on the table for a Feldenkrais lesson," I offered.

In reporting her thoughts following this new experience, she described her initial response in lying down on the table. She was expecting still another "bogus, new-agey" healing experience. She closed her eyes, her head full of thoughts about the errands and chores awaiting her once the session was over, but as the "lesson" progressed, she was surprised to find herself increasingly focused internally on herself and her body. Ordinarily so out of touch with her body, she reported being astounded to find herself thinking, "She's touching my leg. Oh . . . I have a leg." "She's touching my arm. It's weird to think that I have an arm and that it is attached to me." At the end of the 30-minute lesson (the word lesson describes the process of teaching the brain), her body, mind, and emotions had been differentiated, reorganized and reintegrated. She reported feeling "uplifted and calmed." Her physical stance was visibly changed, and the jacket that had hidden and enclosed her was flung over her squared, free, and unrestricted shoulder as she strutted out the door.

Another client, P, was a 23-year-old woman with bulimia (restricting type) and an Axis II diagnosis; when she was younger, she had been gang-raped by her brother and his friends. After being in and out of hospitals for extended periods over a decade for treatment of her eating disorder, depression, dissociation, and self-mutilation, she became part of a psychotherapy support group I ran for adult women. One snowy evening, when only she and only one other person showed up, I decided to offer a Feldenkrais breathing lesson to the two of them. I began with the instruction "Close your eyes." P was too frightened to close her eyes, knowing something unexpected was about to happen concerning her body. In response, I suggested that she leave her eyes open and only "imagine" breathing deeply, only "imagine" her rib cage and chest expanding with each breath. She surprised me the next day by calling to say that she had discussed the experience with her individual psychotherapist and was ready to begin doing this work with me.

I worked with P slowly and purposefully, describing everything that I planned to do with her first, in an attempt to increase her trust in herself and in me in the context of this new experience. For the first several lessons, she sat in a chair, as lying on the table in a prone position would have been too threatening. I began by working gently in moving her hands and feet, the parts of her that were furthest from her core self. Her bodily sensitivity was extreme, having lived through early trauma; as I gently separated two of her fingers, for example, she revealed that the slight movement brought back painful bodily sensations associated with her past abuse.

She came to intensely enjoy her weekly Feldenkrais lessons, and while lying on the table, she would bring up issues that she ordinarily would not have felt comfortable owning and discussing. She spoke of her previously rigid rib cage, not unlike her eating disorder, as having felt like a "prison." As the work uncovered previously buried parts, feelings, and memories, she would at times describe feeling shooting pains in her vagina. Once, when I asked her to gently move her pelvis, I believe that we lost contact with each other for a short time as she went into a dissociative trance.

P reported that the Feldenkrais work gave her choices that she never knew she had. Following these few lessons, this previously withdrawn and starving woman would become extraverted and friendly in the supermarket while purchasing ingredients for her dinner, then go home to make a four-course meal. She described the food entering her body as no longer feeling like "the enemy"; instead, she visualized it traveling throughout her entire system, nourishing, sustaining, and giving life to her cells and tissues as it went. After lessons, she could sleep soundly without medication, and her purging and cutting behaviors diminished and ultimately ceased. About the work, she said,

> I know that on your table I am safe. I know where I am, I know who you are, and I know I will know who I am when we are through. The work makes me feel that it is OK for me to be changing. I also know that if I am capable of making these kinds of changes through these lessons, there should be nothing to stop me from making other kinds of changes in my life as well.

She went on to change her career and to recover completely.

Other Mind–Body Techniques

The power of imagination and visual imagery can be effective treatment devices: "Everything your immaterial mind imagines leaves material traces. Each thought alters the physical state of our brain synapses at a microscopic level. Though we aren't yet certain how it happens, it seems clear that thoughts actually change brain structure" (Doidge, 2007, p. 214). From a neuroscientific point of view, imagining an act can produce the same results for the brain as doing it. Brain scans show that in action and imagination, many of the same parts of the brain are activated. A client whose broken leg was confined to a cast was warned about the possibility of muscle atrophy. He imagined his leg in movement using the Feldenkrais and Anat Baniel techniques, and when the cast was removed, he found that he had prevented atrophy to his leg muscles. In an experiment, the researcher found that mental piano practice alone produced the same physical changes in the motor system as actually playing the piece and that the imagining players were as accurate in their subsequent playing as the actual players. Visualizing can improve performance and is a concentration skill that has proved to be an invaluable asset to competitive athletes.

Rational emotive imagery, a technique often used with clients who have eating disorders, demonstrates the relationship between thinking, imagining, feeling, and behavior. Imagery allows the client to use the same faculty (imagination) that previously generated anxiety to elicit calm, secure, and confident feelings. In becoming familiar with irrational ideas, the client pictures herself disbelieving these ideas and feelings and acts in accordance with new rational challenges.

I often apply the use of images and the imagination to qualify and add substance to therapeutic interventions. As an example, a client with bulimia (restricting type) who had stopped vomiting and laxative abuse and started to gain momentum in refeeding herself, occasionally lapsed into bingeing behaviors. In an effort to prevent a relapse into purging, I suggested that in her recovery, she might add a new "voice" or "signal" to her internal repertoire. Initially, her only internal advisor had been her eating disorder in the guise of her stomach, which demanded dysregulated amounts of food and chaotic means of undoing indiscretions. Now, I explained, she had the benefit of a second voice, to be imagined as an "editor," that resided in her brain's frontal lobe (I pointed to her brain) and that she could count on to comment ("If you eat the next few bowls of cereal, might it frighten you?") helping rein in her impulses before she ate to excess. The presence of the editor could be helpful in reminding her of her alternative to be kinder to herself.

Eye movement desensitization and reprocessing (EMDR) is a comprehensive, integrative psychotherapy approach that contains elements of psychodynamic, cognitive–behavioral, interpersonal, experiential, and body-centered therapies. As an information processing therapy, it attends to past experiences that have set the groundwork for pathology; the current situations that trigger dysfunctional emotions, beliefs, and sensations; and the positive experience needed to enhance future adaptive behaviors and mental health. During treatment, various procedures and protocols are used to address the entire clinical picture, one of which is "dual stimulation" using bilateral eye movements, tones, or taps. During the reprocessing phases, the client attends momentarily to past memories, present triggers, or anticipated future experiences while simultaneously focusing on a set of external stimuli. The client, by following a moving light with her eyes, activates the healing process of the brain, much as what occurs in sleep. As a result, the painful memories are reprocessed and the original beliefs that sprang up from them are eliminated and new, healthy beliefs replace them. During that time, clients generally experience the emergence of insight, changes in memories, or new associations.

A form of movement therapy that has been reported to bring about a sense of integration and self-awareness is neuromuscular integration aerobics (NIA). One of my clients reported, "It frees up my mind, connects me to myself, and in so doing is a little like psychotherapy. Sometimes, I find myself crying while I am doing it."

Energy psychology holds that emotional problems are caused by the body's disrupted bioenergetic system. One woman who suffered with anorexia for 10 years and who made a complete recovery, discovered that even after her weight was more than fully restored, her period did not return. It took eight months of acupuncture, along with omitting dairy products and Diet Coke from her diet, to rebalance her internal chi energies sufficiently to bring back her reproductive function. Today she is the mother of two beautiful, healthy breast-fed children.

CONCLUSION

Every client and every brain is different, and there is much to be learned from each. Science-based, evidence-based research has emerged in the field of eating disorders over the past 40 years, providing a rich and invaluable source of learning and structure. We are becoming increasingly aware that there are a myriad of other forms of treatment capable of augmenting real-life experience as an additional source of learning. No unique treatment outcome is insignificant, even if it is anecdotal or seemingly irreproducible. The neuroscientist V. S. Ramachandran has repeatedly shown that individual cases have everything to contribute to science and that by explaining neurological "oddities," one can shed light on the functioning of normal brains (as cited in Doidge, 2007).

Professionals in the eating disorder treatment field need to remain open to methods that work even sometimes and only for some people. As adjunctive treatments, such methods deserve to be investigated further for ameliorative effects; the real danger of such techniques is only when they are used in place of primary modes of eating disorder treatment. When enough practitioners achieve enough positive outcomes enough of the time, accrued common experience creates legitimacy in a whole that becomes vastly greater than the sum of its parts. It is time that treating professionals begin to harvest their own personal and professional discoveries, respecting common experience for its own significant contribution to an evolving field of practice.

12

Structuring Eating Disorder Treatment: Laying the Foundation of Care

The great end of life is not knowledge but action.

—T. H. Huxley

A t the start of treatment, the therapist engages in a delicate dance with a disorder that inevitably and inextricably partners with the client's disinterest in engaging in the treatment that would cure it. In addressing the client's ambivalence and resistance to treatment, the therapist must create and stimulate the client's motivation to discover healthier ways to secure her personal goals. This chapter reviews techniques for ensuring a positive start to treatment, navigating the client's stages of change, motivating clients throughout the stages of change, and interviewing clients to motivate change.

GETTING OFF TO A GOOD START IN TREATMENT

Chapter 6 describes the initial diagnostic assessment that launches the treatment process. The more precise and dynamic the diagnostic process, the better the opportunity to conceptualize the treatment and action plan. As noted in Chapter 6, diagnosis is an ongoing process, and treatment must respond to accommodate an evolving diagnosis. It is crucial that treatment gets off to a good start even if the diagnosis is still unclear, as the amount of change that occurs in the first few weeks of treatment is a strong indicator of eventual outcome (Fairburn, 2008).

At the start of treatment, I invite the client to describe the personal experience of starting the process, surveying her hopes, fears, agendas, and secret wishes and welcoming any projections from past treatment experiences that might shed light on our current direction. This practice sheds significant light on the client's priorities, thought processes, and coping devices, as well as the nature of her fondest hopes and dreams. One of my clients, a young psychologist who had a history of anorexia, bulimia, and compulsive overeating, had been through therapy many times before. At the end of our first session together, he asked "How do you practice, what is your philosophy, and what are your expectations for care?"

In response, I looked back with him over the process of this session we had just shared, observing the clarity of the goals we set, the action orientation, and the quality of our collaboration. I spoke of my commitment to change, to the therapeutic moment, to a pioneering and mindful use of both of ourselves within the context of our relationship to foster his own mindfulness and readiness to learn. He wanted to know if together, we could "make this work for him;" if this time things could be different. His fondest wish was to redevelop a sense of optimism and hope for a better life. He went on to ask "whether I felt confident enough in my own capacities and in his. Could I envision healing as a realistic option for him? Of course, I could.

At the start of our second session, I asked about any further reactions to our first session together. He expressed heartfelt relief and gratitude for having felt a clear and immediate connection, a sense that I "got it" and that I knew what to do to get this job done. But most of all, he said, I gave him hope and confidence for the first time that change would be possible. A sense of hope and change lies at the heart of motivation and positive outcomes. "Can do" is the most poignant of motivational messages. This client asked if I thought the biological, genetic, and chemical nature of his disorder implied intractability or hopelessness. On the contrary, recognizing the origin and nature of these diseases as biological offers the opportunity to treat and heal them with precision and understanding.

Clarifying Logistics

In approaching the new (and usually ambivalent) client, it is preferable to "strike while the iron is hot"; when a client seeks an appointment, it is critical to fit that client into a scheduled appointment time as soon as possible, before her motivation abates, potentially altering her motivation to enter treatment.

It is also recommended at the start of care to determine the span of time that circumstance and finances will allow for treatment together. For example, will the client be treated while at home over a three-week break from college or over the summer? Will she take a semester off from school to engage in long-term care? The task remains to set up a realistic plan that accommodates the limits set by reality and to consider post-care plans at the outset. The therapist must pace the initial encounter with the intention to educate, advise, and refer, assessing for risk and motivating the client to return for additional treatment. It is often beneficial to set up a double session to accommodate all of those requirements.

Because close to 90 percent of people with eating disorders are under the age of 20 years of age, many will be entering or returning to college away from home. In determining readiness for independence, expectations must be realistic, decision making sound, and challenges anticipated and prepared for. A support system needs to be in place, with a backup plan should the methods provided by the academic institution not be adequate to sustain recovery. Box 11.1 provides guidelines for assessing whether the client with an eating disorder can safely return to college.

In establishing the initial action plan, it is critical to know ahead of time the limits on the number of outpatient sessions permitted by insurance companies and caps on payment amounts covered by insurance for inpatient and outpatient care. If insurance covers inpatient care more liberally than outpatient care, a more restrictive treatment environment may afford the client an initially greater advantage; by offering the potential for more rapid and consistent refeeding,

---

BOX 11.1

A 10-Point Guide to Returning to College With an Eating Disorder

1. Recovery from the eating disorder must be seen as the first priority; earning a college diploma can take place anytime.
2. The student needs to recognize and accept her own readiness to be released from the containment of her ongoing care and to independently handle the triggers that exist in a peer-intensive environment.
3. The student must find a workable team that will monitor her medically and weigh her regularly, keeping her accountable to recovery. If the home team needs to be kept in the loop, a system for doing so must be put into place via e-mail and phone.
4. Readiness has to do with the client's ability to self-regulate and to commit to eating at least three meals a day with snacks.
5. Sleep hygiene is a critical factor in establishing a circadian body rhythm so vital to establishing healthy eating and reliable hunger and satiety cues.
6. The student should determine a game plan for using the cafeteria or restaurants that may involve reviewing the menu for the day, choosing her protein first, and consuming sufficient carbohydrates with meals so as to eat fewer of the less nutritious "snacking" carbohydrates.
7. The most critical skill is for the student to be prepared, in the face of a slip or relapse, to get back on track with the next meal or snack, not waiting until the next day to start anew.
8. The student should prepare herself to eat foods such as chips and salsa, burgers, fries, or pizza with a definitive and finely executed plan if attending bars is a regular aspect of her recreational lifestyle.
9. For every caffeinated drink she consumes, the student should drink two glasses of water to prevent dehydration.
10. Clients in college need to be cognizant that extremes in behaviors that drive eating disorders may show up in other life spheres as well. Staying up all night, abusing alcohol regularly and recreationally, engaging in promiscuous sexuality, or compulsive studying may be indicative of such behaviors.

clients acquire a greater readiness and preparation to benefit from subsequent outpatient care.

Ethically, a therapist should not take on a case that he or she feels unprepared to treat effectively. The social work *Code of Ethics* (National Association of Social Workers, 2008) requires therapists who do not feel capable of providing care for at-risk clients to make appropriate referrals to another professional or institution capable of better suiting her needs. In the event that the at-risk client refuses a treatment referral, it is up to the therapist to inform the family before withdrawing from service. By law, an at-risk client remains technically under the therapist's care until she is transferred into responsible hands elsewhere; follow-up with the client is critical to ensure that she has taken appropriate steps to secure her safety.

Determining Treatment Approaches

At the start of treatment, the therapist offers a combination of treatment approaches and modalities of care, the most appropriate treatment milieu, and the initial frequency of therapy sessions. Following that, the therapist remains flexible and open to directional or strategic changes needed to accommodate changing circumstance and the recovering client's changing needs. Treatment methods and approaches are discussed in detail in Chapter 12.

Session length is a factor significant to the pacing of therapeutic dynamics, both for the practitioner and the client. When a client brings up an important issue late enough in the treatment hour so that there is no opportunity to address it, you can be assured that this was hardly a coincidence and might be addressed as a therapeutic issue. Depending on circumstances (e.g., the client's geographic proximity to the treatment team, the pivotal nature of a session, the presence of other family members) certain sessions should be prearranged to be double or even "marathon" in length, with frequency determined by need and possibility. Anticipating time availability and using it to best advantage becomes a critical treatment/management skill as well as a motivating factor. On occasion, I have become aware of the potential of a session to lend itself to a breakthrough; as the clock winds down, I might note, "Important things are happening here today. I am aware that we are running out of time. Might you be available to stay for some additional time?"

Laying the Ground Rules for Treatment

Stated simply, psychotherapy is about change. Because of their need for control and predictability, clients with eating disorders are particularly uncomfortable tolerating the changes required for recovery and the unknowns that characterize them. It is the clinician's first task to understand and address the client's fears and concerns at treatment outset in an effort to calm them. In describing the treatment process, I typically lay down a few basic ground rules that include:

- "Simply show up" to attend sessions consistently and responsibly, allowing the treatment process to emerge and the healing therapeutic relationship to evolve.

- Engage with me collaboratively in planning treatment strategies and making decisions consensually. It is a relief to the client to understand that as long as she remains physiologically stable, it is she who will determine the pace of this treatment journey. For many, it is just as much of a relief that I make the demands and set the standard at the outset, before she is capable of determining that safe road for herself. We are collaborators, with direction provided as needed or when sought out.
- Understand that anything that is said between us remains in my complete confidence, except when the client may inflict potentially life-threatening harm on herself or others.
- Understand the efficacy of bringing in members of the family for regular or even occasional contacts where possible.
- Remain honest and open in offering ongoing feedback about feelings and any concerns about the process of treatment that need sharing. I encourage clients to confront me candidly about things I might say that could inadvertently hurt their feelings, frighten, or anger them, modeling the reality of human miscommunications and ways to rectify them; this can go far to avert the potential for treatment interruption.
- Call me at any time of the day or night in an emergency or from an emergency room in the event of serious self-harm or thoughts of suicide.
- Discuss the logistics of fees, financial arrangements, and the possible limits of service due to the restrictions of third-party payers and plan accordingly. Brief eating disorder treatment is better than no eating disorder treatment.

Involving Families

Parents, early in treatment, are a boon to the process in sharing and discussing observations and symptoms and demonstrating behavior patterns that the child may be unaware of or not facile enough to articulate. Parents have as much to learn as their children about eating disorders, the treatment and recovery processes, and how to become the most effective supports for their child. Two or more sets of ears can be counted on to hear more accurately than one set, and in many instances, parents learn how to listen and support their child best by modeling after the therapist. Moreover, when the child is extremely resistant to change, the parent needs to be educated to provide a round-the-clock voice of reason and concern at home, at least until the child is substantively engaged in care on her own. With adults and young adults, whether they live with or apart from their family, I encourage attendance by parents, siblings, boyfriends, and fiancés, when possible, regularly or on an ad hoc basis, in the hope of enriching learning for and about the client and the support process.

Bringing parents into treatment (sometimes to the exclusion of the uncooperative or resistant child) can facilitate changes within the wider family system substantive enough at times to effect positive change within the afflicted and absent child. When parents have lost their footing or have been rendered impotent in the face of an overly powerful child, their reinstatement in their child's life and treatment can become a particularly powerful intervention.

A., a 15-year-old girl with anorexia, was oppositional, abusive to her family, unengaged in treatment, manipulative, and noncompliant with her food plan after several months of treatment. I encouraged her parents to leave her at home for a while and to come in by themselves for consultation instead. In this context, I offered insights into the dynamics of their daughter's functioning but most importantly about how their lack of consistent responsiveness to her manipulating and out-of-control behaviors was exacerbating her eating disorder.

As the eating disorder tyrannized A.'s life, so she tyrannized her parents' lives. She refused to speak to her father to avoid the risk of confrontation. When her mother forbade the use of the phone in the very early hours of the morning, A. declared that her mother would have to come into her room every night to enforce the ruling. If her parents went out on Saturday night, A. would threaten to purge, leaving them unable to decide how to respond to her divisive behaviors and typically leading to arguments. In addition, although A.'s peers had reported her purging and the parents themselves had observed her pathological rituals and food restriction, they were not even able to agree on whether A. had an eating disorder.

The goal of establishing a united front between these parents took precedence over everything else during this pivotal time. By teaching these parents to set limits and say "no," they gathered their confidence to set their own limits with A. By releasing the teenager of the burdensome power of controlling their lives, she became freer to assume more appropriate controls over herself, with positive implications for her recovery.

Addressing Unsuccessful Former Therapies

When a client transfers from one therapist to another, as so often occurs in eating disorder treatment, a successful transition depends on the therapist's ability to explore and build on the client's past learning. It is important to discuss why she chose to transfer, and why now. If, at the start of treatment, the client remains under the care of another therapist, the therapist needs to know this and to help the client decide how to proceed, particularly if unresolved termination remains at issue. Some clients intend to work with both treating professionals at once, either by choice or by the recommendation of the other treater. Working simultaneously with two therapists, however, can be confusing and counterproductive for clients, leading to split allegiances and to sabotaged team function and client outcomes.

A critical part of eating disorder therapy is to encourage the client to take responsibility for resolving old treatment relationships through proper termination techniques before engaging with another treating professional, offering an early opportunity to practice pivotal problem-solving and interpersonal skills. If the client refuses to make a choice between two primary psychotherapists, one or both therapists should refuse to treat.

Where a client shows a pattern of sudden, unexplained terminations during past therapies, I frequently bring this pattern to the client's awareness as a therapeutic issue in an attempt to avoid its repetition. I request that if and when the client feels the first considerations of abandoning ship, she promise to come into treatment one last time to inform me of her intent so that we can augment her learning, sending her off with a plan for her future, and provide the option to say goodbye.

Projecting hope in the treatment process and optimism about the client's capacity to change and heal is perhaps one of the most treasured (relationship-based) aspects of the early provision of care. The therapist's capacity to comprehend and speak directly to the client's core conflicts as well as needs is the basis upon which trust, connection, and optimism are founded. The accuracy of the therapist's interpretations appears to be associated with the development of the therapeutic alliance (Luborsky, Barber, Siqueland, McLellan, & Woody, 1997). I believe that one of the reasons that eating disorder specialists do better than non-specialists with these clients is that they have seen enough to know that most people, when treated effectively, do recover, appreciably, if not totally. A therapist's feeling of helplessness in the face of an intractable problem can undermine treatment, as a lack of confidence can prove contagious. Novices in the field with a less successful track record in facilitating recovery may be more likely to lose faith in themselves, the process, and the client's capacity to recover.

Treating Clients in Their Own Environment

Contrary to an apparent trend these days that the provision of mental health care occurs in the client's own milieu, at home, eating disorder treatment generally takes place in treatment offices or in an intensive care milieu. There is, however, a significant place for an occasional session to be conducted in the client's home, in her own environment, around her own table, along with her family. Both positive and negative transference are typically intensified through therapy conducted in a home setting, which if handled skillfully, can lead to enhanced learning opportunities.

There are times when it might be appropriate for a practitioner to meet a young person at school to join her for lunch, offering critical input about the child's school experience and her response to it. I have frequently attended my clients' play performances, dance recitals, art exhibits, and weddings; it generally means a lot to them to have their therapist interested enough in them as a whole person to see them shine in other aspects of their life. There is always something to be learned from a new environment—a new sensing, a new opportunity for depth of connection, and a new understanding of the client through her own perceptions of and response to that process.

The Mindful Eating Disorders Therapist Is a Motivational Therapist

The prominence of resistance in the treatment of eating disorders clearly differentiates this treatment from that of other diseases. Of greatest relevancy for the eating disorders therapist are the pre-contemplative and contemplative stages of change, which allow professionals to develop therapeutic relationships with their resistant clients while minimizing or eliminating the battles for control for which eating disorders in particular have been noted (Leichner, 2005).

In treating eating disorders, you can anticipate that the patient's fear and ambivalence about recovering remain present right up to the last moment before achieving it . . . and even after it has been accomplished. Motivating a patient to grow beyond the pre-contemplative and contemplative stages is a critical first move for the eating disorders practitioner. Motivational enhancement interviewing skills further this end, featuring the practice of empathy with acceptance. In its likeness to aspects of mindful psychotherapy, motivational interviewing allows therapists to be with patients differently, more productively than with former practitioners. Understanding the stages of change is relevant to promoting and sustaining the patient's incentives to heal and stay healed throughout all the stages of eating disorders treatment.

The strategies of motivational interviewing are more persuasive than coercive and more supportive than argumentative, with the counselor creating a positive atmosphere conducive to change, allowing the client to present the arguments for change (Miller & Rollnick, 1991). An empathic therapist style has been shown to be associated with low levels of client resistance and with greater long-term behavior change (Miller & Rollnick, 1991). Conversely, overtly directive and confrontational therapist styles tend to evoke high levels of client resistance (Miller & Rollnick, 1991). The therapist sees resistance, ambivalence, and commitment as factors best understood and addressed within the context of readiness (Miller & Rollnick, 1991). According to the Prochaska–DiClemente stages of change model, motivation can be defined as the patient's state of readiness for change. DiClemente describes the therapist as "a midwife to the process of change; the therapist's role is to assist the patient within her own unique process," providing the motivation to shift from one stage to the next (cited in Miller & Rollnick, 1991, p. xxx). After determining the appropriateness of a treatment milieu, the first goal for the therapist is to harness and transform the energy of resistance to the energy of motivation. "Throughout the course of counseling, wherever pre-contemplative issues appear, strategies that focus on *how* to change (action stage) may be detrimental by distracting the (contemplator) from the crucial issue which is the *commitment* to change" (Miller & Rollnick, 1991, p. xxx). Motivational interviewing is not a set of techniques for *doing* counseling but rather is a way of *being* with the patient.

Upon returning to me for eating disorder care after several years and substantial weight gain, during a young anorexic woman's first session back with me she declared her commitment to Empowered Action now. Despite her motivation however, being unable to quiet the voices that say she does not "deserve" to be recovered, her second session saw her ambivalence grow. "I shouldn't, be needing therapy anymore after all these years." Ultimately when she approached the dreaded 100 pounds at 5′6," she panicked. As well as she was doing in her recovery, she was considering turning back now and retreating into the pre-contemplation stage once again. We spent a substantive session dealing with this dynamic, understanding her need to differentiate her weight from her accomplishments; her *own* strengths from those of her eating disorders; her weight from the quality of her life on a day-to-day basis; recovery progress from recovery failure.

M needed re-education about set point theory to reassure her that if she were to restore her normal weight, she would not become fat but *would* escape victimization by these tyrannical voices. She worked on becoming more mindful of herself and her goals in the moment, letting go of her morbid preoccupation with a future that would find her alone, unloved, and abandoned by her eating disorder. We also discussed her need for a medication re-evaluation, as well as the origins of emotional dependency on the eating disorder within the context of her family system. She left that session with concrete tasks for self-observation and journaling, bringing her to a renewed self-awareness and a re-entry into the preparation and action stages.

Tip: Never fight with an eating disorder, as there will be no way to win. I would strongly recommend that all therapists who deal with eating disorders become intimately aware of Prochaska and DiClemente's stages of change model which includes the pre-contemplative stage, the contemplative stage, the preparation stage, the action stage, the maintenance stage and the termination (or relapse) stage.

NAVIGATING THE CLIENT'S STAGES OF CHANGE

Prochaska and DiClemente's (1984) stages of change model, also called the *transtheoretical model*, outlines the natural sequence of behavioral change and how it happens. The stages of change model helps health care professionals develop therapeutic relationships with their resistant clients while minimizing or eliminating the battles for control for which these disorders previously have been known (Leichner, 2005).

Understanding the stages of change can help the therapist promote and sustain the client's incentives to heal and stay healed throughout all stages of eating disorder treatment. The model at first appears linear and sequential, though in fact it represents a dynamic, circular configuration. The systemic nature of change suggests that it is natural for a person to go through these various processes and stages more than once before achieving a stable state. Reminding the client of this circular path to recovery from an eating disorder is an optimistic way to reassure and encourage her in the face of the convoluted realities of the healing process. Motivational enhancement interviewing, composed of components of cognitive–behavioral therapy, psychoeducation, client-centered therapy, and narrative therapy, takes the therapist and client through these stages with the requirement that the therapist understand his or her own countertransference reactions to the client.

Santucci (2004) modified the stages of change to apply to eating disorders, as follows:

1. *Precontemplation:* The client is in denial that she is ill. The eating disorder has a continued hold over the individual, lending her a sense of control and confidence. The client may say, "I don't need to change; I don't have a problem" (p. 2).
2. *Contemplation:* The client begins to consider the possibility that she has an eating disorder, although she remains reluctant to engage in change and unprepared to consider recovery. She begins to explore the costs and benefits of treatment. The client may say, "I know I need to change, but . . ." (p. 2).
3. *Preparation:* The client recognizes that the eating disorder controls and diminishes her quality of life and moods. Its cost to her relationships and life function lead her to consider options for and commitment to change. She may say, "I've decided to change" (p. 2).
4. *Action:* The client engages in behaviors to effect positive change and modify her behavior. She may say, "I am doing what is needed to change" (p. 2).

5. *Maintenance:* The client applies the strategies she has learned. She may say, "I am committed to my recovery lifestyle and prepared for relapse" (p. 2).
6. *Relapse* (or *termination,* according to Prochaska and DiClemente's model): The client reviews issues and options and prepares for further action—in other words, for continued learning should she not be secure in a complete recovery. She may say, "I need to review what I need to do for change to occur" (p. 2).

The therapist takes different approaches with a client depending on where she is in the process of change, requiring different skills (Miller & Rollnick, 1991, pp. 14–15), with the goal of being able to help the client negotiate the passage from one stage to the next as seamlessly as possible. Knowing what stage your client is in and knowing when and how to switch orientation and strategies to match her needs requires purpose and timing with interventions at incisive moments: "Jumping too far beyond what a patient is prepared to do can turn into interpretations that can act as a roadblock" (Miller & Rollnick, 1991, p. 17). When remediated behaviors jump ahead of readiness and emotional preparedness, the odds are that these behaviors are but temporary. Early behavioral changes do, however, stack the cards in favor of a good prognosis, creating a more balanced and healthy lifestyle for the physical body along with a greater capacity to benefit from psychotherapy.

Echoes of resistance to healing can be expected to resound throughout the course of eating disorder treatment and recovery as the client's cognitive choices inevitably fall out of sync with her physical, chemical, or emotional needs. Resistance must be viewed not as willful opposition, but rather as an indicator of where the client is in the stages of change (Miller & Rollnick, 1991, p. 101).

As the client moves within and through the stages, the therapist is called on to be attentive to which stage the client currently is in. Therapists need to do the following:

- stay the course, warding against battle fatigue by finding support and motivation through consultation and peer dialogue.
- recognize that understanding the past becomes important principally as it relates to the present.
- visit and revisit the client's ambivalence and resistance, welcoming it as a reality to be dealt with, brainstorming with the client about what it means, where it comes from, and how best to respond to it.
- never lose sight of the client's physiological risks; stay on the lookout for cutting, abuse of laxatives or other substances, and other impulsive or self-injurious behaviors
- do not refrain from addressing the difficult issues, asking the tough questions, and "holding the line" for a focused and sustained recovery.

Stage 1: Precontemplation

Clients in the precontemplation stage need the therapist to motivate them to consider change. In this stage, clients are in denial about having an eating disorder and resistant to separating from its perceived benefits. Active listening allows the treating professional to search for common ground (Leichner, 2005). It takes a skillful therapist and team and a strong therapeutic relationship to motivate a resistant client to develop a readiness to change. The therapist establishes an empathic connection not only by identifying "where the client is," but also by recognizing "where the disorder is," in its hold over the client. The therapist recognizes the eating disorder as a palpable presence in the room, a pivotal third party in the triangulated treatment relationship. To establish a common ground with the client, the therapist can point out that everyone present in the counseling room, on her team, and in her home wants the same thing for her as she wants for herself—happiness and a feeling of acceptance, as well as a fit and healthy body. For example, a 16-year-old with anorexia had difficulty eating what her parents fed her. Unclear about what she needed in order to grow, and about how to satisfy a hunger she could not recognize, she had become undifferentiated from her eating disorder. To begin to enable her differentiation herself from her disorder, I said,

> I know I am sitting here with the "two of you," and I am painfully aware that because I end up speaking to both of you in the same breath, there is always some part of you that is not feeling supported by me. What's that like for you?

Clients in the precontemplation stage need the following:

- to receive information and feedback to raise their awareness of the disorder and the possibility of change
- to understand that the therapist walks a thin line in remaining sensitive to the client's needs and issues while being obligated to confront the eating disorder
- to be assured that she is not "crazy" but is merely seeking a way to survive
- to recognize her goals and see that there may be a more effective way to attain them
- to engage members of the treatment team, including her parents.

Giving prescriptive advice or making assumptions about the client's readiness for change at this stage can be counterproductive (Miller & Rollnick, 1991, p. 116). When a client with anorexia returned to me with severe anxiety and depression, I assumed that she was returning with the goal of finally taking action against an eating disorder that was apparently continuing to take a toll on her life quality. It was a mistaken assumption, however, and following this discussion about her unhealed eating disorder, she chose not to return for treatment. There was clearly a mismatch between the stage I thought she was in and the stage she actually occupied.

Stage 2: Contemplation

Clients in the contemplation stage begin to think about what the benefits of recovering might be and what the process would realistically entail. Many clients enter treatment at this stage. The contemplation stage is characterized by ambivalence; the client considers change but rejects it. DiClemente (cited in Miller & Rollnick, 1991) made a point of warning therapists to recognize that "contemplation is not commitment" (p. 113).

With clients in this stage, the therapist needs to know how to recognize and interpret forms of success that may be camouflaged and elusive. The therapist begins to more actively recognize and connect with the client's internal resources that represent strengths and can be rallied as defense forces against disease. The therapist also needs to attempt to tip the balance in favor of change; if a client takes action at a point where she expresses motivation, change becomes inevitable.

The client in the contemplation stage needs the following:

- to have previous change attempts positively reframed as "some success" rather than "a failure" in order to encourage further action (Miller & Rollnick, 1991, p. 196).
- to work through "ambivalence, to anticipate the barriers, to decrease desirability of the problem behavior, and to gain increased sense of self-efficacy to cope with this specific problem" (Miller & Rollnick, 1991, p. 196).
- to review the benefits of the change process
- to be reminded that coming to therapy and recognizing some aspects of the need to change are evidence of her strengths.

Stage 3: Preparation

During the preparation stage, regardless of whether a client enters a restrictive treatment milieu or remains in outpatient care, this is the time to prepare the patient for what she can anticipate in treatment. Parents and other resources need to be tapped, brought in, and guided to support the child through feeding tasks. Strategies employed in the precontemplation and contemplation stages should be maintained during Stage 3 (Miller & Rollnick, 1991).

Therapists can help clients in the preparation stage by teaching skill development, anticipating problems and pitfalls, and discovering alternative solutions in problem solving (Miller & Rollnick, 1991, p. 197). In developing a new sense of companionship with the client, and in leaving ample room for ambivalence and its accompanying forward and backward movement, the therapist helps the client understand that they alone can do it, but they cannot do it alone (Leichner, 2005).

The client in the preparation stage needs the following:

- to review her needs, willingness, and capacity for change
- to have the therapist think out loud in modeling effective problem solving
- to negotiate a plan and set goals: What would she like to see different? What might be a first step?
- to avoid overprescription to the plan
- to keep expectations for the therapy process and timing of healing realistic
- to have parents and families increase their capacity to listen and respond.

Stage 4: Action

In the action stage, the client is ready to make a public commitment to change; she needs to rally support for her plan and to enlist external monitors for her activities. The therapist helps the client in the action stage implement strategies and problem solve while providing encouragement. Recognizing, anticipating, and preparing the client to handle barriers to successful action are critical so that the client is able to sustain any changes she makes.

The client in the action stage needs the following:

- to understand recovery as an action
- to become attuned to recognizing and acknowledging progress
- to be prepared to confront relapses, identifying them as new opportunities to gain
- understanding the need for further change
- to keep her goals clearly in mind
- to set the pace of change in a forward direction
- to be subject to authoritative and loving limits that lead to the development of self-controls
- to develop strategies to support and sustain behavioral change: What did you do, what might you have done? What worked and why? What didn't work and why? What else might you do now? If you cannot, why not? What might you try next time?
- to maintain accountability through the assignment of behavioral tasks
- to listen actively to herself, leading to self-appreciation and understanding
- to discuss past change attempts that can be enlightening and reassuring
- to note partial successes where they may exist
- to discover how to make things different this time around
- to learn more about herself through her own projections. Encourage this process through active listening, realistic feedback, and encouragement.

Stage 5: Maintenance

During the maintenance stage, new behaviors become firmly established, and the threat of relapse is less frequent and intense. The challenge is to sustain the change accomplished in the action stage, preventing relapse (Miller & Rollnick, 1991, p. 23). During this period, strategies may be modified and monitoring diminished. Maintaining a change may require a different set of skills and strategies than were needed to accomplish the change in the first place.

The client in the maintenance stage needs the following:

- to learn that self-observation leads to self-control and that self-awareness leads to self-determination
- to understand that differentiating small changes is a more potent weapon than striving for rapid and unsustainable changes
- to be encouraged to experiment with new strategies on a trial-and-error basis

- to keep in mind that failure is a normal element in recovery progress and in life, as well as an important learning tool; the presence of failure is often a sign of progress.
- to never lose sight of physiological risks

Stage 6: Relapse or Termination

Slips and relapses are normal as clients attempt to change long-standing patterns. It takes time for new pathways in the brain to form. Stage 6 is a time of practicing new behaviors, of continuing to develop self-awareness and insight, and of deepening the connection between therapist and client to ensure recovery and prevent relapse.

The client in the relapse stage needs to do the following:

- anticipate her barriers to change, decrease the desirability of problem behavior,
- work through any slips, honing coping skills,
- be reassured that regressions are normal for the stage. This knowledge can be motivational.

The best course for relapse prevention is a realistic understanding of the nature of recovery. Anticipating a client's worst fears about relapse can be a form of advance problem solving, in preparing the client to deal with them. The therapist can help the client explore her fears by asking the following:

- What might be a first sign of difficulty for you?
- Would you know it when you see it?
- What would be your knee-jerk reaction?
- What might be a more effective response?
- What do you think would be the greatest obstacle to your awareness that you might relapse?
- What can you do if you notice yourself beginning to slip?

Clinicians should not be surprised if the client's waning disorder rears its ugly head just before recovery. Most clients grieve their disorder as they would a death, and a client on the verge of recovery may feel an urgent impulse to starve herself one last time.

Case Study

Y is a bright and emotionally healthy young college student who has a genetic history of eating disorders in her family. A vegetarian, she came to me after suffering with bulimia (restricting type) for over a year. We worked well together, establishing a meaningful and trusting relationship; I attempted to motivate her to attend a day program before going back to college in an attempt to bring her beyond the contemplation stage in which she was firmly grounded. She refused, and to my surprise, abruptly left my care without discussion.

She returned for therapy with me during the following summer, having engaged in successful treatment at college; as a result, she had restored some of her lost weight, begun to eat regular meals, and felt more in control of her life. In coming back to my care, she sought "not to lose ground" in her recovery. During the course of our work together, she appeared reluctant to accept weekly challenges, and exhibited continuing inordinate fear of gaining weight and getting fat. Though we enjoyed a relationship that was versatile and substantive, she expressed to me that she was loath to hear my sometimes gentle, sometimes not so gentle, psycho-educational urgings about the life she could have (and that she deserved to have) without her disorder. It was after the session where I encouraged her to try to "kick" the disorder once and for all, explaining that achieving her set point weight would allow her to be a thin and healthy person for the rest of her life, that she left my practice precipitously once again. For Y, action and maintenance stages were riddled with contemplative issues and would remain that way.

It is not uncommon for people with eating disorders to lose their emotional footing at some arbitrary weight. In still another example of a return to contemplation after action and maintenance, H, a restricting bulimic, had stopped purging, recovered from alcohol and laxative abuse, and had begun to eat regular meals. After gaining 28 pounds, she remained 25 pounds underweight, but decided that she "simply could not gain another ounce." Though her choice was to "maintain and manage" her eating disorder at this point, the disorder caught up with her, re-took control, and she found herself abusing laxatives compulsively once again.

In another example of motivational psychoeducation, when an anorexic client put the skids on her weight restoration at 99 pounds, in encouraging her to "go for the three digits." I reminded her that once she got to 100 pounds, it would be her choice to relose that weight if she found it intolerable. She ultimately found the courage to cross that barrier and continued her weight restoration solidifying her progress, progressing through the stages as she approached set point weight and complete recovery.

MOTIVATING CLIENTS THROUGHOUT THE STAGES OF CHANGE

Of greatest relevance for the eating disorder therapist are the pre-contemplation and contemplation stages, whose prominence in treatment clearly differentiates eating disorder treatment from that of other diseases. Motivating the resistant client to grow beyond the pre-contemplation and contemplation stages is critical; motivational interviewing skills, which take on aspects of mindful psychotherapy, further this end. "Motivational interviewing," discussed in more detail later in this chapter," is not a set of techniques for doing counseling, but rather a way of being with the client. The strategies of motivational interviewing are more persuasive than coercive and more supportive than argumentative; the counselor creates a positive atmosphere that is conducive to change and that allows the client to present the arguments for change" (Miller & Rollnick, 1991, p. 52). An empathic therapist style has been shown to be associated with low levels of client resistance and with greater long-term behavior change. Conversely, overtly directive and confrontational therapist styles tend to evoke high levels of client resistance. One can never fight with an eating disorder, as there is no way to win.

Preparing the Client for Engagement in Treatment

Because the most unique and challenging aspects of working with eating disorders is the client's tenacious resistance to healing, the therapist needs to be prepared to motivate clients, creating, then sustaining, their incentive to recover. Motivational interviewing begins the process of inspiring the client to pursue change; in fact, every stage requires motivational coaching and enhancement.

If the therapist hasn't made a substantive and viable initial connection with the client within the first pivotal five minutes of care, when first impressions are pivotal and the client is seeking to know if she is in the company of an ally, the client is likely not to return for a second session. The therapist needs to "hit the ground running," leading the client to feel safe, heard, and "felt," in beginning to develop a sense of common ground. The goals addressed during the first five minutes of care must be the client's goals; she must perceive the work of therapy as self-enhancement, which will take place at her own pace in collaboration with the therapist's assistance.

When the goals of the client, therapist, and parents are not similar enough to be declared mutual, interim goals can be devised to motivate movement forward. A client's goal may be to get nagging parents "off her back;" the interim goal might be to educate the parents in a conjoint family session with the child. The client's goal might be to lose weight; the interim goal may be to discover how weight can be lost in a healthier manner without dieting, and/or to discover and experience what "healthy eating" really means.

Recognizing and Addressing Resistance

Therapists create motivation for change and healing by redirecting and deflecting the energy of resistance as seen in the client's arguing, discounting, interrupting, denying, disagreeing, excusing, minimizing, being unwilling to change, ignoring, being inattentive, refusing to answer, and sidetracking (Miller & Rollnick, 1991). At any point, when the client appears to be resisting, a change in strategy is called for. The clinician's task is to double back, find out where the client began to show resistance, and begin working from that point, taking a different tack. As Miller and Rollnick (1991) noted, "Differences in client resistance have been shown when the same therapist takes different approaches or even switches styles within the same session with reduced resistance associated with long-term change" (p. 100). The therapist's capacity for nonjudgmental and radical acceptance determines his or her potency in redirecting the forces of resistance.

In treating resistance, keep in mind the following concepts:

- Resistance is a survival tool; it is the client's way to pace her work.
- Clients need to have other coping tools in place on which to hang their survival before letting go of resistance or the eating disorder.

- In the face of resistance, the word "no" must be seen as the start of a conversation, not the end of it.
- By identifying resistance and calling it by its name, you allow the client to take ownership, make choices about it, and gain accountability and control of the process.
- Resistance can take many forms, such as the refusal of medications and of nutritional services. Both may be critical for the success of the recovery process.

Moving Beyond Resistance: Motivating Readiness for Change

Eating disorder therapists can anticipate encountering the greatest resistance in the early phases of treatment, though the peak might not arise until the middle phase of care, when commitment is being strengthened. The client's readiness to recover, an internal state influenced by external factors, is virtually unquantifiable; it is an ever-changing dynamic based on accruing knowledge, maturity, and personal growth; on timing, life experience, and confidence; on fear and desperation; and on preparedness to trust oneself and the team. The client's readiness for change will vary too, with personality structure, ego strengths, diagnosis, and the quality of environmental and familial supports.

Like learning to play a musical instrument, readiness and recovery require extended opportunities for rehearsal and skill practice. For treatment to evoke complete and lasting recovery changes, clients need to have acquired not only the recovery tools but the courage to risk using them consistently, time after time. The therapy relationship is pivotal in its capacity to motivate readiness for change. The therapist's sense of timing and of when and how much to push the client is critical, as is knowing when to back off. It is incumbent on the practitioner to continually assess and shepherd readiness for change by suggesting realistic goals that remain within the client's reach. At the same time, clients need to experience an internal preparedness to accept help; most importantly, they require a growing faith that they have the capacity to accomplish what they set out to achieve.

The following is an example of creating readiness to heal while mediating the anxiety that accompanied it. N sat with her family in weekly sessions, refusing to accept responsibility for making any of the changes her parents were actively fostering. She demanded that her parents leave their jobs on a daily basis to join her for lunch at school if they expected her to eat it. Her father suggested changes around the lunch routine; in response, N's anxiety level led to emotional shutdown, as seen in her eyes and body language. At this juncture, I offered her some slack, relieving her mounting tension with the assurance that our discussion had merely been an exchange of ideas and that any decision to take action would largely be her own. Significant internal movement became immediately evident; N became a collaborator, negotiating the pacing and circumstances that this risk-taking experiment might take. She began to eat lunch on her own at school within a week's time.

Factors contributing to a client's readiness to recover include the following:

- effective treatment and a quality relationship between client and therapist
- high-quality communication within the outpatient treatment team

- a working relationship with the family
- active and appropriate parental involvement
- realistic expectations that can be maintained throughout a protracted recovery process
- creative use of cognitive–behavioral tasks such as contracts
- behavioral challenges that are kept small and manageable
- creative use of adjunctive therapy techniques, including eating disorder support groups, self-help devices, mind–body work, and therapeutic milieus where clients communicate with like-minded individuals in different stages of recovery
- recognition of resistance as an inevitable aspect of the growth process, evident through the very last stages of recovery
- flexibility in the use of self in exercising autonomy, intention, and control to accommodate the changing needs of circumstance.

INTERVIEWING STRATEGIES FOR ENCOURAGING MOTIVATION

Addressing Past Treatment Experiences

If the client speaks of her distrust in psychotherapy because it had never worked for her in the past, hear her carefully, investigating her past experiences in the interest of making this experience better this time around. Show the client that her input is valued and heard:

Therapist: Tell me more about what happened in your past treatment. What did you like most about your therapist? What did you like least? What aspects of your care would you like to see be different this time around?

Therapist: Your therapy experience now will be different, must be different, from past experiences that did not work for you. The way I see things, if changes aren't happening as they should, we need to figure out new and different ways to make sure they do. We need to keep our eye on the ball so this experience can be a genuinely worthwhile one for you.

Meeting Resistance With Reflection

Use the client's own incentives and logic, impaired as they may be, as a place to start. In helping the client see that she is blocking her own way to healing, I might ask, "So are you saying that if you lose weight, you will be more popular at school? In playing the devil's advocate, let me ask you this—as you have become thinner, have you noticed that you have also become happier?"

A client of mine, P, was resistant to care. She wanted her life back, but on her own terms only, without weight gain. In educating and connecting with P, I offered her a trusting haven in which to hope and heal. The following is the start to a session that ultimately evolved into a motivational dialogue:

Therapist: So what's it like to be here today?

P: I'm not at all happy about being here. I think this is silly and unneces-sary. There's nothing wrong with me.

Therapist: It seems as though you feel things are going pretty well for you, that you like how things are going in your life right now. Even so, I won-der if there might be anything at all that you might consider wanting to change about any aspect of your life? If so, what might that be? The time we share together today is for and about you; it would be great if we could find something that you can walk away with today, that will have made this experience worth your while.

P: I just want to be thin so I can feel confident, run better on the track team, and be more popular at school.

Therapist: Can I ask how you have set about trying to achieve these goals? Might these goals be behind your decision to eat so little these days?

P: Well, I have begun to eat healthier and somewhat less these days, so I can perform better.

Therapist: So this all makes perfect sense: You want to become a happy, pro-ductive, loved, fulfilled individual. These are great goals. I wonder if you are aware that, in light of the way the human body works, the path you have chosen to achieve these goals (all good ones) actually runs counter to your wishes. Did you know that dieting and skip-ping meals is the worst way to lose weight and to keep it off? Or that young people who diet are more prone to be overweight adults? I believe I could help you achieve your goals for yourself more effectively.

If the client is forthright and able to share her anger, fear, or at least ambiva-lence, the therapist can salute her honesty and integrity in being so forthright, confirm that her feelings are normal and legitimate, and applaud her ability to access them and her courage in disclosing them. If she is unable to articulate her feelings, the therapist can allude to the courage it takes to come to a new place and to talk to a total stranger about a clearly uncomfortable topic. The client's motivation builds when the clinician acknowledges that it is difficult for most people, normalizing the dynamic of the moment and stimulating her trust that the clinician understands what she feels. When a client is really stumped about how she feels or incapable of expressing herself, the therapist might consider offering information about what other people in this situation have reported feel-ing (frightened, angry, misunderstood, or some other emotion,) and wonder aloud if any of those descriptions might resonate with her.

As you read on, be aware that treatment interventions discussed here are rel-evant not only at the start of treatment, where the therapist seeks to enhance the client's engagement in the process, but to all stages of subsequent care.

Letting Reality Guide Your Discourse

Create a clear differentiation between scaring or threatening the client and confronting her with reality. Confronting reality requires problem recognition, leading to problem resolution. G made it clear that she preferred not to talk about the discomfort she had experienced in our previous session, because "thinking about tough issues just makes me feel bad, and my goal in life is to feel as good as I can."

Therapist: How does that help you to recover from your eating disorder?

   G: It doesn't.

Therapist: May I ask what kinds of things you discussed with your last therapist, with whom you felt so comfortable?

   G: We spoke together only about school and my tests, my friend problems, and what I did that day, because I refused to talk about food and eating.

Therapist: Did you find that helpful to you, and is that a pattern that you would like to duplicate here? Do you believe that would be the best use of your time?

   G: Not really.

Listening Reflectively and Reframing

Many therapists think of listening as a passive process. Motivational interviewing requires active listening with the "third ear" to hear what is meant, which may be different from what has been spoken. "The therapist defers judgment in the effort to accept what the client needs to share, appreciating the legitimacy of any declaration she may make. The crucial element in reflective listening is how the counselor responds to what the client says" (Miller & Rollnick, 2007, p. 173) in order to help her to better know herself. Such responses form the basis of therapeutic dialogue.

   In reflective listening, the professional first makes a guess as to what the client means. By offering several possibilities, the therapist provides the client with an opportunity to decipher and give words to her own meaning, thereby connecting with, and speaking, her own voice. For example,

Therapist: So, are you saying [first guess]? Or [alternative guess]? I'm not certain that I fully comprehend what you mean. I want to understand better—please tell me more.

Therapist: So what I hear you saying is that you are ready for change, you can't tolerate another year like this, and you are sad and frightened and living only half a life. But you are also saying that you will not consider making the smallest foray into recovery. It sounds a little contradictory; is that what you really mean to say?

Reframing is a highly motivational tool that acknowledges the validity of the client's feelings and observations while offering a possible new meaning or interpretation for them. By casting ideas in a new light, the therapist can be helpful in supporting change.

A 40-year-old client with anorexia who had given birth to four children was obsessed with thoughts about tiny bits of "fat" that she could pinch at her waist. In offering a cognitive reframing, I asked if she had ever tended a garden . . . Mother Nature's metaphor for the natural cycles of life, representing continuity and predictability, season after season. The rounded belly that has borne children offers a spiritual testimony to the wonders of creation, to having experienced life fully, to having known intimacy and the love of parenthood. "I wish I could think that way," she replied, "but whenever I am outdoors, I never take the time to tend to my garden; going for a run has always been my first priority."

Asking Open-Ended Questions Instead of Drawing Conclusions

Asking open-ended questions stimulates the client's self-awareness while shaping and clarifying the therapist's accurate perceptions; drawing conclusions runs the risk of making counterproductive projections. This same mother of four who had anorexia described a pivotal interaction with her previous therapist. The therapist, on learning that the client had four children under the age of nine, rolled her eyes and proclaimed how hard that must be for her to manage. The client loved parenting her children, the only area of her life where she felt ease and pride in the quality of her functioning. She was put off by the therapist, who had projected her own past parenting experience. An open-ended question in response—"So, you are one busy lady! What is it like for you to parent four children?"—surely would have led to a more productive discussion.

Motivating Through Example

We have noted that the client who lacks self-awareness may benefit from a description of how others might react in a similar situation. For example,

Therapist: Other youngsters in your position have spoken about reacting with anger or hurt feelings; others speak of embarrassment or shame when this kind of thing happens to them.

Therapist: If you were to try to describe your feeling right now, which might be closest to it—mad, sad, glad, or scared?

In helping a client envision alternative problem solutions, I will typically ask a young person how *she* might handle a similar situation if her *own* child was struggling with such a problem, and *she* were the parent. The change of perspective can be eye-opening for the client.

On occasion, in the context of a long-term and trusting relationship with a client, I might share a personal experience of my own that offers additional permission or incentives to be real, spontaneous, and human. In so doing, I remain highly attuned to what my self-disclosure might feel like for that client and how it might affect her feelings about me and our relationship.

Motivating Through Psychoeducation

The transference of knowledge is one of the most effective ways to motivate change. As an example, most clients appreciate knowing that the origins of eating disorders, as well as weight and shape, are in genetics, not in mental illness, presenting an opportunity to introduce the concept of size acceptance. In addition, a constant threat to the integrity of diagnosis and treatment is ambiguity and misunderstanding about the implications of weight management for the client and for recovery. The most important piece of education you can give clients and families is simply that eating and weight management issues are not the crux of the eating disorder problem and can easily become treatment distractions.

J, a woman with anorexia, began to make progress in feeding herself, eating more diverse and nutritionally dense meals regularly throughout the day. She noted that her weight was going up one pound per week. To reinforce J's motivation, I summarized other effects of the progress she had experienced:

> So let's take a look at what you have learned so far from your efforts. First, it takes some doing to put on weight. You have to really stay motivated and eat a lot of food, and even then, the weight comes on very slowly and gradually. In the one week when you were sick and couldn't eat as much, though you still ate regularly, you lost a pound, showing you how easy it is to lose weight. This awareness should go far in helping you to feel less frightened and anxious in the face of eating.

Providing Personal Validation

It is reassuring for clients to understand that their eating disorder has served a legitimate purpose in having provided a sense of security as a coping mechanism It is also reassuring to know that there are far more productive and efficient ways to solve problems. Clients need to be reminded that comfort is never a natural part of change and that eating disorder treatment gets easier only after things get a whole lot harder, first. For example,

Therapist: I understand how you feel. It's no picnic having to face the idea of letting go of something in your life that feels so precious to you. Though it may be hard to imagine at this point, somewhere along in this process not only will the recovery become easier, but your life will begin to feel dramatically better."

"A general goal of motivational interviewing is to increase the client's perception that she will be able to cope with this adversity and to succeed in making real change" (Miller & Rollnick, 1991, p. 61). When a client expresses discouragement about her own capacities, I legitimatize her feelings and then, when appropriate, respectfully disagree with her logic, citing unrecognized aspects of her strength and character that I have seen and that she may have lost sight of. "The therapist's own expectations about a client's chances for recovery can have a powerful impact on outcome" (Miller & Rollnick, 1991, p. 61).

A client who had recovered from anorexia was a successful and highly functioning businesswoman. But she felt depressed about a difficult interpersonal challenge within her family system. "Everybody in my family is special in some way except for me. I am always a disappointment to them," she observed. "I don't mean to be contrary, but I have to differ with you there," I interrupted her,

> Please don't think that I am not taking your current pain seriously, but this theory just doesn't hold much water with me because of what I know about you. We've been together a long time, and I believe I clearly see who you are and how you function. This thinking about yourself simply no longer applies. So let's get real here by taking a look at who you have become, and what you have accomplished. Better yet, I'd like to hear this from *you*! I have a sense that in thinking about this, you are about to punch some holes in your own theory, which no longer has a heck of a lot to do with reality.

Giving permission to disclose negative feelings, even powerful ones, is another way of providing validation. As the client–therapist relationship is a reflection to varying degrees of all other interpersonal relationships, facing conflict in the therapy relationship provides a poignant opportunity to model healthy conflict resolution:

Therapist: In an earlier example, I explained to a young woman recovering from anorexia that sometimes when people feel anger, it's hard to know precisely what the anger is about or whom the anger is directed toward. "Just as an aside," I asked her, "can you remember anything that has ever transpired between us, in the process of our work together, that has ever made you angry? Would you be willing to talk about it now? [If she decided not to confront me at the time], do you remember how you handled it instead? Might it have affected the way you felt about me or how we have worked together?

Therapists can also encourage clients to devise self-affirming statements that provide self-validation and self-motivation, particularly when tied to their expanding self-knowledge. Statements like the following, tacked up on the refrigerator door, can inspire confidence in recovering clients:

- I am just "P-M-S-ing," not fat, so that's why I feel this way.
- I'm not getting fatter; I'm getting healthier.
- I have so many more strengths than my eating disorder gives me credit for.
- Eating disorder, I'm onto your tricks!

A client spoke of getting into a self-pitying funk and asked herself, "Why me!?" I suggested that she never ask herself this question without also providing herself with the reality-based answer that she sought: "I have an eating disorder because that is how I am put together genetically. I have it now because I have not yet finished recovering from it. Soon enough, I can and will be done with it once and for all."

Offering Objective Feedback and Using Leverage

A person needs a clear vision of "where she is at " in order to recognize the direction in which she wants to go. In clarifying a client's options and stimulating motivation for change, "expressions of concern from family members have been shown to be an important form of feedback, as are objective tests, self-monitoring diaries or food logs, or stepping on the scale" (Miller & Rollnick, 1991, p. 26).

> Even confrontational feedback can be motivating; its purpose is to help the client see and accept reality so that she can change accordingly, amplifying discrepancies between present behavior and broader goals motivates change by introducing a seed of doubt in the client's current thinking. (Miller & Rollnick, 1991, p. 56)

Therapist: Think about what you want your life to look like in 10 years. As you think of marriage and having a family, how will you achieve these dreams if your eating disorder has made you infertile? Might you think of a better, more reliable way to get you closer to your dreams? You realize that choosing to hold on to your eating disorder is a decision you make now, but are you as aware that the disorder could become capable of dictating the quality of your life in the future. I know how hard it is to think so far in advance. . . .

When reason, education, cajoling, demanding, scaring, and any other form of incentive cease to work to motivate a client to recover, any leverage that will work should be used. W made no attempt to curtail her bulimia and anorexia until her parents told her definitively that they would not permit her to return to college for her senior year unless she stopped purging. Although it did not cure W's eating disorder, that incentive was sufficient to stop her purging and inspire her to get help before leaving for school. This early care became her incentive to seek ongoing help at school.

Handling Silence in Sessions

> Silence is a form of communication that can mean many things. As rests that appear in musical compositions, the spaces between sounds can take on meaning and significance at least as great as the sound itself. Silence is a natural part of every discussion; like sleep, silence can be a time for integrating information, but when it happens too often or seems excessive, it may indicate resistance or manipulation. Like sleep, silence can be a time for integrating information. Human connection may be felt more deeply in silence, in the space between words. (Germer et al., 2005, p. 101)

Silences can have a variety of meanings:

- "Some silences feel like walls erected for protection. We attempt to create a sense of safety by inviting the patient to talk about the choice not to talk" (Germer et al., 2005, p. 101).

- Some silences are avoidant or defensive, indicating the client's refusal to remain present within a difficult experience. Challenge such mindless silences.
- Other silences are angry and resistant. Comment on the anger, and welcome its expression.
- A young child client's silence may reflect a lack of assurance, self-knowledge, insights, or capacity to express herself sufficiently to speak for herself, particularly at the start of treatment. Silence in that situation may signal a need for a parent spokesperson.
- "Fertile silences are teeming with life and are best left undisturbed, as the client conveys a sense of "being" in our presence. Joining with this activity is seen as active support for the freedom to be quietly alone with oneself. Wordlessness can be transformative" (Germer et al., 2005, p. 138).

Fertile silences are a useful part of therapy. The client may divert her attention from you to look away, staring at nothing in particular. By watching her eye movements, you can tell whether she is seeing within herself. The timing of the therapist's intervention in the face of silence is critical so as not to extinguish a response, or dismiss a unique opportunity. It is a nuanced judgment that leads the practitioner to know when to break a client's elongated silence. By investigating what the silence is about, you become a catalyst for the client to learn more about herself. I typically ask, "So what are you thinking about? A penny for your thoughts . . . anything that might be worth sharing?"

If a client is obviously struggling with the decision about whether to reveal a confidence, I ask, "Is there anything that might be stopping you from sharing your thoughts with me?" I invite her not to disclose whatever it is, but instead to imagine that she has spoken the secret. Following that, I invite her to share her feelings about what it was like to have shared her secret (still in her imagination), what she might regret, what she fears, what she might find rewarding, and so forth.

The therapist can also consider how the client perceives the therapist's own silence. Whether the client recognizes the therapist's silence as fertile or as a form of disconnection, fatigue, or disinterest is a potential subject for discussion.

CONCLUSION

By offering the client the opportunity to know what the therapist knows, to see what the therapist sees, and most poignantly, to want what the therapist wants, the therapist begins the process of treatment engagement. He or she establishes a dialogue with the client's compromised ability to think, reason, perceive, and exercise sound judgment, then juggles the client's known deficits with her potential to realize her strengths. By establishing the power of the therapeutic relationship, the client becomes motivated to make the changes that will lead to recovery.

13

Eating Disorder Treatment Methods and Approaches: Differentiating and Integrating Methodological Techniques

If the treating professionals are lost at sea, the clients and families, too, remain adrift.

The generic therapeutic tools already in the therapist's treatment box are all applicable to the treatment of eating disorders. This chapter takes an integrationist look at treatment approaches, helping practitioners learn when and how to call up these comfortable "old shoes" to make them relevant and useful to each unique case in a framework of eating disorder applications. Combined treatment approaches offer the greatest odds of achieving healing outcomes once nutrition and eating patterns are normalized. It is for the practitioner to devise his or her own unique system of approaches, custom tailored to the unique needs of each client.

This chapter introduces therapists to the staples of eating disorder care: cognitive–behavioral therapy (CBT) techniques and its variants, a technique replete with invaluable and practical strategies and skills, and mindfulness in psychotherapy, a tool essential to the therapist's (and ultimately the client's) versatile use of self. The combination of these methodologies, together with a motivational bent and a family systems perspective, becomes the heart of the eating disorder treatment process.

COMBINING COGNITIVE AND BEHAVIORAL TECHNIQUES

In the past, the brain was considered to be essentially unchanging in structure and capacity. With this perspective, therapists strove to achieve better coping by maximizing clients' strengths and accommodating their weaknesses, a technique that in many respects remains applicable in best practice. Recent advances in understanding and appreciating the brain's capacity to change (i.e., plasticity) indicate that newly learned coping capacities both influence behaviors and prompt change in the brain's ability to continue influencing ever-improving behaviors. Therapy now seeks not only to accommodate what the brain can already do but also to augment its capacity to do more and do it better.

Eating disorders are marked by distortions in cognition that lead to dysfunctional behaviors and by dysfunctional behaviors that exacerbate distortions in cognitions. The task of cognitive therapy is to access automatic, dysfunctional thought patterns and modify longstanding distorted beliefs; the task of behavioral treatment is to decrease maladaptive behaviors while increasing adaptive ones. The combination of behavioral and cognitive concepts into a unified methodology known as CBT and CBT–Enhanced (CBT–E) has provided the best cognitive and behavioral tool for defining eating disorder problems, trying and achieving solutions, and solidifying behavioral gains.

Cognitive–behavioral therapy is a form of psychotherapy that emphasizes the important role of thinking in how we feel and what we do. CBT is not a distinct therapeutic technique but is a general term describing therapies with certain similarities. CBT is based on the cognitive model of emotional response—on the idea that our thoughts result in feelings, and our feelings motivate our behaviors. All three concepts are interchangeable, as behaviors influence thoughts, which in turn, influence feelings. CBT has sometimes been called "BCT" (behavioral–cognitive therapy), as cognitive awareness often follows behavior change. In the context of an eating disorder, malnourishment leads to damaged perceptions, damaged perceptions lead to physiological changes, and physiological changes lead to brain chemistry (serotonin) imbalances that further damage perceptions. Brain chemistry imbalances affect mood regulation and promote further behavioral dysfunction. The benefit of the technique is that it empowers clients to change the way they think, feel, and act regardless of their external situation.

Eating disorders create all manner of problems that demand solving—physical, emotional, cognitive, and interpersonal. Well-suited to eating disorder treatment, manualized CBT approaches offer a wealth of understanding about what eating disorders are and how to approach solving the diverse problems that they create. Eating disorder treatment requires action-based changes; CBT requires that newly learned concepts and cognitions become translated into action/behaviors and practiced through homework, task assignments, logging, journaling, and other forms of self-motivated self-expression. The tasks of eating disorder recovery and CBT teach clients *how* to behave and think, not *what* to do and think. By minimizing distortions in what a person thinks and feels, CBT prepares the individual to behave in ways that foster healthier living and problem solving.

How CBT and CBT–E Work

The use of CBT in eating disorder treatment originated in the 1970s as a theory-driven outpatient-based treatment for adults with bulimia. Throughout the 1980s and 1990s, the techniques were defined and refined by Christopher Fairburn, professor and researcher at Oxford University and colleagues. Under the assumption that eating disorders share common maintaining mechanisms and core pathologies (Fairburn, 2008, p. 12), Fairburn and his colleagues extended the work to accommodate all forms of eating disorders. To the original treatment model addressing body weight and shape and dietary restraint, Fairburn and colleagues added the treatment of low self-esteem, clinical perfectionism, mood intolerance, and interpersonal difficulties to form CBT–E (Wilson, 2005). Because CBT–E uses a systems model based on changing behavior, physiology, emotions, and cognitions, a CBT–E intervention that addresses any one of these four elements influences all of them.

A basic tenet of CBT–E is that "second- or third-tier issues such as preoccupation with food and eating or with shape and weight, compensatory vomiting and laxative abuse, calorie counting, and overexercising are issues that will resolve when the key features of the core psychopathology are addressed" (Fairburn, 2008, p. 47). (See Chapter 5 for a description of core psychopathology.) Fairburn (2008) likened eating disorder psychopathology to a house of cards; identifying and removing the key structural cards cause the house to fall.

CBT–E encourages clients to learn to de-center from their eating problem and "to observe themselves enacting their formulation live, and to become intrigued by the effects and implications of trying different ways of behaving" (Fairburn, 2008, p. 28). "By learning to 'spot shifts in their mindset,' clients learn to manipulate their frame of mind and deal more effectively with setbacks that might otherwise develop into full-scale relapses" (Fairburn, 2008, p. 28).

Awareness, novelty, and distinguishing differences facilitate new learning. M, a client with anorexia, felt it was "useless" and "foolish" to think about pleasantness when it did nothing to stave off problems in the future. To engage her cognitive brain, I asked her to consider how often she thought these thoughts, in whose voice she heard them (hers or her eating disorder's), what triggered them, and what her responses were to the thoughts. I suggested that when she first notices herself falling into this thought pattern, she mark it by snapping an elastic band against her wrist. By bringing about an awareness of the moment, this behavior would remind M that she had free choice to create a new and different thinking and behaving, allowing her to feel less distressed.

The Case for and Against Pure CBT–E

CBT or CBT–E procedures are currently the empirically based treatment of choice for clients with bulimia; these procedures have been shown to eliminate binge eating and purging in roughly 30 percent to 50 percent of all cases (Wilson, 2005). In addition, CBT–E has been shown to reliably decrease dysfunctional dieting and improve clients' body image, reducing the level of general psychiatric symptoms and improving self-esteem and social functioning. As a technique, it has been shown to be more effective than either psychodynamic psychotherapy or antidepressant medication alone, especially in producing a complete cessation of binge eating and purging (Wilson, 2005).

CBT–E, however, was created as an exacting discipline, and it is rarely implemented by eating disorder practitioners in its pure form, as an irrevocable and integrated set of practices to be followed within routine clinical practice (Keel, Mitchell, Miller, Davis, & Crow, 1999). Reluctant practitioners criticize it as a boilerplate method not suited for application in treating vastly diverse symptom configurations. In bypassing the psychological aspects of care, including the healing aspects of the treatment relationship, many believe that using CBT–E exclusively might promote the resurfacing of underlying problems in other symptoms. Critics describe the manual-based therapy as proceeding in an "unchanging, lockstep fashion" and failing to incorporate the self-correcting nature of real-world clinical practice (Wilson, 2005). As such, it runs counter to the professional sensibilities of many professionals who believe that predetermined protocols limit their freedom of function.

On the other hand, by precisely following CBT–E protocols, even unseasoned practitioners can avail themselves of a valuable treatment method that has been proved effective. CBT–E must also be appreciated as an incomparable tool for professional self-education, providing practical and creative solutions for problems that may otherwise appear to be unresolvable. I strongly recommend that eating disorder practitioners read Fairburn's (2008) definitive treatise on CBT–E; those who do not familiarize themselves with the basic precepts of CBT–E risk expending energy in "reinventing the wheel" of eating disorder clinical practice.

Although CBT–E remains at the very core and foundation of best eating disorder practice, it is my sense that no singular practice technique has the capacity to be integrative and comprehensive enough to fully and adequately address the diversity of these complex disorders and client populations. Throughout the course and confines of a single evolving case, the practitioner needs to use an integrative, eclectic approach to care, capable of accessing different methods and modalities at different times, and in different combinations, to ensure effectiveness.

The Maudsley Method

The Maudsley approach (also called "family-based therapy") is an evidence-based, manual-based approach to family treatment of eating disorders developed in London at the Maudsley Hospital. This method combines elements of structural, strategic, and narrative approaches to family therapy and places a special focus on parental control of the child's refeeding early in treatment rather than on addressing more general family processes. Studies have shown that for adolescents with short-term anorexia, the approach was superior to individual supportive therapy and to ego-enhancing individual approaches (Lock, 2006). The approach coaches parents to become their child's "food police," similar to the role of inpatient nurses.

This prescribed mode of treating families essentially replaces an overcontrolling eating disorder with parental control. Particularly in treating eating disorders in young childen, the approach has a great deal of value. In some cases, particularly with older teens and young adults, I believe that it has the potential ultimately to stifle the capacity of the client for self-determination, particularly if she is not given the freedom to accept responsibility for her own eating choices once she has achieved the capacity to do so. "There remains a need to determine the relative efficacy of the Maudsley approach as compared to a more psychodynamically oriented family therapy in order to understand whether outcomes are related to the involvement of the family or if they are specific to the interventions of this therapy" (Lock, 2006).

COMBINING CBT AND MINDFULNESS IN EATING DISORDER TREATMENT

Mindfulness in psychotherapy coexists brilliantly with CBT–E and other manualized approaches, which provide the foundation on which therapists can construct layer upon layer of treatment nuance and relationship quality in successfully treating clients with eating disorders. In CBT, the emphasis has traditionally been on identifying and changing irrational patterns of thought that lead to maladaptive behaviors. Irrational thoughts are labeled, challenged, and replaced with more rational thoughts and more satisfying behavior. Mindfulness-based CBT "borrows from ancient mindfulness practice the idea that learning to accept painful experiences, rather than seeking to be rid of them, can be transformative" (Germer, Siegel, & Fulton, 2005, p. 34). "By reducing the anxiety that deters learning, mindfulness offers the potential to inform cognition, bringing the protocols of CBT into a dynamic mechanism for change. The client's mindful, self-monitored attention to the reality of his or her current moment cultivates an awareness of what has worked in the past, affecting what might work in the present, and what may be worth trying in the future" (Germer et al., 2005, p. 153).

Mindful psychotherapy circumvents the current impasse that threatens the eating disorders treatment field with divisive priorities (science vs. art of care, scientific vs. anecdotal evidence, technical protocols vs. relationship building) offering the possibility of the emergence of a more unified model of psychotherapy (Germer, 2005, p. 20). In *Mindfulness and Psychotherapy*, Germer et al. (2005) speaks of mindfulness as a construct that draws clinical theory, research, and practice closer together, identifying this technique as "a key element in treatment protocols as the crucial ingredient in treatment protocols, and as technology for therapists to cultivate personal therapeutic qualities and general well-being" (p. 11).

Introducing Mindfulness Into Psychodynamic Practice

"Practicing clinicians are reminded regularly about the importance of the therapy relationship in treatment outcome. Clinicians also struggle with "transfer of technology"—making a bridge between treatment protocols developed in our universities and their application in the field. Germer et al. (2005) predicts that in the coming years, mindfulness practice may prove to be a tangible means for building empirically supported relationship skills." He presents something that we can do to improve the therapeutic connection. How we plan interventions may even be guided by a common therapeutic principle—the simple mechanism of mindfulness (p. 12). Inseparable from the formation of bonded relationships, mindfulness creates connections between people. Mindfulness requires a sense of presence in the moment; psychotherapeutic change takes place in the present. "The acceptance of self, other, and reality facilitates cognitive change, increases tolerance of pain, uncovers emotions, and increases the client's capacity to choose whether to act on his urges. Mindfulness practice allows people to feel less resistant to and threatened by the vicissitudes of life experience" (Germer et al., 2005, p. 187).

On the basis of the assumption that problems are rooted in developmental anxieties, social pressures, and separation issues, the effectiveness of psychotherapy depends on the therapist's heightened awareness of self, other, and the dynamics of the unfolding therapeutic process and moment, along with the importance of the unconscious. "Any method that develops empathy in the therapist would support a positive treatment relationship and therefore improve outcome" (Germer et al., 2005, p. 82). "Empathy, the ability to identify with a person's experience, is a learnable skill that helps the therapist understand the other's meaning through the use of reflective listening" (Miller & Rollnick, 1991, p. 26), which is also a powerful means of helping the client to better hear and understand herself. Germer describes empathy as "learning to let one's self go into the other person with a willingness to be changed in the process" (p. 82).

In listening to M, a client who had made a breakthrough in her recovery work, it occurred to me that what she had achieved was the result of her mindful striving to stay in the moment. My first impulse was to blurt out excitedly what I discovered to be such significant learning, the fruits of her strivings. I restrained this impulse, instead spending the next 10 minutes having her rethink how she had put learning and action together to arrive at her successful outcome—In helping her to become mindful of her own learning and change, I asked, "So what might this be about?" "Does any part of this decision-making recall other things you have been learning and doing in your recovery?" "What does it feel like to be discovering these things about yourself?" Through her own self-discovery, she walked away with something she truly "owned." It was hers now, an investment in her emotional future and a resource that would serve her well in her continued recovery and in all of her life functions.

> **Client:** Things are going better this week.
> **Therapist:** So what in particular is different for you this week? What part did you play in actively bringing about those changes? What did making those changes help you to discover about yourself? Were you aware of those parts of yourself before?
> **Client:** I am so much better off when I keep busy.
> **Therapist:** What might that be about? Might it have more to do with providing distractions for yourself, or about recognizing the benefits of actively creating a structure for yourself both in your eating lifestyle and in your life in general?

Client: I think my relationship with my Dad is improving.

Therapist: So how do you understand that change happening at this particular time in your life and recovery? Do you think that he has changed, or might there be something different about you?

In respecting and accepting a client's pain, the therapist helps her to respect and accept her own. The mindful practitioner brings the client's relationship with her abandoned past into awareness, evoking a greater degree of emotional integrity. Mindful treatment helps the therapist

> observe with the patient when he or she self-abandons, by noting that his or her voice has dropped off in describing some aspect of experience, or in observing an attitude of self dismissal of their own pasts and narrative histories. (Germer et al., 2005, p. 136)

One of the limitations of psychotherapy is that thoughts and feelings must be symbolically represented in language in order to be communicated. Language is an imperfect and disguising vehicle for subjective experience. The advantage of mindful practice is that "The mindfully engaged psychotherapist becomes capable of listening *beyond* the spoken word with the 'third ear' to hear the unspoken, the accidental, the avoided—to find the reality that lies imperfectly revealed and disguised in thought" (Germer et al., 2005, p. 36).

Case Study

L was healing. Her weight was gradually being restored, her eating patterns had changed, and she was communicating better with her parents, who were together with her in her session this day. They had been supportive, dedicated to the treatment process, and always loving to their daughter. At one point, L snapped at her mother after her mother appropriately spoke of her concern about a meal her daughter had chosen to order at a restaurant: "That's none of your business," L replied, "and you have no right to question me, especially since I am doing better."

I asked her to stop for a moment and listen to the sound of her voice. Could she hear how quick she was to anger? I then asked her to consider the genuine, supportive, always well-intentioned role her parents had consistently played in partnering with her throughout her recovery. I pointed out that in light of their joint responsibility in her recovery, in fact, L's mother had every right to notice a behavior that concerned her and to express it honestly. I went on to suggest that L look into herself to more fully understand where her virulent anger came from and to whom it might more appropriately be directed. My sense, I noted, was that she might have been feeling disappointment and angry at herself for continuing to give in to her disease. As an aside, I wondered aloud if she had ever been aware of experiencing anger toward me during our sessions, and if what I was saying now might be difficult for her to hear.

I suggested that she needn't be so hard on herself, as uncomfortable eruptions of feelings are part of the natural process of recovery, and that the deeper she came to know herself and her feelings, the better a psychotherapist she would eventually become. She sat quietly for a long stretch of time, tears welling up. This reality-based confrontation marked a turning point in her treatment: From this point on, she would recognize and mediate the previously mindless hostility she had continually shown her family throughout her illness. Her new cognitive mindfulness would bring her closer not only to her parents, but to herself.

A month later as she began her social work graduate education, she moved out of her parent's house into her own apartment. Her mother came for a visit soon after she moved in, with a small house gift in hand. She had painstakingly chosen the kind of bagels L liked best from her favorite bagel deli. In the past, L would have perceived such a gesture as her mother's attempt to manipulate her into eating more and gaining weight. Now her response was of gratitude, as she perceived this act as one of kindness and caring, not as a lack of confidence.

Learning to "Not Know"

"Mindfulness helps therapists hold their theories and practice protocols more lightly. By allowing themselves to be attentive to the 'now,' therapists tacitly admit that they simply do not know what the next moment will bring." Modeling for the client, "they surrender—albeit temporarily—their wish to know and control by allowing themselves not to know. The invitation of mindfulness to 'not know' should be taken not as license to abandon all of their clinical training but as a process of learning to cling less firmly to imagined certainty and to trust that an open and attuned mind (fortified by substantive clinical training) will be far more responsive to the demands of the moment than one resting on concepts alone. Mindfulness grants therapists access to all the tools at their disposal, based on the needs of the present, and allows them the freedom to jettison them when they are unhelpful" (Germer et al., 2005, p. 72). There is a marvelous irony in the parallel between the therapist's mindful need to let go of controls and predictability and the roots of eating disorder pathology in a pathological fear of the unknown.

"Tranquility is based on the acceptance of whatever is arising, on concentration, and on equanimity" (Germer et al., 2005, p. 77). Accepting moment-to-moment experience makes available energy that was formerly used to control or defend. Perhaps some of the most important learning that the client accrues during recovery comes from modeling herself after the therapist's facility for mindful "letting go" as experienced through the client–therapist connection.

Accepting the Therapist's and Client's Self

"For the therapist, self-acceptance precedes acceptance of others. When mindfulness becomes a vehicle for the professional's own personal development, the mindful therapist models and invites the client to develop similar skills and insights in approaching life and healing changes" (Germer et al., 2005, p. 96). When therapists are not intimidated, and when they can feel comfortable disclosing the self in appropriate, boundaried, and clearly intentional ways, "clients are offered the opportunity to bring forward more of their own seemingly intolerable experience. Therapists' receptivity assures clients that they need not censor themselves; emotions lose some of their threat" (Germer et al., 2005, p. 61). More mindful awareness of their own struggles allows practitioners to more readily empathize with patients.

Valuing Caring and Connected Moments

Neuropsychiatric research has confirmed that

> working in the here and now has the greatest potential to bring about change in another. "Sloppiness," the product of two minds working together, is inherent in the process, and can lead to eruptions of *now moments*—new states coming into being or threatening to come into being. This refers to a mounting emotional charge in the consultation room when the usual way of being with each other is implicitly called into question." (Germer et al., 2005, p. 101)

The moment when the therapist is moved to make a creative, authentic response has been called the "moment of meeting," where both parties are moved by the momentum of the new connection The therapist's genuine interest and close attention to the client and the process are palpable and contagious. The quickening of the therapist's energy not only captures the client's attention but becomes riveting (Germer et al., 2005).

During a discussion about P's need to eat more, the 10-year-old jumped up out of his chair and started to walk out of the session. His parents attempted in vain to stop him. At this pivotal moment, the client had lost trust and the connection to the process. I began to speak with fervor, making it clear that his feelings were valid but that to express them by walking away would be self-defeating. I told him that my relentless drive, as well as his parents', to defeat his eating disorder had been a vote of our confidence in him and an investment in the quality of his life; it was a tribute to him—as a resourceful, talented, and highly intelligent human being. I told him he deserved to enjoy all the things he dreamed of—accomplishing . . . family, love, acceptance, and normalcy. He saw that I meant what I said in my body language, sitting as I was at the edge of my chair. He heard it in my voice and felt it through my eyes.

P turned around and sat down once again, surprised but reconciled. This impassioned demonstration of caring provided important instruction and modeling for his parents, who tended not to show how much they valued him. By infusing energy into the session, I caught his attention, evoking a surge of his own motivation. "But don't you say this to all 50 of your clients?" he asked. "Great question!" I replied. "So glad your asked! So now I'm going to turn that question back to you for your answer. Listen to your instincts—can you not sense my sincerity on a deep level? What might be some indicators that I mean what I say? Can you trust what you are feeling now? Can you share your feelings about what is happening at this very moment?"

Improving Boundary Versatility

Through an empathic yet boundaried projective identification and merging with the other both in flaws and in strengths, client and therapist are drawn into each other's energy system, arriving at full acceptance and mutual growth. Mindfulness allows treating professionals to be engaged, yet disentangled, from the client's experience; to enter a family system while remaining objective enough to foster insight and change; and "to pop in and out of [the client's] reactions to learn from what their mind is doing without losing connection with the client (Germer et al., 2005). With mindfulness, "there is an awareness of the potential of each new moment. . . . We are trying to find the pulse of someone's experience, beat by beat, and provide deep company in whatever challenges arise in experiencing the pulse more directly" (Germer et al., 2005, p. 134).

Mindfulness takes practice and intention. By consulting their own internal cues and their own wandering inattention through the psychotherapy process, therapists are better able to comprehend and guide the client to attend to the relational dynamics, facilitating the client's insights and learning. The therapist does well to take his or her own intermittent inattentiveness as clinical information, inviting the question, "What might be happening in the dynamic of the session right now that is making it hard for me to stay focused, that is causing my mind to wander, my eyes to want to close?" (Germer et al., 2005, p. 59). In the face of an awareness of my own boredom or anxiety, I sound a small alarm in my head to discover what dynamic may be resulting in my sense of being fatigued, overused, underused, or otherwise manipulated. This is my cue to say to the client, "You know, somehow I feel as though you have me working awfully hard today, perhaps too hard. Are you aware of that? What might be going on within you right now?"

Likewise, it is sometimes necessary to catch the attention of a client in preparation to facilitate learning. The anticipation of what is to come alerts the brain to attend with curiosity and intention. I typically invite the person to attend through conversational "appetizers" such as the following:

- "So here are my thoughts about what you just said."
- "I want you to think about something together with me."
- "What I am about to say may be hard to hear."
- "I am going to ask you a really tough question now that I don't expect you to be able to answer at this point, but I want you to start thinking about it anyway; the answer is less important than how you approach thinking about it."
- "Here is what leads me to ask you this question now."
- "I understand that you have no idea about how you feel, but let me share with you some reactions that others in your shoes typically have had in response to similar situations."

Stimulating Awareness and Learning in Clients

It is virtually impossible to separate any aspect of mindfulness from the quality of a therapist's presence in any psychotherapeutic moment. R refused to take responsibility for her own recovery in deference to her loyalty to her disease; instead, she relied on her parents to "force" her to eat what she needed to stay alive. During family sessions, she preferred to defer to her mother to begin the discussion and determine the agenda for the meeting. After I pointed out this pattern to client and family, it became a therapeutic issue and learning tool. On humid days, when the door of my Victorian home office sticks and demands a great effort to open, R would stand aside to let her Dad use his strength to grapple with it. I stopped allowing this to happen: "R, you know how to handle that big old door yourself. Let's see you do it."

B chose not to call for an appointment during the last month before she was to leave for college. I invited her to come in for a good-bye session, during which she spoke of her mortal fear of being "forgotten" by her friends whom she believed would "move on" without her. Despite her claim of having been "too busy" to call, I helped her consider whether her anxiety about separation from home and friendships might have generalized to our own relationship, as well, in her concern that I, too, might forget her, and somehow invalidate our four-year relationship. We spoke of how hard it might be to say good-bye . . . to me, to her childhood, to a dependency on family and friends . . . and to her eating disorder. Transitions are not easy for anybody, with or without an eating disorder.

Always seeking a "way in" and always available in the dynamic process of the here and now with the client, it is a rare occasion when I won't shepherd otherwise meaningless "filler chatter" (always respecting the legitimacy of the client's needs at the moment) to a more relevant conversation relating to mindfulness of purpose in addressing the eating disorder. Z sat down in my office, declared that she was "freezing," and wrapped herself in an afghan and turned up the heater. "Are you cold a lot?" I asked, after we finished commenting on the weather. In the discussion that followed, she revealed that in opposition to her parent's directives, she had refused to stop wearing her cotton summer cargo pants, even as Chicago's winter began. She favored this pair of pants as she had been using its deep pockets to hide snacks until she could dispose of them,. One of the family's homework tasks for the week was to buy Z warm pants as well as snow boots, which she wore to her next session.

Mindfulness allows entry into the dynamic process of the treatment moment; likewise, engaging with the dynamic process promotes mindfulness. I asked S, who had spent the summer in treatment with me and was about to begin graduate school in a nearby city, whether she planned to make the commute to remain in treatment with me or find a different therapist at school. "I haven't begun to think about it yet," she replied. "I've been too busy. I can't say." I responded as follows:

> It might be helpful to think about it together, then, to discover what issues may be standing in the way of your thinking—the sooner the better, I would think, so we can prepare to terminate our work together should that be your choice. Am I imagining what seems to be some discomfort on your part in my approaching you with this question? Could we discuss what might that be about?

In considering the underlying dynamics and full meaning behind the apparent anger in her response, I wondered aloud if she might be feeling unduly "pushed"; if she might be struggling with some unspoken aspect of her feelings about me, about her own progress, or about our treatment experience together; or if she might be toying with the idea of taking a break from treatment altogether after her progress that summer. Such probing offered inroads into her understanding of herself and into the significance of the therapy moment. She continued her treatment with me and went on to enjoy full recovery.

Striving for Mindfulness in Eating Behaviors

Mindless eating is ritualized eating that is directed by habit or emotions, not by bodily senses and cues. Mindless eating tends to fulfill goals and tasks that are essentially beyond the individual's consciousness and includes "comfort" eating, eating standing up, eating to punctuate life activities (walking in the door, turning on the television), eating to avoid or procrastinate, eating hurriedly, eating in front of an electronic device, and eating to satiate emotional hunger.) When a client's weight gain or weight loss is not the result of consistent, intentional, consciously self-determined changes in eating lifestyle, it becomes mindless; it represents arbitrary change and therefore does not represent recovery.

Mindfulness in eating can be reinforced by self-determined choices. Behaviors that promote mindfulness might include setting the breakfast table the night before; sitting down to eat a meal; "designing" one's plate with all the foods one intends to eat during that meal and in the appropriate amounts; chewing each mouthful slowly; savoring smells, tastes, and textures; punctuating the end of a meal with a hot drink; and clearing the table and washing the dishes. Mindful eating can be an important tool in managing compulsive eating.

Mindless learning (the kind that happens when multitasking) changes brain maps but not necessarily lastingly (Doidge, 2007). Distractions such as anxiety, incessant television noise, or the nagging criticism of the eating disorder can contribute to a mindless state. Any behavior that is mindless can be brought into mindfulness by the client's decision to exercise choice and her own voice.

Mindfulness in Parenting

Central to the growth and development of a child who has an eating disorder is a healthy relationship with his or her parents. Teaching mindfulness to parents in facilitating a healthy relationship with their child is critical. Mindfulness allows parents to have greater presence, awareness of connection and disconnection, openness to a child's nonverbal communications, and ability to join with the child in play, all of which help children to experience their parents' love and understanding more fully and help parents deal with conflict and set appropriate limits more skillfully (Germer et al., 2005).

RELATED THERAPIES THAT INCORPORATE MINDFULNESS

Dialectical Behavioral Therapy

Dialectical behavior therapy, developed by Marsha Linehan, validates the patient's current emotional, cognitive, and behavioral responses and balances them with active problem solving. Dialectical behavioral therapy (DBT) can be considered a bridge between acceptance-based (rather than change-based) CBT and the incorporation of mindfulness in treatment. As "a variation of CBT, the central dialect of the therapy balances a focus on change with one of acceptance" (Wilson, 2005). In acceptance-based treatments, the client learns to allow disturbing sensations and thoughts to come and go; "patients are asked to imagine that the mind is like a big sky where thoughts and feelings pass by like clouds" (Germer et al., 2005, p. 125).

The focus of DBT is to help clients live a more successful life, particularly interpersonally, in spite of how they may feel (Germer et al., 2005). DBT, which has become the preferred treatment for borderline personality disorder, especially parasuicidal behavior, and is typically used for affect regulation, generally takes place in groups; the group therapist uses mindful techniques to stimulate feelings of acceptance, to validate and legitimize behaviors, and to transfer focus from pathology to the dynamics of the session in progress. While differentiating objective and subjective realities, DBT considers all perceptions true and real as they relate to the subjective internal reality of the client.

DBT is well suited to treating eating disorders because it supports action to effect and cement change; is predicated on motivational development; focuses on behavioral and cognitive interventions, skill development, and problem-solving; and emphasizes learning mindfulness skills for staying present in the moment. Through the technique, the therapist prioritizes the most pressing crisis in the client's chaotic emotionally dysregulated life, treating that behavior first while helping the client tolerate the subsidiary distresses in her life. As an example of the preference for behavioral attention, DBT differentiates suicidality from depression, treating the behaviors before attending to the mood instability.

DBT skills related to mindfulness practice include the following:

- focusing awareness on present activity
- labeling feelings
- letting thoughts slip in and out
- practicing nonjudgment
- doing one thing at a time
- practicing radical acceptance of feelings.

DBT teaches interpersonal skills, improved self-regulation, and distress tolerance, but the most unique aspect of this form of therapy is its emphasis on mindfulness strategies of relaxation, breathing, and self-awareness.

Acceptance and Commitment Therapy

Acceptance and commitment therapy (ACT) is a branch of cognitive therapy that incorporates mindfulness as a core skill. "ACT focuses on full acceptance of present experience and mindfully letting go of obstacles as clients identify and pursue their life goals" (Germer et al., 2005, p. 132). ACT is different from traditional CBT in that rather than trying to teach people to better control their thoughts, feelings, sensations, memories, and other private events, it teaches them to "just notice," accept, and embrace their private events, especially previously unwanted ones. Mindfulness practice makes a continuous effort to set aside or not be caught up in thinking but instead watching the arising and passing of sensory, perceptual, and cognitive events . . . as one might note an itch or a passing sound. "No symptom or state can (or should) be held indefinitiely" (Germer, 2005, p. 30).

The efficacy of ACT is attributable to a reduction in the believability, rather than the frequency, of negative thoughts (Germer et al., 2005). In response to a young woman who spoke about how readily she translates all her feelings of anxiety and depression into the sensation of being "fat and ugly," I suggested that she become aware of this dynamic as it happens, that she place "a tiny version of herself" on her shoulder to watch out for when this distorted transference of negative energy takes place, then invite this small observer to sound a chime to promote an awareness of when she may be falling into this deceptive habit.

Internal Family Systems Therapy

Family therapist Richard Schwartz developed a unique approach to treatment, Internal Family Systems Therapy (IFST), which is a derivative of mindfulness in the context of family systems theory. A psychospiritual approach to treatment, IFST recognizes people's potential to heal themselves through their own internal resources. Schwartz describes parts of ourselves that become "like internal families, constraining and protecting the Self from leadership in the face of trauma" (R. C. Schwartz, 1995). "Each seeks opportunities to tell their stories, through flashbacks and fleeting tastes of pain, thus obscuring the self's leadership qualities, and causing the Self to be separated from the sensations of the person's body" (R. C. Schwartz, 1995). When, through the technique, true leadership is achieved, the 'true Self' or core self is revealed, releasing the parts to find and adopt their preferred roles in a unified integration of the self. The role of parts, which carry emotions, memories and sensations from past experiences, may be determined by childhood trauma or the patient's family values and interaction patterns that create internal polarizations, which escalate over time and are played out in other relationships. When parts differentiate and then reunite to become part of an integrated whole personality, the individual becomes his or her own caretaker to his or her own inner families, ultimately healing parts that swam in their inner pools of pain and shame (R. C. Schwartz, 1995).

CONCLUSION

In overriding the limitations of manualized CBT–E and broadening its focus, mindfulness in psychotherapy tailors treatment more precisely to the unique qualities of the individual. This chapter is designed to whet therapists' appetite to learn more about applying mindfulness practice in supporting their current "meat and potatoes" care protocols, which include cognitive–behavioral, psychodynamic, and systems-oriented care.

14

Practical Building Blocks of Strategic Interviewing: Borrowing Freely From Diverse Treatment Approaches

It is our choices, Harry, that show what we truly are, far more than our abilities.

—J. K. Rowling

Throughout this book, I have offered interviewing strategies and tips as they relate to various techniques and circumstances described. This chapter deals with other types of practical tools and mindful strategies to use when face to face with clients with eating disorders. The chapter is solely about doing and addresses in greater depth what to say, when, and how to facilitate learning and change that leads to healing. Each unique strategy or tool forms part of the larger framework of comprehensive care. The chapter provides behavioral and Gestalt strategies, strategies to reinforce learning and increase mindful attention, psychoeducational techniques, and finally, strategies for treating clients with Axis II disorders.

BEHAVIORAL TOOLS AND STRATEGIES

Written and Self-Expressive Tools

Journaling and logging feelings, behavioral patterns, and the outcomes of concrete behavioral homework tasks facilitate self-awareness, self-determination, and accountability. These activities help the client become accountable to herself and others, practice sound judgment, and use her imagination to anticipate and prepare for future challenges. Writing provides a check on reality, and tracking in the support of problem solving. Diary keeping externalizes learning, so the client can more clearly see and accept herself in the process of becoming. By offering concrete evidence of emotional patterns that trigger dysfunctional behaviors or give rise to more functional ones, journaling, diary keeping, and scrapbooking provide the client a sense of stability in a sea of powerful disease-directed compulsions and compelling recovery demands.

Therapists should be sure to discuss outcomes of homework assignments to validate and reinforce the process. Taking action and then discussing what has been learned supports the retention of information.

Logging Food Consumption

The food plan is a key treatment device to teach and enforce normalized eating. (Chapter 9 discusses the role of the nutritionist as part of the treatment team.) If the client follows a food plan, logging the outcomes of her attempts to follow the plan is crucial. Food logging may provide a critical point of entry into an expansive system of symptoms as a first step toward change, a means of pacing recovery, and a stimulus to self-awareness and choice making. It also provides a chief source of motivation for change and for self-observation in the process of so doing, and a unique diagnostic tool for guiding and monitoring nutritional interventions and, in some instances, milieu placement. How a person abides by the plan indicates how she learns, approaches tasks, and solves problems. The plan inspires, rewards, and augments change in eating habits, encouraging the discovery of joy in the smallest details and the recognition that we learn from our "failures" as readily as from our successes. As a musician would do when practicing a new piece of music, the client can break down the plan into smaller units of concentration based on her capacities and focus on a few manageable "measures" at a time.

The commitment to log one's eating lifestyle provides structure and realistic limit setting for a life in flux. C was close to 300 pounds when she started treatment for binge eating disorder. As she began to follow a regularized eating lifestyle, her log indicated that she was also becoming more in control of other spheres of her life as she began to feel happier and more empowered. With a renewed sense of self-determination and organization, she found herself able to make clearer decisions about when she needed to eat and when to stop, when to exercise and when to stop, when to work and when to stop, all with a sense of balance and moderation.

Food plans require consistency, above and beyond compliance. Beyond achieving eating-related goals, the client must *sustain* the changes she achieves without relying on compensatory behaviors such as purging, overexercising, or laxative abuse. Without a written record, the client's memory is likely to fail her, and her viewpoints more apt to become distorted. In response to an inquiry about how the food plan is being attended to, beware of the response "Fine. It's going well." Be sure to get the particulars, in such a case, as they provide the stuff of learning.

A typical reason for a client's reluctance to log what she eats is the fear that it will put her in a compulsive mode of counting calories or challenge her distorted perspective of reality. In handling problems with logging, deal with the process (the resistance underlying the refusal to comply) along with the difficulty in facing food issues. Does resistance appear in other areas of her life as well, or only around the issue of her eating disorder? What is its meaning for recovery? Might noncompliance indicate intention, fear, or lethargy?

Use Action of Any Kind to Reinforce Change

Reinforce mindful awareness and learning through encouraging the client to take action; behaviors go a long way toward reinforcing cognitions. As homework, you might consider asking the client to do the following:

- Pretend to be three pounds lighter and then imagine the confidence she would feel under these circumstances. For the brain, imagining that an outcome and doing it can have the same effect.
- Anticipate or rehearse a feared activity to prepare for alternative solutions to potential problems. Note and record instances of "brain speak" in the interest of diffusing and negating it. The eating disorder voice inside one's head, which typically preaches self-hatred and can be brutalizing in its constancy, creates a critical self-perception and crowds out new learning. Awareness and anticipation can help prepare a client to fight the voice of the disorder. For example, M's voice reminded her of the "futility of trying to recover" because she "doesn't have the strength to survive without her anorexia"; that any progress she made "just set her up for a more painful fall"; and that if she felt connected and positive in treatment, not to be fooled because "it's only an illusory and temporary sham." Her efforts to fight the force behind this voice needed to be active and constant.

A client who experiences compulsive self-flagellation might benefit from the following behavioral strategies:

- Identify her inner critic and write down examples of its voice throughout the day. Report them during therapy.
- Learn a response to the banter of the critic, such as "Pipe down. I've heard this before; I know the drill."
- Differentiate how she speaks to herself. Instead of telling herself "This is what I really believe," the client can learn to say, "I am being told this by my eating disorder," or "I never realized I had the option to believe something else." Instead of telling herself "These are the changes I am hoping for," she can learn to say, "These are the changes I am determined to make."

One of my favorite behavioral (as well as cognitive) tools is to have the client draw a pie chart illustrating the proportion of her time she spends doing life activities—work, study, recreation, relaxation, and so forth—as compared with activities related to her eating disorder. Seeing how much of her day the eating disorder takes up in obsessing and preparing gives the client a strong incentive to make different choices. Recreating the pie chart as recovery occurs can be an enlightening and motivational device.

Contracts

Contracts are behavioral promises that carry consequences in holding the client accountable for her actions. An example is the following: "I promise to gain one pound a week for the next month or acknowledge that I am unable to heal myself without the assistance of a more restrictive treatment environment." For a client who chooses to remain under the care of an outpatient team against medical advice for not having achieved sufficient or timely enough progress, a time-limited "consent to treat" contract such as the following may be drawn up by the professionals to be signed by client and family members to protect the treating parties:

> By the authority of this contract [client's name], the client, and her family agree to hold harmless the professional team treating the client for her eating disorder in the understanding that the client has refused at present to enter a more restrictive treatment care facility as advised by her professional team to ensure her physical safety. This contract is good for a period of [specify time period], during which time, according to the client's own wishes, she has promised to gain [number of] pounds while being monitored weekly by a physician. If the client does not meet the requirements of this contract, or if her condition becomes worse, she will seek care in a more restrictive treatment environment immediately or as need dictates."

Any contract with a client with an eating disorder is dictated by the reality of how sick and at risk she is and what it would take to improve her health. G, on vaction with her parents, called to ask about what would be appropriate input from her parents about her eating on their cruise. I suggested that if she felt ready and committed to monitoring herself, she could do so. A verbal contract that came out of the conversation stipulated that upon her return, if she had lost any weight on her trip, she would agree to take a leave of absence from her high school track team to enhance her recovery efforts. When she returned she had lost three pounds, and she stopped participating in track until she had gained the weight back and made progress in recovery.

Exercise

The subject of exercise for clients with eating disorders can be a difficult issue but is an important learning tool that relies heavily on the therapist's use of timing and capacity to create understanding. About three quarters of individuals with eating disorders use excessive exercise as a method of purging or of reducing anxiety. A multidisciplinary treatment team should determine the appropriateness of exercise during the recovery of a client who is malnourished or who has binge eating disorder and lacks internal controls, and such clients should have close medical monitoring.

Clients need to understand that rescinding exercising rights is a temporary and nonpunitive recovery tool to minimize stress to an already highly stressed body in an attempt to prevent harm. The use or prohibition of exercise is a superb diagnostic tool, even well into the recovery process; the therapist can raise a client's self-awareness by confronting her with the extent of her own compulsions. The client needs to know that as soon as her mind and body are adequately prepared for safe exercise, and as soon as she can reliably supplement her food plan to accommodate calories burned, exercise becomes a privilege restored, moderately and mindfully. Recovering clients require guidance in preparing to resume exercise; the environment of health clubs may challenge their newly acquired capacity to appreciate and moderate their exercise.

Clients need to learn to approach exercise as a way of reconnecting to their bodies pleasurably instead of as a device to serve the eating disorder's demands, to burn calories or to quell anxiety. Redirecting the client's attention to how her body feels in movement, as opposed to how many repetitions she can muster, is an important differentiation that brings a client face to face with her body and herself in a meaningful way. In becoming a kinder and more generous offering to the body, exercise becomes a mode of self-nurturance. Clients need permission to do less and to have fun. A supervised graded exercise program, such as nonaerobic yoga or the Feldenkrais or Anat Baniel method, can be highly beneficial.

GESTALT STRATEGIES

The Empty Chair Technique

On the basis of the theory that emotional dysfunction is largely based in parts of the self that have been exiled or nonintegrated, the empty chair technique is a useful tool in individual or group therapy sessions for clients who need to reconnect with their estranged part or parts. The client sits face to face with her alienated part in the opposing chair, which may be the client's own exiled part, an absent family member who needs to be addressed, or the voice of the eating disorder that dictates the client's actions and thinking. In a dialogue initiated by the client, the voice and the message of the absent part becomes heard and defined, allowing the client (with the guidance of the therapist) to mediate divisiveness and negotiate an internal truce, ultimately reintegrating a fragmented inner world. The integrating self becomes increasingly capable of developing the emotional versatility to bend and flex with the ever-changing requirements of life, leading the way to maturity and recovery. Confronting the feared part in the chair demands courage, acceptance, insight, and inventiveness.

In the example of the empty chair technique that follows, the client, F, engages her disease in dialogue, facilitated by the empathic responses of the therapist:

Therapist: What is the eating disorder in the chair telling you?

F: It's saying, "How can you even consider eating a piece of pizza? You're worthless as an anorexic! You're fat, undisciplined, and weak. You don't deserve to ever eat again."

Therapist: It looks like this diatribe is causing you a great deal of pain. Can you tell the anorexia how hard it is for you when it speaks this way about you? How it makes you feel?

F: It makes me feel awful to hear those things. But I feel really guilty for letting my anorexia down. I'm afraid the anorexia will punish me for abandoning it, and I'll become totally out of control and obese. I'm afraid that I am in this thing for life and that nothing will ever come of all my hard work at recovery.

Therapist: What might it be like for you to tell the anorexia that you need it to be quiet? That it must stop, or it will kill you? Can you tell your disease that you understand that its intentions are good and that you understand that it only seeks to protect and serve you, but that you have begun to develop other skills of your own now that are fortifying you and that you might like to give this recovery effort a go on your own for a bit?

F to chair: You have to let me do this on my own! You know, you can let go a little now . . . I am feeling a bit safer now than I was before. You must give me a chance to prove myself to myself. You have been a help to me when I needed you, but now I need a chance to see who I am and what I can accomplish on my own.

Therapist: What's it like to speak up for yourself, to confront the anorexia with your true feelings? Has there ever been anyone else that you have protected from your deepest feelings, as you do your anorexia,? Has there ever been anyone else who has been as protective of you?

In the course of this dialogue, F began to access her true feelings, which had previously been camouflaged by her eating disorder. She was able to express anger at the disorder for the first time, and at the same time, in appreciating its caretaking role, she was able to forgive it even as she distanced herself from it.

The Interpretation of Dreams

Generally seen as the stuff of the unconscious, of Freudian psychoanalysis, or Jungian psychotherapy, remembering dreams can be key to accessing parts of the individual as they emerge into the realm of consciousness. Using another Gestalt device, I suggest to the client that every part of a dream represents an aspect of herself. I invite her to take turns "being" the various parts of the dream she has dreamt, sensing and speaking them, in all of their emotional ramifications, and in as much detail as possible.

As an example, if the client reports a train going into a tunnel, I ask her to "be" the train, the tracks, the tunnel, "the darkness inside the tunnel," and to describe those experiences separately and mindfully. "What is it like for you as tracks to be carrying that train into that tunnel? As the train, are you in control of the speed at which you are traveling?, I inquire of the tunnel what it feels like to be receiving that barreling train, to be harboring the unknown in your eternal darkness.

Eating disorder treatment is about reaching as deeply into the client's conscious and unconscious as possible to help her to discover, accept, understand and forgive all parts of herself. It is the merging of the fragmented self that represents a true and complete recovery.

STRATEGIES TO REINFORCE LEARNING, CHANGE, AND THE INCENTIVE TO HEAL

Motivational strategies not only inspire treatment engagement, but sustain the client's desire to remain in treatment and ultimately initiate changes on her own. Eating disorder treatment inevitably involves numerous interruptions, plateaus, and backslides, and these tools can help get treatment back on track.

Communicating Acceptance

In efforts to encourage the client's feelings of acceptance and incentive to work, the therapist gently taps the accelerator, while leaving the driving to the client. The following statements communicate the therapist's acceptance of the client as a partner in treatment:

- "I want you to fully understand why I feel this is the time to be asking this of you. What is your sense about this?"
- "I want you to understand that I have spoken my thoughts about what might be going on with you in declarative statements; in fact, I am envisioning a question mark at the end of each statement! Does what I am saying make sense to you? Does it apply, in your opinion?"
- "None of what I say has any relevance unless it means something to you. "If it does not, we'll toss it, and move in another direction."

Stroking is an empathic device often useful in motivating a client's capacity to listen and hear challenging information and accept herself. As a strategy to soften what might be considered criticism or judgment, it presupposes that the therapist sees and appreciates the client's strengths as well as weaknesses. Stroking is different from flattery, as there is nothing ingenuous about the former; stroking it is based purely on reason and backed by concrete illustrations. Clients tolerate strokes more easily as they develop trust in the therapist and themselves. T's new boyfriend ordered cheese fries and insisted that she eat them with him. Having newly recovered from anorexia, she described the act of eating the fries as being "out of control" As a greater advocate for this young woman than she could be for herself at this juncture, I responded, "Nope—spontaneous, maybe, but certainly not out of control. It sounds to me as though you decided to break an anorexic rule that had already become obsolete and that no longer applied. You're just not yet used to appreciating the quality things that you do and decisions you make."

In the presence of family members, I often speak to the strengths and attributes of the child client, for the benefit of parents as well as the child. Many parents, in their frustration and anger, temporarily lose sight of the whole child, seeing only a "walking eating disorder." I invite parents to appreciate with a refreshed awareness the strengths of the child's intellect, uniqueness, artistic talent, value system, and so forth, which also praises their strengths as parents. In deference to the quality of the child–parent relationship, on more than one occasion I have assigned joint homework tasks for parents to come to know their child better by visiting museums, doing home-based projects and creating quality time.

Negotiating With the Client

Teens and young adults living at home with parents typically harbor unresolved issues with their parents that may interfere with their recovery and require attention. In motivating these clients to become self-advocates in defining and attending to these issues, I will carefully rehearse alternatives for future dialogues between these youngsters and their parents, and when necessary, will encourage them to bring their parents into a treatment session with them so that they might have the advantage of my backing and support during such a confrontation.

To avoid inadvertently jeopardizing a client's motivation, therapist and nutritionist must be vigilant in not sending food-related messages that could inadvertently exacerbate the client's fears. A client may construe "If you have eaten a good size dinner and feel overly full, it is fine to skip dessert" as "dessert is unhealthy and fattening at best." A more appropriate comment might be, "Why not try next time to eat just a few bites of the dessert before calling it quits? We know you are capable of doing it now; it's up to you to decide when you are ready to try."

Negotiating a food plan should not be about deal-making or tradeoffs that allow the client to cut corners with calories or restrict fat intake. If a new client has eaten only 500 calories a day, the nutritionist begins the task of teaching her to consume more calories gradually so the client feels safe and is able to complete the tasks. The client whose plan permits her not to ingest fats or desserts indefinitely or who is never asked to consume more than 2,200 calories in a single day is one who will never fully recover.

J, in 45 years of struggling with anorexia, bulimia, binge eating disorder, and overweight condition, had had past experiences with nutritionists without success. After seeing my nutritionist partner, however, she began to believe that this time it could be different. The two of them spent a short time discussing the logistics of healthy eating, with which she was well familiar. Their more meaningful focus, however, was on J's emotional investment in and physical sensitivity to sugars and carbohydrates. J described what made this treatment relationship different and special:

> Restriction of fats and sugars, which is the battle cry of most nutritionists, tends to backfire on me, where one behavioral extreme leads to another and I invariably end up bingeing.

Lynn saw and understood the "rebelliousness" I harbor toward sugar as the forbidden fruit that had always been denied me. My binges have become a conflicted expression of anger and self-nurturing." When J felt ready, Lynn suggested that she introduce sugars slowly and gradually, within the context of a full and healthy meal, and that initially she consume sugar only while in the company of others, divesting the situation of shame and the powerful takeover of compulsive overeating. Once her "sugar thermostat" had become regulated, her acclimatized body craved it less.

Encouraging Self-Initiated Experimentation

A weight chart is a technique used in cognitive–behavioral therapy that helps eating disorders understand the relationship between caloric intake and weight gain, the stability of the set point weight, and the natural phenomenon of weight fluctuation brought on by endocrine system changes, retention of fluids, and so forth. This technique highlights the client's distortions about the reality of weight management and the fears that keep a self-destructive eating system in force. For the client who fears that knowing her weight will trigger an overwhelming loss of control and compulsion to restrict, gathering evidence for a weight chart exposes her to, and potentially extinguishes that fear.

A weight-related activity involves the client's estimating how much weight she is likely to gain on any given day based on the food items she has consumed. The client then begins tracking specific dietary changes, the anticipated gain and actual weight shifts. Will a 40-calorie rice cake produce a 10-pound weight gain? The client provides her own proof to disprove her worst fears in the course of discovering how much food it really takes to gain weight and sustain that gain. For best results, weigh-ins should take place over a period of time, as weight fluctuates on a day-to-day basis. Because of the degree of self-initiation and control required, this experiment may not be appropriate for clients in the very early stages of treatment.

E, a client with anorexia, ate only three quarters of her school lunch each day. I suggested that she use a weight chart to see if she would become fat by eating the rest of her lunch. We agreed that she would see how close she could come to finishing her lunch, documenting her efforts to do so every day and her weight every few days. I invited her to predict how much weight these few extra bites of food might amount to and then compare her predictions to the actual numbers on the scale. As a result of this experiment, she grew more confident about her ability to eat more freely without becoming fat.

D had lost control of her life. She refused to monitor her own eating, and would fulfill her daily life tasks, such as studying, recreation, exercise, home chores, and therapy, only when her mother forcibly insisted that she do so. Although she resented her mother's interference, she relied upon it. I suggested that mother and daughter consider engaging in an experiment at home that might free them both of the confining restraints of their relationship. D would soon be required to structure her own life at college, so I suggested that she practice structuring her own use of time during the hours after school and before bed, with no one's interference. She would be required to structure the time she spent doing sports, homework, meals, bathing, home chores, television watching, and communication with friends and accept the consequences of her outcomes. With practice and over time, D became empowered to manage her own life, creating a healthy and balanced lifestyle that carried her successfully into her upcoming college experience.

Experiential Therapy

In the course of my work with my clients, I conduct experiential therapy sessions over lunches and dinners, at restaurants or at my home, with clients who are afraid of food and weight gain. The prerequisite for going out to dinner together is that the client commits to ordering a dish that represents a true challenge in order to intensify her learning through novelty and reaching. As part of an adult treatment group series that I run, I incorporate a potluck dinner to be eaten on laps, as well as a homemade turkey dinner with all the fixings to be shared together over my dining room table. Clients confirm that these kinds of personal connections resonate powerfully in spheres of learning and loving. Client readiness for the challenge of experiential activity is critical; in early stages of treatment, such activities might lead to increased fear and obsessiveness. It is critical that therapists be aware of the appropriateness of timing of treatment interventions and make choices on the basis of the client's stage of readiness to change.

PSYCHOEDUCATIONAL TECHNIQUES

Knowledge is a powerful motivator. By increasing clients' knowledge, therapists can help them develop the wherewithal to make change. At the risk of nagging and not being heard, I do not hesitate to reiterate important knowledge over and over again, within the context of each unique treatment experience, as clients need time and "recovery mileage" to gradually gain enough trust in the treating professional and process to wrap their minds around sensitive issues that have been previously cloaked in denial. The message may be the same, but the person in recovery is constantly evolving and changing.

I will openly discuss with clients the redundancy of my efforts to turn attention to the critical nature of this knowledge. I tell them, "I know you've heard these same words out of me so many times, but I feel compelled to say it once again in this context . . ." The recovering client is at a different place developmentally with each "telling" in terms of brain function, attitudes, and perspective, decreasing resistance to recovery and increasing capacity to listen and to hear. The learning brain is a changing landscape of receptivity.

Dietary Education

Basic dietary education sustains and empowers recovery. Clients need to hear reassuring information time and time again. There are many dietary concepts that therapists can never repeat too many times. I might say:

- "In seeking to achieve your recovery goals, you need to keep in mind certain obstacles that might throw you off course. Knowing them should help to prepare you to confront and move beyond them."

- "You do know that if you fail to consume enough calories, your body will resort to using your muscle mass for energy and to feed your brain. This can result in a dangerously slower pulse, low blood pressure, and potentially a weakened and diminished heart."
- "You do realize that in order to become thin and fit, and to stay thin and fit, you have to eat lots of nutritious foods, consistently and regularly on a daily basis." When it comes to anorexia and food, more is definitely better."
- "You do realize that if you restrict food and don't eat regular meals, you are damaging your metabolism that is designed to burn fat."
- "You do know that the more you restrict food, the hungrier and more out of control you become, predisposing you to binge eventually.

Confrontation

Honest confrontation keeps reality at the forefront. The purpose of confrontation is for the client to see and accept reality so that she can make changes accordingly. This awareness-raising process is a critical aspect of the change and helping process, acknowledging the truth in the face of the distortions that all too frequently emerge from the mind of the client with an eating disorder.

In response to a young client's complaints about her parents' insistence that she recover, I observed,

> You know, if I were your parent, I believe I would do the very same thing. As I think about this, I believe it would be irresponsible of them to allow you the freedom to destroy yourself without putting up a fight. If you had cancer or diabetes, no parent would let you go untreated. Can you see their concern in any way as an expression of their love? What do you think you might do if you were the parent in this situation? I believe that the novelty of my confronting her so honestly with these realities caught this client unaware. Though it may have felt jarring initially, the result was a visible softening in her attitude towards her parents and a change in her motivation to invest herself in this work.

Honest confrontation strengthens the quality of the therapeutic connection. T revealed that she felt I "disapproved" of her when I confronted her honestly about the disproportionate strength of the anger she expressed toward her parents. Her sharing this prompted me to express why I chose to confront her with this issue when I did. Based on the recovery strides she had made, I felt confident in her capacity and readiness to hear and integrate this information about herself. By speaking to her strengths, I reinforced her positive feelings about herself, increasing the therapeutic bonds between us. What at first sounded like criticism was ultimately taken in as my faith in her and in her capacity to heal. Later in treatment, she was to own this belief for herself.

Affirmation of Strengths

Therapists are educators about "what works" in life and in recovery. In affirming a client's strengths, the therapist acknowledges and reinforces "what works" for the client. In finding that she had reached 99 pounds, R e-mailed me in a panic about the fear she felt at the prospect of reaching the dreaded "three figures." She wrote,

> Gaining the weight feels like I'm totally out of control; my membership "in the anorexia club" is truly gone. I'm sorry—I know intellectually that gaining weight is a positive step, but the way my thighs, stomach, and arms feel tell me a different story.

The following was my response:

> Thank you so much for sharing your true feelings with me. It is evident from your work here that you are a real trooper and have what it takes not only to hang in there and beat this disease, but to succeed at everything you choose to do in life. Just think about doing one day and one moment at a time, putting one foot in front of the other. You know you can always choose to reverse the situation at will; you are still and always in control. There are an awful lot of people out there who love and care about you, and I think it is safe to say that we are all pulling for you.

In affirming clients' strengths, I freely comment on the qualities that I wish to reinforce. I tell them what I like best about what they are saying or about how they are thinking when it comes to solving problems. I assure them that this kind of thinking and problem solving bodes well for a successful recovery, and I acknowledge both the difficulty and importance of the work they have done. It's never hard to find some evidence of a client's strengths. In one session, Y's backbones hurt against the wicker of her chair, so she stood up and changed chairs, midsentence. "I like that! Good for you!" I exclaimed. "It shows that you know what you need and want and how to take action to accomplish it." This validated a strength she didn't recognize she had.

Transparency

Therapist transparency models healthy thought processes, problem solving, decision making, and ego function and furthers collaborative change. In working with clients, I am prepared to explain and discuss the goals and intentions behind each of my interventions or statements. The following are examples of "speaking" the process actively:

- "I need to ask about something you just said because it brings me back to something you spoke about last week."
- "My intention in saying this is not to frighten or threaten you, but rather to inform you."
- "You know, I've been thinking about something you said last time we were together."
- "I am wondering about how you may have interpreted what I just said."
- "I am going to say something now that I don't want you to misinterpret; it may be easy to do so."

- "Tell me what you just heard me say, because sometimes the eating disorder has a way of distorting things we hear."
- "But do you *really* know that in no way is it my intention to be critical or to judge you?"

In another valuable form of transparency, therapists reveal their own vulnerability, modeling for clients the ability to accommodate human error. To be human is to err. The goal in life is not to be perfect; it is not about living a mistake-free existence. To attempt to live such an existence would be to commit oneself to never taking educated risks that could lead to growth and learning. Life is about learning to behave with resilience and to recover from one's mistakes as quickly and as gracefully as one can. Fortunately for us, eating disorder treatment is not a concert performance. Being the distinctly human endeavor that it is, this work allows participants plenty of room for error, for gaffes in relationship, for leeway to skip a beat here and there, only to regain our balance a few minutes or a few weeks later through the intention to redo, revisit, and repair.

Ego Lending

Client learning occurs through the borrowing and lending of the therapist's ego function and value system. The therapist's generosity in offering his or her total self provides a reflected vision of the client's own recovered self. Y began to discuss how carefully she measured out her cereal at breakfast time. When I suggested that there may be a better way than measuring to gauge serving sizes, she asked how I eat a bowl of cereal. I described it as follows:

> I start off with the first round of flakes with milk. After finishing, there's milk left in the bowl, so I add another dump of cereal until this too is gone, along with more fruit. I always end up needing more milk to accommodate all the extra servings of cereal and fruit. And so it goes; I keep adding cereal, milk, and fruit until I've had enough. My cereal is always best with tea and toast with salted butter. This is how a "relaxed eater" enjoys breakfast.

Y reported feeling reassurance and trust in herself when she replayed my voice in her head, which urged, "So when you make yourself a bowl of cereal in the morning, make it a *big* bowl, Y, a *big* bowl; no measuring!" Her mother and sister sometimes gently remind her, "Remember what Abbie said about how much cereal a normal eater eats?" Another client told me, "You were in my head last night, telling me not to get up to go to the kitchen in the wee hours."

U, was able to stop bingeing and purging as she got better at mindfully differentiating her feelings, which led to more effective and lasting problem solving, emotional versatility, and internal resourcefulness. In retrospect, she told me, "Whenever I would have 'a bad day' you would help me separate out my feelings . . . like from a ball of twine. You'd always chalk up days like this to being normal and human and OK. I believed you and gave myself the same permission to feel as crummy as I needed to feel." U realized that she no longer had to go through life overwhelmed by a global sense of defeat and shame, as she continued to practice differentiating, monitoring and accepting her feelings.

Paradoxical Interventions

The following statements can help the therapist get the client's attention: A paradoxical intervention is one that catches the client's attention through an element of surprise and implicit contradiction. As an example, by suggesting that she cannot do something, she realizes that she can and sets out to prove it.

- "Perhaps this might be asking too much of you . . . but let me just run something by you and see what you think you might be capable of." The patient thinks, it won't be. I can accept the challenge.
- "This may be hard for you to hear . . . but I feel I can say this to you anyway." I already feel relieved that you feel you can trust me with the truth.
- "So, listen carefully now to what I am about to say." I'm all ears.
- "This next question is a tough one. I don't expect you to be able to answer it now. You may want to think about it; if thoughts begin to come to you when you are standing in the shower or while stopped at a red light, make note of them, and bring them back to our next session so we can discuss them." I will, but I can already think of an answer here and now.

Playing the "devil's advocate" can inspire positive learning. To play the devil's advocate is to unexpectedly support the "other side" of an issue as stated by the client. The technique helps the client to become more honest with herself as she feels compelled to refute your statement. Consider the following examples:

- "I know you believe you can't do anything right. So the way you handled yourself with your boss last week in that very dicey situation was just a fluke?"
- "It appears as though you think everybody else has life really easy except for you. Am I right about that?"

When a client who began to restore weight decided prematurely that she was done with treatment and was planning to leave, I discussed with her the benefits of continuing her work. When she insisted upon leaving, I offered, "Why not take a break now and then plan to come back in a month so we can see how things are going for you on your own?" In this case, I actively chose to support what I considered to be a premature, but inevitable, judgment in favor of terminating in the hope of ultimately refreshing her treatment experience if the decision were to have proven precipitous.

Behavioral Rehearsal

Afterthoughts and forethoughts are a form of behavioral rehearsal or anticipation that prepare the client for a novel use of self. The mindful anticipation of risk, through advance thinking and preparation, inhibits emotional arousal and promotes planning and the creation of more flexible cognitive responsiveness. The therapist can lead the forethought process with questions like the following:

> So, let's imagine together what it will be like for you when you walk into that party. How might you be feeling? What might you have done in the past when you felt this way? Can we think together of some other, more effective way to handle your classmates' cruel comments?

> Let's think together of a way to handle the temptations that you know await you there and the urges that might come over you to respond to them?

The afterthought dialogue between therapist and patient, and ultimately between the patient and herself might sound like this:

> So what have you learned about yourself from observing your reactions in that situation? How would you have preferred to see yourself respond, in the best of all worlds? Next time you find yourself in this kind of situation, might you be able to sound a small internal alarm in your head to indicate that "it is happening once again" so this time, you can make a different choice about your response? Where might you have your next opportunity to try out a new response?

K spent two days mentally preparing for Thanksgiving dinner. We anticipated her difficulty in handling the day and arrived at a plan to get her through the most stressful part of that event: serving herself food from a buffet table. (forethought) Her task would be to "design" her plate, dividing it into four sections containing protein, fresh vegetables, a cooked vegetable, and a starch or grain. Her dessert plate was to have three small slices of samplings of interesting choices. We celebrated her successes after the fact (afterthought), and her next task was to remember the things she did to prepare herself and then to recall them during subsequent occasions.

Goal Setting

Small changes lie at the foundation of the broad-based transformations that occur for the client over the course of treatment. Well on her way to getting her anorexia under control, G quipped, "So, I decided not to weigh myself this morning. I said to myself, 'You are feeling pretty good now; why spoil it by sabotaging yourself on the scale and creating a frenzy of anxiety?'" A small step in terms of her daily functioning . . . a giant leap for her recovery.

In describing the process of recovery, I have alluded to the metaphor of dropping coins into a piggy bank, one small achievement after another small achievement. The effects grow and matter, but they may not register as "recovery" as such, with all of its benefits of happiness, well-being, freedom from fear and recidivism, until they reach a critical mass, an amount substantive enough to assume the shape, form, and function of healing.

As she sat in her psychotherapy session, G developed the courage to acknowledge some things about herself that she had never been able to admit before. As she did so, I helped her to do the following:

- notice what gave her the impetus at that particular moment in time to use herself differently and to observe how it felt.
- see the benefits such action had on the pace of her learning and on the quality of her search for problem solutions
- anticipate similar opportunities or circumstances that might come up for her in the course of daily living and consider what it might be like to use herself courageously outside the therapy context as well
- anticipate that her plan to use herself in this way may vary in its outcomes and to consider such inconsistency part of a normative process of change.

Metaphors and Imagery

Speaking the "language" of the client enhances communication. In their role as educators and life coaches, therapists need to understand that people learn differently, uniquely, in accordance with the wiring of each individual brain. Auditory learners learn best through what they hear; visual learners comprehend better from what they see or words that paint pictures. In an effort to speak the language best understood by clients who are visual learners, I use imagery and metaphors and draw graphics in the air to drive home an image, mapping out a concept that may be best construed visually.

In pointing out that normative eating becomes second nature after a while, I have used the imaged metaphor of a skier making turns down a mountain slope. Following a food plan begins by rigorous and precise compliance with following rules, as does learning the form and fundamentals of executing a turn; initially, the task is committed to the left brain. With practice and skill development, the cognitive exercise becomes increasingly right brained and instinctual, offering new freedoms (flexibility and use of the integrated self) even within the constraints of "correct" form. Eventually, rule following safely gives way to approximation and "feel"; "sensing" recognizes and accommodates the requirements of the moment, allowing the naturally occurring bumps in the ski hill to dictate the nature, form, and timing of the initiation of each turn. Similarly, eating dictates a flexible spontaneity in accommodating to life circumstances.

When I treat clients who play tennis, I might use the metaphor about the importance of estimating where an approaching ball might land, how fast it is coming, and with what kind of spin, to best facilitate one's own stance in setting up a successful return. For client, athlete, and therapist alike, skill development and physical and mental preparedness can and will optimize a person's potential; fate and the vicissitudes of life and happenstance will determine the rest . . . as it should.

Is the client capable of reversing a backslide without help? I offer the image of her car's wheels spinning atop an icy snowbank. There are occasions where the driver can "rock" a car out of a bank to freedom; other times, nothing short of a crew of supportive others pushing from the rear is sufficient to create the required adjustment.

The use of a formalized food plan is never static. As with steering a car, driving in a straight line requires constant adjustments of the wheel, which is never still as it accommodates the slight though constant deviations in the road. Healthy normalized eating involves deviation, too, always without fear or compulsivity, in the effort to arrive at a healthy balance.

Rewards from an eating disorder recovery experience are in some cases enhanced by more intensive exposure within a treatment milieu. When recovery progress slows to a halt or even reverses, the option to enter a more restrictive treatment milieu may be compared to plunging into a cold ocean, immersing oneself, and starting to swim, developing one's own internal heat in mitigating the shock of the sudden exposure; choosing to walk into a cold ocean (as into recovery) inch by inch, only prolongs the agony.

Clients need to be reassured that once they have reached their set point weight, they will stop gaining. I speak of the set point weight as being a kind of "cruise control" that dismisses the option of extreme gains or losses, keeping the body within a homeostatic and constant self-adjusting balance.

A client with a black-and-white thinking style determined that she could not return to college if she put on as much as a single pound over the summer. Often, however, what appears to be weight gain is actually the result of water retention or another highly temporary condition. An accurate number requires weighing over the course of time. I asked her, "Why not think of the 'weight's-up' syndrome as a 'bad-hair day' for your weight. Factors as arbitrary and as temporary as the timing of the weigh in, the clothes you are wearing, the amount of salt in your system, and the time of the month will all have an effect."

Thought and Behavior Shaping

Cognitive restructuring, or "thought shaping," is the process by which a client can become aware of thought patterns that lead to ineffectual behaviors, enabling him or her to change these thought processes to more productive ones. "The client analyzes what worked in the past and what parts of those real-life successes might be reapplied to the present" (Lange & Jakubowski, 1976, p. 144).

> The more a patient can think rationally, the greater the likelihood of her acting assertively. A person cannot change her history, but she can change the "stories" she tells herself about her history and the way she thinks about herself based on these stories/mythologies. One's "internal dialogue," what she says to herself just before, during and after an incident, is an important determinant of how she will act. (Lange & Jakubowski, 1976, p. 141)

Once a negative thought is stopped, the client makes positive affirmations to replace it. Such affirmations are not mindless, arbitrary, or ritualized prescriptive statements, but rather a way to promote mindfulness in daily problem solving, thereby creating new neuronal pathways to reinforce thoughts and feelings.

I ask clients to think through scenarios like the following:

> Can you remember a time when things were not so hard for you, when you
> better liked how you interacted with your peers, how you approached food,
> how confident you felt about yourself and your problem-solving? What might
> you have done then that you might consider doing once again? It is important
> to try not to forget who you were, where you've been, and what you are capa-
> ble of in assessing who you are today.

Behaviors are shaped by reinforcing successive approximations that increasingly resemble a desired behavior. Eating disorder recovery is about approximation. In eating, as in life itself, the lesson of recovery is that we cannot predict life,
or how we live it from moment to moment; the best we can do is to cope as best
we can, with our realities and the full range of resources we have available to us
at any given time. Success can be seen not only in achieving positive outcomes,
but also in the process that leads to them. Through Socratic questioning, the client
arrives at her own answers, gently shaped and formed by the soft power of the
litany of well-chosen considerations.

In shaping thoughts and behaviors, clients grow and their goals change, session by session, day to day, week to week, month to month and sometimes year
to year. Through the therapist's help in reassessing, differentiating, refining, and
redefining new goals, all goals are kept clearly and intentionally in mind and
sight. Diffuse goals and foggy vision cause clients to lose their way, deterring
healing.

In her recovery from bulimia, M began to awaken at night to drink large
glassfuls of acidic juices and to purge them. Together, we identified the problem:
M was going to bed at 4:00 P.M., before eating a healthy dinner, leaving her hungry and not prepared for undisturbed sleep. We discussed various options for
her to begin to bring about change, including how to occupy herself productively
at the end of the day, how to handle her fear of eating healthfully at dinnertime,
and how to regulate her thirst at the end of the day by satisfying her body's need
for liquids throughout the day. In addition, we discussed the implications of her
bedtime on her relationship with her husband and her eating disorder. We
decided collaboratively that she would choose one small aspect of these behaviors that she would try to alter at least three times before our next appointment.
She chose to walk her dog at 4:00 to get her blood flowing and hold off bedtime.
The following week, she would begin to alter her intake of liquids throughout
the day.

By informing cognition, remediated behaviors reshape clients' goals. O had
only a short time in treatment before returning to school out of town. Her initial
goal was to stop purging sufficiently to return to school safely, by order of her parents, but her secret personal goal was to lose weight. As she became engaged successfully in treatment and started a healthy eating regimen with a nutritionist, she
revised her initial and primary goal to that of recovering fully from her eating disorder and learning to eat healthfully. Once she returned to school, she sought out
a treatment team to help her continue to recover.

STRATEGIES TO INCREASE MINDFUL ATTENTION TO THE SENSES

The client with an eating disorder has difficulty sensing herself accurately; hunger signals and internal demands become lost to a visceral lack of awareness, and misperceived sensations result in distorted cognitions. The eating disorder client with an eating disorder typically chooses foods by computational skills, through reading nutritional labels (e.g., calories fat and sodium levels) rather than using her senses. Portion sizes become determined by food scales and other measuring devices, where normal eaters gauge amounts through feeling or sensitivity to bodily or social cues. Body image distortions, like disturbances in the client's capacity to love and feel love, can be attributed to the client's inability to sense accurately. By teaching the client techniques to enhance moment-to-moment self-awareness, the therapist potentially offers sensory awareness,

G felt capable of having only one significant relationship: with her eating disorder. Attachments require the use of feelings, and she would not allow herself to feel. She struggled against the closeness and attachment that she felt developing within our treatment relationship. "I am afraid to speak these feelings," she admitted. "No need, then," I replied. "Just concentrate on your sensing them and the awareness of what stops you. Just try to stay in the current moment and 'be.'"

Therapists can encourage clients to observe the senses that become reactivated during eating, through chewing, smelling, noting the aesthetics of food presentation and table design, taste, and texture in their attempt to fully savor the process. Learning what it feels like to step out of oneself to observe and sense oneself can prompt the awareness that "if this is what is happening (or not happening), then I might as well ask why, and then decide to do something different. As noted in Germer et al. (2005), relabeling allows the client to establish enough distance from the content of the obsession, to observe its effects and slightly separate herself from it, thereby helping her to obtain a sense of increasing closeness to herself (p. 171).

The therapist can help the client sense the moment by directing the client's awareness. With V, I instructed, "Close your eyes. What do you sense at this very moment?" "I feel the cat on my lap." she replied. I continued, "Now can you begin to hear the clanging of radiators, to sense the light from the window through your closed lids, the warmth of the cat on your lap, and the softness of his fur in your fingers?" I asked V to try sitting quietly for 20 minutes each day, doing nothing but sensing herself and her environs.

Mindfulness, in regulating attention, brings the unconscious into consciousness, offering the potential for awareness, choice, and action in addressing otherwise intractable symptoms of anxiety and body image disturbances. Action-based behaviors help ground cognitions and contain anxiety; clients who write their anxieties down on a list have the option of putting them aside, literally and figuratively, for later attention. As placing dirty dishes in the sink makes for the appearance of a clean and organized kitchen, putting compulsive thoughts on a list makes for a clearer mind, enhancing learning.

When negative thoughts become compulsions, they require attention, tracking, and acceptance for what they are—the replaying of repetitive thinking that is deeply entrenched in neuronal pathways. Such thoughts need to become diverted into different thoughts or activities. In treating symptoms of obsessive–compulsive anxiety disorder with mindfulness, Schwartz suggested relabeling and reattributing what is occurring. The client might say to herself, "Yes, I do have a real problem right now. But it is not from paranoia or craziness; it is simply my OCD talking. My brain just isn't turning the page" (Doidge, 2007, p. 176). He recommends "refocusing (the client asks herself, 'Why not do something useful, like studying for my history test?') and revaluing ('These repetitive thoughts are disturbing and a waste of time')" (Doidge, 2007, p. 176).

> This approach makes plastic sense because it grows a new brain circuit that gives pleasure and triggers dopamine release which rewards the new activity and consolidates and grows new neuronal connections. This new circuit can eventually compete with the older one, and according to use it or lose it, the pathological networks will weaken. Rather than breaking bad habits, we replace them with better ones. (Doidge, 2007, p. 170)

A client whom I had treated for anorexia four years earlier returned for therapy following her full recovery. She had developed a relationship with a boyfriend and was consumed by jealousy and paranoid thoughts about his imagined interest in other women. Her increasing anxiety and obsessive–compulsive symptoms warranted a reevaluation with the psychopharmacologist; in addition, she needed to diffuse her obsessive retracing of paranoid thought networks by attending to the present moment, thereby creating a new network of responses around the familiar stimulus. Together we reviewed and listed all the reasons that her boyfriend might have chosen to say hello to an otherwise unknown young woman for whom he held a door, a logic-based tactic that offered her relief.

L, who was six months into a full recovery from anorexia, described having to manage her intermittent anxiety about thinking she looks too fat:

> In response to my thinking about how bloated my face looks, I step outside of myself a bit, attempting to calm myself by repeating to myself how good I feel, how I feel better than ever before within my recovery, and how I would never want to go backwards, remembering again what it had been like to be starving with anorexia. So I step into my cognition, and I say, "Look how happy you are!" Then I ask myself, "Why do you *do* this to yourself!?"

Schwartz contended that "it is not what you feel while applying the technique that counts, it is what you *do*. The struggle is not to make the feeling go away; the struggle is not to give in to the feeling" (Doidge, 2007, p. 173) by acting out a compulsion or thinking about the obsession. "The goal is to 'change the channel' for 15 to 30 minutes per day, though any time spent resisting is beneficial even for only a minute. That resistance, that effort, is what appears to lay down new circuits" (Doidge, 2007, p. 173).

A, in her newly recovered state, admitted to excessive worrying about handling life, approaching and surviving her future, achieving her goals, managing her relationships, and so forth. The worrying dynamic, in taking her outside of the moment, interrupted any attempts on her part to find sound and healthy solutions to problems as they arose. Together we observed how worrying took on a function parallel to that of the eating disorder, giving the illusion of doing something "constructive" in an effort to remain in control of a situation that is beyond her control, creating the illusion of predictability. Understanding that the function of worrying stifles the very outcomes that it appears to achieve helped her to let go of the habit.

STRATEGIES FOR CLIENTS WITH AXIS II DISORDERS

Psychodynamic psychotherapy has been shown to be least effective with clients who have Axis II personality disorders. Because such clients may have difficulty reading the therapist's nonverbal signs and seeing beyond their own projections in what the therapist says, they require clear and consistent language, limits, and boundaries. Concrete and specific language and visual metaphors hold the client accountable to fulfilling defined behavioral tasks. Dialectical behavioral therapy, which balances a focus on change with one of acceptance, has been proven to be the most effective form of treatment for Axis II diagnoses (Wilson, 2005, p. 444). This section discusses strategies for the treatment of clients with such disorders.

Negotiating Problems of Attachment

Attachment problems are common in clients with eating disorders and especially in those who suffer from Axis II disorders. Therapists need to anticipate and intercept abrupt and unexplained terminations. Because clients are reluctant to face and resolve conflict, particularly in social situations, misunderstanding, disappointment, or hurt feelings (narcissistic injury) are easier to walk away from than to resolve face to face. It is within these pivotal moments where the most teachable moments lie.

T, a compulsive overeater in her mid 20s, came from a dysfunctional family, and she had learned to cut herself off from early object relationships to survive their intrusiveness and simultaneous abandonment. She carried interpersonal mistrust and a resistance to attachment into her adult life. One day, she failed to show up for an appointment and did not call to explain or reschedule. Aware of these sensitivities in her relationships, I understood that this failure could have had a deeper meaning. In processing the no-show with her, she described having first felt guilt and embarrassment for the failure to attend the session; then, by default, she had numbed herself with food, avoiding facing herself and me. In exploring this deeply entrenched learned behavioral pattern, T came to recognize that she felt incapable of responding responsibly. She admitted that in other treatment relationships that meant less to her, she probably would have dissociated herself further and never returned to treatment at all. Following this teachable moment, she made a point of always giving me as much advance notice as possible if unable to attend sessions.

Therapists should be alert to the possibility of attachment problems when clients describe past tendencies to transfer from therapist to therapist, miss appointments, or show reluctance to setting up future appointment times. I tend to be assertive and proactive in reaching out to "fragile" clients (with narcissistic or borderline personality disorders, or whose eating disorder leads her to behave as if she had one) whose tendency would be to disconnect from treatment. The therapist's response to premature leaving or irregular attendance is critical in helping the client recognize the feelings that give rise to the motivation to flee, the dynamics behind her reluctance to confront the pattern, the generalizability of the pattern in her other life relationships, the ramifications for recovery timing, and the potential lost opportunity for the client to learn about herself.

Engaging Withdrawn Clients

Because any form of confrontation or reality testing might be assimilated as a narcissistic injury, I actively initiate contact with withdrawn clients, who may feel slighted, abandoned, or have misinterpreted some communication. For such individuals, premature termination is often the result of the client's inaccurate perception that the therapist has withdrawn his or her connection, having lost hope in her ability to succeed. For such clients, I might convey the following message:

> I haven't heard from you yet this week. I'm worried that I might have unintentionally hurt your feelings. Am I right or wrong? How about giving me a call back and letting me know what you are thinking? I am looking forward to hearing from you.

Therapists can help prevent distortions and disturbances in vulnerable personalities by predicating their words with phrases such as, "What I am about to say is in no way meant to be a judgment or criticism; I just want to share with you something I think I am seeing."

Using Active Listening

As the archetypal mother of all relational experiences, the therapy relationship packs its punch by simultaneously replicating the dynamics of other human relationships, even while intentionally diverging from them in an attempt to remediate and heal. In this way, the treatment relationship encourages the client's capacity to create more healthy attachments. Whatever got "broken" in human connections in the past will need to get fixed within the context of the therapeutic relationship. Active listening is the stuff of healthy relationships and the stuff of relationship repair.

The active listening response is intended to permit the client to hear and to take ownership of herself. For example, with a client who asks, "Am I fat?" a response like "Are you kidding?" or "No, don't be silly!" would lead her not to trust that you are being honest and would forfeit a golden teaching moment. A better response would be, "What is your own thinking about this? Why are you wondering about this now? What is it like for you to feel this way? Are you hoping to lose weight? If so, how do you propose to accomplish this?"

ACTIVE LISTENING: AN EXERCISE

In teaching the techniques of active listening to clients and families seeking to learn to communicate more effectively, I hate that they may do the following:

Stop the discussion.

Each party states what he or she believes the other person is *feeling* (rather than discussing the content of what has been communicated). The listener confirms, denies, or otherwise informs the speaker how accurate he or she is in his or her assessment. By revealing one's feelings to oneself and the other, problems are more apt to get resolved at their source. Most of the time, people speak in truncated "topic sentences," missing the essence of what they genuinely need to communicate. Words are free; they need to be used as the invaluable commodity that they are in nuancing meaning and creating a sense of understanding and well-being between people.

In teaching parents to become active listeners to their child, therapists should encourage them to speak to the child from the "I" perspective, as feelings become legitimized simply by virtue of their existence and cannot be negated. The parent is more effective saying, "I found this behavior difficult to watch. I believe you could be making better choices. These are my feelings. As your parent, I need to share them honestly with you", than "These behaviors are bad; you are making bad decisions." The latter statements are more threatening and less likely to lead to a constructive conversation.

In working with children and parents together in family therapy, I make it a point to support the child in the eyes of frustrated parents and to support the parents' intentions and efforts in the eyes of their child in recovery. The young client needs to learn to actively listen and to hear her parents, to appreciate their role in her life and recovery, and to understand the worthiness of their intention and their loving concern, just as parents need to learn to listen to their child.

CONCLUSION

Borrowing from diverse treatment approaches, the strategies provided here are designed to sustain the client's motivation to heal. Mindful techniques that foster a healthy connection between practitioner and client provide ideal vehicles for offering incentives to heal.

SECTION 5

THE REALITY OF RECOVERY

15

Recovery, Aftercare, and Relapse: Sustaining the Integrity of the Healing Process Through the Long Haul

Maintenance is not an absence of change, but the continuance of change.
—Pierre Leichner

Eating disorder recovery is difficult not only to achieve but also to track, in its convoluted and inconstant course. Once recovery is achieved, *sustaining recovery* gains can be a rigorous challenge, particularly when the recovery process is not carried to completion. This chapter discusses the elusive nature of eating disorder recovery, offering skills in recovery assessment and facilitation, as well as strategies to motivate clients to heal completely and to stay healed. Having been restored to themselves, to loved ones, and to the capacity to live a full and gratified existence, most recovered clients contend that the healing process, despite its intense challenges and trials, is well worth the effort it takes in restoring and upgrading life quality.

WHAT IS EATING DISORDER RECOVERY?

Recovery is as broadly based in its healing as is the eating disorder in its capacity to disable. The jury remains out among eating disorder professionals about what constitutes full recovery and which standards most accurately measure recovery progress. I believe a person is recovered when she has learned to trust her body to

---

BOX 15.1

Unique Characteristics of Eating Disorder Recovery

- Recovery is marked by reconnection, refeeding, and repair.
- Recovery progress is hard to discern as its course is convoluted, at times stagnating or regressive, and at times taking on the appearance of failure. The process occurs through steps so small that they sometimes escape notice.
- The client is typically unable to discern the process of her own growth because of lack of self-awareness and difficulty recognizing and accepting personal strengths. In many instances, she struggles to withstand the inevitable anxiety that comes with weight gain or the cessation of anxiety-reducing activities.
- The emotional tools and resourcefulness required to fix what is broken evade most clients. The therapist is responsible for introducing and providing these tools and motivating clients to experience them within the context of the depth and quality of the treatment relationship.
- Recovery occurs through taking action.
- In ED recovery, feeling worse is a prerequisite for getting and feeling better. Recovery can be considered combat training for life itself.
- As the client moves ever closer to a breakthrough to cure, the eating disorder will frequently rear it ugly head for its last licks. Clinicians can anticipate that the time of greatest healing can also appear to be a time of great ambivalence and regression.
- Two steps forward and one step back is the form that eating disorder recovery progress takes.
- Eating disorder recovery is elusive, challenging and ever-changing, a metaphor for life itself. It is essential that clinicians learn to see evidence of success as it begins to emerge. Signs of recovery appear as emotional resiliency, cognitive processes, self-love, self-care, mood changes, and problem solving.
- Recovery changes need to be evident from the very outset of treatment.
- The practitioner needs to become capable of seeing the whole recovery puzzle, even with some of the pieces missing.
- Treatment from outset to recovery occurs over the long haul. Longer-term cases will be those in which there are co-morbid diagnoses, dysfunctional families or where the eating disorder remains "managed," or partial, rather than fully cured.
- Recovery is the process of preparing one's inner self how to heal.
- The lesson of recovery is that one can't predict life, but must instead develop an inner trust of one's capacity to handle whatever life may bring.

---

send dependable signals about its needs and to trust herself to interpret and abide by those signals—in other words, when she has learned how to feed, nurture, and care for herself responsibly and completely.

Eating disorders do not heal in the absence of human connection. The healing process transfers a pathological dependency on the client's relationship with food to supportive, loving, limit-setting, and reality-testing human beings; it is through these close and loving human connections that the client experiences an evolving sense of self, self-regulation, and self-determination. "The self organization of the developing brain occurs in the context of a relationship with another self, another brain" (Schore & Schore, 2008).

The benchmark of recovery is emotional maturity . . . the flexible use of self in the face of uncertainty (a defining characteristic of life itself), with the internal resiliency and resourcefulness to weather and grow from it. Recovery immerses the client in the unknown, in risk taking and the unpredictable, the antithesis of what the client with an eating disorder tolerates comfortably. Full and complete recovery has occurred when the authentic personality becomes simply too spontaneous and healthy to continue to support core aspects of eating disorder psychopathology.

Prior to fully recovering from her anorexia, L believed that she had recovered from her eating disorder on three separate occasion in the past, between stints at hospital programs and through a series of outpatient therapists. Now, four years later, having made a genuine and complete recovery through her work with me, she recognized that those past experiences had been totally unlike her current one. Her previous healing could not be considered true recovery as these instances were not complete recoveries. This young woman stated,

> As recovered as I am, I feel I am still on this journey. Last week, when I looked at my schedule for school and work, I started to get that awful overwhelmed feeling again, which scared me. The difference is that now I am aware of what this sensation is and what it means. Now I can attend to it, rather than get bowled over by it. Now I have a choice as to how to behave in the face of problems. Before, I had nothing but my anorexia.

For clients with anorexia, recovery resides in the *process* by which weight restoration occurs (how it is done and why), not in the weight restoration by itself. Though nutritional restoration and physiological optimization of brain and body function are prerequisite to healing, these are but a few facets of a wider recovery picture that includes the client's accruing capacity for self-care, self-regulation, intelligent decision making, and sound judgment in problem solving.

Recovery Is About Resourcefulness

"Could I survive without my eating disorder?" This is a question commonly asked by clients undergoing recovery changes. In turning the question back to the client, I demand that she take a stab at providing her own answer.

Client: I don't know . . . what if I have to face the death of a loved one, a job loss, a divorce? What would I do? How would I take care of myself?

Therapist: So, were you to need to face a problem without the safety net of your eating disorder, let's think about it together. What *would* you do?

Client: Well, I suppose I could get professional help, look for a new job, talk to a friend. It sure is easier and more foolproof to use food, but I suppose somehow I'd muddle through. But it would be very scary for me.

Therapist: Of course you would figure out a way; that is the human condition and it is well within your capabilities. It might feel pretty painful for some time, but you would have the wherewithal and intelligence to figure out how to make your way and move forward. Can you think of other times in your life when you used yourself resourcefully, when you were able to turn things around for yourself? Do you remember what it felt like to have faced life full-on and to have prevailed? I wonder if you can picture yourself doing so again.

It is imperative that the client begins to own her capacity to think through problems and cope in response to inevitable life problems that require solutions. She cannot and need not know the unknowable; she only needs to recognize that whatever the challenge or occasion, she will somehow be able to rise to it. F, a young woman in active recovery from anorexia, demonstrated her healing progress in spheres that extended far beyond food and weight management. Her decision to fly to New York to interview with an executive of a prominent marketing firm with less than a day's notice illustrated the spontaneous and risk-taking use of self that emerged side by side with her weight gain. She got the job and moved to New York, where she found her career and eventually her life partner. Her openness to new opportunities and her confidence in herself to handle them enabled her to participate in life fully for the first time since the onset of her disorder three years previously.

Recovery Is an Odyssey

Clinical eating disorders and a healthy, normalized eating lifestyle, as different as they may appear to be, comprise opposite ends of a common continuum; what seemingly starts out as a benign enough sign of good values and healthy self-discipline carries the risk of ultimately evolving into a pernicious and life-threatening disease in the individual with genetic susceptibilities who experiences triggering factors in the environment. The backwards and forwards dynamism of the healing process simulates a true odyssey for the client, as recovery calls participants to action, demanding that they overcome temptations and obstacles, rely on the support of others, and experience rock bottom before being able to enjoy the rewards of their efforts. The recovery journey varies from person to person in its pace and timing, in how it is attained and experienced, in the client's willingness and motivation to heal and stay healed, and in the level and comfort of its completeness and acceptance by the client. Among my own clients, most have recovered appreciably within six to 18 months; tougher cases can take years or even decades. The pacing of guiding an eating disorder recovery process forward is critical. Too fast can frighten the client and increase resistance; too slow can bring a loss of momentum and motivation. The rhythm and pace of recovery change must keep up with, and eventually overcome, the pace of disease. Within the recovery process, whenever windows of opportunity for forward movement present themselves in the form of resources and/or client readiness, it is time to take action.

The elusive nature of the recovery process demands that the therapist is skill-ful in recognizing and interpreting ephemeral signs of recovery as they appear and before they recede, only to re-appear once again. Positive change needs to begin to occur in one form or another from the very outset of treatment. From the first session onwards, your client needs to walk away from your office feeling somehow touched, heard, understood, joined. The vigilant therapist keeps a methodical finger on the pulse of change through progress, regression, and fam-ily involvement, always with an eye to the possible need for more extensive or different interventions and services from session to session.

Practitioners need to determine when signs of a stagnating process may be indicators of the client's need to moderate the pace of progress in an effort to inte-grate current changes or of a resistance to recovery strong enough to demand an upgrade in the level of care. In an ongoing assessment of the progress of recovery, clinical dialogues may open with such questions as: "So how is it going with your food? What goals did you work on this week?" "What worked well for you, and what did you find to be difficult? Do you have any notion about why?" Such dis-cussions convey the critical message that there needs to be an active and ongoing accountability of progress in recovery behaviors from the very start of treatment, that efforts to achieve goals are the stuff of making changes, and that transparency and sharing can increase self-awareness and lead to the creation of more effective and practical goals.

Recovery and Food, Weight, and Eating

What does recovery from an eating disorder have to do with food, weight, and eating? A great deal, through these factors aren't everything. The litmus test for a true and complete recovery is the client's capacity and commitment to reach and sustain her body's normal set point weight. Feeding the brain and nourishing the body (behavioral tasks) are prerequisite to medical stability, which enables the client to benefit maximally from the psychotherapy process. However, as in the chicken–egg paradox, one's capacity to eat healthfully and to achieve medical sta-bility requires good problem solving, self-acceptance, sound judgment, accuracy of self-perception, and responsiveness to feelings and needs, all products of the mind and emotions.

Treating professionals must be careful not to mislead themselves, their clients and families, other professionals, and/or insurance companies about the signifi-cance of weight in determining diagnosis or recovery. Misinterpretation of the influence of weight in recovery is sufficient to cause premature discharge from treatment, ineligibility for care, financial losses, and other negative outcomes.

Therapists should never lose sight of the reality that the client's developing autonomy and judgment regarding what, when, and how much she eats general-izes to her growing capacity to live an empowered and self-determined life in all contexts. As C became less afraid to eat, she became less afraid to ask for what she needed in all spheres of life, standing up for herself in the face of her abusive brother and boss. Conversely, a young anorexic girl refused to take charge of her-self or her food choices; she was unable to go to sleep by herself, crawling into bed with her mother instead, and refusing to practice her piano unless her mother sat on the bench beside her.

In recovering from an eating disorder, the client ultimately "recovers" the following:

- the capacity for self-determined and self-regulated self-care
- a mind free to participate in thoughts beyond food
- the capacity to eat healthfully and without fear
- the capacity to solve problems effectively
- genuine internal controls replacing the client's compulsion to overcontrol her external environment
- the capacity to live in the moment, letting go of yesterday's regrets and the dread of what tomorrow might bring
- responsible problem solving and "response-ability"
- the capacity to let go of debilitating compulsions and perfectionism
- appropriate developmental milestones, filling in emotional voids to achieve maturation
- new habits and attitudes and, with them, newly forming neuronal pathways in the brain
- enhanced relationships with food and others
- access to feelings
- feelings of optimism and hope
- a return to normal metabolism and body composition (Dellava, n.d.)
- weight restoration, but only if it is accompanied by other remediated factors.

Recovery Progress Comes in All Shapes and Forms

A client with bulimia who had been working with me for four weeks bemoaned the fact that she was "failing" at regulating her eating. She was surprised when my response to her description of her efforts was positive. What she saw as failure held many signs of progress:

- Her despondency and frustration indicated that she was starting to experience real feelings.
- She could say "no" to herself prior to the start of a binge, even though she could not yet abide by her own warnings.
- She was able to stop her binge–purge cycle even after being more than halfway through it.
- Her feeling of relief after her purges had diminished.
- She was able to acknowledge her edema as a side effect of her purging and laxative abuse

Recovery Through Willpower: Does It Exist?

It is not unusual to hear parents of children with eating disorders speak of their own related experiences as children and claim that they "healed themselves" or just "grew out of it." Many of these parents do not understand the impact of their own behaviors (and genetics) on their children, who model themselves after them. Some children in recovery describe envying their parents' ability to "get away with" behaviors that the requirements of their eating disorder recovery will not permit them.

Two mothers of daughters with bulimia suffered eating disorders when they were in college, and both reported that they had "just stopped" the behaviors. One mother continues to run 11 miles a day in below zero-degree Chicago winters, and the other continues to compare her recovering daughter to her daughter's skinny classmates, fearing that her child would become "too fat" in consuming all the food her treatment required of her. Do these mothers have eating disorders? Probably not. Do they remain disordered in some of their thoughts, behaviors, and attitudes and in the messages they send their daughters? They do. Was this an issue for the recovering children to deal with? Certainly it was and deserved discussion, either with or without the parent present.

PROMOTING SELF-ADVOCACY IN CLIENTS AND PARENTS

E discontinued treatment for obsessive–compulsive anxiety disorder and anorexia when she left town to start her third year of medical school. For several years, despite several interventions with distraught family members, she remained entrenched in her eating disorder and was emaciated. She married and was doing well in her medical residency, though nothing would touch her eating disorder until her department head asked her to leave her position for two months to "de-stress" and "get her life back in order." It was the result of this young woman's intelligence, functionality, and skill that she had not been dismissed from her residency. Four years after our last previous contact, she called me for a phone consultation.

Confronted with a number of treatment options, it became apparent to E, finally, that here was a window of opportunity to make something of this part of her life that remained so chaotic and beyond her reach despite all of her accomplishments. In this conversation, my goal was to inspire her to become an advocate for herself and for a quality her life. We discussed her option to participate in an eating disorder program that was currently demanding a six-week inpatient commitment. She balked at leaving her husband for such an extended period of time, so we considered alternative out-patient care solutions, contingent upon her commitment to upgrade her level of care if the less restrictive treatment environment failed to achieve timely changes. The decision would be collaboratively based, but solely her own. Her parents solicited my help to learn how to better support her, as she strove to support herself through this recovery

E's success in meeting her personal goals would ultimately determine her ideal course of treatment and milieu. Her goals for the next two months were as follows:

- to achieve significant weight restoration
- to sustain her relationship at home

- to connect with a highly competent medicating psychiatrist
- to connect with a highly competent outpatient therapist
- to begin to recognize, confront, and resolve her underlying anxiety, anger, and other unresolved issues with her family of origin.
- to return to work in two months, having made substantive cognitive and behavioral changes.

Though E expressed relief at being offered this option to save herself from a compromised existence and an early death, from racing thoughts, compulsions, and job loss, she experienced deep internal conflict between her fear of letting go of the eating disorder and her determination to put her anorexia behind her.

Parents must be actively prepared for the stretching of their child's "emotional muscle." At times, what may feel like a verbal attack on a parent may actually be a healthy attempt to throw off the emotional constraints of the eating disorder. The child may need help and direction to express the newly discovered feelings that may be bubbling to awareness. Conversely, what may feel like the parent's attack on the child ("You can't leave this table until you have finished your dinner!") needs to be interpreted to the child as an attack on the disease; it is hard to separate the two.

In coaching parents to better deal with their child's illness, professionals can teach them the following:

- the value of discerning the voice of the eating disorder (as opposed to that of the child)
- the capacity to recognize small and sometimes hard to recognize positive changes in their recovering child, and to use them to convince the child of her capabilities; the smaller the change, the more likely it is to have been made through purposeful choice, and that it will be retained.

Therapists can also help parents develop a nose for recognizing recovery derailment. A child with anorexia, was not making substantive progress toward recovery with her current therapist. As her daughter's advocate, her mother approached the therapist in an effort to better understand and facilitate the process and status of the treatment. The psychologist refused to discuss the girl's treatment with this mother or in any way support her effort to support her child. Because her daughter was comfortable with this clinician, her mother was afraid to consider the alternative of a change in therapist for fear it might create a major setback In response, I communicated the following:

- Families need to know that professionals have clearly honed goals and that they are seeing positive outcomes.
- Families need to know the standards professionals use to assess progress, as their child's life may be at stake.
- Families need to communicate with the treatment team about whether their child's health is improving. They deserve answers.

- Therapists need to be family inclusive, for the sake of both the parents and the child. They need to involve parents in the healing process as recovery advocates.
- Parents need to talk to their child about their concerns, preferably together with the therapist, so as not to violate confidentiality rights.
- Parents need to exercise their power and obligation to do something different if the treatment is not working and changes are not being made to accommodate everyone's needs.

DO CLIENTS EVER FULLY RECOVER FROM AN EATING DISORDER?

Twelve years after treating a young woman for anorexia, I met her parents at a concert. They were eager to report how wonderfully their daughter's life had been going, though they admitted that they were still fearful; every time she would call home, they were afraid that she might report the return of her eating disorder. "We feel a permanently entrenched fear that she will be haunted by these issues for the rest of her life," they reported. "Is she cured? Will she ever be? Is anyone ever cured?"

When full recovery has taken place, the client is cured. In most cases, particularly when co-occurring problems are not severe and the personality has effectively grown beyond its need for this dysfunctional life prop, the eating disorder will be gone forever. Once recovery has been fully achieved a person does not emotionally "undevelop." Like riding a bicycle or learning to swim, once the brain has "got it," it's there for good. The problem comes where clients believe that recovery has fully occurred, when in fact it has not. Recovery is complete only if the client has reached, and fearlessly sustains, her full set point weight along with a sense of well-being and normalcy. According to one client, "Recovery did not happen until I decided that these behaviors of mine were crazy. The better I feel, the more I realize how miserable and dysfunctional I was all those years with this illness."

A mother came to speak with me about her daughter, who "had recovered but was starting to relapse." In questioning this mother, I learned that even after her so-called "recovery," the youngster had not been able to eat comfortably and without fear, had never attained her full body weight, had never stopped exercising compulsively, and had tenaciously held on to her vegan lifestyle. As I see it, never having fully recovered in the past, this child was hardly suffering a "relapse."

Managed Recovery

The lack of readiness to heal may lead to a partial recovery or in other words, a "managed" disorder. A managed maintenance of the eating disorder is marked by a continuing fear of food and fat and lack of full weight restoration, despite improved emotional functioning. Recovery marks a fearless and comfortable relationship with food following a fearless and comfortable relationship with the self;

anything short of that represents something else. There is no real recovery short of full recovery. Typically, people confuse weight restoration with recovery. Those who choose to recover partially (or who choose not to recover fully) may contend that the progress they have made is "sufficient" and they are "recovered enough." In other words, they fool themselves. No "breathtaking views" are available to the mountain climber until she arrives at the peak; invariably, the last stages of the climb are the most grueling. During the final leg of the climb, the climber's vision is restricted to the last menacing slab of vertical rock, sapping her resiliency. It is not until she reaches the pinnacle that the climber is rewarded with the expansive perspective of a world unfolding before her.

Managed recovery can be more difficult to endure than the disorder itself. Representing the worst of both worlds, clients lose their freedom to enjoy the benefits of eating without fear, despite having restored some or most of their lost weight. By depriving themselves of an eating disorder diagnosis, those who choose partial recovery deprive themselves of the capacity to fully heal; in so doing, they indefinitely leave themselves unable to experience joy or well-being. The partially recovered client with anorexia believes that having gained some weight, she should feel some sense of relief. Instead, she feels fat and depressed, recognizing no benefits at all.

To ensure that partial or imminent recoveries become complete and lasting, it is up to the therapist to carry the *vision* of complete wellness and to inspire and shepherd the process all the way to fruition. The therapist must recognize obstacles to complete recovery and motivate the client to remain fully engaged all the way to the finish line, devising ways to help her circumvent the detours all along the road. Recovery is attainable for the vast majority of clients who receive optimal care. "The belief that clients cannot fully heal but are 'always recovering' can set up the expectation of relapse, possibly creating a self-fulfilling prophecy of failure" (Costin, 2002).

The partially recovered patient may have gained back a significant amount of weight, may have diminished or ceased certain self-destructive behaviors, and may eat healthy food in the form of meals, though not enough of the right kinds of foods, enough of the time, and in the right proportions. The client will probably:

- engage in internal battles with herself at some or most meals
- limit her calories or restrict certain food groups within the context of her food plan
- deal with "head noise" or the eating disorder voice
- engage in noncohesive eating habits
- pre-plan her "eating day" and worry about conforming precisely to the plan
- develop other dysfunctional compensatory behaviors to replace eating disordered behaviors
- rearrange her day to get to the gym and exercise as a chief priority
- be disappointed if she cannot remain at size 0 or 2, refusing to buy a larger size
- experience little empathy from family members or friends who haven't any notion that she still has the eating disorder.

In carrying the vision of total healing, the therapist needs to

- be capable of gauging the recovery progress as it stands
- anticipate that the rhythm and pacing of recovery progress waxes and wanes in different ways and at different times
- recognize at what point anticipated slow progress becomes stalled progress; the pacing of change can jeopardize the recovery of an unremitting disease
- understand that eating disorder recovery, like eating disorder treatment and diagnosis, has its own clearly definable stages that must be recognized, addressed, and accommodated.

D, a brilliant law student, chose to terminate her treatment for anorexia and body image disturbances after she gained as much weight as she was comfortable gaining and chose to gain no more. She considered herself "recovered enough," though I made it clear to her that despite a strong start on recovery, premature termination would leave her saddled with a managed and ongoing eating disorder. D held her own against her disease during the first year of law school, exercising compulsively, studying compulsively, and managing to maintain her restored weight until she hit a wall. Rapidly sliding downhill, she lost weight precipitously and became overwhelmed with anxiety and depression. She returned to treatment for a second try at recovery, until the anxiety of weight gain knocked her off her recovery course once again. Relying on the strength of our relationship, at this point I confronted her with what we both knew was a pattern of withdrawal from anxiety and discomfort. Her disease would impair her functioning in all aspects of her life and career, now and in the future, affecting her choice of a marriage partner and function as a parent, her work ethic as a professional, and relationships with colleagues and clients. D took an extended break from treatment after this potent session that had apparently touched an uncomfortable cord within her.

She returned to law school after Christmas break and did not contact me during a long siege of final exams and unsettled feelings. I chose to initiate contact with her after a time by leaving her a voice message, followed by a succinct e-mail inviting her to express her feelings toward me and recovery if and when she felt ready. After a month, she called to say she was ready. She had already begun to make significant changes and to experience newly emerging high anxiety in the face of her choice to "eat through her fear." We resumed treatment via phone therapy, focusing on her capacity to face and manage the anxiety that real recovery brings. Not only did she begin to prioritize changes in her eating lifestyle, but she also mustered the strength to confront and separate from her now mismatched boyfriend of five years. She modeled her confrontation with him after my own firm but loving confrontation with her.

Timing and readiness are important. D's recovery efforts and progress reflect the normal, disjointed, and convoluted nature of the recovery process, the changing quality of support that emanates from a versatile use of the therapist's self, the impact of life experience and circumstance on a client's drive to recover, and the limitless and spontaneous opportunities for variation and flexibility within each treatment process. D soon became a fully recovered individual. The strength of our relationship over the years and across the miles, as well as my demands that she hear and integrate realities that were hard for her to stomach, kept her coming back for help through the uncomfortable times. Eventually, in bringing her newfound emotional maturity to her longstanding love relationship, the couple was ultimately able to resolve the obstacles between them.

At certain points along the way, another therapist might have considered this young woman's progress to be a success and released her as a recovered individual; others might have considered her efforts a failure because she returned to treatment with what she described as a relapse. To me, this case was an example not of relapse but of the natural course of growth and change and of this woman's potential to enjoy a full and complete recovery along with the full and complete life that she so richly deserved. Every element of the treatment process, even the plateaus and regressions, were about her learning—about herself, her strength and versatility, and her options for using herself in the face of adversity. The character and fortitude she displayed with regard to her eating disorder recovery would carry over into every other life function and sphere.

Distinguishing Between Regression and Relapse

Even fully recovered individuals who suffer co-occurring issues that preceded the onset of the eating disorder, such as obsessive–compulsive anxiety disorder, body image disturbances, mood disorders, and personality disorders, may be more prone to experience resurgences of regression following recovery, for which they may require ongoing or ad hoc treatment to prevent a full-blown relapse. Once a client has fully recovered, however, any aspect of the eating disorder that is called up after the fact can be counted on to be a mere shell of its former self; the disorder loses its power to cause lasting physical, behavioral, or emotional havoc, particularly if the client gets help at the first sign of trouble.

A client who had been in psychotherapy for years with a colleague of mine had recovered fully from her eating disorder. After the colleague moved away, this young woman had begun purging again and came to me for a quick refresher course in herself. In fact, within a three-session tune up, she was able to revisit and resolve the underlying issues that had begun to plague her. Through a quick and substantive therapeutic connection, reality testing, and cognitive reshuffling, she regained her balance and returned to her sense of self. The purging would be again eradicated, perhaps forever this time.

In another instance, a young woman with a diagnosis of eating disorder not otherwise specified struggled with a pattern of submissive powerlessness in various contexts of her life. As she journeyed toward recovery, she became increasingly empowered in feeding and exercising her body, in mediating the intrusiveness of her parents, and in handling manipulating peers. In ultimately having to deal with an emotionally abusive boss, she began to feel herself regressing into an acute loss of self-confidence. It took no more than one session to remind her ego of its powerful capacities to cope; she left prepared with a plan for action and a sense of relief.

In the face of normative backslides, I

- depathologize the process, then problem solve recurring dysfunction, noting triggers;
- create client self-awareness to break routine habits;
- re-access which internal resources may have worked for the client previously in other contexts and determine the differences between those earlier experiences and the current one;
- brainstorm what to do in the future to avoid this pattern repetition.

Recognizing small successes is an effective way to help a client own and cement her gains. Even during backslides, there are always elements to be found that shine with the promise of change, warranting the comment, "Here's what I like about what I see." This is a comment that I enjoy making with clients whenever it is appropriate to do so.

In one instance where parents joined their teenager in a treatment session to complain of her resistance to eating, I reinforced their honesty, their frustration, and their efforts to be supportive and involved and, most of all, their daughter's apparent efforts to change. "Rome was not built in a day," I told them, "but the foundation of this recovery is being built right under all of our noses . . . and it's all good." I encouraged their patience, persistence, and ability to identify recovery progress, as well as their flexibility in using themselves to accommodate the child's recovery needs. I also helped them keep their expectations for treatment and recovery changes realistic.

WHAT FULL RECOVERY IS LIKE: CASE STUDY

L, mentioned earlier in this chapter, thought she had "recovered" on several occasions in the past. Never fully attaining set point weight, and always hearing the "head voices" of her eating disorder, she remained vulnerable to relapse, unable to consider letting her anorexia go completely. This time would be different.

During the summer between college and graduate school, she came to me for treatment, individually and with her parents. Initially, the war she waged was against her parents for their "unfounded concerns" rather than facing the true battle against her anorexia. Within three months of treatment, however, she had completely restored her weight and was on track for a complete recovery. She experienced a huge burst of authenticity and happiness with the return of her true self.

As she became increasingly well, she described having

a glimpse of what life is like again . . . of what it feels like to be "me" again. I realize now that there's so much I want to do that I can't do if I'm sick. I wanted my eating disorder to ensure life quality, to take care of me so I could live long and avoid death. Now I see for the first time that by protecting my anorexia, I was sabotaging my life quality and bringing myself ever closer to death. It's so weird!

L grew beyond her prior coping mechanisms, which simply did not work for her anymore. In the process of letting go of her eating disorder, she reported "missing my flat stomach," though she admitted that a part of her knew it was well worth it. As her depression lifted, she became more open to taking food risks that would move her forward; in balancing her meals, she noted balance and intelligent risk taking becoming evident in every life sphere. She spoke with satisfaction of happily juggling school, work, friendships, family time, and professional responsibilities, with the ever-burgeoning capacity to smile and laugh. "I can still remember how good I felt at that bar meeting new people the other night with my friends, and I can now look forward to my future without dread and shame," she said. "My priorities are different now. To enjoy myself is no longer a crime."

The client in recovery can be expected occasionally to experience a fear of getting fat but, despite this, to "eat through the fear," not letting it deter her. For L, her distorted thoughts were the last remnants of the disease to go. "These thoughts would say, "Don't give in to yourself, not even an inch. Always say no. Not one extra sip—not one little bite." Now, she defied those dictates, trying to "fake it till she makes it," and found herself succeeding most of the time. She described these experiences as follows:

> Before, I believed the thoughts and voices of the eating disorder . . . now, not so much. I am able to think about things differently now, proving these voices wrong, quieting them. Sometimes a thought comes to me about eating something that scares me. In the past, it would stop me from eating. Now I meet it head on with the question, "Is this a disordered thought?" "Am I still eating well?" In the end, I am doing my own self-monitoring, and my eating disorder is being shunted by the wayside. I talk to myself . . . I think, "What good is it to have this disorder? Enough already! Move on; live your life. If my parents and friends are eating the pickles on the table at the restaurant, maybe it's normal and I should do it, too."

L reported having become newly aware of "the choice now about how I will respond when I am upset or angry; there is a voice of reason inside me." In describing her ever-strengthening resiliency and feelings of genuine self-control, she reported, "When I was sick, I had no capacity for self-soothing, no internal mediator. Everything upset me." Though she described her eating disorder and most of her anxiety as having been "turned off like a spigot" (although "the faucet is still drippy now and then"), she admitted that "it will still take effort and thought on my part and probably will for a long time."

On the road to a permanent recovery this time, L was committed to staying in treatment to practice her new skills as the "new person" she had become. The control that she felt was less "head control" and more of an inner sensation that came of her ever-deepening belief that she can and will accomplish anything she determines to do—that she can and will find a way, fully aware that she now has a future to look forward to. Increasingly able to take in more than food, she is able to let in more people and life experience as well. "I know I could have a boyfriend now; I believe I can do anything that normal people do. My mind and myself are back to stay." With her weight fully restored, L described enjoying a "taste now of what's on the other side," knowing "how good it feels to feel good again."

L described the odd sensation of being perceived at her new workplace as "a robust, normal girl, with energy, present in the moment, positive. . . . "Who are they referring to? Could this be the me that I am now, though better, more mature, and more confident?" She speaks now from a place of honest self-appraisal and with no pretense. Her father, a bit confused about who she had become, confessed how worried he had been typically about her one day in the past when she had been unreachable by phone at a certain time of day when she could be expected to be at home. "But, not any more!" she quipped. "I've got places to go and people to see and the flexibility to wing it," she explained to him.

In looking back over the quality and style of care she received from me, though my demands were clear and my approach brutally reality based, she easily sensed how much I liked and cared about her. Time and again, she heard my hard-nosed but loving "You deserve better than this in life" speech. More than once, she struggled with conflicting feelings of shame and anger in the face of my toughness and brutal honesty. These pivotal moments were indicators of my commitment to her, and they ultimately translated into her commitment to a good life.

TROUBLESHOOTING THE RECOVERY PROCESS

"Doing Better" Versus "Being Better"

When you hear "Fine" or "Better" in response to the open-ended question, "So tell me how are you doing this week," you haven't heard enough. The client may be deflecting further conversation in an attempt to divert an uncomfortable focus on the eating disorder, or she may not yet have the awareness she needs to become an eye witness to her own process of change. The client may claim to be eating "more" foods or "new" foods . . . a good sign, though less meaningful if she is not eating *enough* of these foods, *enough* of the time, in the context of consistent meals. Eating a bite of key lime pie is not the same as eating the whole slice. Food risks need to be repeated consistently; the true test of doing better is one's ability to repeat the ameliorated action again and again, and to do it for and by oneself, rather than to please or placate others. "Doing better" implies intentionality . . . the existence of a pace, a purpose, and a direction . . . as established by the client. It is for you and the client to determine together what these are and what they may eventually need to become.

A mother observed that her child ate one good meal that day; she reported feeling confident that her child was "doing well." Before she could rightfully assume this, however, she needed to consider how well the child ate earlier, and later, that same day. Might the child have skipped a meal or restricted food that day to compensate for the "good meal" consumed? Accountability to the change process can be seen in the client's motivation to "keep up the good work."

Having gained 20 pounds, R described herself as "better." Yet she couldn't figure out why she still felt increasingly miserable. Although she still had 30 pounds to gain, in her mind, there was "no more anorexia." She explained, "I gained weight and I eat, and now I am left without self-discipline, pride in my capacity for self-deprivation, and my trusty eating disorder. I am nowhere." Misguided, R believed that she had conclusive evidence that recovery feels horrendous, that she looked fat, and that increasing her weight would give her a greater compulsion to eat and continue her weight gain. She assumed that once she arrived at her "weight goal," she would need to start restricting food again in an effort to sustain that weight, preventing obesity.

R did not realize that she was not by any means recovered, though she had made an appreciable start on the process that would lead her to it. She needed to be reminded that she could expect to feel worse for a long time before she started to feel better; that once she reached her set point weight, her body would naturally sustain its own self-regulated constancy.

The Importance of an Accurate Diagnosis

A client who transferred to my care from that of another therapist was finally able to make a leap into health after many years of minimal success. To what did she owe her new readiness? There were only two factors that had changed for this young woman that summer: beginning her relationship with me, which led to receiving to a proper diagnosis, which had been lacking for the three years of her previous treatment. By finally recognizing her diagnosis of eating disorder not otherwise specified and co-occurring mood disorder, this young woman was finally able to understand and accept herself without judgment. She not only discovered that she was not "crazy after all," but also began to reframe an appreciation of her resiliency and strength as demonstrated by her perseverance in treatment despite years of inaccurate diagnosis and appropriate medication.

Self-Determination . . . not Compliance . . . as the Goal

The practitioner's goal is not to seek compliance for compliance's sake but to help the client understand and respond to the obstacles that stand in the way of her attempts to make changes. A client with binge eating disorder reported "failing" her nutritional appointments because of her shame in not being able to comply with the food plan. I explained to her that the significance of the food plan lies less in the client's compliance and more in the process of her learning potentially important lessons about herself. I anticipated that the nutritionist's response to her "failure" would have been excitement and relief that the client had shown insight into herself, commitment to the process, and the courage to face and admit her problems. The client left my office determined to make an appointment to see the nutritionist soon and to begin to log her daily food consumption, feeling massively relieved.

This client needed to be reminded when she flagellates herself for not being able to change, she has lost sight of the reality of the human condition: change, as challenging as it is, remains a constant in all of our lives. Through life experience, and self-determination, whatever the client was, she is not now; whatever she is she will no longer be.

Relapse Versus Failure to Recover

In many cases, premature termination from eating disorder treatment occurs because the client believes she has "achieved enough recovery." In reality, premature termination is more likely to be a matter of denial and resistance to recovery. Clients who choose to leave treatment before achieving full recovery risk disease resurgence. With eating disorders, short of a full recovery there is no "remission," . . . only tolerable lulls in a continual storm. Not all "failed" treatments or premature terminations represent poor treatment or opportunities squandered. Sometimes, the client (or family) is simply not emotionally prepared to let go of the eating disorder. Timing is critical, and in some instances, pivotal external supports or resources for healing may not yet be in place.

The raging fire of S's eating disorder had been reduced to a small flickering flame, but it was never fully extinguished. The disorder needed nothing more than to catch a dry wind to be reignited into a small blaze. S had suffered for two years with anorexia and obsessive–compulsive anxiety disorder. Through intensive outpatient individual and family therapy, the counsel of a nutritionist, psychotropic medication, a partial day program, cognitive mediation for reading and learning problems, and Feldenkrais therapy, she made good progress, achieving what was close to full weight restoration. She displayed increased emotional flexibility, reduced anxiety, improved judgment, and a healthier balance in lifestyle. Now able to re-enroll in college and to function well there, away from home, she made friends and became a leader among her peers.

She ultimately chose to leave her productive two-year treatment relationship with me somewhat precipitously, just shy of her weight being fully restored. The nature of that termination foreshadowed the prognosis for that recovery effort. Despite her lingering obsessive–compulsive symptoms, she also decided to stop taking medication on the advice of a relative who believed it would be "best to go through life "medication free" (and because some medications can result in weight gain).

S returned to treatment 18 months later at the start of a significant backslide. She described her eating as having been close to normalized for several months following treatment, though she remained ever fearful and vigilant about eating certain foods and in certain amounts. With the advent of "bathing suit weather" and in the face of a mounting sense of self-consciousness and guilt, she began to restrict certain foods from her diet. Her re-emerging fears, body image concerns, and increasing food restriction, in tandem with her intensified obsessive–compulsive preoccupations, resulting in excessive calorie counting, compulsive viewing of food websites, and the ultimate drive to exercise off all the calories she consumed each day. She became increasingly socially isolated and began to suffer panic attacks about attending classes at college. Slowly, her life imploded and grew smaller. She lost her period as she steadily continued her weight decline. The more weight she lost, the more she wanted to lose. The happier she became with her weight, the unhappier and the more dysfunctional she became in every other sphere of her life.

Having "gone the miles" of recovery once, one might assume that her accrued therapeutic learning would be readily recalled in response to appropriate cues and that "square one" would be nowhere within her recovery landscape. But, this is not how eating disorder recovery works. Although S's past attempts at recovery had accomplished approximately 93 percent success, the last 7 percent of unattained goals began a slide down a slope that would become steep and slippery. Is this an example of relapse? Initially, I had come to believe that she had achieved true recovery. I ultimately understood that it might be more accurately described as a recovery interrupted in the 11th hour.

What causes relapse? People relapse for the following reasons:

- Clients may be discharged from inpatient to less restrictive care before they are clinically ready. Insurance coverage may necessitate such premature reductions in care.
- Clients transferring from greater to lesser restriction in treatment environments may lack continuing motivation and support from expert professionals and loving and enlightened families.
- Clients may give verbal assurances that they are managing well on their own, even while they continue to struggle.
- Aftercare or postrecovery care on a regular or as-needed basis may be unavailable.
- Often, when clients with co-occurring substance abuse and [eating disorder] begin rehab and stop abusing substances, their eating disorder intensifies (Wall, Eberly, & Wandler, 2007). For this reason it behooves such individuals to undergo attempts to heal both conditions simultaneously.
- When recovering clients are part of a marital system, if the client's partner is not prepared to make parallel changes, either the marriage or the recovery may be at risk of becoming sacrificed.

The best form of relapse prevention is learning to engage in a normalized, healthy eating lifestyle, allowing for a full restoration of body weight. Recognizing early signs of potential relapse becomes a powerful antecedent to taking action to avoid regression. It is critical to help the client learn to become sensitive to her own hunger and satiety cues, to feel her sensations, to recognize when she is in trouble, and know when and how to ask for assistance. Antidepressants and other psychiatric medications that may be used to treat comorbid disorders will improve the client's capacity to sustain recovery gains.

BEYOND RECOVERY: POSTRECOVERY TREATMENT

Although clients with co-occurring pathology have poorer outcomes in therapy, healing resources within the community, such as a supportive family system, the availability of strong treatment team professionals, or the presence of a conveniently located day program, can contribute to sustaining a successful recovery. Perhaps the most significant factor in sustaining recovery, however, is the continuation of therapeutic care following full recovery (Morgan, Purgold, & Wellbourne, 1983). Postrecovery care may be considered a kind of insurance policy for the recovered client who seeks to secure her recovery gains.

The aftercare treatment cushion provides the wiggle room clients require to learn to handle naturally recurring ambivalence, to practice new life skills, to deepen new neural pathways in reinforcing change, and to learn to right themselves when life throws them off balance. Postrecovery care can take the form of individual or family treatment; clients also benefit greatly from educative, support, or psychotherapy groups in which individuals who have recovered from eating disorders come together, sometimes with families, to share experiences and support each other through the tough times, buoying each other up through their personal life experiences, trials, successes, and failures.

Postrecovery Case Study

V, who had recovered from anorexia, made a superb adjustment to life far away from home at a challenging job. Her transition to her new life had been successful, her food and exercise were under control, and she had started to date men. Despite having achieved a meaningful balance in her life, two years postrecovery, a crisis of confidence and a jaw problem that hampered her ability to eat normally resulted in weight loss; this, in turn, led to a perseveration fed by an obsessive–compulsive anxiety disorder, about her dread of the unknown and intolerance of life's ambiguities. V decided to return to weekly phone treatment

V's yearning for formulaic and definitive solutions to complex problems interfered with her effective problem solving in the here and now. In noticing how little of her true self currently resided in the moment, I assigned her the task of becoming aware of "being," of her presence in the "now" of daily living. Within a week, she reported feeling gratified in enjoying her work with Excel spreadsheets, as well as her walk to work in lovely fall weather. These new insights put a new spin on how she felt about her potential to experience joy in the moment and optimism about the future. She learned to recognize a yet undisclosed part of herself (rational, comforting, and optimistic), which offered her a feeling of reassurance and calm.

Like many other members of her generation, V grew up with little ambiguity in a life that was programmed for success. As part of the "millennium generation" (Alsop, 2008), her path through life had been preprogrammed for her, marked by the best schools, sports teams, vacations, and university, leaving little need for autonomous self-determination or decision making. After college, she found herself left on her own to make her way for the first time in her life. Discovering answers that lay buried within the process and fabric of living each day, V ultimately realized that she was capable of thriving in ambiguity, that she could move with and beyond unpredictability to maintain her balance if she could hold fast to a clear internal vision of who she is and what she needs.

In the course of postrecovery care, she came to understand that obsessive worrying offered the *illusion* of being in control ("At least I can worry about this; at least I can *do* something") just as her eating disorder had done for her at another time. She learned that real control (recovery) is not found in black-and-white solutions, but in learning to trust herself and her own potential to respond spontaneously and purposefully to the moment, whatever that might require. For V in postrecovery, self-trust would replace compulsive worry; authenticity and action would replace fear.

Postrecovery Care With Couples

Postrecovery treatment feeds and repairs the deeper levels of the self that become newly exposed in the absence of the eating disorder. In recovery's aftermath, some of the underlying issues that initially drove the eating disorder may still exist and resurface in less toxic forms. A recovered anorexic came back for more treatment three years after her eating disorder had vanished without a trace. In her relationship with her boyfriend, she had found herself attempting to cover up real and uncomfortable feelings in vain attempts to avoid rather than confront and work through her pain. Believing that romantic trust and love were conditional, they entered their relationship with an unwritten contract never to argue or disagree with each other. My recommendation for them was to get real and off the eggshells if they were seeking increased intimacy.

Through her treatment for her eating disorder, the young woman had learned that there is no place for perfection in recovery, in human beings, or in expectations for a relationship. She needed a reminder that the courage and flexibility it takes to experience and express true feelings within the context of her recovery also applies to bringing people closer to each other. Her young man needed to learn how to support her; she needed to learn how to ask for what she needed. By doing away with their secrets, the couple became closer, and she further cemented the learning she had begun in her eating disorder treatment.

Aftercare Following Residential Treatment

The term *aftercare* generally refers to continued treatment following a client's release from a hospital, day program, or residential care. At the end of a milieu tenure, aftercare consolidates and integrates the learning and changes that occurred during treatment. Aftercare typically takes the form of intensive outpatient treatment by a team of professionals, or a residential stint in halfway housing, providing group care and transitioning assistance to independent living. What can be misleading about the concept of aftercare is its implication that the recovered client is in remission for a disorder that is not curable, which is not the case with eating disorders.

An important task of hospital-based inpatient teams is to anticipate and prepare for discharge and aftercare from the very outset of the client's tenure, which may involve addressing such issues as transitioning into and out of the hospital, sustaining the consistency of outpatient care (or not) following release and navigating the logistics and technicalities of insurance funding. If the client does not have an outpatient team in place, it is up to the inpatient care program to find one. If the client has a working relationship with an outpatient team upon entry into the milieu, the quality of caregiving will determine the efficacy of retaining the existing team. The decision to seek a new outpatient team should be a collaborative one, made between hospital staff, the client, and the family.

CONCLUSION

By banishing the eating disorder from the client's core, recovery facilitates the re-association and reconnection with previously dissociated, exiled, or disabled parts of the self. This process represents the transfer of dependency from the eating disorder to supportive and educative human relationships, including therapist and family; that dependency is ultimately transferred to a trusting place of well-being and genuine self-control within the client, leading to a reintegrated core self. Through recovery, clients get their personality back; parents of child clients get their children back.

Anat Baniel defines our authentic self as someone we grow into. The young mother who puts so much effort, love, attention, and nurturance into her newborn baby expects nothing back initially, but soon the effects of this loving nurturance take form in a smile, eye contact, recognition, ever-accruing responsiveness, and physical and social development. So it is with healthy eating and the process of growing out of an eating disorder: The process happens slowly, unassumingly, and sometimes tediously, but the potential outcomes are nothing short of marvelous.

Perhaps one of the most difficult aspects of providing psychotherapy is that for the most part, when clients leave treatment healed, therapists rarely hear from them again. Much we wish to know about their continuing lives eludes us by virtue of the nature of the therapy relationship. Among my past clients who have remained in contact through the years, I have been privileged to witness recovery go hand in hand with self-actualization; so many of these individuals have made their mark on the world as human beings, as professionals, as life partners, and as parents. It has been a privilege to inspire and be part of such healing in others.

References

Academy for Eating Disorders. (2006, December 6). *Eating disorders are biologically based mental illnesses* [Press release]. Deerfield, IL: Author. http://www.eatingdisorderhope.com/ed-biological-mental-illnesses.html

Adolescent Medicine Committee, Canadian Paediatric Society. (1998). Eating disorders in adolescents: Principles of diagnosis and treatment. *Journal of Paediatrics and Child Health, 3,* 189–192

Alsop, R. (2008). *The trophy kids grow up: How the millenium generation is shaking up the workplace.* Somerset, NJ: Jossey–Bass.

American Psychiatric Association. (2000). *Diagnostic and statistical manual of mental disorders* (4th ed., text rev.). Washington, DC: Author.

Andersen, A. (2004a). Males with eating disorders: The gender factor. *Eating Disorders Today.* Available at http://www.gurze.com/client/client_pages/newsletteredt10.cfm

Andersen, A. (2004b). Recognizing and responding to binge eating in children. *Eating Disorders Today.* Available at http://www.gurze.com/client/client_pages/newsletteredt10.cfm

Ann, S. (2007, January 26). *Understanding eating disorders among college women.* Available at http://www.associatedcontent.com/article/124611/understanding_eating_disorders_among.html?cat=70

April, D., & Nicholas, L. J. (1996). Premature termination of counselling at a university counselling center. *International Journal for the Advancement of Counselling, 19,* 379–387.

Arehart-Treichel, J. (2005). Strong link found between anxiety, eating disorders. *Psychiatric News, 40,* 34.

Association for Advanced Training in the Behavioral Sciences. (2008). *Ethical and professional considerations.* Ventura, CA: Author.

Attia, E., & Walsh, T. (2009). Behavioral management for anorexia nervosa. *New England Journal of Medicine, 360,* 500–506.

Baniel, A. (2009). *The special needs child—A cutting edge approach to treating developmental disorders.* Available at http://www.anatbanielmethod.com/help-children-overview.htm 2009

Banker, J., & Klump, K. (2007). Toward a common ground: Bridging the gap between research and practice in the field of eating disorders. *AED Forum, 14*(4), 7–9.

Barbarich, N. C. (2002). Lifetime prevalence of eating disorders among professionals in the field. *Eating Disorders: The Journal of Treatment and Prevention, 10,* 305–312.

BBC News. (2005a, January 5). *Brain theory of eating disorders.* Available at http://news.bbc.co.uk/2/hi/health/4144755.stm

BBC News. (2005b, February 7). *ED care criticised.* Available at http://news.bbc.co.uk/2/hi/health/4237055.stm

Bennett, J. (2008, September 6). It's not just White girls. *Newsweek.* Available at http://www.newsweek.com/id/157574?tid=relatedcl

Bernstein, B. E. (n.d.). *Eating disorders: Anorexia.* Available at http://emedicine.medscape.com/article/912187-overview

Bulik, C., Devlin, B., Bacanu, S.-A., Thornton, L., Klump, K., Fichter, M., et al. (2003). Significant linkage on chromosome 10p in families with bulimia nervosa. *American Journal of Human Genetics, 72,* 200–207.

Campbell, A., McGilley, B., & Tyson, E. (n.d.). *Eating disorders: A guide to medical care and complications.* Baltimore, MD: Johns Hopkins University.

Carey, B. (2006, June 14). Study sees no gain in using antidepressant to treat anorexia. *The New York Times.* Available at http://www.nytimes.com/2006/06/14/health/14prozac.html?pagewanted=print

Cedric Centre for Counselling. (n.d.). Victoria, British Columbia, Canada: Author. Available at http://www.cedriccentre.com

Connors, M. E., & Morse, W. (1993). Sexual abuse and eating disorders: A review. *International Journal of Eating Disorders, 13,* 1–11.

Costin, C. (2002). Eating disorders. *The Journal of Treatment and Prevention, 10,* 293–303.

Dalle Grave, R., Calugi, S., & Marchesini, G. (2008). Underweight eating disorder without over-evaluation of shape and weight: Atypical anorexia nervosa? *International Journal of Eating Disorders, 41,* 705–712.

Davis, C., Shuster, B., Blackmore, E., & Fox, J. (2004). Looking good—Family focus on appearance and the risk for eating disorders. *International Journal of Eating Disorders, 35,* 136–134.

de la Rie, S., Noordenbos, G., Donker, M., & van Furth, E. (2006). Evaluating the treatment of eating disorders from the patient's perspective. *International Journal of Eating Disorders, 39,* 667–676.

Doidge, N. (2007). *The brain that changes itself: Stories of personal triumph from the frontiers of brain science.* New York: Viking.

Eating Disorders Coalition for Research, Policy & Action. (2008). *Victory in passing mental health parity!* Washington, DC: Author. Available at http://www.eatingdisorderscoalition.org/

Eberly, M. (2005). Understanding self-injurious behavior in eating disorders. *Remuda Review, 4,* 26–30.

Eddy, K., Dorer, D., Franko, D., Kass, A., Thompson-Brenner, H., Sears, M., et al. (2008, May). *EDNOS or partial recovery? A longitudinal examination of subthreshold presentations in women with lifetime anorexia nervosa or bulimia nervosa.* Paper presented at the conference of the Academy for Eating Disorders, Seattle, WA.

Emergency Economic Stabilization Act of 2008. H. R. 1424 (110). Available at http://www.eatingdisorderscoalition.org/documents/bailoutbillandmentalhealthparity2008.pdf

Engel, B., Reiss, N. S., & Dombeck, M. (2007). *Prevalence, onset, and course of eating disorders.* Columbus, OH: Mental Help Net. Available at http://mentalhelp.net

Engel, S. G., Wittrock, D. A., Crosby, R. D., Wonderlich, S. A., Mitchell, J. E., & Kolotkin, R. L. (2006). Development and psychometric validation of an eating disorder-specific health-related quality of life instrument. *International Journal of Eating Disorders, 39,* 62–71.

Estes, C. P. (1992). *Women who run with the wolves: Myths and stories of the wild woman archetype.* New York: Ballantine Books.

Fairburn, C. G. (2008). *Cognitive behavior therapy and eating disorders.* New York: Guilford Press.

Fairburn, C. G., Cooper, Z., Bohn, K., O'Connor, M. E., Doll, H. A., & Palmer, R. L. (2007). The severity and status of EDNOS: Implications for DSM–V. *Behaviour Research and Therapy, 45,* 1705–1715.

Family dinners mean better nutrition for children. (2000, May). *Tufts University Health and Nutrition Letter, 18*(3), 2.

Fat-phobia in the Fijis: TV-thin is in. (1999, May 31). *Newsweek.* Available at http://www.newsweek.com/id/88437

Feldenkrais, M. (1949). *Body and mature behavior.* New York: International Universities Press.

Feldenkrais, M. (1972). *Awareness through movement: Health exercises for personal growth.* New York: Harper & Row.

Fetissov, S. O., Harro, J., Jaanisk, M., Järv, A., Podar, I., Allik, J., et al. (2005). Autoantibodies against neuropeptides are associated with psychological traits in eating disorders. *Proceedings of the National Academy of Sciences of the United States of America, 102,* 14865–14870.

Field, A. E., Austin, S. B., Taylor, C. B., Malspeis, S., Rosner, B., Rockett, H. R., et al. (2003). Relation between dieting and weight change among preadolescents and adolescents. *Pediatrics, 112,* 900–906.

Fraker, C., Walbert, L., Cox, S., Fishbein, M., & Barker, S. C. (2007). *Food chaining: The proven 6-step plan to stop picky eating, solve feeding problems, and expand your child's diet.* New York: Marlow.

Franzen, L., Ackard, D., Cronomeyer, C., Lesser, J., Lesse, J. N., & Mangham, D. (2008, May). *Does use of laxatives for weight control purposes affect treatment outcome? Analyses for a long-term follow-up of eating disordered patients.* Paper presented at the conference of the Academy for Eating Disorders, Seattle WA.

Gardiner, R. (1973). *The talking, feeling, and doing game.* (Available from Creative Therapeutics, 155 County Road, Cresskill, NJ 07626)

Garner, D. M. (1997). Psychoeducational principles in the treatment of eating disorders. In D. M. Garner & P. E. Garfinkel (Eds.), *Handbook of treatment for eating disorders* (pp. 145–177). New York: Guilford Press.

Gendall, K., Joyce, P., Carter, F., McIntosh, V., & Bulik, C. (2005). Childhood gastrointestinal complaints in women with bulimia nervosa. *International Journal of Eating Disorders, 37,* 256–260.

Germer, C., Siegel, R. D., & Fulton, P. R. (Eds.). (2005). *Mindfulness and psychotherapy.* New York: Guilford Press.

Gersema, E. (2003, September 26). *Diet guidelines aimed at healthy people.* Available at http://www.redorbit.com/news/science/9043/diet_guidelines_aimed_at_healthy_people/

Gibson, L. (2006, April). Mirrored emotion. *University of Chicago Magazine,* pp. 34–39.

Ginott, H. G. (1969). *Between parent and child.* New York: Avon Books.

Graham, J. (2006, June 27). Answers missing in anorexia fight: Medications, therapy of little help to those with disease. *Chicago Tribune,* p. 6.

Guarda, A. S. (2008). Treatment of anorexia nervosa: Insights and obstacles. *Physiology & Behavior, 94,* 113–120.

Guarda, A. S., Pinto, A. M., Coughlin, J. W., Hussain, S., Haug, N. A., & Heinberg, L. J. (2007). Perceived coercion and change in perceived need for admission in patients hospitalized for eating disorders. *American Journal of Psychiatry, 164,* 108–114.

Halmi, K. H., Heebink, D. M., & Sunday, S. R. (1995). Anorexia nervosa and bulimia nervosa in adolescence. Effects of age and menstrual status in psychological variables. *Journal of the American Academy of Child and Adolescent Psychiatry 34,* 378–382.

Health matters—women's & men's health issues: Womens health. (n.d.). Taft CA: Taft College Counseling Center. Available at http://www.taftcollege.edu/newtc/studentservices/health/women_issues.htm

Henig, R. M. (2004, November 4). Sorry. Your eating disorder doesn't meet our criteria. *The New York Times.* Available at http://www.nytimes.com/2004/11/30/health/psychology/30eat.html

Holm-Denoma, J., Witte, T., Gordon, K., Herzog, D., Franko, D., Fichter, M., et al. (2008). Case reports of anorexic women's deaths by suicide as arbiters between competing explanations of the anorexia–suicide link. *Journal of Affective Disorders, 107,* 231–236.

Hudson, J. I., Hiripi, E., Pope, H. G., Jr., & Kessler, R. C. (2007). The prevalence and correlates of eating disorders in the National Comorbidity Survey Replication. *Biological Psychiatry, 61,* 348–358.

Hurst, P. S., Lacey, J. H., & Crisp, A. H. (1977). Teeth, vomiting and diet: A study of the dental characteristics of seventeen anorexia nervosa patients. *Postgraduate Medical Journal, 53,* 298–305.

Iacoboni, M. (2008, May). Mental mirrors. *Natural History, 34–39.*

Johnson, C. L., Connors, M. E., & Tobin, D. L. (1987). Symptom management of bulimia. *Journal of Consulting and Clinical Psychology, 55,* 668–676.

Johnson, C. L., Lund, B. C., & Yates, W. R. (2003). Recovery rates for anorexia [Letter to the editor]. *American Journal of Psychiatry, 160,* 798.

Johnson, C. L., & Maddi, K. L. (1986). The etiology of bulimia: Biopsychosocial perspectives. *Adolescent Psychiatry, 13,* 253–273.

Johnson, C. L., & Sansone, R. (1993). Integrating the 12-step approach with traditional psychotherapy for eating disorders. *International Journal of Eating Disorders, 14,* 121–134.

Johnson, C. L., Sansone, R. A., & Chewning, M. (1992). Good reasons why young women would develop anorexia nervosa: The adaptive context. *Pediatric Annals, 21,* 731–737.

Judson, O. (2008, October 21). Weighing the vote. *New York Times.* Available at http://judson.blogs.nytimes.com/2008/10/21/weighing-the-vote/

Kaplan, A., Levitan, R., Yilmar, Z., & Kennedy, J. (2008, May). *Bulimia nervosa and ADHD: Shared phenomenological, psychometric and genetic variables.* Paper presented at the conference of the Academy for Eating Disorders, Seattle, WA.

Kartini Clinic (n.d.). *Bones and anorexia nervosa: Osteopenia/osteoporosis.* Available at http://www.kartiniclinic.com/node/7057

Katzman, D. K., Morris, A., & Pinhas, L. (n.d.). *Canadian Paediatric Surveillance Program: Early-onset eating disorders.* Available at http://www.cps.ca/ENGLISH/Surveillance/CPSP/Studies/early onseteatingdisorders.htm

Kaye, W., Bulik, C., Thornton, L., Barbarich, N., Masters, K., & The Price Foundation Collaborative Group. (2004). Comorbidity of anxiety disorders wth AN and BN. *American Journal of Psychiatry, 161,* 2215–2221.

Kaye, W. H., Lilenfeld, L. R., Berrettini, W. H., Strober, M., Devlin, B., Klump, K. L., et al. (2000). A search for susceptibility loci for anorexia nervosa: Methods and sample description. *Biological Psychiatry, 47,* 794–803.

Keel, P. K., Dorer, D. J., Franko, D. L., Jackson, S. C., & Herzog, D. B. (2005). Postremission predictors of relapse in women with eating disorders. *American Journal of Psychiatry, 162,* 2263–2268.

Keel, P. K., Mitchell, J., Miller, K. B., Davis, T. L., & Crow, S. J. (1999). Long-term outcome of bulimia nervosa. *Archives of General Psychiatry, 56,* 63–69.

Kolata, G. (2007, May 8). Genes take charge, and diets fall by the wayside. *New York Times.* Available at http://www.nytimes.com/2007/05/08/health/08fat.html

Krishnan, K. R. R. (2005). Psychiatric and medical comorbidities of bipolar disorder. *Psychosomatic Medicine, 67,* 1–8.

Krug, I., Treasure, J., Anderluh, M., Bellodj, L., Cellini, E., de Barnardo, M., et al. (2008). *Lifetime co-morbidity of tobacco, alcohol and drug abuse in eating disorders: A European multicenter study.* Paper presented at the annual conference of the Academy for Eating Disorders, Seattle, WA.

Lask, B., & Bryant-Waugh, R. (2000). *Anorexia nervosa and related eating disorders in childhood and adolescence* (2nd ed.). New York: Psychology Press.

Laurance, J. (2005, April 7). Anorexia could be caused by brain dysfunction. *New Zealand Herald.* Available at http://www.nzherald.co.nz/technology/news/article.cfm?c_id=5&objectid=10119226

Ledford, J. R., & Gast, D. L. (2006). Focus on autism and other developmental disabilities; feeding problems in children with autism spectrum disorders: A review. *Focus on Autism and Other Developmental Disabilities, 21,* 153–166.

Leichner, P. (2005). A quiet revolution in the treatment of youth with eating disorders [Guest editorial]. *BC Medical Journal, 47,* 22.

Lilenfeld, L. R. Kaye, W. H., Greeno, C. G., Merikangas, K. R., Plotnicov, K., Pollice, C., et al. (1998). A controlled family study of anorexia nervosa and bulimia nervosa: Psychiatric disorders in first-degree relatives and effects of proband comorbidity. *Archives of General Psychiatry, 55,* 603–610.

Linehan, M. (1993). *Cognitive–behavioral treatment of borderline personality disorder.* New York: Guilford Press.

Lock, J. (2006, Winter). Update on Maudsley type family therapy for eating disorders. *Renfrew Perspective,* 19.

Luborsky, L., Barber, J., Siqueland, L., McLellan, A. T., & Woody, G. (1997). *Establishing a therapeutic alliance with substance abusers.* Available at http://www.nida.nih.gov/pdf/monographs/Monograph165/233-244_Luborsky.pdf

Lucka, I. (2006). *Anxiety disorder in children suffering from anorexia nervosa.* Available at http://www.ncbi.nlm.nih.gov/pubmed/1675603

Lund, B., Johnson, C., Hernandez, E., Yates, W., Mitchell, J., & Mckee, P. (2008). *Eating disorders and suicide attempts: Independent risk factor or marker for mood disorder?* Paper presented at the conference of the Academy for Eating Disorders, Seattle, WA.

Lunde, A. V., Fasmer, O. B., Akiskal, K. K., Akiskal, H. S., & Oedegaard, K. J. (2009). The relationship of bulimia and anorexia nervosa with bipolar disorder and its temperamental foundations. *Journal of Affective Disorders, 115,* 309–314.

Madden, S., Morris, A., Zuryaski, Y. A., Kohn, M., & Elliot, E. J. (2009). Burden of ED in 5- to 13-year-old children in Australia. *The Medical Journal of Australia, 190,* 410–414.

Mahaffey, B. A., & Granello, P. F. (2007). Therapeutic alliance: A review of sampling strategies reported in marital and family therapy studies. *Family Journal, 15,* 207–216.

Manley, R. S., O'Brien, K. M., & Samuels, S. (2008). Fitness instructors' recognition of eating disorders and attendant ethical/liability issues. *Eating Disorders, 16,* 103–116.

Maslow, A. H. (1966). *The psychology of science: A renaissance.* New York: Harper & Row.

Mathur, R. (2008). *Diabulimia—Eating disorders.* Available at http://www.medicinenet.com/script/main/art.asp?articlekey=81960

Matzkin, V. B., Geissler, C., Coniglio, R., Selles, J., & Bello, M. (2006). Cholesterol concentrations in patients with anorexia nervosa and in healthy controls. *International Journal of Psychiatric Nursing Research, 11,* 1283–1293.

McCune, N., & Walford, G. (1991). Long-term outcomes in early onset anorexia nervosa. *British Journal of Psychiatry, 159,* 383–389.

McLaren, L., Gauvin, L., & Steiger, H. (2001). A two-factor model of disordered eating. *Eating Behaviors, 2,* 51–65.

Mehler, P. S., & Andersen, A. E. (1999). *Eating disorders: A guide to medical care and complications.* Baltimore: Johns Hopkins University Press.

Mehler, P. S., & MacKenzie, T. D. (2009). Treatment of osteopenia and osteoporosis in anorexia nervosa: A systematic review of the literature. *International Journal of Eating Disorders, 42,* 195–201.

Mertens, M., & Vandereycken, W. (1998). History of prepubertal overweight in adolescent girls with a pronounced body dissatisfaction. *Eating Disorders: Journal of Treatment and Prevention, 6,* 225–229.

Michelle's Law H.R. 2851; Public Law 110-381. (October 9, 2008; 122 Stat. 4081).

Miller, W., & Rollnick, S. (1991). *Motivational interviewing: Preparing people to change addictive behavior.* New York: Guilford Press.

Miller, R., & Rollnick, S. (1992). *Motivational interviewing: Preparing people to change addictive behavior.* New York: Guilford Press.

Mitchell, J. E., Agras, W. S., Wilson, G. T., Halmi, K., Kraemer, H., & Crow S. (2004). A trial of a relapse prevention strategy in women with bulimia nervosa who respond to cognitive–behavior therapy. *International Journal of Eating Disorders, 35,* 549–555.

Monson, K., & Schoenstadt, A. (2007). Prozac and suicide. *eMedTV.* Available at http://depression.emedtv.com/prozac/prozac-and-suicide.html

Moss, E., & Von Ranson, K. (2008). *An examination of eating disorders symptoms in women with alcohol dependence.* Paper presented at the conference of the Academy for Eating Disorders, Seattle, WA.

Myers, M. D. (2004). *Compulsive overeating (binge eating disorder).* Available at http://www.weight.com/bed.asp

Natenshon, A. (1999). *When your child has an eating disorder: A step-by step workbook for parents and other caregivers.* San Francisco: Jossey-Bass.

Natenshon, A. (2005). *Feeding disorders and picky eating in infants and children.* Available at http://www.parentingbookmark.com/pages/AN01.htm

National Association of Anorexia Nervosa and Associated Disorders. (n.d.). *ANAD School Guidelines Program.* Highland Park, IL: Author. Available at http://www.anad.org

National Association of Social Workers. (2008). *Code of ethics.* Washington, DC: Author. Available at http://www.socialworkers.org/pubs/code/code.asp

National Center on Alcoholism and Substance Abuse at Columbia University. (2004). *Eating disorders, substance abuse linked.* Available at http://alcoholism.about.com/cs/nutrition/a/blcasa040128.htm

National Eating Disorders Association. (n.d.). *Statistics: Eating disorders and their precursors.* Available at http://www.nationaleatingdisorders.org/p.asp?WebPage_ID=286&Profile_ID=41138

Nichols, P. (1999, April). Arbiter of taste. *University of Chicago Magazine,* p. 22.

Night eating syndrome. (n.d.). Retrieved from www.ultraprevention.com.

Parry, D. (2000). *The Essene book of days.* Bainbridge, WA: Earthstewards Network.

Penn State Hershey, Milton S. Hershey Medical Center. (2008). *A–Z topics: Health and disease information.* Available at http://www.hmc.psu.edu/healthinfo

Pettus, A. (2006, July–August). Psychiatry by prescription: Do psychotropic drugs blur the boundaries between illness and health? *Harvard Magazine,* 38–44, 90–91.

Pinheiro, A., Thornton, L., Strober, M., Kaye, W. H., & Bulik, C. (2008). *Alcohol and drug use in women with anorexia nervosa.* Paper presented at the annual conference of the Academy for Eating Disorders, Seattle, WA.

Plessinger, A. (2008). *The relationship between ED and athletic participation.* Available at http://www.vanderbilt.edu/AnS/psychology/health-psychology/AnnieP.html

Poppink, J. (2006). *Joanna Poppink's eating disorder resource list: Inpatient treatment programs worldwide.* Available at http://www.joannapoppink.com

Potter, B. K., Pederson, L. L., Chan, S. S. H., Aubut, J. L., & Koval, J. J. (2004). Does a relationship exist between body weight, concerns about weight, and smoking among adolescents? An integration of the literature with an emphasis on gender. *Nicotine and Tobacco Research, 6,* 397–425.

Prochaska, J. O., & DiClemente, C. C. (1984). *The transtheoretical approach: Crossing traditional boundaries of therapy.* Homewood, IL: Dow Jones-Irwin.

Pukley, F., Midtsund, M., Losif, A., & Lask, B. (2007). PANDAS: Anorexia nervosa—Endangered, extinct, or nonexistent? *International Journal of Eating Disorders, 41,* 15–21.

Quindlen, A. (2007). *Good dog. Stay.* New York: Random House.

Ramsey, R., Ward, A., Treasure, J., & Russell, G. F. (1999). Compulsory treatment in anorexia nervosa: Short-term benefits and long-term mortality. *British Journal of Psychiatry, 175,* 147–153.

Rayworth, B. B., Wise, L. A., & Harlow, B. L. (2004). Childhood abuse and risk of eating disorders in women. *Epidemiology, 15,* 262–263.

Reed, C. (1993). Implications at intervention strategies for physically challenged children for the child's perspective. *The Feldenkrais Journal, 10,* 35–45.

Reindl, S. M. (2001). *Sensing the self: Women's recovery from bulimia.* Cambridge, MA: Harvard University Press.

Richards, P. S., & O'Grady, K. A. (2008, May). *Exploring the role of spirituality in treatment and recovery from eating disorders: A qualitative interview study.* Paper presented at the annual conference of the Academy for Eating Disorders, Seattle, WA.

Ruder, D. B. (2006, January–February). Life lesson: Gravely ill patients teach medical students about listening and compassion. *Harvard Magazine,* pp. 44–49.

Rudolph, C. D., & Link, D. T. (2002). Feeding disorders in infants and children. *Pediatric Clinics of North America, 49,* 97–112.

Santucci, P. (2004, Fall). Stages of change—Where are you? *Working Together Newsletter.* Available from National Association of Anorexia Nervosa and Associated Disorders, Highland Park, IL.

Scalzo, K. (2001, Winter). Polycystic ovary syndrome. *After the Diet, 1*(4). Available at http://www.afterthediet.com/atd-winter01.pdf

Schmidt, U., Lee, S., Perkins, S., Eisler, I., Treasure, J., Beecham, J., et al. (2008). Do adolescents with "eating disorder not otherwise specified" (EDNOS) or full-syndrome bulimia nervosa differ in clinical severity, co-morbidity, risk factors, treatment outcome or cost? *International Journal of Eating Disorders, 41,* 498–504.

Schore, J., & Schore, A. N. (2008). Modern attachment theory: The central role of affect regulation in development and treatment. *Clinical Social Work Journal, 36,* 9–20.

Schwartz, M. B., Chambliss, H. O., Brownell, K. D., Blair, S. N., & Billington, C. (2003). Weight bias among health professionals specializing in obesity. *Obesity Research, 11,* 1033–1039.

Schwartz, R. C. (1995). *Internal family systems therapy.* New York: Guilford Press.

Seidenfeld, M. E., & Rickert, V. I. (2001). Impact of anorexia, bulimia and obesity on the gynecological health of adolescents. *American Family Physician, 64,* 445–450.

Setnick, J. (2005). *The eating disorders clinical pocket guide: Quick reference for healthcare providers.* Dallas, TX: Snack Time Press.

Severson, K. (2007, October 10). Picky eaters? They get it from you. *New York Times.* Available at http://query.nytimes.com/gst/fullpage.html?res=9C05E6D6153BF933A25753C1A9619C8B63&n=Top/Reference/Times%20Topics/People/S/Severson,%20Kim

Shroff, H., Reba, L., Thornton, L. M., Tozzi, F., Klump, K. L., Berrettini, W. H., et al. (2006). Features associated with excessive exercise in women with eating disorders. *International Journal of Eating Disorders, 39,* 454–461.

Siegel, R. (2006). An interpersonal neurobiology approach to psychotherapy. *Psychiatric Annals, 36,* 248–256.

Spicer, K. (2007, April 8). My 6-week journey to the land of thin. *Sunday Times.* Available at http://women.timesonline.co.uk/tol/life_and_style/women/diet_and_fitness/article1625715.ece

Stice, E., Cameron, R., Killen, J., Hayward, C., & Taylor, C. B. (2000). Naturalistic weight-reduction efforts prospectively predict growth in relative weight and onset of obesity among female adolescents. *Journal of Consulting and Clinical Psychology, 67,* 967–974.

Suisman, J., Bart, A., & Klump, K. (2008, May). *Weight-based teasing: A non-specific risk factor for disordered eating.* Paper presented at the 2008 International Conference on Eating Disorders, Seattle, WA.

Tiemeyer, M. (2008). Is Prozac (fluoxetine) helpful for anorexia? Available at http://eatingdisorders.about.com/od/treatmentstrategies/f/anorexiaprozac.htm

Tyre, P. (2005, December 5). Fighting anorexia: No one to blame. *Newsweek.* Available at http://www.newsweek.com/id/51592

von Ranson, K., & Robinson, K. (2006). Who is providing what type of psychotherapy to eating disorder clients? A survey. *International Journal of Eating Disorders, 39,* 27–34.

Wall, A. D., & Cumella, E. J. (2005). Anxiety and eating disorders: An introduction. *Remuda Review, 4,* 38–43. Available at http://professionals.remudaranch.com/pdf/remuda_review/Fall_2005.pdf

Wall, A. D., Eberly, M., & Wandler, K., (2007). Substance abuse and eating disorders: The Remuda review. *The Christian Journal of Eating Disorders, 6,* 2–9.

Wandler, K. R., & Lee, Y. B. (2007, September/October). What are eating disorders patients taking? *Addiction Professional,* pp. 46–49.

Weighing the facts—Eating disorders: Information and resources. (2008, March 5). Available at http://weighingthefacts.blogspot.com/2008/03/eating-disorder-statistics.html

Weisberg, H. I., Hayden, V. C., & Pontes, V. P. (2009). Selection criteria and generalizability within the counterfactual framework: Explaining the paradox of antidepressant-induced suicidality? *Clinical Trials, 6,* 109–118.

Weltzin, T. E., Weisensel, N., Cornella-Carlson T., Riemann, B., & Bean, P. (n.d.). The importance of addressing OCD and other anxiety disorders symptoms in the treatment of eating disorders. *Eating Disorder Hope.* Available at http://www.eatingdisorderhope.com/ocd-in-ed-treatment.html

Wilson, G. T. (2005). Psychological treatment of eating disorders. *Annual Review of Clinical Psychology, 1,* 439–465.

Westin, D., & Harbden-Fischer, J. (2001). Personality profiles in eating disorders: Rethinking the distinctions between Axis I and Axis II. *American Journal of Psychiatry, 158,* 547–562.

Work Group on Eating Disorders. (2006). *Practice guideline for the treatment of patients with eating disorders* (3rd ed.). Washington, DC: American Psychiatric Association. Available at http://www.psychiatryonline.com/content.aspx?aID=139788

Yanovski, S. Z. (2003). Binge eating disorder and obesity in 2003: Could treating an eating disorder have a positive effect on the obesity epidemic? *International Journal of Eating Disorders, 34*(Suppl.), S117–S120.

Zabinski, M. F. (2001, May). *A synchronous, computerized intervention to reduce body image and disturbed eating concerns among college-aged women: A pilot study.* Paper presented at the conference of the Academy for Eating Disorders, Vancouver, British Columbia, Canada.

Zeeman, C. (1976). *Catastrophe theory: Selected papers.* Reading, MA: Addison–Wesley.

Zerbe, K. J. (1993). *The body betrayed: A deeper understanding of women, eating disorders and treatment.* Washington, DC: American Psychiatric Press.

Index

In this index, *b* denotes *box* and *f* denotes *figure*.

About the Author

Abigail H. Natenshon, MA, LCSW, GCFP, is an expert in the treatment of eating disorders who has treated children, adults, couples, families, and groups for the past 35 years. The author of *When Your Child Has an Eating Disorder: A Step-by-Step Workbook for Parents and Other Caregivers* (Jossey-Bass, 1999) and the e-book *Doing What Works: A Professionals Guide for Treating Eating Disorders*, Abigail is the founder and director of Eating Disorder Specialists of Illinois: A Clinic without Walls.

Abigail is also a Guild Certified Feldenkrais Practitioner. She is a leader in the use of this neurophysiologic approach to augment more traditional approaches to treating patients with eating disorders and body image disturbances. The Feldenkrais Method, based on the work of Dr. Moshe Feldenkrais, uses gentle, pleasurable movements and directed attention, to create a novel and remediated experience of the body and the self, offering patients enhanced self-awareness, stress-relief, and new options for personal growth and change.

Abigail has appeared on national television as an eating disorder expert on *The Oprah Winfrey Show, The John Walsh Show, Starting Over* (NBC), as well as on MSNBC and National Public Radio. She will be featured in the fall of 2009 as an expert in a documentary about eating disorders produced by Fox TV.